Foundations of Liturgy:

An Introduction to Its History and Practice

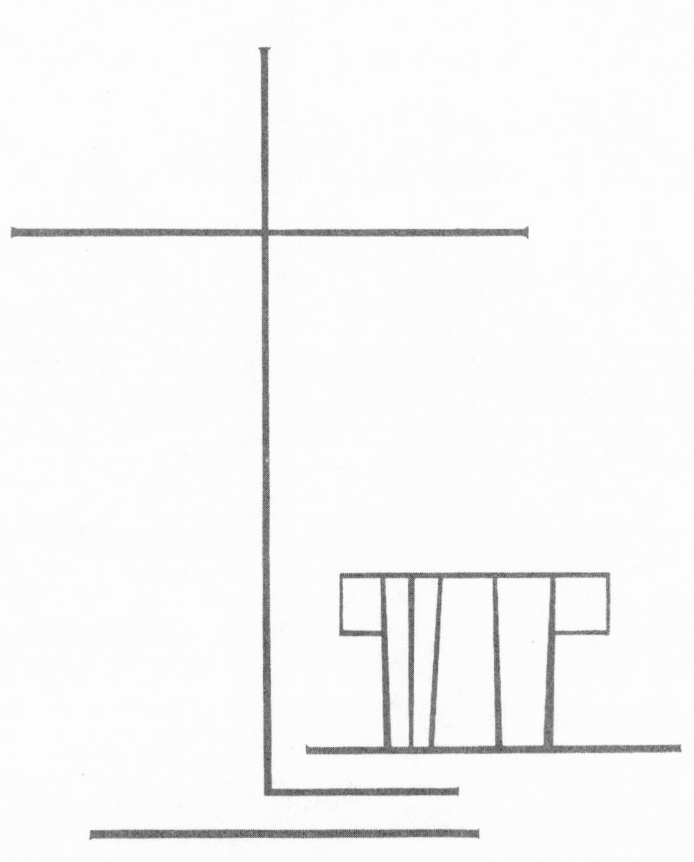

Adolf Adam

Foundations of Liturgy:

An Introduction to Its History and Practice

A PUEBLO BOOK

The Liturgical Press Collegeville, Minnesota

A Pueblo Book published by The Liturgical Press

Foundations of Liturgy: An Introduction to Its History and Practice was originally published by Verlag Herder under the title: Adolf Adam, *Grundriss Liturgie.* © 1985 Verlag Herder.

Design by Frank Kacmarcik

American adaptation by Alan F. Detscher

Printed in the United States of America.

Library of Congress Cataloging-in-Publication Data

Adam, Adolf, 1912–
[Grundriss Liturgie. English]
Foundations of liturgy : an introduction to its history and practice / Adolf Adam ; translated by Matthew J. O'Connell.
p. cm.
Translation of: Grundriss Liturgie.
"A Pueblo book."
ISBN 0-8146-6121-1
1. Liturgics. I. Title.
BV176.A3213 1992
264'.02—dc20 91-28515
CIP

CONTENTS

Preface

All who know and love the liturgy as "the summit toward which the activity of the Church is directed [and] at the same time...the fount from which all the Church's power flows" (*SC* 10) must deeply regret that interest in it and esteem for it seems to be on the wane in broad sections of the Church. The phenomenon is certainly connected with a widespread decline in the strength of Christian and ecclesial faith. For faith alone can open the eyes of the mind and focus them on the value and high dignity of the Christian liturgy. The old saying, "No one loves what he/she does not know," holds true in regard to the liturgy.

The purpose of this book is to make known the nature and structure of the liturgy and to present the most important information about the numerous areas that make it up. Despite the necessary conciseness of the presentation, this "Outline" endeavors to give a careful survey of the wideranging and many-faceted realm of liturgical actions. In any effort at a deeper understanding of the present-day liturgy it is necessary and helpful at every step to be conscious of its historical evolution. Nor have I failed to take note of the forms of liturgy practiced in the Churches separated from Rome.

The book is a scientific compendium and as such it seeks to meet the needs primarily of students of theology and others whose task it is to communicate the Christian message and the Christian life. But it will also be of service to those who are looking for a more comprehensive knowledge of the liturgy. May it help to make the Christian liturgy once again known and loved as "the most important, the most urgently needed, and the most glorious activity that can take place on earth" (Karl Barth).

Mainz Adolf Adam

Part I

Liturgy in General

Chapter One

Nature and Importance of the Liturgy

MEANING AND HISTORY OF THE WORD

The Greek word *leitourgia* (verb: *Leitourgein*) is made up of the noun *ergon* = "work" and the adjective *litos* = "belonging to the people" (derived from *los*, Ionian *laos* ="people"). Literally translated, then, *leitourgia* means "work of the people." In practice, it was understood to mean services performed for the good of the people, whether by affluent citizens or by whole cities, as, for example, the equipping of a chorus in a Greek theater, the fitting out of a ship, the feeding of a tribe at national festivals, and so on. Later on, the term included any public service; from the second century on it included cultic service as well.

The Septuagint (the Greek translation of the Old Testament, dating from 250-150 B.C.) uses the word for the service given by the priests and Levites in the temple. The word occurs several times in the New Testament with this meaning (Lk 1:23; Heb 9:21; 10:11), but it is also used there with other meanings, for instance, caritative activity (e.g., 2 Cor 9:12) or the service rendered to the communities by the angels (Heb 1:7, 14). It may also mean "worship of God" (Acts 13:2). Christ is once called "minister of the sanctuary and the true tent" (Heb 8:2), and his service as mediator is called a "liturgy" (Heb 8:6).[1]

The postapostolic period used *leitourgia* to mean both service of God and service of the community. Gradually, however, the Greek-speaking East reserved the word for the celebration of the Eucharist; it has kept this meaning in the East ever since. The word was originally unknown in the West and in its place numerous Latin expressions were used for the activity of worship; these have survived down to our time in inherited prayers.[2] The word "liturgy" (*liturgia*) was introduced into the West only in the sixteenth century, chiefly through the influence of the humanists, and was adopted even by the Churches of the Reformation in the seventeenth and eighteenth centuries; in its Western use it included all of Christian worship. It had this comprehensive sense in the 1917 Code of Canon Law, which stated that it was for the Apostolic See alone "to order the sacred liturgy and approve liturgical books" (Can. 1257).[3]

It may be mentioned for the sake of completeness that the term "liturgics" is based on the Greek adjective *leitougik*, which in this context needs to be completed by the noun *epistme = "science"; "liturgics" thus means "liturgical science." Two senses of the word "liturgist" must therefore be distinguished: student of liturgy and celebrant of liturgy. The former investigates the historical development, essential structures, contents, effects, and manifestations of the liturgy; the latter performs liturgical actions.*

NATURE OF THE LITURGY

In attempting to understand the nature of the liturgy we will be best advised to begin with the statements of Vatican II or, more accurately, those found in its Constitution on the Liturgy, which was the fruit of a decades-long effort to gain a correct understanding and practice of the liturgy. The final sentences of Article 7 can be regarded as one of the most important statements of the council:

"Rightly, then, the liturgy is considered as an exercise of the priestly office of Jesus Christ. In the liturgy by means of signs perceptible to the senses, human sanctification is signified and brought about in ways proper to each of these signs; in the liturgy the whole public worship is performed by the Mystical Body of Jesus Christ, that is, by the Head and his members.

"From this it follows that every liturgical celebration, because it is an action of Christ the Priest and of his Body which is the Church, is a sacred action surpassing all others; no other action of the Church can equal its effectiveness by the same title and to the same degree."

This passage makes it clear that the liturgy is not primarily a human activity but a continuation of the redemption which God has accomplished in Jesus Christ through the Holy Spirit. "As

Christ was sent by the Father, he himself also sent the apostles, filled with the Holy Spirit. Their mission was, first, [to] preach . . . the gospel to every creature . . . . But the work they preached they were also to bring into effect through the sacrifice and the sacraments, the center of the whole liturgical life" (Art. 6). "To accomplish so great a work, Christ is always present in his Church, especially in its liturgical celebrations" (Art. 7).[4]

It follows from these statements that the initiative in the liturgy belongs to God; that in it the history of salvation is being continued; that the chief agent and primary actor in the liturgy is Christ the high priest. To that extent liturgy is primarily a grace event, both in the proclamation of the divine message and in the sacraments (mysteries) with the paschal mystery of Christ that is contained in them. The purpose of the liturgy is the sanctification of human beings. Liturgy as word and sacrament has therefore a primarily *descending (katabatic) structure*.

This does not mean, however, that the human beings participating in the liturgy may remain entirely passive. Because they are creatures possessing freedom and intelligence they are required, first of all, to be ready to hear and believe, to listen and heed. God's word presses for an answer, his love for a return of love; his gracious action demands that human beings thank and praise him. But this praise and thanksgiving is the activity not of isolated individuals but of members of a far-reaching society that is described in the theology of St. Paul as a mystical body whose head is Christ himself. The response to God's saving action is thus the praise offered by the entire Church, in which Christ joins.

To this extent liturgical action also has an *ascending (anabatic) structure*. Liturgy has a secondary agent, a secondary acting subject, namely, the Church. The following key sentence can therefore serve as a handy definition: *Liturgy is the joint action of Jesus Christ, the high priest, and his Church for the salvation of human beings and the glorification of the heavenly Father*. This action has also been rightly described as a "dialogue between God and human beings."[5] Liturgy is thus not a one-way street but a "holy exchange" (*sacrum commerciuum*).

In light of this insight into the essence of the liturgy the insufficiency, and even falsity, of many conceptions of it becomes clear.

This is true especially of the widespread defective view that the liturgy is the sum-total of all the ceremonies and rubrics for divine worship. Pius XII had already opposed this superficial view in his Encyclical *Mediator Dei* (1947), in which he wrote:

"It is an error, consequently, and a mistake to think of the sacred liturgy as merely the outward or visible part of divine worship or as an ornamental ceremonial. No less erroneous is the notion that it consists solely in a list of laws and prescriptions according to which the ecclesiastical hierarchy orders the sacred rites to be performed."[6]

In the Protestant world, too, there are those who tend to regard the liturgy as simply a set of regulations governing the exercise of office or as a "mantle of prayer" thrown over it.[7] A completely mistaken assessment of the liturgy, found in many depth psychologists and sociologists, regards it as simply a set of highly developed symbols of socialization; even an enlightened atheist like A. Lorenzer laments the (supposed) destruction of these symbols.[8]

Widespread, too, is the identification of liturgy with cult, or worship. By "cult" (from *colere* = to cultivate, to honor) is meant the honoring of God in praise and thanksgiving, signs and symbols, song and music, and the most diverse kinds of sacrificial rituals. The focus here is on what human beings or the Church does to honor God and win divine favor; that is, it is on the ascending movement, the *actio* of human beings. Pius XII still accepted this understanding of liturgy when he wrote in *Mediator Dei*:

"The sacred liturgy is, consequently, the public worship which our Redeemer as Head of the Church renders to the Father, as well as the worship which the community of the faithful renders to its Founder, and through Him to the heavenly Father. It is, in short, the worship rendered by the Mystical Body of Christ in the entirety of its Head and members."[9]

It must however be said in defense of the encyclical that the descending movement not mentioned here is given its due in other passages. In general, one receives the impression in reading the documents of the Church that the word "cult," contrary to its proper meaning, has increasingly been given a more comprehensive sense that includes the descending movement of sanctification. Thus the supreme Roman authoritative body that was first established after Vatican II to deal with liturgical questions was given the name "Congregation for Divine Worship" (*Congregatio pro cultu divino*). It is gratifying that the new Code of Canon Law (1983) takes over both elements in the definition of the liturgy given in the Constitution on the Liturgy: Exercise of the priestly office of Christ, who sanctifies humankind, and "the whole of the public worship (*cultus*) of God that is carried on by the mystical Body of Jesus Christ, that is, by the Head and the members" (can. 834).[10]

The dialogical nature of the liturgy is also a commonplace in many Evangelical theologians. Thus E. Lohmeyer writes: "All cultic activity on the part of man is merely *re-actio* to God's *actio*, the response (*Antwort*) to His preceding word(*Wort*)."[11] P. Brunner, who is familiar with the idea of "salvation-event in worship,"[12] writes: "The side of spiritual activity in worship immediately directed to God is based exclusively on that activity through which God addresses Himself to man and offers him and conveys to him His gift of salvation. The Word evokes the response, the gift of God evokes man's devotion to God."[13]

The single German word that best expresses this understanding of liturgy is doubtless the word *Gottesdienst*, "service of God." But then the phrase "of God" must be taken not only as an objective genitive but also as a subjective genitive; that is, not only does the community serve God, but God also serves the community, in the saving service he has performed for it in Christ, who said that he had come "not to be served but to serve" (Mt 20:28; Mk 10:45). It is with this twofold meaning in mind that P. Brunner entitles two sections of his book on worship: "Worship as a Service of God to the Congregation" and "Worship as the Congregation's Service Before God."[14]

Liturgy thus understood is one of the essential expressions of the Church's life; it is one of the Church's basic functions, the others being the proclamation of the faith (*martyria*) and the service of assistance to others (*diakonia*). The Constitution on the Liturgy does not hesitate to assign it the highest place of all, for it describes it as "the summit toward which the activity of the Church is directed" and "the font from which all the Church's power flows" (Art. 10).

"No other action of the Church can equal its effectiveness by the same title and to the same degree" (Art. 7). These superlatives initially made many of the council Fathers and theologians feel uneasy. But if we reflect that the liturgy springs from the paschal mystery of Christ and makes the fruits of this mystery (salvation of human beings and supreme glorification of God) effectively present, then no other action of the Church can be said to be more valuable, more efficacious, or more necessary. (This is not to deny that among the specific parts of the liturgy the celebration of the Eucharist takes first place.) The same high value is also set on the liturgy by some Evangelical theologians; Karl Barth, for example, writes: "Christian 'service of God' is the most important, the most urgently needed, and the most glorious activity that can take place on earth."[15]

The high rank assigned to the liturgy is not equivalent to a claim of exclusivity in the Church's life. The council Fathers knew that many other things had to precede the liturgy; for example, missionary preaching, the conversion and turning of human beings to Christ, and readiness to become part of a community of brothers and sisters. In addition, liturgical activity may not be left in isolation. Those who are constantly being more fully incorporated into Christ in and through the liturgy know that like him they have a duty to seek the salvation of all human beings. The liturgy gives the right motivation and strength to overcome self-centeredness and to devote oneself unselfishly to the service of one's fellow human beings and the salvation of the entire world. The gift received in the liturgy must never lead to self-satisfaction but must rather become a task to be accomplished in and for the kingdom of God. These considerations clearly show how ungrounded is the objection that high regard for the liturgy leads to "a cultification of Christian life." On the one hand, the liturgy embodies the "vertical" dimension (human beings—God) that can never be eliminated; on the other, it imposes the obligation of striving for a correct living of the "horizontal" dimension (human being—fellow human beings—building of the world) and the strength to do so.

SCOPE OF THE LITURGY (ITS SUBDIVISIONS)

Liturgy as dialogically understood service of God has a wide variety of manifestations. At the center is undoubtedly the Eucharist which renders present the paschal mystery of Christ and thus brings salvation. Because the Eucharist is the basis and fountainhead of all liturgy, the other parts draw their life to a greater or lesser extent from the Eucharist, are measured and crowned by it, and are located like concentric circles around it. This centrality of the Eucharist is also emphasized by Evangelical theologians: "The Holy Communion worship service is the hidden, vibrant center of all worship services. If these detach themselves from this center, if the Holy Communion worship service is no longer preserved as the center supporting the entire worship life, then these detached services will necessarily become stunted and dwarfed."[16]

The other sacraments form as it were a circle around the Eucharist. First in time are the sacraments of rebirth (initiation), namely, baptism and confirmation, which incorporate believers into the communion of the Church and bring all the effects of grace that this process entails. The sacrament of penance and the anointing of the sick bring help to Christians in special situations. The sacraments of orders and marriage summon them to special forms of service in the Church and equip them for these ("sacraments of states of life"). A further important area of liturgy is the proclamation of God's word through reading and preaching, whether in connection with the celebration of the sacraments or in independent services of the word. Vatican II speaks of the "table of the word," which it decreed should be set more lavishly (Liturgy Constitution 51). The prayer of the Hours likewise has an important function as a daily service of prayer and readings. Another area of the liturgy is the sacramentals, that is, consecrations and blessings of the most diverse kinds. Finally, liturgy in a broader sense includes special gatherings for worship (devotions, ceremonies, processions) which "particular Churches" undertake "according to customs or books lawfully approved" (Art. 13). These forms of worship can with good reason be described as diocesan liturgies, although the Liturgy Constitution seeks to distinguish them from the liturgy proper, which "by its very nature far surpasses any of them" (Art. 13).[17]

Centralized regulation of the liturgy in even its smallest details has been a reality in the Church especially since the Council of Trent, and it certainly has a positive value in as much as it helps obviate excesses and aberrations. Complete centralization is not, however, to be considered an essential principle of the liturgy; this is quite clear from the way the liturgy developed during the first centuries of the Church's life. For this reason the question of what is to be regarded as liturgy, that is, as ecclesial worship, should not be approached in too narrow and timid a spirit. Whenever a local Church under its bishop, or even a limited community or group that accepts the teaching of the Church, gathers to hear God's word and to pray and sing together, Christ the high priest is present (see Mt 18). Therefore such a service is also permeated by the paschal mystery and is for the glorification of God and the salvation of those who celebrate it. Why, then, should not the essential definition of liturgy apply to such services?

AGENT (SUBJECT) OF THE LITURGY

Reflection on the nature of the liturgy has already made it clear that the two essential agents of Christian worship are Christ and the Church. In a concrete liturgical celebration the Church is the gathered community or group. In these gatherings the office holders who are appointed such by the sacrament of orders with its three degrees, namely, bishops, priests, and deacons, have a special position. Numerous liturgical actions are reserved exclusively to them; in many areas of the liturgy the reason for this reservation is not simply legal regulation but the possession of sacramental power. But the laity too, by reason of the universal priesthood bestowed on them in baptism and confirmation, are active agents in the liturgy; they are "a holy priesthood, to offer spiritual sacrifices acceptable to God through Jesus Christ" (1 Pet 2:5; see v. 9). The individual believers present at liturgical services are therefore called upon to open themselves to the word of God, to unite with the community in offering its prayer of praise, thanksgiving, and petition, and to be witnesses to Christ in faith, hope, and love both during and after the service.

Vatican II sums up all this in the phrase "active participation" (*participatio actuosa*). The Constitution on the Liturgy speaks in no less than 16 passages of this attitude that is required of the faithful, and describes it in greater detail as a full, conscious, active, devout, and communal participation which is called for by the very nature of the liturgy and to which the faithful have "a right and duty by reason of their baptism" (Art. 14). An interior spiritual and mental participation is unconditionally required and is primary; but because the human being is a composite of body and soul, the interior seeks a visible and tangible bodily expression. This active participation can, of course, take many forms and be manifested in a variety of ways: for example, acclamations, responses, prayers, and songs of various types; corresponding postures, such as bowing, genuflecting, kneeling, standing, and sitting; gestures with the hands; and external actions such as the provision of the eucharistic gifts and charitable contributions. Nor should attention of ear and eye and, as required, meditative silence be omitted from this list (see Art. 30). It is undoubtedly an important responsibility of a truly pastoral liturgy to help the faithful to this kind of participation and to show them its deeper meaning.

Certain groups among the laity play a special role as agents of the liturgy. The Constitution on the Liturgy expressly says that "servers, readers, commentators, and members of the choir . . . exercise a genuine liturgical function" (Art. 24). To be added are those who assist at communion; the appointed leaders of services at which there is no priest; organists, cantors, and, in a sense, even sextons or sacristans. These services undoubtedly presume not only the requisite skills but a solid liturgical formation.[18]

An important part is also played by the liturgical committee, which represents the parish council in this area of activity; its function is to work closely with the parish priests for the best possible liturgical services.[19]

Chapter Two

History of the Liturgy

In the following survey it is impossible to do more than trace the main lines in the development of the Christian liturgy. In order to avoid repetitions, I shall as far as possible leave developments in specific areas of the liturgy to the discussion of those areas in Part II of this book. Furthermore, the emphasis will be on the history of the Western liturgy.

The development of the liturgy has been compared to the growth of a tree that has its roots in the primitive community but partly too in the pre-Christian period and especially in Jewish worship. In the course of the centuries it has put forth new branches but then dropped many of them again; it has grown "in great variety, but nevertheless is a single whole that derives its nourishment from the vital soil that is Jesus Christ."[1] Another comparison often used is a building—a castle, for example, or a church—whose original plan has been notably altered in the course of time by conversions or additions and by new interior decors. The original form is often not recognizable at first glance and can be brought to light only by intensive study.[2] Such study alone can also provide criteria for determining whether the alterations are coherent with the original form and intention and whether and how reforms are to be undertaken.

THE BEGINNINGS

The Liturgy in the New Testament Writings

The New Testament gives no systematic description of the original Christian liturgy, but it does provide many details and allusions that required nuanced interpretation.

The verbs regularly used in the New Testament for the liturgical celebrations of the primitive community are "come together" and "assemble".[3] The place in which the primitive community of Jerusalem gathered at the beginning was the temple, where Christians joined their fellow Jews for the traditional periods of prayer.[4] Meanwhile, however, the gatherings in the homes of Christians were becoming increasingly important. The temple had ceased to be, for Christians, the only place of liturgical assembly. The accounts of meals taken with the risen Christ and the miracle on Pentecost make it clear that communion with the risen Lord and the sending of his Spirit were not tied up with the temple.

What was done at these domestic gatherings? The Acts of the Apostles speak of the breaking of bread and meals taken "with glad and generous hearts" (2:46). In the light of other passages of scripture (e.g., Acts 20:7; 1 Cor 10:16ff.; 11:17-34) we can go further and say that these meals included both fraternal agapes and eucharistic meals. Connected with them were the praise of God and prayer of petition (e.g., Acts 2:14, 24, 42, 47; 4:24-31; 12:5b). It went almost without saying that Jewish forms of prayer such as the *Berakoth* ("blessings," "praises") and individual words such as "Alleluia," "Amen," and "Hosanna" should be used. The community knew that they were assured of the presence of the Lord (Mt 18:20; 28:20) and of his promised Spirit at all of their liturgical gatherings. In addition, the memory of God's saving deeds was kept alive by the preaching of the apostles and the other eyewitnesses to the life of Jesus. This "school of faith" enabled the individual disciple not only to hold fast to the teaching of the apostles (Acts 2:42) but to become in turn a witness to the good news.

The liturgical assembly on Sunday became particularly important at an early stage. This first day of the week was also the day of Christ's resurrection; it was consequently the appropriate day for recalling this basic object of faith in Christ (see Acts 20:7; 1 Cor 16:2; Rev 1:10). From 1 Corinthians 5:7, where Paul, with his eye on the Jewish ritual of Passover, says: "Christ, our Passover lamb, has been sacrificed," we may infer that Easter became known at a very early time as the "annual [Christian] Passover." Due to the saving event that occurred on that day the Jewish feast of Passover took on a new meaning for Christians, although it is probable that Jewish-Christian communities only gradually broke away completely from the Jewish feast as a commemoration of Old Testament salvation history.[5]

A basic form of liturgy in the New Testatment was the administration of baptism. Whether the ceremony was already linked to the weekly or annual "Pasch" is a question that cannot be answered with certainty from the New Testament writings.

Another fact of which the New Testament shows a keen awareness was that Jesus, who himself forgave sins, had given his Church authority to forgive sins by the power of the Holy Spirit (Mt 16:19; 18:15-18; Jn 20:23).

There is no doubt that the primitive Christian communities established a close link between their Lord's word and example regarding loving service of neighbor and their liturgical services and that they carried this link over into their everyday lives. Passages such as Acts 4:32, 34; 6:1; Romans 12:10, 13, make this clear. This is the attitude to which Paul exhorts Christians when he urges them to make of themselves "a living sacrifice, holy and acceptable to God," and which he describes as "spiritual worship" (Rom 12:1).

No fixed ceremonial for worship is discernible at this early period. On the contrary, the Acts of the Apostles and the Pauline and post Pauline letters give evidence of a wide range of Spirit-inspired (charismatic) activities involving many members of the congregation. Paul wants plenty of room allowed for these charisms of the Spirit: "Do not quench the Spirit; do not despise prophesying, but test everything; hold fast to what is good" (1 Thess 5:19-21). A call for what we today speak of as "active participation" by the members of the congregation is implicit in this passage: "When you come together, each one has a hymn, a lesson, a revelation, a tongue, or an interpretation" (1 Cor 14:26). The same rich multiplicity was also manifested in the postPauline communities, as we learn, for example, from Ephesians 5:19-20: "Be filled with the Spirit, addressing one another in psalms and hymns and spiritual songs, singing and making melody to the Lord with all your heart, always and for everything giving thanks in the name of our Lord Jesus Christ to God the Father." Contributions to liturgical gatherings got out of hand at times and were overly eccentric; Paul's response was to insist that "all things be done for edification. . . . All things should be done decently and in order" (1 Cor 14:26, 40).

As heretics and pseudocharismatics appeared on the scene toward the end of the first century there was an increasing concern for purity of doctrine and liturgy. The concern is especially clear in the Pastoral Letters.

"Only office-holders—and specifically *episkopoi, presbyteroi* and *diakonoi*—who have their place in the line of apostolic succession through the laying on of hands, have the right to act in the name of Jesus, even in worship. The functions previously belonging to the teachers and prophets have now passed to these men. . . . Prophecy is mentioned only in passing (1 Tim 1:18; 4:14). This development had as an inevitable consequence a stress on the official and juridical side of the liturgy." [6]

The Liturgy in the Documents of the Second and Third Centuries
The *Didache,* or *Teaching of the Twelve Apostles,* which was discovered only in 1873 and is considered one of "the earliest Christian writings of the postapostolic period,"[7] provides us with some important information about liturgical life between 80 and 130 A.D.[8] It has chapters on the administration of baptism (7), fasting and prayer (8), and the celebration of agape and Eucharist (9-10), especially on Sundays (14); the Eucharist is described as a "sacrifice" (*thysia*), Malachi 1:11, 14 being cited to this effect. In 15, 2 there is an exhortation to assemble frequently for the sake of the soul's salvation.

The Letter which Pope Clement wrote to the community at Corinth in 96 A.D. exemplifies the growing practice of putting Jewish prayers to Christian use (chapters 59-91).

The seven Letters written by Bishop Ignatius of Antioch in about 110 express with special clarity the concern, already seen in the Pastoral Letters, to protect the liturgy against distortion by heretics. To this end, baptism and Eucharist, agape and marriage are to be celebrated only in agreement with the bishop. "Only what he has tested is acceptable to God; this ensures that everything done is sure and reliable."[9] Since Ignatius considers it characteristic of heretics that they stay away from "the Lord's Supper and prayer,"[10] he exhorts the community of Ephesus to gather more frequently for the Eucharist and praise of God, so that "the power of Satan may be broken and his pernicious attacks on your unanimity in faith may be repelled."[11] This exhortation, like those in *Didache* 15, 2 and Hebrews 10:25, is probably aimed at an incipient indifference and laxity in regard to participation in the liturgy.

A Letter of Pliny the Younger, governor of Bithynia, to Emperor Trajan in 112 tells of Christians gathering twice for worship on an appointed day. The first gathering took place before daybreak; here hymns were sung antiphonally to Christ "as to a god," and the Christians bound themselves by oath to obey certain commandments. The other gathering was in the evening, for an innocuous meal. J. A. Jungmann and others consider the first assembly to have been for the Eucharist, the second for an agape.[12] Others interpret the predawn celebration as a liturgy of the word or a baptism, and the evening meal as the Eucharist.[13]

The first *Apology* of Justin, philosopher and martyr (d. ca. 165), provides valuable information about the Christian liturgy around the year 150. In addition to chapter 61 on baptism, chapters 65-67 are especially interesting, because they describe the eucharistic celebration. This begins with a liturgy of the word at which the "memoirs of the Apostles" and the writings of the prophets are read. The readings are followed by a homily of the president and prayers of the faithful. After the preparation of the gifts (bread, wine, and water are brought up) the president speaks the "prayer of thanksgiving," and the congregation signifies its agreement with an "Amen." "Then takes place the distribution, to all attending, of the things over which the thanksgiving has been spoken, and the deacons bring a portion to the absent."[14]

The first texts for liturgical use that have come down to us are in the Church Order of Hippolytus (d. 235), a Roman priest and later antipope, who wrote about 215; he was a representative of conservative circles and was anxious to preserve the "Apostolic Tradition" (as his little book is called in Greek) from distortions. The texts he gives are for baptism, the Eucharist, the three degrees of orders, some blessings and prayers, and the agape. There is, among other things, a eucharistic prayer that in somewhat adapted form would be introduced into the post-Vatican II Roman Missal as the Second Eucharistic Prayer. But even though Hippolytus provides texts for use, he acknowledges the right of the bishop to compose his own prayers if he has the ability to do so.[15]

The tradition that Hippolytus passes on regarding baptism, the Eucharist, and the transmission of office in the Church is essentially confirmed by the writings of Tertullian (d. ca. 220) and Cyprian (d. 258).

In summary it may be said that in the first three centuries, despite all the variety in texts and individual rites, the Christian liturgy had one and the same structure everywhere in the Church. This was true in particular of the Eucharist. "Despite all the diversity in details it is legitimate to speak of a single basic structure for the Lord's Supper. The differences are not fundamental but matters of emphasis."[16] One scholar (L. Fendt) speaks of a "Justin Martyr pattern" that even today still underlies the eucharistic celebrations of most of the liturgical families. It is quite understandable, therefore, that when Bishop Polycarp of Smyrna visited Rome in 154 he should have celebrated the Eucharist there at the invitation of Pope Anicetus and that this gesture of communion should later be recommended by the Syrian *Didascalia* (ca. 250) for similar situations.[17]

CHRISTIAN LITURGY IN THE FOURTH TO THE SIXTH CENTURY

As a result of the program of toleration which Emperor Constantine mapped out with Licinius at Milan in 313 and communicated to the governors of the provinces in a rescript ("Edict of Milan"), Christianity gained complete freedom and equality with other religions. As time went on, Christians were granted various privileges, until finally in 380 Emperors Gratian (in the West) and Theodosius (in the East) proclaimed Christianity to be the sole legitimate religion of the state. The once persecuted Church had become the privileged imperial Church.

Effects of the "Constantinian Revolution" on the Liturgy

The change in the Church's situation under Constantine also influenced the liturgy. This is already obvious from the external appearance of churches. Especially in the large cities the liturgy was now celebrated in magnificent basilicas that were built chiefly with the aid of the Emperor and members of his family (e.g., his mother Helena).[18] The change of venue inevitably led to the development of a more solemn liturgy as well. Furthermore, bishops were now treated as the equals of the highest officials in the empire. As in the ceremonial of the imperial court, they were accompanied at their solemn entry into their basilicas by ministers carrying lights and incense and were conducted to a throne. Bows and the *proskynesis* (prostration with forehead touching the floor) were the signs of reverence given to them as to the emperor himself and his highest officials. The high social status of bishops and their clergy also led to the wearing of festive garb with special insignia, such as stole, pallium, and maniple; it was from this garb that the later liturgical vestments developed.

"So far as we know, only a few bishops were doubtful of ascribing great importance to their official insignia and privileges and of making use of them in worship. These few were certainly among the best of their time: Hilary of Poitiers, Martin of Tours, Fulgentius of Ruspe, and Augustine. The majority were of the opinion, however, that it could only enhance the Church's authority if those who exercised this authority were invested with official badges of rank and surrounded with the splendor of the ceremonials of state." [19]

While the Church was thus open to an extensive display of the splendor derived from other areas of public life, it tended to reject the rich musical culture of antiquity. The chief reason for this was probably the fact that musical instruments played a significant role in the many varieties of pagan sacrifice, where their use was regarded as part of the worship. "According to the concepts of antiquity, music was a part of each sacrifice, even when only incense or a libation were offered. Flutes, various stringed instruments, noisy kettle-drums, trumpets, and little bells, the so-called *sistrum*, were employed. The music was meant to ward off the demons and to invite the coming of the gods."[20] Christians contented themselves instead with responsorial songs; antiphonal singing was added at a later date. Church singing was advanced especially by Ambrose of Milan, who not only practiced psalmody with his congregation but also composed "hymns" of his own. No less a person than the newly-converted Augustine listened to these compositions with deep emotion and tears (*Confessions* IX, 8) and extolled the great value of the custom (X, 33). "Ever since then the custom has been retained, and the example of Milan has been followed in many other places, in fact in almost every church throughout the world" (IX, 7).[21]

Attendance at the Sunday liturgy was made significantly easier by a law which Constantine issued on March 3, 321. It declared "the venerable day of the sun" to be a day of rest for all judges, city folk, and business people. The rural populace were allowed to go about their work in order not to waste the hours of good weather. A few months later (July 3) a further law exempted the manumission of slaves—an action regarded as desirable—from the law of Sunday rest. As time went on, rest from work became increasingly the focal point of the sanctification of Sunday. "Servile work" (*opera servilia*) on Sunday was considered a serious violation of both civil and ecclesiastical law and was harshly punished. In justification, an appeal was also made to the sabbath legislation of the Old Testament, even though at an earlier time many ecclesiastical writers had made it clear that these laws were part of Jewish ceremonial law and did not bind Christians.[22]

In consequence of the struggle against Arianism and its denial of Christ's divinity many forms of prayer were altered. Thus the widespread prayer "to the Father through the Son in the Holy Spirit" gave way to the concluding formula "to the Father and to the Son and to the Holy Spirit." In addition, many prayers were addressed directly to Jesus Christ and no longer to the Father. Reverence before the Lord present in the Eucharist became even more profound now that he was thought of explicitly as the consubstantial Son of God. Writers spoke of the *mysterium tremendum*, the "terrifying mystery," which is to be approached only with fear and trembling.[23] The fourth century already provides examples of the words of institution and the prayers immediately before and after (Postsanctus and Anamnesis) being spoken only in a low voice. The line of demarcation between altar and congregation was emphasized by heightening the enclosure around the sanctuary and (in the East) providing it with drapes so that during the key prayers of the anaphora(=eucharistic prayer) the altar could be hidden from view; it was from this practice that the later iconostasis developed in the Byzantine Church. The most regrettable consequence, however, of the new attitude to the Eucharist was the decline in the reception of communion. By the fourth century Eastern Christians were already content to receive only once or twice a year; Western Christians adopted the same practice not too long after. This was certainly not Christ's intention in instituting the Eucharist, and one must agree with W. Nagel, Evangelical historian of liturgy, when he writes: "How far removed the celebration of the Lord's Supper now was from the joy once felt in communion with the Christ believed to be present and from the joyous expectation of the day of his return!"[24]

To the extent that the privileges given to the Church and its elevation to the position of obligatory religion of the state brought the masses in large numbers into the Church, there was the further danger of superficiality in liturgical participation. We learn of this from, for example, Augustine. Not only does he complain with deep feeling that many are satisfied to enroll as catechumens and then defer their baptism; he also reproaches "the masses of theater-goers" for attending the liturgy on feast days more because of its externals than because of inner devotion. "Has not so great a multitude been gathered together in the Church that the chaff at the moment entirely hides the wheat? . . . When some spiritual advice is given, or some spiritual duty is laid down, they oppose it and they resist. They follow their flesh and withstand the Holy Spirit."[25]

Once the Constantinian revolution put an end to persecution of Christians the martyrs for the faith became the object of special attention and veneration. The beginnings of this veneration are to be found much earlier, especially in the East, where, for example, in the middle of the second century the community of Smyrna in Asia Minor annually celebrated the anniversary of Polycarp, its martyred bishop (d. 155 or 156), "with joy and gladness."[26] In the West, too, the veneration of the martyrs became increasingly popular. Their death as witnesses was seen as linked to the paschal mystery of Christ, and the invocation of the martyrs was regarded as extremely effective, especially at their tombs. Later on, other communities inserted the celebration of important martyrs into their festal calendars and replaced the inaccessible tomb with relics (including *brandea* or pieces of cloth touched to the martyrs' tombs) and, at a later period, with images as well. [27]

The growth of monasticism in the fourth century gave it an especially important role in the organization of prayer, in particular the daily prayer of the Hours. From the fourth century on monks and consecrated virgins everywhere began to form communities.

"Such monasteries were generally erected in isolated places; a famous example was Monte Cassino. . . . But it was precisely in Italy that such monasteries were also erected in towns, preferably in the vicinity of some famous martyr's grave. . . . These foundations had obviously arisen from the pious desire that the horary prayers, performed according to the manner of the monks, should never cease either day or night in the basilicas erected over the graves of the martyrs." [28]

The Formation of Liturgical Families in East and West

Of great importance for the further development of the liturgy was the influence—theological, disciplinary, and liturgical—which the great ecclesiastical centers exercised in an increasing measure after the Constantinian revolution. This did not mean that regional diversity was everywhere eliminated. Quite the contrary: this period saw the rise and consolidation of new groups of rites, a growth in which theological disputes about the Trinity and Christ as well as ethno-cultural and political factors all played a part. Careful examination is required if students are to pick their way through this "maze of liturgical practices" in East and West.[29] The present limited survey does not allow me to describe in detail the contents of these various liturgical groups; a good deal of information regarding them will however be given in discussing the several parts of the liturgy.

The Eastern Liturgies

The oldest patriarchate and the dominant ecclesiastical center in the East was Antioch, the capital of the Roman-Byzantine province of Syria. The city itself and the coastal regions were Greek in language and culture, but the hinterland and the areas bordering on Persia spoke Syro-Aramaic dialects. The liturgy that developed in Antioch in the first centuries (= the West Syrian liturgy) is also known as the liturgy of James after the Anaphora of James, which originated in Jerusalem. We meet this liturgy in the *Didascalia*, the *Apostolic Consti-*

tutions (end of the fourth century), and the sermons of John Chrysostom (d. 407) and Bishop Theodore of Mopsuestia (d. 428).

This Liturgy of James, which was celebrated in Greek, is to be distinguished from the Jacobite Liturgy of the sixth century, which took its name from its organizer, James Baradai (d. 577). The Jacobite Liturgy put the Liturgy of James into Syriac and combined it with Monophysite tendencies and East Syrian elements. Later on it also underwent various Byzantine influences.

The Melchites are those Christians who remained orthodox, cultivated close ties with Byzantium, and in the twelfth century accepted the Byzantine rite in its totality. The Maronites of Lebanon, who took their name from Maro, a monk, have a liturgy of the West Syrian type but with some East Syrian peculiarities. Since union with Rome at the time of the crusades this liturgy has been extensively Latinized.

The East Syrian area, with centers at Edessa and Nisibis (Mesopotamia = modern Iraq), fell under Persian control at an early period and thus became very much isolated from the West. After the Council of Ephesus (431) these regions adopted Nestorianism. Their liturgy, which is also known as the Syro-Mesopotamian, retains numerous original elements and sets many problems for scholars. The widely used "Anaphora of the Apostles" (the Apostles Addai and Mari), for example, has no words of institution.

The energetic missionary activity of this "Nestorian Church" spread Christianity to, among other places, the southwest coast of India (Malabar Coast, modern Kerala), where it has outlasted the centuries. Because the Indians of this region trace their faith back to Thomas the Apostle, they also call themselves "Thomas Christians." When the Portuguese gained a foothold there in the sixteenth century, they began a rigorous Latinization of the rite; some of the Malabar Christians therefore rejected Rome and, under the name of "Malankers," joined the Syro-Antiochene patriarchate. In 1962 and especially in the period after Vatican II the Malabar Christians were allowed to revive their ancient rite.[30]

The "Chaldeans" are those Christians of the Syro-Mesopotamian rite who are in union with Rome. They are found chiefly in present-day Syria and in Iraq, but also on Cyprus.

The patriarchate of Alexandria originally used a form of the "Liturgy of Mark," which was strongly influenced by Syria. One of the few documents that have survived from the early period is the Prayer Book of Serapion, Bishop of Thmuis (in the Nile delta), which dates from the middle of the third century. This patriarchate joined the Monophysites after the Council of Chalcedon (451). The Coptic (Egyptian) and Ethiopian (Abyssinian) rites developed from a revision and translation of the Liturgy of Mark. Those Christians who remained orthodox (chiefly in the coastal areas) cultivated closer ties with the Byzantine rite and became known, like their counterparts in West Syria, as Melchites ("the emperor's people").[31]

Jerusalem has played an especially important role in liturgical history. It acquired the canonical status of a patriarchate only at the Council of Chalcedon (451), but its connection with Christian salvation history had already made of it (especially from the fourth century on) a favorite place of pilgrimage and "center of devotion." Constantine and his family had splendid churches built in the holy places; in these churches crowds of pilgrims gathered throughout the year, and services were celebrated daily. Egeria (Etheria), a pilgrim from southwest France or northwest Spain, has left us a detailed description of these services in about 381-384.[32] Other countries, too, acquired knowledge of these services from homebound pilgrims and gladly imitated them. Another important source of information about the liturgy of Jerusalem comes to us in the *Mystagogical Catecheses* that used to be attributed to Cyril of Jerusalem but today are usually ascribed to his successor, John of Jerusalem. The Anaphora of James was the one mainly used in the Eucharist; it made its way then from Jerusalem to other regions. The prayer of the Hours and the festal cycle that were used in Jerusalem also played a decisive role in the liturgical development of other Churches (Holy Week and Easter, Ascension, Pentacost, and various feasts of Mary). The takeover introduced a strong historicizing element into the liturgy; this element is clear in, for example, the selection of readings for the various feasts.

Of the various Eastern liturgies the Byzantine became the most widespread. There were several reasons for this. Because the emperor resided in Constantinople the patriarch of that city acquired precedence over all the other Eastern patriarchs (officially so in 451). In addition, the patriarchates of Antioch and Alexandria adopted Monophysism and then came under Muslim control at an early date. An important factor in the further spread of the Byzantine liturgy was the missionary activity of Sts. Cyril and Methodius; as a result of this activity the Byzantine liturgy was translated into Old Slavonic (second half of the ninth century) and was eventually adopted in the Kingdom of Russia (987).

The Byzantine liturgy has its roots chiefly in Antioch and Cappadocia, secondarily in Jerusalem. The eucharistic liturgy most frequently used is the one named after St. John Chrysostom (354-407) but in fact completed only in the eighth century. On twelve days of the year the liturgy of St. Basil (329-379), one of the Cappadocian Fathers, is celebrated. In addition the "liturgy of the presanctified" is used on special days.[33]

The Armenian liturgy closely resembles the Byzantine. It derives in part from the same Antiochene and Cappadocian roots, but it has also undergone direct Byzantine influences.

To be mentioned, finally, is the Georgian liturgy, which is common in the present-day Soviet Republic of Georgia (capital: Tiflis). Originally very dependent on Armenia and Syria, this liturgy was later "Russified," that is, it came under the influence of the Russo-Byzantine liturgy. The Church of Georgia is today a member of the World Council of Churches.

The Western Liturgies

Two basic types of liturgy can be seen as operative in the history of the Western Church: the North African-Roman and the Gallican.

The shape of the North African liturgy is known to us chiefly from the writings of St. Augustine.[34] The language used was probably Latin from the beginning, in contrast to Rome where Greek (see the *Apostolic Tradition* of Hippolytus) yielded to Latin only during the fourth century.[35] We learn from a Synod of Hippo in 393[36] that the same texts were not used from see to see. Each bishop could use his own compositions or those of others; they were, however, to be checked in advance by learned fellow bishops. The same regulation was subsequently repeated in a number of African synods.[37] In its overall structure, however, and especially the structure of the Mass and the liturgical year, the North African liturgy closely resembled the Roman.

We know many details of the Roman liturgy during the fourth to the sixth century, but, contrary to what we might expect, actual liturgical texts have come down to us only from a relatively late period. The earliest document is the *Verona Sacramentary*, which for a long time was attributed to Pope Leo I (440-461) but in fact did not come into existence until the second half of the sixth century. This sacramentary is a collection of older *libelli* ("little books"), that is, individual sheets or booklets that recorded the texts for particular Roman liturgies in the course of the year; for many feast days there are several formularies (twenty-eight for the feast of the Apostles Peter and Paul). The texts for the months of January through April (including Lent and Easter) have not been preserved.[38]

The second sacramentary that has come down to us is known as the *Old Gelasian*, because it was attributed to Pope Gelasius I (492-496); in fact, it probably originated around the middle of the seventh century as the sacramentary of one of the titular churches of Rome.[39] The *Gregorian Sacramentary* was probably compiled by Pope Gregory I (590-604) in about 592, as a book containing the papal liturgies (stational liturgies) of the entire year. Pope Hadrian I (772-795) sent a revised copy of the Gregorian to Emperor Charlemagne. A Supplement (*Hucusque*) was added to this sacramentary in order to meet the needs of the Frankish Church. In the eighth century and later numerous sacramentaries came into existence that combined elements from the older compilations; these became known as *Eighth-century Gelasians*.[40]

Scholarly research has shown that although the sacramentaries as such originated at a relatively late time many of the texts can by traced back to Pope Leo I, and others to Popes Gelasius I and Vigilius (537-555). Pope Gregory I played an especially important part in the reorganization of the Roman liturgy. In all the ancient Roman prayers we find language that is terse, soberly objective, almost juridical in character, and a rejection of elements that would give the rite a poetic and emotional tone. One outstanding scholar has spoken of the "puritanism of the Roman liturgy."[41] This language reflects the kind of Roman rhetoric that was highly esteemed at that period.

"Another device of the Roman oration [= presidential prayer] deserves mention: the *cursus*. By *cursus* is meant the arrangement of words at the end of phrases and clauses so that their accents produce a beautiful rhythm. . . In the more ancient orations, the rules of the *cursus* have been regularly observed: . . . "mirabilius reformasti" (*cusus velox*); "eius divinitatis esse consortes" (*cursus planus*); "qui humanitatis nostrae fieri dignatus est particeps" (*cursus tardus*)." [42]

Characteristic of the Roman Mass was the use of a single eucharistic prayer (the Canon), which allowed only minor alterations in a few of the prayers making it up.

The Gallican type of liturgy includes all the Western rites outside the area associated with Rome. Despite all the differences between them they are at one in being heavily influenced by the Eastern rites, especially the Byzantine; the language (Latin) is more prolix and colorful, the ceremonial more dramatic. As a result of the struggle against Arianism they quite often address prayers directly to Christ in contrast to Roman custom).

Within this group the following are to be distinguished:

The Old Spanish liturgy, which is also known as the Visigothic liturgy and, in the period after the Islamic Arabs occupied southern Spain, the Mozarabic liturgy.

The Old Gallic or Gallican liturgy, which was celebrated in Gaul and showed many local peculiarities because there was no outstanding center that could have imposed a degree of unity.

The Celtic liturgy among the Irish, Scots, and Welsh. This liturgy is heavily marked by Old Spanish, Gallican, and Roman elements. In the form in which it has come down to us it shows many lacunae and dates from a rather late period. The most important document is the Stowe Missal (eighth and tenth century).

The liturgy of Milan is still celebrated today throughout the ecclesiastical province of Milan. In the eighth century it was attributed to St. Ambrose and is therefore also known as the Ambrosian liturgy. Its real origin is still obscure to us. It may have had the same primitive form as the Roman. Numerous details of its older form are given to us in two writings of Ambrose (ca. 340-397): the *De mysteriis* and the *De sacramentis*. The Canon is essentially the same as the Roman; in other areas this liturgy has many traits in common with the Gallican liturgy.[43]

THE WESTERN LITURGY IN THE MIDDLE AGES

In this and the following sections I shall be concerned chiefly with the development of the Roman liturgy.

The Period of Liturgical Exchange

In the area north of the Alps the seventh century saw the beginning of a far-reaching process of amalgamation of the Roman and Gallo-Frankish liturgies; these were therefore centuries of transition. The motives at work were a general high esteem of the Roman Church because it had been founded by Peter, and an uncertainty and dissatisfaction, widespread among bishops and abbots, with the many variations to be found in the Gallican liturgy. Boniface, an Anglo-Saxon missionary bishop, thought it important to bind the Germanic tribes more closely to Rome and its liturgy. The same goal marked the efforts of King Pepin, who in 754 prescribed the Roman liturgy for his kingdom. In 785-786 Charlemagne issued the laws that would bring the Romanization to completion. As a matter of fact, however, the liturgy thought to be Roman was already interspersed with Gallican elements; in the following period it underwent further Gallo-Frankish adaptations and revisions. These can be seen especially in the taste for dramatic actions, for the multiplication and lengthening of prayers and rites, and for the subjective elements found in the many prayers said silently by the celebrating bishop or priest.

Toward the end of the eighth century the custom slowly grew of saying the Canon of the Mass in a low voice. The reason given for the practice was that the priest had now entered into the holy of holies and that the holy words he was speaking had to be protected against profanation.[44] Allegorical explanations determined the way in which the liturgy was understood. The faithful were instructed to see behind each detail of the liturgy a deeper meaning that was often artificial and far-fetched.

"Everything receives a significance—persons, vestments, church vessels and utensils, dates, actions, and motions. Different types of signification are employed: ethical admonitions (moral allegory), fulfillments of the Old Testament (typological allegory), events in the economy of salvation (rememorative allegory) or allusions to the consummation at the end of time (eschatological or anagogic allegory)." [45]

The principal representatives of this kind of allegorical explanation in the Carolingian period were Alcuin and his disciple Amalarius, Bishop of Metz; these two men were also Charlemagne's chief advisers.

The people of this period seem to have had a strong sense of unworthiness and sinfulness. This led to, among other things, the introduction of numerous confessions of sin ("apologies") into the prayer literature of the time and especially into the Mass.[46] This was also the period when Irish and Scottish monks were spreading the practice of private confession on the continent. Around 800 this practice was prescribed for the entire Frankish kingdom. The ancient practice of public penance that had been inherited from antiquity took a secondary place.

"Public penance and private confession battled for the favor of the members of the Church during Carolingian times. The hierarchy demanded public penance; the people asked for confession. It is understandable that most local pastors began to follow the latter practice. Initially public penance would still be required for great public sins, but for great secret sins confession was permitted. It was simply a matter of course that the practice of confession finally won the day, totally vanquishing public penance." [47]

The old Roman liturgical books had contained almost nothing but texts; no descriptions were given of the course of the service. Now books began to appear that gave directions for the rites; we today would call them books of rubrics or ceremonies, at that time they were known as *ordines* ("methodical arrangements"). Most of them appeared north of the Alps. The few authentically Roman *ordines* that are intermingled with them can be isolated only with difficulty.[48] Comprehensive liturgical books were then compiled from collections of such *ordines*. The most important of these inclusive books was written around 950 by Benedictines of the Abbey of St. Alban in Mainz and later became known as the *Romano-German Pontifical*. In addition to the *Ordo Romanus Antiquus* the book contained Gallo-Frankish texts and rites along with some additions of the copyist. In the time of Otto I (second half of the tenth century) the *Romano-German Pontifical* reached Rome, where ecclesiastical and cultural life was in a desperate state (the tenth century is known to historians as *saeculum obscurum*, "the dark century"). Because liturgical manuscripts were rarely written in the ninth century and the first half of the tenth,[49] the Church of Rome received the new book with grateful willingness and adopted it as supposedly containing the authentic Roman liturgy. Other manuscripts were given a similar reception. As a result the old Roman liturgy returned to Rome, but now in Gallo-Frankish form, and from there, as the "liturgy of the Roman curia," began its victorious effort to become the one, uniform liturgy of the entire West.

Once the Spaniards, with French help, had driven the Arabs (Moors) from their country, the Old Spanish (Mozarabic) liturgy surrendered its pride of place to the (neo-) Roman and eventually came to be celebrated only in a single chapel in Toledo. The Celtic liturgy too had to make way for the Roman. In Scotland the shift took place in the eleventh century, in Ireland at the Synod of Cashel in 1172.[50] The Roman liturgy had gained a hold in England at a much earlier period, due to the efforts of Augustine, the Benedictine abbot whom Gregory I had sent to evangelize the Anglo-Saxons.

During this period the building of churches proceeded at a quick pace under the Carolingian and Ottonian rulers. A first climax was reached around 1100 with the Romanesque style.[51]

From Gregory VII to the Eve of the Reformation

Under Pope Gregory VII (1073-1085) a phase of consolidation began at Rome; it extended not only to ecclesiastical life generally but to the liturgy as well. Gregory and his successors required all bishops to follow the liturgical practice of the Roman curia. The goal was in fact not reached until the thirteenth century, when the Franciscan Order and its thousands of itinerant preachers adopted the "liturgy of the Roman curia" and promoted it everywhere. With the coming of Gothic, which was not simply a style of building but a style of thinking and living that embraced the whole of the public and private spheres, new forces and forms also made their way into the liturgy. The characteristic traits of this new outlook were individualism, subjectivism, and ethicism. "These are the roots of everything that is creative and fruitful in Gothic; they are also the primal source of all its efforts, doubts and despairs; in them slumber the seeds of both the rise and the fall of the Gothic."[52] "Even Gothic realism, which increasingly turned into naturalism, was a child of individualism."[53]

While the liturgy, in keeping with its nature, was still understood and celebrated as a communal activity, individualist and subjectivist tendencies now made their appearance. The complete missals that came into existence at this time made it possible for the priest to celebrate a "private Mass," that is, one which he said all by himself, without reader and choir. Yet even when he had reader and choir to assist him at solemn Masses, he felt obliged to read all the readings and songs quietly to himself while they were being proclaimed and sung. The liturgy became increasingly a "clerical liturgy" at which the clergy alone did everything; this tendency was strengthened by the presence of the choir screen, which divided the church into a "church for the clergy" and a "church for the congregation" and thus at the architectural level already broke the unity of the one community of Christ that includes both clergy and laity. It is true that on the side of the screen facing the people an altar was set up for "the people's Mass," but the "silent Mass" that was celebrated there did not allow any active participation by the faithful.

A similar tendency to privatization showed itself in the prayer of the Hours. The introduction of the "breviary," which contained all needed texts, made possible and promoted an individual celebration of the Hours, even though this prayer was originally public and involved the entire community.

The liturgical year was greatly expanded by the introduction of new feasts of the Lord, Mary, and the saints. The crusades intensified veneration of the humanity of Christ and all the phases of his earthly life. The Lord's passion, in particular, had a profound appeal for the people of the Gothic age; the result was a flowering of devotion to the passion and of mysticism centering on the passion. Works of art depicting the passion adorned not only churches and chapels, but public and private buildings as well.

Hand in hand with growth in veneration of the saints went an increase in veneration of relics and in pilgrimages. Whenever a community or some private individual (a nobleman) gained possession of a (supposedly) important relic, people felt blessed and surer of salvation. To the ancient places of pilgrimage many new ones were added, usually as a result of stories about appearances, miracles, and extraordinary happenings. Many of the faithful made extreme efforts to reach these places and pray there, not only for temporal needs (and there were plenty of those) but also and above all for the salvation of their souls.

Preference for the realistic and concrete begot a great desire to gaze upon what was holy and divine. People wanted as far as possible to see with their own eyes that which faith proclaimed and promised. As a result, Gothic cathedrals became overwhelming representations of the heavenly Jerusalem.[54] In the mind of the people of that day the Mass reached a new high point when the consecrated host was elevated after the words of institution (a practice first attested shortly after 1200 in Paris).[55]

From the second half of the thirteenth century on, the feast of Corpus Christi with its procession joined Christmas with its crib as the favorite feasts of the year. Even during the celebration of Mass people wanted to be able to gaze continually on the "Savior" in the consecrated host. The desire led to "Masses before the exposed Blessed Sacrament," which despite Rome's reservations continued down to the middle of our own century and whose cessation many of the faithful still regret. To the detriment of the genuine celebration of Mass the isolated adoration of the Blessed Sacrament developed in various forms. Even the reception of communion declined to an alarming extent, so that the Fourth Lateran Council (1215) had to order reception at least once a year.[56] The reason for the decline was not so much a falling off in devotion as an excessive reverence for the sacrament. This reverence was also one reason why the celebrant no longer put the host in the hand of communicants but on their lips and why communion from the chalice fell into disuse; it was feared that even a single drop might be spilled (there were other reasons as well).

Extravagant notions of the efficacy of the sacrifice of the Mass led to widespread quantitative thinking and behavior. As a result, the "Autumn of the Middle Ages" (J. Huizinga) saw the rise of ever new votive Masses and numerous Masses-in-series, which were regarded as having extraordinary effects. The frequency with which Masses were "said" increased greatly, as throngs of priests were ordained (after a very poor training) who were simply "altarists," that is, had no other duty than to celebrate a "founded" Mass each day. Thus at the Cathedral of Strasbourg in 1521 there were no less than 120 Mass foundations,[57] and in fifteenth-century Breslau there were 236 altarists at two churches.[58] The result was, of course, that any given church had to have a vast number of altars; this in turn promoted the grotesque custom of "boxed Masses."[59] These and similar abuses caused many thoughtful Christians to call for a "reform in head and members."

These regrettable distortions must not make us forget, however, that during this period deep faith, interiority, and a spirit of self-sacrifice characterized large groups of people. These traits are documented even for the devotional movement known as "mysticism," that is, the art and practice of absorption into the deepest "ground of the soul" or the "apex of the soul," in order there to have a profound experience of the divine. Bernard of Clairvaux (1090-1153), Hildegard of Bingen (1098-1179), and Elizabeth of Schönau (1129-1164) may be mentioned as some twelfth-century representatives of this movement. Above all, however, it was the new Franciscan and Dominican Orders that fostered the mystical attraction from the thirteenth century on. The high point of the German mystical movement came in the fourteenth century; it is enough to mention such outstanding figures as Meister Eckhart, John Tauler, and Henry Seuse. From their ranks, too, came the repeated call for an interiorization of all religious life.

A similar striving for interiority marked the movement of renewal known as the Devotio Moderna, which originated in the Netherlands at the end of the fourteenth century (Gerard Groote, mystic and preacher of repentance, d. 1384) and spread throughout Western Europe. It strove to promote a deeper devotion to and following of Christ; this spirit found its classical expression in the famous *Imitation of Christ* of Thomas à Kempis (1379-1471).

Both movements had a fruitful influence not only on the life of prayer but on the worship of the Church, since they promoted a more deeply interior participation. Yet such efforts could not alter the fact that the liturgy had become a clerical liturgy. The faith of the laity sought and found expression and nourishment in peripheral areas, for example, in the numerous mystery plays that were celebrated chiefly on the great feasts of Christmas, Epiphany, and Easter, but also in honor of the patrons of churches and cities. People sought and found a patron saint for every need; not infrequently, however, veneration of the saint was accompanied by superstitious ideas and practices.

"Veneration of the saints and their relics—genuine or fake—is often quite unrestrained. Protections and blessings are sought in ever new ways: the *rituals* become full of new benedictions. Confraternities are founded and new devotions spring up all around. Religious life becomes more and more complicated. A growing insecurity and many-sided discontent is apparent everywhere." [60]

FROM THE COUNCIL OF TRENT TO VATICAN II

The Council of Trent and the Liturgy

In face of the abuses current in the whole of ecclesial life and in the liturgy, which is an essential part of that life, the call for a "reform in head and members" had become increasingly loud as early as the beginning of the sixteenth century; see, for example, the petition addressed to Pope Leo X in 1513 by V. Quirini and T. Giustiniani, who later became Camaldolese monks.[61] Explicit mention must be made, for Germany, of the reports on reform which Georg Witzel (1501-1573) wrote for the prince-abbot of Fulda in 1542. Witzel urged a reform of the Church by means of a reform of the liturgy, and he stressed in particular the need of explaining the liturgy to the ordinary people. "This would satisfy the murmurers, because they would hear that the Church they despise contains such good things."[62] There was an ever louder call for revised liturgical books that would be uniform throughout the Church. For the time being, however, nothing happened. The Renaissance popes would have had to change themselves first.

The Reformers were thus able to link their serious complaints with a demand for radical changes, and, in doing so, could count on widespread agreement and readiness for change. After great difficulties the Council of Trent finally met (1545-1563, with lengthy intermissions). The final session (1563-1565) was important for the liturgy. A commission was charged with drawing up a list of current "abuses in the Mass"; the most succinct list ran for six quarto pages[63] and was " the most comprehensive collection of ideas for liturgical reform."[64] But because time was short the Council could not go into these matters in detail. It did, however, take the important step of instructing the pope to compile a new catechism and revise all the liturgical books with the help of a commission of experts. The *Roman Catechism* appeared in 1566; then, under Pius V (1566-1572), the *Roman Breviary* (1578) and *Roman Missal* (1580) were also published. The accompanying Bulls decreed that these books were henceforth obligatory, unless a diocese or religious order could show that their special usages were at least two hundred years old. The Congregation of Rites was established in 1588 to see that the decree was faithfully followed. In the words of the Bull *Quo primum tempore* that was prefixed to the Missal, "nothing" was "ever to be added, removed, or changed" in the new rite; this, however, was a disciplinary decree and could not legally bind subsequent popes or general councils. Liturgical standardization was also promoted by other liturgical books: the *Roman Pontifical* (1596), the *Ceremonial of Bishops* (1600), and the *Roman Ritual* (1614).

A uniform liturgy was thus prescribed for the entire West; it was not, however, the old Roman liturgy, but a hybrid Roman-Gallican-German liturgy. What the Council had in mind was a reform of the divine office "according to the ancient order of prayer" and of the Mass "according to the norm of the holy Fathers and the ancient rites," but this was "a goal that remained out of reach with the means available at the time and given the contemporary state of liturgical science."[65] The post-Tridentine liturgy was "a continuation—even if a purified continuation— of the medieval liturgy . . . a liturgy reserved to the clergy and, in the beginning, frequently still hidden behind the roodscreen. . . . Except in the sermon, little attention was paid to the people."[66] They "attended Mass," and their participation was limited to "listening" and "watching." For the ordinary people the liturgy remained a mystery that was for the most part not understood, even though the Council of Trent had urged that pastors should "frequently . . . explain during the celebration of Masses some of the readings of the Mass, and among other things give some instruction about the mystery of this most holy sacrifice, especially on Sundays and feastdays."[67]

The Catholic hymnals (e.g., those of Michael Vehe, 1537, and Johannes Leisentritt, 1567) that were published at this time made a valuable contribution to popular piety. In the beginning the songs were sung outside of Mass in processions and devotions, but gradually they found a place in the Mass as well. Peter Canisius (1521-1597) said that these popular German hymns, which were now much used due to stimulus from Reformed Christians, were "a pious practice and salutary for the Church."[68] The Cantual of Mainz, published in 1605, already provided songs in the vernacular at the Gradual, after the consecration, at the Agnus Dei, and during communion.

The Liturgy in the Baroque Period

The liturgical books, and especially the Missal, that were published under commission of the Council of Trent, inaugurated "the age of a rigid unified liturgy and of rubricism."[69] "From the seventeenth to the twentieth centuries liturgical legalism and casuistry took an ever greater place in the practice and teaching of liturgy."[70] Under the influence of the baroque attitude to life, the official liturgy of the Church was celebrated with an ever greater display of splendor. Elements in this were not only the magnificent interiors of the baroque churches but also the polyphonic singing and the instrumental music. The celebration of Mass was experienced as a "feast for eye and ear." This splendor found its greatest manifestation in the Corpus Christi processions, the many other processions and pilgrimages, and the spiritual plays on feastdays. The element of subjectivism was little changed since the high and late Middle Ages, if we prescind from the elimination of the grossest abuses. During the Mass the faithful would say the rosary or the prayers of the "devotions during Mass" that were to be found in the numerous prayerbooks (flowering of the art of printing). The effort of J. de Voisin, a French priest, to make the texts of the Mass available to the people in the vernacular translations was sharply condemned as a "profanation of the sanctuary" by Alexander VII in a Brief of 1661.[71]

The ever more common bad practice of not distributing communion until after Mass, in order that the faithful who did not receive might leave the church sooner, only accentuated still more the isolation of a communion-centered piety from the Mass proper. The sermon was usually preached before Mass, with the result that it could easily be omitted entirely. "The devotion to the Son of God, present in the tabernacle on the altar, to his most Sacred Heart, and to His Passion, and equally the almost infinite number of forms of devotion to Our Lady—all these were more congenial to the pious than the existing forms of the liturgy which for the most part were not properly understandable."[72] "At every point in the liturgical life there is a strange but unmistakable attraction to the peripheral. Medieval developments continue, but people do not look back to their origins."[73]

One gratifying phenomenon of the baroque period was the development of liturgical science. Many scholars, especially in Italy and France, published source material and treatises on liturgical themes. Deserving of special mention are Benedictines U. Menardo (d. 1644), J. Mabillon (d. 1707), and E. Martene (d. 1739), Theatine Cardinal B. G. M. Tommasi (d. 1713), historian L. A. Muratori of Modena (d. 1750), Pope Benedict XIV (d. 1753), and Benedictine abbot M. Gerbert of St. Blasien in Germany (d. 1793). To a much greater extent than in the past, scientific documentation was available for comparing the earlier liturgy with the liturgy of Trent and for stimulating efforts at renewal. In France numerous dioceses returned to the pre-Tridentine "Gallican" liturgy; many published new missals and breviaries incorporating a good many changes. Because these books were connected at least regionally and in time with Jansenism and Gallicanism, Rome soon suspected them of heresy and forbade the use of some of them. The liturgical reform planned by Benedict XIV did not become a reality.

The Liturgy in the Period of the Enlightenment

Under the influence of a new intellectual outlook that replaced the baroque attitude to life these efforts at renewal took on new vitality. People now looked at the liturgy more in terms of its pastoral usefulness; they emphasized its communal character and strove for a greater simplicity and "reasonableness." In the process, however, they succumbed to the risk of reducing worship to a tool of moral formation, an educational aid. Especially notable in this context is the 1786 Synod of Pistoia. Despite its many valuable suggestions for reform Pius VI harshly condemned it in 1794.[74] Demands for liturgical reform were also expressed at the Congress of Ems in 1786, but the archbishops of Cologne, Trier, Mainz, and Salzburg were concerned primarily with resisting the papal claim to primacy.[75]

In addition, there were many theologians who took up the cause of sound liturgical reform and in some cases carried its banner far into the nineteenth century. This period may be called the cradle of the liturgical movement.[76]

The Liturgy and the Catholic Restoration of the Nineteenth Century

The Romantic movement in the first decades of the nineteenth century represented a swing of the pendulum away from the Enlightenment. In reaction to rationalism it was individualistic and subjectivist, overemphasizing feeling and mood, even in the realm of religion. "The whole nature of the Romantic religious spirit was opposed to the spirit of the liturgy. It is therefore not surprising that the real Romantics . . . had practically no time for the liturgy and things liturgical. . . . At best, they regarded the liturgy as a historical datum or as a source of esthetic pleasure, but the true nature of the liturgy was wholly alien to them."[77] Romanticism was, of course, not a Catholic movement and must not be confused with the subsequent Catholic restoration, even if some Romantics who later encountered the Catholic restoration found certain Romantic elements in it.

As the name indicates, the "Catholic restoration" aimed at rebuilding what had supposedly been destroyed by the Enlightenment. In the process it sought to align itself closely with Rome and the High Middle Ages. As a result, it developed connections with historicism, as may be seen, for example, in the revival of Scholastic theology (Neoscholasticism) and the imitation of medieval architectural styles (especially Romanesque and Gothic). This outlook also marked its attitude to the liturgy: it cultivated the supposedly early Roman form of the liturgy as something worthy of veneration and tried to stir enthusiasm for it.

The spokesman for this restorational view of the liturgy was Prosper Guéranger (1805-1875), Benedictine abbot of Solesmes in France. In his two principal works, *Institutions liturgiques* and *L'annee liturgique*,[78] he sought to bring out the dignity and beauty of the liturgy. In doing so, he strongly emphasized its esoteric character. It is "by its nature reserved to the clergy, to a greater extent even than the sacred scriptures."[79] "The liturgical books are intended for priests. . . . The faithful, therefore, have no right to complain that what was not written for them is kept from them."[80] He regarded any change in the "formulas and rites" as an offense against the Church itself and as a want of the Catholic spirit.[81] This applied to any attempt to create a liturgy in the vernacular. Because he regarded the Roman liturgy alone as free of all error, he bitterly resisted the Gallican liturgies that were followed in many dioceses, and he was completely successful. He even hoped that "the time will come when the language and faith of Rome will be the sole means of achieving unity and renewal in the East no less than in the West."[82] The re-introduction of the Roman liturgy into France meant, unfortunately, that a great deal of value in the local liturgies was lost. Guéranger's efforts at centralization reached beyond the borders of France and led to the loss of valuable local customs in Germany (e.g., Trier) as well.[83] Despite all that Guéranger did to foster, in principle, a high esteem for the liturgy, he can hardly be ranked among the fathers of the liturgical movement insofar as this aimed at promoting an intelligent participation of the entire Christian people. Guéranger and his abbey deserved special praise for the study, cultivation, and spread of Roman liturgical singing.

Solesmes did play an important part in the modern history of the liturgy inasmuch as the brothers Maurus and Placid Wolter from

Cologne stayed there from 1862 to 1863 in order to gain a closer knowledge of Benedictine life in that monastery and then to return to Germany and reopen the abbey of Beuron. Beuron became a center of liturgical celebration and study and then spread this spirit through new foundations which it established (the Beuron Congregation). Of these Maredsous in Belgium (1872) and Maria Laach (1892), as well as Mont-Cesar at Louvain, which was founded by Maredsous, would all play a decisive role in the liturgical movement of the twentieth century.

Another feature of the restoration period that would be important for later liturgical renewal was its scientific cultivation of liturgical history. Extensive collections of the Fathers and liturgical sources were published (Migne, the German Library of the Church Fathers, the *Analecta hymnica* of G. M. Dreves and C. Blume), along with many textbooks on the liturgy. These included the works of F. X. Schmid (d. 1871), V. Thalhofer (1825-1891) and F. Probst (1816-1899), "who became the real founder and pioneer of modern liturgical science."[84] The way was thus prepared for a critical appraisal of the medieval-Tridentine liturgy, which had often been so unilaterally praised in the restoration period, and for a better grasp of the liturgy as being by its nature a concern of the entire people of God.

The Liturgical Movement of the Twentieth Century (Down to Vatican II)
In a document published at the beginning of the twentieth century Pope Pius X (1903-1914) wrote a sentence that was to mark the beginning of the properly pastoral phase of the liturgical movement, or of what has also been called "the classical liturgical movement."[85] In his Motu Proprio *Tra le sollecitudini* on church music (November 22, 1903), the pope called for "active participation in the holy mysteries and in the public and solemn prayer of the Church."[86] A Belgian Benedictine, Lambert Beauduin of Mont César, picked up the expression "active participation" (Latin: *participatio actuosa*) of the laity in the liturgy and made it the slogan for his pastoral liturgical work. He spoke of the need of "democratizing the liturgy," that is, making it the concern of the entire congregation. At the annual Catholic Day of the Archdiocese of Mechlin in 1909 he had the opportunity of presenting his views to a wide audience. He spoke of the liturgy as being the authentic

prayer of the Church, the bond of unity between priest and people, and the great medium for the Church's preaching. The resolutions he proposed were unanimously accepted: dissemination of vernacular translations of the texts for Sunday Mass and Vespers; the focusing of all piety on the liturgy; annual retreats for church choirs. This "Mechlin event" may be regarded as the birth of the classical liturgical movement.[87] Only a few weeks later Beauduin began to publish a kind of popular missal in the form of a monthly periodical (from 1911 on, as a Sunday missal); in 1910 the first "liturgical week" was celebrated at the Abbey of Mont-César with many participants and in a contagious spirit of enthusiasm.

In Germany, the Abbey of Maria Laach, under Abbot Ildefons Herwegen (from 1913 on), was the chief promoter of liturgical understanding and participation. It directed its efforts first at academics, who in 1913 were invited for the first time to join in the celebration of Holy Week at the abbey. Among the participants were the later imperial chancellor of Germany, H. Bruning, and the later French prime minister, R. Schumann. While the First World War was still going on, editor I. Herwegen inaugurated the series *Ecclesia orans* with the publication of R. Guardini's *The Spirit of the Liturgy*, which is regarded as a classic of the early liturgical movement and has stimulated liturgical understanding through numerous editions down to the present day.[88]

After the First World War numerous scientific studies of the liturgy appeared both in Germany and abroad; for example, the series "Liturgiegeschichtliche Quellen und Forschungen,"[89] the *Jahrbuch für Liturgiewissenschaft*,[90] the publications of F. J. Dölger (especially his *Antike und Christentum*) and his school, including among others Th. Klauser (who founded the *Jahrbuch für Antike und Christentum*), and, in Italy, the multivolume *Liber sacramentorum* of I. Schuster, Benedictine abbot and later cardinal of Milan.[91] One of the outstanding German liturgical scholars was Odo Casel (1886-1948), a monk of Maria Laach, whose studies in the Fathers and the sciences of religion convinced him that the liturgy is to be regarded as a mystery celebration ("the mystery of worship") in which the "primordial mystery," Jesus Christ, becomes redemptively present with his saving activity.[92] Among the praiseworthy servants of the liturgical movement in Germany the following may be mentioned among others: J. Pinsk (Berlin), J. A. Jungmann (Innsbruck), L. K. Mohlberg (Maria Laach), and J. Quasten (Washington, D. C.). Important scientific and practical work was also done by the members of the Leipzig Oratory of St. Philip Neri (from 1930 on; later in Munich as well), among them Th. Gunkel, J. Gulden, H. Kahlefeld, and K. Tillmann.

While the monks of Maria Laach directed their attention chiefly to academics, R. Guardini carried " the spirit of the liturgy" into the world of young students, who under his direction formed the Quickborn association at Burg Rothenfels.

New ways of celebrating Mass played an important part in the liturgical revival after World War I. As early as 1921, the *Missa recitata* (i.e., read rather than sung) was being celebrated in the crypt at Maria Laach; in this Mass the priest celebrated facing the people, while the congregation stood close around the altar and gave the Latin responses (*Missa dialogata*, or "dialogue Mass").[93] Out of this form of celebration grew the later "community Mass," during which a leader of prayer spoke the prayers and readings in German while the priest was reading them in Latin, and the people present prayed many parts together. Once German songs were introduced, the celebration was called a *Betsingmesse* (a "prayed and sung Mass"). Pius Parsch had already introduced, quite early on, the "choral Mass" and the "congregational choral Mass." In all these types of celebration there was a considerable amount of "active participation." As a result of these various forms of the Mass, which had youth groups as their original setting, many parishes also acquired a concern for the liturgy.

The liturgical revival did not fail to arouse opposition and suspicion. Many resisted it as being superficial frivolity and a fad of the young; others objected that it was dividing communities and promoting eccentricity. Two books in particular raised serious charges and disturbed not only the German bishops but the Roman authorities.[94] The result was the so-called "crisis of the liturgical movement" during the Second World War.

Romano Guardini helped to clear the air somewhat with a letter which he wrote in 1940 to Bishop A. Stohr of Mainz.[95] In it he clarified many misunderstandings, rejected some extreme views, and warned against the dangers of liturgicisms, pragmatism, and dilettantism, on the one side, and, on the other, of conservatism and an overhasty reaction by the authorities. In that same year the German bishops established a liturgical commission under the leadership of Bishops A. Stohr and S. Landersdorfer (Passau), which was to direct the liturgical movement from that point on and to prevent a crisis within the Church at a time of serious pressures from without (the Nazi regime and its persecution of the Churches; World War II).

1943 saw a new crisis when a Roman commission of cardinals that had been established precisely to deal with these liturgical tensions sent the German episcopate a letter in which it spoke of Rome's apprehensions and asked the German bishops to put an end to all unauthorized liturgical activity. A week after this letter became public knowledge Archbishop K. Gröber of Freiburg heightened the tensions with his "Seventeen Causes for Concern," which in their basic tenor resembled the apprehensions voiced in the Roman letter. While Cardinal Innitzer of Vienna (Austria was at that time regarded as the "Eastern Marches" of "Greater Germany") in a response of his own declared that the Roman anxieties did not apply to Austria, and distanced himself from Grober's "concerns," the other German bishops sent their answer on April 10, 1943, via their president, Cardinal von Bertram (Breslau). Frankly and persuasively they set Rome straight with regard to its charges or at least showed these to be less serious. On December 24, 1943, the Roman secretariat of state replied in more conciliatory tones that the bishops should henceforth curb unauthorized activity, but at the same time it allowed the "community Mass," the *Betsingmesse,* and the "German High Mass" in which the celebrant recited all the parts in Latin, but at the same time German songs appropriate to each part were sung. Thus the danger which Guardini had feared, of overhasty reaction by the authorities, was averted.[96]

A further turning point in favor of the liturgical movement came in the Enclyclical *Mediator Dei* of Pius XII in 1947, which gave approval in principle to the efforts of the movement. As a result of the encyclical, "Liturgical Institutes" were established in many countries. Numerous national liturgical congresses and international meetings on study of the liturgy were held; especially important was the Congress of Pastoral Liturgy at Assisi in 1956.[97] In his greetings to this congress the pope expressed a deep appreciation of the liturgical movement: "The liturgical movement is thus shown forth as a sign of the providential dispositions of God for the present time, of the movement of the Holy Ghost in the Church, to draw men more closely to the mysteries of the faith and the riches of grace which flow from the active participation of the faithful in the liturgical life."[98]

In the early decades of the century the liturgical movement was concerned with a renewed participation of the faithful in the current Tridentine liturgy. As mid-century drew near, however, it was becoming increasingly clear that the liturgy itself was in need of reform and renewal. A start was made with the new Latin translation of the psalms, which Pius XII released in 1945 (*Psalterium Pianum*). Around mid-century Rome approved a number of national rituals in which the vernacular of the country was used to an ever greater extent. On February 9, 1951 the decree on the reform of the Easter Vigil liturgy appeared; it moved the service from Holy Saturday morning to the beginning of the vigil night. Initially, this was done cautiously and "as an experiment," the change being left to the decision of each bishop. Thus the "Mother of all Vigils" once again acquired an important place in the consciousness of the faithful. The reform of the Easter Vigil was followed on November 16, 1956, by a reorganization of Holy Week in its entirety; this time the change was made obligatory for the whole Church beginning in 1956. There was a sudden feeling that the armor of Trent's "rigid unified liturgy" had been forced open. Although the 1958 Instruction *De musica sacra et sacra liturgia* of the Congregation of Rites was regarded as a setback, the pressure for further reforms was now irresistible.

VATICAN II AND POSTCONCILIAR DEVELOPMENTS

The time was ripe for a radical and comprehensive reform of the liturgy. This came more quickly than expected, due to John XXIII's surprising announcement (January 25, 1959) of a general council and to the spirit of freedom and honest search for the best possible solutions that characterized the work of this council.

The great breakthrough came, despite the final efforts of curial circles that would only too gladly have held on to a rubricized, centralized, and rigidly immutable liturgy. This attitude of the Curia explains the hasty publication of the *Codex rubricarum* of July 27, 1960. "It was impossible not to see in this publication a work intended to forestall later decisions of the council; it subsequently became clear how well-founded this suspicion had been."[99] On April 15, 1961, a new *editio typica* of the Breviary was published, and on June 23, 1962, a new *editio typica* of the Missal; both were produced by the Congregation of Rites, and are probably to be interpreted in the same light as the *Codex rubricarum.* During the preparation of the schema for the liturgical constitution there were still tensions and attempts to organize a last-ditch resistance to profound changes; but the council was able to overcome this opposition as well.

It was an event of epochal importance not only in the history of the liturgy but in the life of the entire Church when on December 4, 1963 (exactly four hundred years after the closing session of the Council of Trent) the liturgical constitution was accepted as the first conciliar document (2147 ayes and 4 nays). The document makes important statements about the nature and meaning of the liturgy and sets the course for a radical reform. Moreover, the document was not the result of motivations peripheral to the main thrust of the council; rather it had a place in achieving the overall goal which the council had set for itself, namely, "to impart an ever increasing vigor to the Christian life of the faithful; to adapt more suitably to the needs of our own times those institutions that are subject to change; to foster whatever can promote union among all who believe in Christ; to strengthen whatever can help to call the whole of humanity into the household of the Church" (*SC* 1).

Only the most important elements in the council's rich and multifaceted treatment of the liturgy can be summarized here. Part II of this book will refer frequently to what the document has to say about particular areas of the liturgy. Among the general aims of the document were the following:

1) to foster a new esteem of the liturgy, because "no other action of the Church can equal its effectiveness by the same title and to the

same degree" (Art. 7);
2) to promote active participation by the faithful (14 and frequently);
3) to promote liturgical science and liturgical formation (15-19);
4) to effect a general renewal in the changeable parts of the liturgy (21-40) insofar as "the good of the Church genuinely and certainly requires" it (23). Special importance is attached to respect for the biblical readings and an increase in their number ("more reading. . . more varied and apposite": 35), to the communal nature of liturgical celebration, to simplification and greater clarity (34), to adaptation to the tradition and special character of peoples, which implies a degree of decentralization (37-40), and to greater consideration of the vernacular (36 and frequently).

These general principles are then applied to various sectors of the liturgy in the later articles of the constitution (47-130). In an appendix the council takes a position on the demand, often heard, that the feast of Easter be assigned to a set Sunday and that a perpetual calendar be developed and followed.[100]

Of decisive importance in carrying out the decisions of the council was the establishment of the *Consilium ad exsequendam constitutionem de sacra liturgia*(Commission for Implementing the Constitution on the Sacred Liturgy = Consilium) by Paul VI in a Motu Proprio of January 25, 1965. Among the most important documents produced by this agency and its successors (see below) were the following six Instructions: three on the orderly implementation of the liturgical constitution (*Inter oecumenici,* 1964; *Tres abhinc annos,* 1967; *Liturgicam instaurationem,* 1970); the Instruction *Musicam sacram* on sacred music (1967); the Instruction *Eucharisticum mysterium* on worship of the Eucharist (1967); and the Instruction *Comme le prévoit* on translation of liturgical texts for celebrations with a congregation (1969). To these must be added the rapid publication of various liturgical rites and books. Here are the rites and books, grouped chronologically under several headings; the titles of the English translations, if they exist, are also given.[101]

CELEBRATION OF THE EUCHARIST
Missale Romanum, 1970, 1975². ET: *The Sacramentary,* 1974, 1985².
Lectionarium Missae, 1969¹, 1981². ET: *Lectionary for Mass, 1970.*

Kyriale simplex, 1965; *Graduale simplex*, 1967. ET: *The Simple Gradual*, 1968.
Ordo cantus missae, 1972. Based on these was the private edition, *Graduale ss. Romanae Ecclesiae* (Solesmes, 1974).

LITURGY OF THE HOURS
Liturgia horarum (4 vols.; 1971ff.). ET: *The Liturgy of the Hours* (4 vols.; 1975ff.)

PONTIFICAL (in separate fascicles)
Liber de ordinatione diaconi, presbyteri et episcopi, 1968. ET: *Ordination of Deacons, Priests, and Bishops*, 1969, 1976.

Ordo benedictionis abbatis et abbatissae, 1970. ET: *Blessing of an Abbot and an Abbess, 1976.*
Ordo consecrationis virginum, 1970. ET: *Consecration to a Life of Virginity*, 1976.
Ordo confirmationis, 1971. ET: Rite of Confirmation, 1971, 1975.
Ordo benedicendi oleum catechumenorum et infirmorum et conficiendi chrisma, 1971. Rite of Blessing the Oils, Rite of Consecrating the Chrism, 1971.
Liber de institutione lectorum et acolythorum; de admissione inter candidatos ad diaconatum et presbyteratum; de sacro caelibatu amplectendo, 1972. ET: *Rite of Institution of Readers and Acolytes; Admission to Candidacy for Ordination as Deacons and Priests; Commitment to Celibacy, 1973, 1976.*
Ordo dedicationis ecclesiae et altaris, 1977. ET: *Dedication of a Church and an Altar*, 1978, 1989.
Caeremoniale Episcoporum, 1984. ET: *Ceremonial of Bishops*, 1989.

RITUAL
Ordo baptismi parvulorum, 1969, 1976[2]. ET: *Rite of Baptism for Children*, 1969.
Ordo celebrandi matrimonium, 1969. ET: *Rite of Marriage*, 1969.
Ordo exsequiarum, 1969. ET: *Rite of Funerals, 1970; Order of Christian Funerals*, 1989.
Ordo professionis religiosae, 1970. ET: *Rite of Religious Profession*, 1975, 1989.
Ordo initiationis christianae adultorum, 1972, 1974[2]. ET: *Rite of Christian Initiation of Adults*, 1974, 1985.

Ordo unctionis infirmorum eorumque pastoralis cura, 1972. ET: *Rite of Anointing and Pastoral Care of the Sick,* 1974; *Pastoral Care of the Sick; Rites of Anointing and Viaticum,* 1983.
De s. communione et de cultu mysterii eucharistici extra missam, 1973. ET: *Holy Communion and Worship of the Eucharist Outside Mass,* 1974.
Ordo paenitentiae, 1974. ET: *Rite of Penance,* 1975.

ROMAN CALENDAR
Calendarium Romanum, 1969. ET: *General Roman Calendar,* 1970.
Instructio de calendariis particularibus (1970). ET: *Instruction on Particular Calendars(DOL; 481).*

In an effort to ensure the most efficient organization of the extensive work entailed in revision of the liturgical books Paul VI, on May 8, 1969, divided the existing Congregation of Rites into a Congregation for Divine Worship and a Congregation for the Causes of Saints. This new arrangement put an end to the work of the Consilium as an independent organization. The latter was initially incorporated as a special commission within the Congregation for Divine Worship, but in 1970 it was dissolved and its work distributed among teams working on specific areas. In his Apostolic Constitution *Constans nobis gaudium* of July 11, 1975, Paul VI combined the Congregation for Divine Worship and the Congregation for the Discipline of the Sacraments (established in 1908) into a single new congregation with the somewhat inappropriate name of "Congregation for the Sacraments and Divine Worship." On April 5, 1984, however, John Paul II dissolved this union and restored independence to each of the parts.

Although most of the books have now been revised,[102] there remains the abiding duty of implementing the basic principles and guiding values in the life of the faithful and of communities. Each generation must tackle anew the task of educating the faithful to an intelligent and active participation in the liturgy.

The faithful by and large welcomed the many liturgical changes as a real improvement and, especially in the parishes, willingly adopted them wherever they were properly implemented. There is no denying, however, that criticism and opposition has been voiced from two different sides. Some people (usually described as "progressives") have regarded the reform as overly timid and limited; they have therefore thought themselves justified in making more extensive changes on their own. Others (the "conservatives") regard almost every change as a betrayal of tradition and a disaster. In particular, the admission of the vernaculars into the liturgy drew especially strong criticism (see the Una Voce groups, for example [103]). Elements of this "conservative" opposition, under the leadership of French (missionary) archbishop Marcel Lefebvre, have come suspiciously close to schism; but this kind of movement has occurred after many ecumenical councils.

To the surprise of many, on October 3, 1984, the Congregation for the Sacraments and Divine Worship issued a papal indult in which bishops were authorized to allow those priests and faithful "who had remained attached to the so-called Tridentine Rite" to celebrate Mass using "the Roman Missal of 1962."

The following norms are to be observed in granting this authorization. Such priests and faithful must "have no ties with those who impugn the lawfulness and doctrinal soundness of the Roman Missal promulgated in 1970 by Pope Paul VI." The celebration must be solely for those who petition it, and the local bishop must determine the time, place, and other circumstances. The Mass is to be in Latin, and there is to be no intermingling of the old rite with the rites and texts of the new missal. Finally, "the indult is to be used without prejudice to the liturgical reform that is to be observed in the life of each ecclesial community." The document is presented as "a sign of the care the common Father has for all of his children."[104]

Chapter Three

The Science of Liturgy

HISTORICAL DEVELOPMENT

The liturgy has not always been the object of scientific study. In Christian antiquity it was thought enough to offer, in addition to the usual homily during services, catechetico-homiletical explanations of the sacraments of initiation, that is, baptism, confirmation, and the Eucharist. Surprisingly, the instructions were given not before the reception of these sacraments at the Easter Vigil, but afterwards during the liturgies of the ensuing Easter week. Explanations of this kind have come down to us from Cyril (John?) of Jerusalem and Theodore of Mopsuestia in the East, and from Zeno of Verona, Ambrose of Milan, and Augustine of Hippo in the West.

The late patristic period saw the beginnings of an allegorical interpretation of the liturgy. This genre had its first golden age in the Carolingian period in the writings of Alcuin and Amalarius of Metz. In the high Middle Ages it experienced a new flowering in, among others, John Beleth, Sicard of Cremona, Innocent III, and William Durandus of Mende. There were few opponents of the method, the most important being Albert the Great.[1]

A scientific approach to the liturgy began with the humanists and their historico-critical method. Disputes with the Reformers likewise led on both sides to a more intense study of liturgical sources and to historical investigations such as those of J. Pamelius and M. Hittorp. Studies of this kind became more numerous and important in the seventeenth and eighteenth centuries (Baroque period). Special interest attached to publications on the Eastern liturgies, for example, those of J. Goar and the scholarly Assemani family.

The development of pastoral theology from the end of the eighteenth century on caused attention to be focused as well on the contemporary liturgy and thus led to the beginnings of a systematic theological science of the liturgy. Deserving of special mention here is F. X. Schmid, a disciple of Sailer; he was probably the first to insist, in his three-volume *Liturgik der christ-katholischen Religion,*[2] that liturgics should be regarded as an independent science (*scientia liturgica*, I, 9). Its object, according to Schmid, is the externals of Catholic liturgy: "the totality of ceremonies, the garb in which catholicism becomes visible and audible" (Preface, VIII), the way in which it "as it were travels the earth in visible and audible bodily form—the way in which it is embodied and lives" (I, 18). But liturgical science is not concerned solely with the origin and significance of the individual "ceremonies" and with a "summary listing of these"; it also endeavors to organize them into "a systematic whole" and to judge their "value or lack of value" in relation to the essence of the Catholic religion and the needs of the faithful (*ibid.*, 9).

In 1899, however, Suibert Bäumer, O.S.B., presented a considerably more profound view of the liturgy, when he defined it as the "science of the praying and sanctifying Church" and as therefore to "be assigned a high rank."[3]

R. Guardini adopted this same view in an essay of 1921: "The object of systematic study of the liturgy is thus the living, sacrificing, praying Church as it carries out the mysteries of grace, and therefore in its actual exercise of worship and its compulsory expressions of this worship."[4] A short time later, Athanasius Wintersig of Maria Laach went a step further when he spoke of the liturgy as "the continuing action of Christ the high priest in the Church" and as "the holy mystery." This mystery, he said, is "the authentic center of the religious life of the believing community"; it is the subject with which pastoral liturgics is specifically concerned.[5]

It thus became increasingly clear that the science of the liturgy is primarily a theological science and deals with key aspects of the faith. Clarification of this point "is doubtless an abiding contribution of O. Casel, O.S.B. (1886-1948), who thus set a standard which liturgical science must continue to meet; this service must be acknowledged independently of how many or few of Casel's controversial premises and statements the individual scholar accepts."[6]

TASKS AND PROBLEMS OF CONTEMPORARY LITURGICAL SCIENCE

The conception of the liturgy that found expression in Vatican II likewise influences the place and tasks of a science of the liturgy. Inasmuch as the liturgy is an exercise of Christ's priestly office and a joint action of Christ and the Church for the sanctification of human beings and the glorification of God (see *SC* 7), scientific reflection on it must attend both to Jesus Christ the high priest and to the Church as Christ continuing his life and work on earth. The object of liturgical science is nothing less than the divine economy of salvation and the paschal mystery of Christ, but it must also include the community of Christ that receives salvation and responds to it. A science of the liturgy must inquire to what extent the mystery of Christ is accomplished in the visible signs of the liturgical celebration and is applied therein to the faithful, and whether and how the faithful in turn give an appropriate response in their liturgical assemblies and outside of these as well. A science of the liturgy is thus an eminently theological discipline.

This theological approach must be accompanied by an historical one that will show which liturgical actions and forms are to be attributed to Christ himself, which have their roots in the first Christian community or, even earlier, in Judaism, and, finally, which ideas, texts, and rites came into existence as the Church developed against the background of contemporary cultures and in the setting of contemporary history. It is necessary to ascertain how the common liturgy of the Church's beginnings took on a distinctive character in each of the liturgical families of East and West.

Since the liturgy is celebrated by local communities and therefore by changeable individuals who reflect the conditions of their time, liturgical science must also take concrete human beings into consideration. This means examining their capacity for liturgy; that is, whether and to what extent they are open to God's care of them; whether they are able to understand the signs that interpret the mystery, and to respond to God's saving call and offer of salvation in word, sign, and the circumstances of life. Moreover they are to understand and respond not simply as individuals but as members of the community of Christ. This new dimension supposes that they have a capacity for community and can move beyond an individualistic or even self-centered attitude. This aspect of the scientific effort to optimize the capacity for liturgy is the object of pastoral liturgics, although the latter is hardly to be considered an independent discipline, as A. Wintersig desired.[7]

In this context it is also the task of liturgical science to inquire whether many changeable parts of the liturgy are not in need of revision. "In this reform both texts and rites should be so drawn up that they express more clearly the holy things they signify and that the Christian people, as far as possible, are able to understand them with ease and to take part in the rites fully, actively, and as befits a community" (*SC* 21) The council expressly requires that any revision be preceded by "a careful investigation" which is "theological, historical, and pastoral" (*SC* 23). When the constitution goes on to say that "the general laws governing the structure and meaning of the liturgy" are to be studied, it is again setting a task for liturgical science.

It was said above that it is concrete individuals who participate in the liturgy. Liturgical science must also be open, therefore, to the authoritative findings of the human sciences. Relevant here are psychology (including group psychology and depth psychology), the science of language and communication, phenomenology, sociology, semiotics (the science of signs), the history of art, and the musical sciences. Since so many disciplines must make their contribution, one can accept the call for an "integrative method" and the "recovery of the empirical dimension,"[8] although in many cases this makes excessive demands of the individual liturgical scholar. On the other hand, the demands become less excessive to the extent that the results of the human sciences can be transmitted in a formation which is interdisciplinary in character. Other sciences too, after all, and especially such practico-theological disciplines as pastoral theology, homiletics, religious pedagogy, and catechetics are similarly dependent on those results. Happily, such an arrangement is already envisaged in the "Program of Priestly Formation of the National Conferency Catholic Bishops"; here provision is made for the study of the behavioral and social sciences, history, culture and literatures and also the natural sciences.[9]

Consistently with the high value which it sets on the liturgy, Vatican II also assigns liturgical science a new rank in the cosmos of the theological disciplines: "the study of liturgy is to be ranked among the compulsory and major courses in seminaries and religious houses of study; in theological faculties it is to rank among the principal courses" (*SC* 16). The council adds that this scientific discipline is to be "taught under its theological, historical, spiritual, pastoral, and canonical aspects" (*ibid.*). The very multiplicity of these aspects shows that liturgical science cannot rely exclusively on some single method. "The fact that there is no specific method for liturgical science shows that this discipline occupies a special place."[10]

At the same time the council requires that the professors of other disciplines, "while striving to expound the mystery of Christ and the history of salvation from the angle proper to each of their own subjects, must . . . do so in a way that will clearly bring out the connection between their subjects and the liturgy, as also the underlying unity of all priestly training" (*SC* 16). This is a clear invitation to promote a theme-oriented interdisciplinary dialogue within the theological faculties themselves. Liturgical science, as "doxological theology,"[11] has a critical function in relation to the other theological disciplines[12]; so too "the neighboring disciplines have the critical function of checking our work and supplying us with material which we cannot provide for ourselves."[13]

Not the least of the duties of liturgical science is to develop and transmit a "liturgical spirituality."[14] This obligation is expressly set down in a passage already cited from *SC* 16, where it is said that the liturgy is to be studied from the viewpoint of the spiritual life, among others. "Spiritual life" is a life lived under the influence of the Spirit of Christ; this means, concretely, a loving self-surrender to God, the following of Christ in everyday existence, and, consequently, a loving concern for our fellow human beings and an effort to shape the world in the light of Christian values. Liturgical spirituality[15] is to a large extent coextensive with biblical spirituality, since the celebration of the liturgy submits the participants ever anew to the word of God. For in the readings "God is speaking to his people, opening up to them the mystery of redemption and salvation, and nourishing their spirit; Christ is present to the faithful through his own word" (*GIRM* 33). The encounter with Christ becomes even closer in liturgical participation in the paschal mystery, especially at the Eucharist. This "liturgical formation in [the] spiritual life" (*SC* 17) is an inherent result of a proper celebration of the liturgy. Liturgical science should open the eyes of students to this and prepare the way for it.[16]

SOURCES AND TOOLS OF LITURGICAL SCIENCE

Chapter II, on the history of the liturgy, also provided many indications of the sources and tools of liturgical science. Later chapters on the particular areas of the liturgy will do the same. All these discussions make it clear that the primary source of information for liturgical science is the writings of the New Testament, although these writings contain no systematic discussion of Christian worship. Also of great importance are the testimonies of the postapostolic period and the gradually appearing descriptions of Christian liturgies, such as we find in, for example, Justin Martyr and Hippolytus of Rome. But if I were to list these in detail, I would be covering the same ground twice. The same must be said of the next period, in which patristic literature provides us with a great deal of information and, in addition, we find documents of many kinds dealing with the worship of the individual liturgical families. Basic for our knowledge of the Roman liturgy are the sacramentaries, the *libelli*, and the Roman *ordines*.[17] The subsequent development of the Western liturgy with its most important liturgical books, documents, and literary expressions is likewise already sufficiently known to us here from the historical survey in Chapter II; we may therefore turn immediately to our own day.

The most recent sources to be used by liturgical science are the documents of Vatican II and of the postconciliar commissions, insofar as they relate to the liturgy. This documentation has found its practical embodiment in the revised liturgical books.[18] Various collections and commentaries help make these sources accessible (for example, Kaczynski, *Documents on the Liturgy, 1963-1979*, and the *Commentary on the Documents of Vatican II* that was published as a supplement to the *Lexikon fur Theologie und Kirche*), as do the numerous monographs on particular questions. Also of service are the many periodicals dealing with the history, theology, and pastoral aspect of the liturgy. I close this brief survey with a list of these periodicals (in alphabetical order). Periodicals that only occasionally deal with liturgical themes are not included.

1. *Archiv fur Liturgiewissenschaft* (Regensburg)
2. *Bibel und Liturgie* (Klosterneuburg)
3. *Communauts et liturgie* (Ottingies, Belgium)
4. *Ecclesia orans* (Rome)
5. *Ephemerides liturgicae* (Rome)
6. Gottesdienst (Freiburg, etc.)
7. *Jahrbuch fur Liturgik und Hymnologie* (Kassel; Evangelical)
8. *La Maison-Dieu* (Paris)
9. *Liturgisches Jahrbuch* (Münster)
10. *Liturgy* (Washington, D.C.)
11. *Liturgy ' 80* (Chicago)
12. *Musica sacra* (Regensburg)
13. *Notitiae* (Vatican City)
14. Questions liturgiques (Louvain)
15. *Studia liturgica* (Rotterdam)
16. *Tijdschrift voor liturgie* (Affligem, Belgium)
17. *Worship* (Formerly *Orate fratres*) (Collegeville, Minnesota)

Chapter Four

The Liturgical Assembly as a Process of Communication

SOME BASIC PRINCIPLES

Two dimensions of activity need to be distinguished when Christian communities (groups) gather for liturgy: the dimension of the mystery of salvation and the dimension of behavior and activity among human beings.

The first of these two activities involves God in Christ turning to the community in love and giving himself to it. Liturgy is primarily a matter of divine giving. To the extent that the faithful open themselves to this self-donation of God and respond to him with grateful praise and with a self-giving in return, liturgy acquires a vertical dimension: the encounter and communion of God and human beings. It is here that the mystery of salvation is accomplished. The full reality of what happens here can be apprehended only by faith and is therefore in great measure inaccessible to empirical observation.

The situation is different in the area of interhuman behavior and activity, which, according to the anthropological sciences, may be understood and examined as a process of communication. "The rediscovery of the communicational structure of all liturgical celebrations is one of the most important results of the liturgical reform that has been going on since Vatican II."[1]

A "process of communication" consists in the transmission of information (facts, appeals of one or other kind) by a communicator (speaker, transmitter) to participants (hearers, receivers) by means of particular signals of a verbal or nonverbal kind. There are laws at work in this process that can determine whether the goal of communication is attained. I shall not list them here in a series of definitions[2] but shall simply apply the most important of them directly to the liturgical assembly and reflect on their relevance to the success or failure of the liturgy.[3]

An important role in the liturgical process of communication belongs to the communicator, who in this case is the presiding minister (leader), that is, the bishop, priest, deacon, or commissioned layperson. His very personality and the total impression he gives (the image he projects) is already decisive for the deciphering (decoding), by the participants in the liturgy, of what he is communicating. If they accept and esteem him, then they will from the outset be more attentive and receptive. His manner of conducting himself must show that he intends to be, not a ruler of the community, but a brother among brethren (see Mt 23:8) and a servant bent upon increasing their joy (see 2 Cor 1:24).

This attitude should be perceptible at the very beginning of the service when he greets the community and introduces them to the liturgy. On this point the *Directory for Masses with Children* makes a statement that should be heeded since it is important for all liturgies: "It is the responsibility of the priest . . . to make the celebration festive, familial, and meditative" by "his manner of acting and speaking with others."[4] It should also be clear to the assembly that the leader's way of expressing what he communicates springs from experience and personal conviction. This is true especially of the sermon (homily), in which the hearers should be able to tell that the priest has himself been touched and apprehended by the word of God before attempting to transmit it to the community. Augustine describes this sequence in a play on words "Territus terreo": "I myself am filled with reverent fear before I try to make others fearful"; "I myself am deeply moved before I try to move others."[5]

The leader's prayer, too—which he usually says in the first person plural ("We . . .") because he is acting as leader of prayer for and with the community—must have a certain character: it must avoid, on the one hand, theatricality and false emotion, and, on the other, cold, unfeeling routine. This prayer is indeed first and foremost "vertical," being addressed to God; but it is at the same time a communication with the community, which must be able to make it its own and join in it. In this area, too, therefore, there can be disruptions of communication.

The leader's behavior is likewise decisive in the area of nonverbal communication (communication by signs). As I shall show in detail later on, liturgical signs and symbols are symbols conveying information. If the manner in which they are sent is wrong, they can distort the intended message and lead to disruptions of communication.

As a communicator, then, the leader must be possessed of a keen sensibility. He must have an eye and ear that will enable him to shape the liturgy in a harmonious way, a feeling for atmosphere that will keep the liturgy from being boring and joyless, and a sensitivity to disruptions of communication should these begin to appear.

The participants in the liturgy, for their part, are not simply mute spectators and passive listeners, but sharers in the celebration ("concelebrants" in the proper sense of the word) who are to contribute to the liturgy by their exterior and interior behavior (see Chapter I). I have already said something about their relation and attitude to the leader.

Also important to the flow of the communication process is the kind of expectations that the participants bring to the liturgy. Statistical studies (among others, the questionnaires sent out for the Würzburg Synod[6]) show that most of the people participating in the service have not yet fully accepted the ideal picture of the liturgy that is set down in the documents of Vatican II. Most of them still look for quiet, personal prayer, and private encounter with God. "This is even more true of occasional churchgoers: in their responses the formula 'Quiet, and personal prayer' is by far the most frequent."[7] Such expectations from a quite unhomogeneous liturgical community certainly cannot supply the norm for structuring the liturgy. On the other hand, they do provide clues to the weak points of the liturgical assembly and reasons for undertaking a more intensive education and motivation of these visitors. Thus the emphasis on the desire for quiet and for personal prayer represents a justifiable rejection of several things: the restlessness and hectic activity often seen in the liturgy; the excessive talkativeness of many priests ("sermonitis"); and the lack of periods of silence during the celebration.[8]

In liturgical assemblies as in all processes of communication the ideas of "transmitter" and "receiver" are often not the same. What the leader is communicating in introduction, reading, or sermon is often received by the hearers in a way not intended. The reasons for this may be a defective capacity for understanding (differences in the "stock of signs" of each person), differences in experiential background or sociocultural context, and even the operation of processes of selectivity that prevent many "messages" from being remembered or perhaps received at all. It is important, therefore, that the leader be alert to sensory responses from his listeners and that in, for example, a subsequent discussion of the liturgy and sermon he accept and evaluate any feedback.

In any process of communication the media used play an especially important role. In the liturgy these media are, above all, language and liturgical signs (symbols). We must therefore reflect more fully on each of these.

LITURGICAL LANGUAGE (VERBAL COMMUNICATION)

As a result of Vatican II, and after a lengthy period in which Latin alone had been used almost exclusively, the liturgy of the Roman rite made room for the vernaculars. This was an event of historical importance. Most of the faithful are glad of the change; a few, however, regard it as a scandal, since they see it as a betrayal of tradition. Here again, knowledge of the beginnings of the Christian liturgy and of its subsequent development can provide criteria for sound judgment on this question.

Historical Retrospect

As the original Aramaic gospel of Matthew suggests, the liturgical language of the first community in Jerusalem was the colloquial Aramaic of everyday life, although many of the formulas and acclamations used in prayer were surely in Hebrew. Outside of Palestine the Church used chiefly Greek. Other languages whose use in the Christian liturgy is attested for the early centuries are Syriac, Coptic, Ethiopic (known as Ge'ez), Armenian, Georgian, Old Slavonic, and, from the tenth century on, Arabic.[9] It can be said that the Eastern Churches have always accepted the current language of the country and, to some extent, have celebrated the liturgy in several languages in communities where several languages are spoken.[10]

Greek, in the form known as "Koine" ("Common"), was the dominant everyday language of Rome down to the third century, and this among the educated as well as among a great many of the ordinary people. It comes therefore as no surprise to learn that the Roman liturgy was celebrated in Greek at least until the third century, as can be seen, for example, from the Church Order (the *Apostolic Tradition*) of Hippolytus of Rome (ca. 215).

The restoration of the Latin language, beginning in the reign of Emperor Decius (249-251), confronted Rome with a problem already experienced elsewhere: the discrepency between the language of the people and the language of the liturgy. In this situation the Roman Church, in a somewhat lengthy transition, adopted the principle that the liturgy must be celebrated in the language of the people. The Latinization process was completed in about 380 under Pope Damasus.[11]

"Ambrosiaster," an anonymous commentator on the letters of Paul and a contemporary of Pope Damasus, tells us in his comments on 1 Corinthians 14 that the people of the day felt it unnatural for Latins to be singing Greek songs whose meaning they did not understand. The pleasure given by the melodious sound of the words did not outweigh the great disadvantage that the whole activity was a fruitless one. Following Paul, who in the passage in question says he would rather speak five intelligible words than ten thousand unintelligible ones (v. 19), Ambrosiaster ends with this admonition: "If you come together in order to build up the Church, you must speak a language the hearers can understand."[12] As the use of Greek spread again under Byzantine rule, readings in both languages were introduced into the papal liturgy from the seventh century on; both languages were also used in important parts of the baptismal rite.

After Cyril and Methodius had come from Constantinople to evangelize the Slavs of Moravia in the second half of the ninth century, a lively controversy arose on the subject of the language to be used in the liturgy. The two missionaries had translated the "Liturgy of St. Peter" into Slavic; to them as Byzantines this seemed a quite normal step. They met with the objection, however, that only three languages were appropriate in the liturgy; namely, Hebrew, Latin, and Greek, because these had been given sacral status by the inscription on the cross of Jesus.

The missionaries were summoned to Rome and interrogated. In the end, however, Pope John VIII declared in 880 that God desired to be honored in every language. It is not (he said) an offense against orthodoxy to sing the Mass in the Slavic language or to proclaim the gospel and the divine readings in a good translation; after all, the Creator of the three prinicipal languages created all the others as well for his honor.[13]

Exactly two hundred years later Gregory VII withdrew the permission given by John VIII and refused the request of King Vratislav of Bohemia for the continued use of the Slavic language in the liturgy. The pope's reason, which looks chiefly to the sacred scriptures, is a surprising one: It has rightly pleased almighty God that the scriptures should remain veiled in certain regions of the world, lest universal accessibility should make them seem ordinary and cause them to be treated with contempt and lest ordinary people misunderstand them and so be led into error.[14]

In the high Middle Ages Latin had acquired such a status in public life that its use as the language of the liturgy drew no objection from the influential classes. At the beginning of the sixteenth century, however, well-intentioned voices were to be heard arguing that the interests of the simple people required the use of the vernaculars. Thus Paul Giustiniani and Vincenzo Quirini, who had become Camaldolese monks in 1512, addressed a petition to Leo X in 1513 in which they recalled the linguistic practices of the patristic period and asked why the Church should not imitate the Fathers in this area, since only a few of the faithful understood Latin. No one of sound mind (they said) could reasonably argue against the translation of liturgical texts as some were doing who wanted to be regarded as the only wise men around. The people would take much fruit home from their churches if they understood what was being read to them there. The pope should therefore put an end to the *latina miseria*, the "impoverishment caused by Latin."[15] —Others, however, like Nicholas Herborn, Guardian of the Franciscan convent at Marburg, regarded the use of Latin in the liturgy as *praecipuum articulum fidei nostrae*, "an important article of our faith."[16]

Although the demands and practices of the Reformers with regard to the vernaculars in the liturgy caused a hardening of positions, the Council of Trent (1545-1563) limited itself to condemning the claim that Mass should be celebrated *solely* in the vernacular[17]; it thus left the door open for further developments. Yet as early as the end of the sixteenth century this canon of Trent was interpreted as meaning that the council had forbidden any and every liturgy in the vernacular; as a result, the Roman position in favor of Latin underwent significant hardening in the ensuing four centuries. Even translations of the Missal for private use were forbidden; thus Alexander VII issued an unusually sharp condemnation (Brief of 1661) of French priest J. de Voisin's translation.[18] In 1851 the Congregation of Rites renewed the prohibition against translations of the Missal; in 1857 Pius IX forbade the translation of the Canon and the words of consecration. In 1891 Leo XIII finally ordered that such translations were no longer to be challenged.[19]

Only around the middle of the twentieth century could a softening of the Roman attitude to the liturgical use of the vernacular be seen, beginning with the Encyclical *Mediator Dei* (no. 59). But a radical change did not come until Vatican II. In *SC* 36 the council said that the use of the Latin language was to be preserved "in the Latin rites" insofar as particular law did not say otherwise; at the same time, however, it allowed more room for the vernacular for the sake of the great pastoral advantage it would bring. The manner in which the vernacular was to be introduced was left to the decision of the regional episcopal conferences with Rome's approval.

The permission thus given was substantially broadened in the ensuing years at the request of a number of episcopal conferences and with the approval of the pope, so that today practically the entire liturgy can be celebrated in the vernacular. This development admittedly goes beyond the wording of the council, but at the same time it must be acknowledged to be implicit in the council's call for conscious and active participation of the people and for the adaptation of the rites to make them comprehensible to the faithful. How can those ignorant of Latin join consciously and intelligently in the celebration of the liturgy, when an unknown foreign language keeps them from grasping the content of the texts? Such a situation represents a radical disruption of communication, in the face of which all the traditional arguments for Latin cease to carry any weight.[20] At the same time, however, bishops and episcopal conferences repeatedly urge that communities not be allowed to lose what capacity they have for celebration of the Mass in Latin; the bishops' appeal is motivatied not least by the thought of liturgies in which the participating faithful speak different languages. For this reason many dioceses have decided that a Latin Mass must be celebrated once a month.

The Problem of Translations into the Vernaculars

The granting of permission for vernacular liturgies quickly led to the discovery that many literal translations of the Latin original were highly unsatisfactory, especially when the original expressed ideas tied to particular historical periods and particular cultures. Even the piety of the early Christian ages had its special historical coloring and cannot be simply carried over into the present. In addition, many theological emphases have shifted to a marked degree, especially since Vatican II. For example: in many of the presidential prayers we ask that we may "condemn what is earthly and love the things of heaven"; our age, however, in agreement with the council, emphasizes the role of Christians in relation to the present world. Christians must take earthly realities seriously; they must regard themselves as divinely commissioned to structure these realities properly and to work for the temporal as well as the eternal salvation of their fellow human beings.

Further problems arose from the fact that the full meaning of many Latin terms cannot be reproduced in a single word of the vernacular (e.g., the Latin *mysterium*) and that many literal translations are ill-adapted for setting to music. The experience of these various difficulties caused a widespread dissatisfaction that seemed to justify the opponents of a vernacular liturgy.

In this difficult situation the Instruction of the Roman Consilium on the translation of liturgical texts (January 25, 1969) provided valuable help.[21] The document was based on the results of an international congress on the translation of liturgical texts (Rome, November 9-13, 1965). It says, among other things, that it is not enough to translate a text word for word; rather "the translator should give first consideration to the meaning of the communication" (no. 8). "A faithful translation, therefore, cannot be judged on the basis of individual words: the total context of this specific act of communication must be kept in mind, as well as the literary form proper to the respective language" (no. 6). "To keep the correct signification, words and expressions must be used in their proper historical, social, and ritual meanings" (no.13 d).

The language (says the Instruction) should be that of elevated common usage. Generally speaking, it is better to create the new language needed "by infusing a Christian meaning into common words" rather than by "importing uncommon or technical terms" (no. 19. 3). As far as prayers are concerned, "the formula translated must become the genuine prayer of the congregation and in it each of its members should be able to find and express himself or herself" (no. 20 c). In prayers to be spoken by the community, and especially in acclamations, special heed must be given to the phonetic and rhythmic qualities of the language (no. 35).

These are but of a few of the document's many important directives and recommendations. The authors of the Instruction were aware, however, that translations alone, however good, are not enough. The document therefore ends with this impressive and significant observation: "Texts translated from another language are clearly not sufficient for the celebration of a fully renewed liturgy. The creation of new texts will be necessary" (no. 43).

This admission sets our age a difficult task. For, on the one hand, the language of the liturgy must be intelligible and true to life, "without lapsing into the language of the newspapers, the sciences, or faddish jargon."[22] On the other hand, it should be the expression of religious experience; it ought to be language that emerges from God and speaks to God; it should strike to the center of the human heart and thus come close to poetry, as has been the case with many psalms and hymns of the past.[23] Texts of this high a quality cannot be produced on order. They require inspiration and time to mature. Our communities must realize this and be patient.[24]

THE LANGUAGE OF LITURGICAL SIGNS

The Meaning of "Sign" and "Symbol"

In addition to verbal language the liturgy also uses a wordless speech: the world of signs that point to specific realities. It is true, of course, that spoken words are, in a broad sense, audible and legible signs to other human beings. In addition, however, there are things, persons, actions, and postures that are perceptible by the senses and that point beyond their own existence and nature to other, invisible realities. In addition to their own native meaning they convey another; they are "sensible images" of invisible realities; they function as signs. Thus Thomas Aquinas in his treatise on the sacraments long ago defined a sign as "something through which a person achieves knowledge of some further thing."[25] Signs are therefore revelatory, although they do not disclose the full existential reality of that to which they point. This relationship between visible and invisible is possible because of a certain similarity between sign and signified.

The word "symbol," which is derived from the Greek, is also used for this kind of sign. Originally, "symbol" referred to the two halves of some broken object (a ring, a staff, a tablet, and so on), which, when fitted together (Greek: *symballein*, "throw together"), served as a means by which the holder of one half could recognize in the holder of the other an authentic guest, messenger, or partner in an agreement. A symbol is thus a sign that consists, so to speak, of two parts: a visible part and an suprasensible reality which the visible part signifies. Only when the two parts are put together does the whole become visible.

There is no agreement on the conceptual definition of symbol or, therefore, on how the word is to be used. As used by many, symbol has a broad meaning and includes in practice the entire range of signs. Others use it in a narrower sense that distinguishes it from the rest of the world of signs: "they limit it strictly to significatory phenomena with two meanings . . ., in which the immediately recognizable meaning urges the mind on to a further meaning."[26] The objection to this view is that every sign is a "phenomenon with two meanings" and points to a "further meaning," even if the element of " immediate" recognition of the significatory thrust can be found only with difficulty or varies in degree.

Also unsatisfactory is the attempt to define a symbol as a "stylized sign" and thereby differentiate it from other signs. A. Verheul, for example, writes: "The more one stylizes, the more the sign approaches the symbol, and the more one passes from sign to symbol. . . . Thus we have here to do with the extreme of spiritualization and stylizing of the image."[27] But in this area, too, the line of demarcation can only be fluid, and it will be difficult to decide in very many instances whether the degree of stylization has been reached that turns a sign into a symbol. Nor is it possible to agree with Verheul when he asserts that "a symbol is never a natural sign, but a cultural sign, and therefore a freely chosen sign."[28] This assertion would lead to the conclusion that such "primal symbols" as water, wind, fire, light, mountain, rock, and so on, which are shared by all peoples and cultures, do not deserve the name "symbol" at all.[29]

All these considerations and critiques suggest the advisability of not looking for criteria to distinguish between sign and symbol and, instead, of using the two words as synonyms.[30] This is not to deny that various signs differ in the intensity with which they carry the mind to the signified reality or, in other words, that they differ in their power of signifying.

The use of signs (symbols) does not at all mean an impoverishment of communication. On the contrary: they are able to express invisible realities with an intensity not often achieved by verbal language. They mediate a quick, intuitive grasp and penetrate into areas largely closed to logical speech.

"Symbolism is a mode of speech that ventures to penetrate the world of the incomparable by means of comparisons, while at the same time maintaining an appropriate distance from it. An expression is symbolic when the cognitive content expressed remains open to various kinds of acknowledgment and appropriation, to affective as well as cognitive access, and to quite varied possibilities of understanding by those who are addressed and share the experience. Symbolism can serve as a bridge between varying levels of linguistic capability and can even leap over quite pronounced linguistic boundaries." [31]

The world of signs that we encounter in everyday life is extensive beyond imagining: we "are confronted with a bewilderingly complex and multifaceted world."[32] This variety is already evident in the immense variety of classifications.

"People speak, for example, of natural and artificial symbols, symbols properly and improperly so called, symbols transparent and opaque. Or a distinction is made between primal symbols springing from nature and history and symbols that are societal or legislated or national or confessional. In reference to the areas of life in which symbols appear a distinction is drawn between psychological, metaphysical, religious, and esthetic symbols. An attempt is made to bring out the nature and role of symbols by distinguishing ontological symbols from functional, representative from expressive, presentational from discursive, symbols that veil from symbols that disclose. It is possible to speak of status symbols; expressive, associative, instrumental, and goal-directed symbolisms; dream symbolism, object symbolisms, and linguistic symbolisms; primary and secondary symbolisms. Yet it is also observable that in all these efforts at schematization the symbols themselves are usually concrete individual realities which can be systematized only with difficulty, at least if logical symbols, culminating in those that are mathematical, are left out of consideration." [33]

In recent times numerous sciences have dealt extensively with this world of symbols and tried to analyze it each in its own technical language. I need only mention linguistics, the science of communication, religious phenomenology and philosophy, psychology (including depth psychology), sociology and social psychology. Most importantly, in the last few decades semiotics, the science of signs, has taken a systematic approach to "the special character, significance, and functioning of the signs through which human beings communicate with one another."[34] Here too a technical terminology has quickly emerged, although the competing systems are far from having reached agreement on terminology. The brevity of the present outline and the desire to be understood by all have led me to avoid this technical terminology (the same holds for the technical terminology of the other sciences I have mentioned).[35]

The Cosmos of Liturgical Signs

In the biblical and Christian understanding of the world every existing thing is a creature and therefore at the same time a sign pointing to the Creator: "The heavens are telling the glory of God; and the firmament proclaims his handiwork" (Ps 19:1). "Even in the anemone and the carnation the kingdom and the glory are present, Lord, for him who sees it and whose gaze embraces all things."[36]

In the incarnation of Christ the incomprehensible fullness of divine being took bodily form. In Christ the glory of God is revealed in a corporeal, sensible way (see Jn 1:14; 2 Cor 4:6). Those who see him see the Father (Jn 14:9). "He is the image (*eikon*) of the invisible God" (Col 1:15; see 2 Cor 4:4). Understood in this way, the God-man, Jesus Christ, is the most profound, the most comprehensive, the richest of all symbols, disclosing as he does the infinite dimensions of God.

The Church as "mystical body of Christ" shares in this corporeality of God in Jesus Christ. Theologians speak of the incarnational structure of the Church: because the Spirit of Christ lives and works in it, the Church exists among the nations as a visible sign of salvation; in and through it the high priest of the new covenant communicates the invisible glory and grace of God through the visible signs that are the sacraments. It is possible to understand in this sense the words of Pope Leo the Great (440-461): "What was visible in Christ has passed over into the sacraments of the Church."[37] And Thomas Aquinas says of the sacraments in the narrow sense of the term that they are signs recalling the past, that is, the passion of Christ (*signa rememorativa*), signs pointing to the present, that is, to the bestowal of grace (*signa demonstrativa*), and anticipatory signs announcing the glory to come (*signa prognostica*).[38]

The cultic activity of the faithful (the ascending line of liturgical action) also displays a wealth of symbolic actions and objects. The very *assembly* of the faithful is clearly a sign, inasmuch as it is not a collection of disparate individuals but the "people of God," the mystical body of Christ, God's partner in the liturgical action, and what is signified and sought is communion (*koinõnia*) with God and one another as one of the greatest of all the blessings included in salvation. The attentiveness, reverence, and thankful response of the community to the word of God and to his sacramental action shows itself not only in spoken and sung words of praise, thanksgiving, adoration, and petition, but also in bodily actions, postures, and gestures as well as in the use of symbolic objects. In what follows here I shall limit myself to a short survey; because I must be so brief I refer the reader to the extensive literature for more detailed information and explanation.[39]

Even bodily *posture* can be an expression of spiritual attitudes and convictions. The postures used in the liturgy are standing, kneeling, and sitting; walking (processions); obeisances or bows, including the *prostratio* or stretching out on the ground, as, for example, on Good Friday or at priestly ordination; and, in many countries, religious dancing and rounds.[40]

Gestures with the *hands* are many: folding, raising, stretching out, imposing, signing with the cross, striking the breast, blessing, giving to others in the greeting of peace, and washing. Numerous, too, are ritual actions in which symbolic objects are used: for example, the pouring of water on a person at baptism, anointings with holy oils. At Mass there is the kissing of altar and gospel book; the preparation of the altar (the holy table); the bringing of bread and wine; the mixing of water with the wine; the breaking of the host; the sacred meal as such; the greeting or kiss of peace; the use of incense on solemn occasions. In the course of the liturgical year there is the signing with ashes, the veiling of the cross, the blessing and procession of palms, the washing of feet on Holy Thursday, the ritual of light during the Easter Vigil (Easter candle), and all sorts of blessings (of foods at Easter, medicinal herbs on the feast of Mary's Assumption, produce at the harvest feasts).

During the liturgical year we also encounter many things that serve as signs: cross, candle, sanctuary lamp, altar veils or banners depicting the passion, and images. The church building, as a whole and in its parts, is full of symbolism: exterior parts such as entrance court and main door, tower and bells; interior parts such as the altar, ambo (pulpit), presidential chair, baptismal font, organ, and so on.[41] The liturgical vestments and their colors are also symbolic; I shall speak of these in the next section.

History and Significance of the Liturgical Vestments and Colors

The early Christians had no special liturgical vestments. On the other hand, the conviction quite soon arose that people should wear festive garments for the celebration of the sacred mysteries.[42] After the Constantinian revolution the higher clergy were put on a par with high imperial officials and were allowed to wear special insignia such as the stole, maniple, pallium, and ring. Liturgical vestments in the proper sense of the term first appeared in the fifth century, when the ancient Roman garb of men—tunic and toga—were replaced by the garments of the Gauls and Germans (trousers and short coat). Since celebrants of the liturgy continued to wear the old festive garments of the Romans, the result was specifically liturgical vestments that over the centuries were increasingly felt to be alien. In what follows I shall limit myself to describing briefly the most important of these liturgical vestments.

The *alb* (from Latin *albus*, "white") is a long white undergarment that was successor to the old Roman tunic (*tunica*) and is worn at Mass by all celebrants in sacramental orders. Under the alb, or over it in many religious orders, is a cloth laid over the shoulders (the amice). This might be described as a kind of scarf; according to the present rubrics it need not be worn as long as the alb fits neatly around the neck. Nor need the cincture (*cingulum*, "belt") be used, provided the alb is so cut that no belt is needed.

The *stole*, a sashlike strip of cloth, was originally a mark of secular office. It is now reserved to those in sacramental orders. Bishops and priests wear it around the neck and hanging down in front on both sides (before the reform, priests wore the ends crossed over their chests). Deacons wear it over the left shoulder and extending diagonally across to the right side in front and back.

The *chasuble* or "Mass vestment" (in Latin: *casula* but also *paenula* and *planeta*) is the outer liturgical garment; it derives from the ancient Roman toga. Originally it was conical in shape and was lowered over the head and covered the entire body ("chasuble" from Latin *casula*, "little house"). In the thirteenth century the garment was shortened at the sides; the result was the "Gothic" chasuble. In the Baroque period it was shortened even further, and heavy brocade was used in making it; the result was a highly ornamental garment (the "fiddle back" chasuble). In 1925 the Congregation of Rites declared this "mini" chasuble to be the only allowable form and prohibited "Gothic" chasubles. The decree was not withdrawn until 1957.

The *dalmatic* (a name probably referring to an outer garment originating in Dalmatia and worn by men and women at the end of the second century A.D.) became the liturgical outer garment of deacons. But it was also an episcopal vestment worn under the chasuble.

The *tunic* was the outer garment worn by subdeacons; it came increasingly to resemble the dalmatic. (The order of subdeacon was eliminated after Vatican II.)

The *pluvial* (literally: "raincoat"), also known as the cope, is worn by bishops and priests for many actions outside the celebration of the Eucharist, for example, in processions, the choral Office, sacramental blessings, consecrations, other blessings, and so on. It is a festive cloak or cape that reaches almost to the ground; it is open in the front but drawn together at the breast with a clasp.

The *pallium* probably developed out of the stole and is now an insignia reserved to the pope and residential archbishops. It consists of a cross-shaped band of wool that is worn on the shoulders over the chasuble. It has a further short band in front and back and is adorned with six crosses. Once the tiara was eliminated by Paul VI the acceptance of the pallium became the sign of a new pope's assumption of the see of Rome.

Anyone beside a bishop, priest, or deacon, who performs a service at the altar may wear the liturgical vestment lawfully approved in each region (*GIRM* 301).[43]

In regard to the *meaning of liturgical vestments*, the *General Instruction of the Roman Missal* calls attention to two aspects. The first is that the vestments "should . . . symbolize the function proper to each ministry. But at the same time the vestments should also contribute to the beauty of the rite" (*GIRM* 297). A further significatory element is connected with the fact that Christ the high priest acts in the celebrants of the liturgy; they are his instruments and represent his person (see *SC* 7). In the celebration of the saving mysteries it is primarily Christ who acts, and to him the person and subjective outlook of the human priest must take second place; this role of the human priest is indicated by the liturgical garb in which he is as it were hidden from view. The vestments have thus a mystagogical meaning, that is, they help the participants to understand and experience the mystery. By any accounting they are meant not to exalt their wearer ("cult of personality") but to show rather that Christ has taken the wearer into his service.[44]

The foregoing considerations are not meant to give the impression that the vestments which have come into use in the course of history should be retained in their present form. As I shall show in detail in the next section, liturgical signs are changeable. The documents of the Church take this fact into account to the extent that they admit a certain decentralization of ecclesiastical competence in this area: "Regarding the design of vestments, the conferences of bishops may determine and propose to the Holy See adaptations that correspond to the needs and usages of their regions" (*GIRM* 304).

In the course of historical development *a canon of colors* came to be associated with the vestments. To understand the colors used in the earliest liturgical vestments we must look to the technology for dyeing fabrics in antiquity. At the time an especially prized dye came from a secretion of a mollusk of the genus *Purpura*; this was acquired drop by drop, thinned, and used to dye material. By varying the amount of secretion used and the length of the dyeing process and the exposure various shades of color could be achieved. The most expensive and therefore the most fashionable was a dark red; Pliny speaks in this connection of a blackish purple. Next in the scale of value came "royal purple." The darker the garment, the more valuable and festive it was. Thus ancient depictions usually show the pope and bishops in dark chasubles, while the vestments of deacons are of a brighter color. In the ninth and tenth centuries the ancient technology was lost and replaced by a less expensive one that used plant saps.[45]

Only around 1200, however, was a strict canon of liturgical colors established, though there were early efforts along this line during the Carolingian period. Innocent III provided the first careful description of the customs followed in his time.[46] This canon was accepted and recommended by Durandus of Mende at the end of the thirteenth century.[47] It did not become obligatory, however, until the publication of the Tridentine Missal in 1570, whence it has been taken over, with minor changes, into the Missal of Vatican II. The *General Instruction of the Roman Missal* says: "Variety in the color of the vestments is meant to give effective, outward expression to the specific character of the mysteries of the faith being celebrated and, in the course of the year, to a sense of progress in the Christian life" (no. 307).

The most important prescriptions are: *white* for the Easter and Christmas seasons, the feasts of the Lord and his Mother, of the angels, and of non-martyr saints; *red* for Palm Sunday, Good Friday, feasts of the passion of Christ, Pentecost, and the feasts of the apostles and the martyrs; *green* for "Ordinary Time"; *violet* for Advent and Lent (also permitted in liturgies for the deceased); *black* in liturgies for the deceased (optional); *rose* on the third Sunday of Advent (Gaudete Sunday) and the fourth Sunday of Lent (Laetare Sunday). As with the liturgical vestments, the episcopal conferences may undertake suitable adaptations (*GIRM* 308). More precious vestments (e.g., vestments of gold brocade) may be used on all festive occasions, regardless of the color of the day (no. 309).

The Eastern rites have no real canonical colors, at least if we prescind from some customs of the Byzantine rite and especially of the Greek Church.[48]

The attitude and practice of the Protestant Churches differ widely from region to region and confession to confession.

"The late medieval tradition regarding liturgical colors was evidently continued, or adopted, most extensively in Lutheranism. The Reformed tradition paid no attention to the question because as early as the sixteenth century it had already completely eliminated the altar and liturgical vestments. . . . Only in very recent years, as a result of the movement of liturgical reform, has it raised the question from time to time. . . Anglicanism, with its strong attachment to tradition, went its own way; in Anglo-Catholicism it once again followed to a large extent the medieval or Roman custom." [49]

In the Scandinavian countries, the Reformation "proved more conservative even than German Lutheranism in the matter of ceremonial. This includes the vestments for Mass and probably, in principle, the canon of liturgical colors."[50] Nowadays the call for greater festivity and enjoyment of color in Protestant worship is becoming ever louder.

The Mutability of Liturgical Signs

Because liturgical signs are meant to signify and shed light on invisible realities, their actual power of signifying must be tested from time to time. Many signs are very old and originate in cultures now long past. Many of these same signs belong admittedly to the so-called "primal symbols" that are common to all peoples and transcend time; others, however, are bound up with historical periods and cultures and suffer some loss of their significatory power with the passage of time or transference to other cultures. This is no less true of many signs and symbolic actions found in sacred scripture than of signs and symbols added later. Think, for example, of Jesus' use of spittle in healing the sick or of the many liturgical signs taken over from the ceremonial of the imperial court after the Constantinian revolution.

For this reason Vatican II was concerned that the texts and rites of the liturgy should "express more clearly the holy things they signify and that the Christian people, as far as possible, are able to understand them with ease and to take part in the rites fully, actively, and as befits a community" (*SC* 21). The same intention finds even clearer expression in Article 34 where it takes the form of a directive: "The rites should be marked by a noble simplicity; they should be short, clear, and unencumbered by useless repetitions; they should be within the people's powers of comprehension and as a rule not require much explanation."

As a matter of fact, the revision of the liturgical books that was commissioned by the council began with a weeding out of the signs used. An example would be the rite of baptism for children, from which the reform eliminated the threefold breathing on the child's face, the placing of some salt in the mouth, the touching of nose and ears with spittle, and so on. At the same time, however, other signs that are still very meaningful today, such as the signing with the sign of the cross and the giving of a white garment and a lit candle, were not only kept but had their meaning further clarified by, for example, the participation of parents and sponsors in the signing of the child with the cross and by the lighting of the baptismal candle from the Easter candle.[51]

It is true, of course, that erudite experts can show the meaningfulness of many signs derived from ancient cultures but found unintelligible today. The need, however, is that the ordinary faithful should be able to understand them quickly and without a great deal of explanation. Otherwise the liturgy risks becoming a museum piece and is open to the objection of archeologism. With this in mind Benedictine A. Verheul urges " that the forms that need an elaborate archeological explanation to make them intelligible and can no longer be made meaningful, be removed or given a new shape. A liturgy that only becomes clear when preceded and accompanied by a lot of explanation is of doubtful value. It no longer speaks to the man of today."[52]

Evangelical theologian K. H. Bieritz is in agreement on this point; he writes with regard to Lutheran worship:

"Contemporary problems of liturgical praxis cannot be solved simply be returning to real or supposed 'origins.' Such a process of restoration fails to take into account that the liturgical signs which are to be restored were originally located in entirely different syntagmas and even in an entirely different cultural and social context and that the meaning they may have been able to convey in that context cannot without further ado be transferred to a new context."[53]

The fact that the ability to signify can undergo change also means, and even necessitates, that the liturgy must be receptive to appropriate *present-day signs* and that in view of the varied cultures within the one worldwide Church there can be no imposed uniformity of liturgical signs. There is a parallel here with church architecture. As late as the early decades of our own century there were influential circles within both great confessions that were energetically opposed to any departure from the architectural styles of the past. According to Lutheran architect Otto Bartner, these disciples of historicism were promoting the impression that the present-day Church is an institution of and for yesterday and therefore lacks credibility.[54] Similar objections were raised against Catholic ecclesiastical bans on the introduction of any new architectural style: "The prohibitions not only were injurious to ecclesiastical architecture but alienated the enthusiastic young from the Church, which inevitably struck them as outdated and as something with which one need no longer be concerned."[55] Vatican II rejected this inflexible clinging to the traditional: "The art of our own days, coming from every race and region, shall also be given free scope in the Church, on the condition that it serves the places of worship and sacred rites with the reverence and honor due to them" (*SC* 123).

The parallel with church architecture and the conciliar declaration are fully applicable to the whole world of liturgical signs. The *tragic history of missionary endeavor* in recent centuries is one long indictment of the unenlightened view that the traditional signs must be uniformly retained at all times and in all cultures. Liturgical signs that are not found in the intellectual world of other cultures or even convey the very opposite of what is intended certainly do not serve the liturgy and the faith but are a hindrance and source of harm.

For example: at the end of the sixteenth century, under the protection of the Portuguese colonial overlords the Latin rite of confirmation was introduced into the Christian communities of southern India (the "Thomas Christians" of Kerala), which had previously been under the influence of the East Syrian rite. Since the ritual of confirmation included as one of its signs a slap on the cheek, the new rite led to violent demonstrations, because this action was regarded as humiliating and degrading. The original meaning—"Be mindful!"—of this sign that was indigenous to the German tribes of the Middle Ages met, in Kerala and elsewhere, with misunderstanding and resistance.[56]

Another illustration of the harm that can be done by an uncritical introduction of culturally conditioned signs is the unqualified use of the Roman canon of liturgical colors. As is now generally known, in China and some other countries white and not black is the color symbolic of mourning. If, then, we want the liturgy to exercise its symbolic power, we must pay heed to the horizon of understanding proper to each culture; in other words, we must accept the principle of inculturation. Vatican II finally took this step: "Provisions shall also be made, even in the revision of liturgical books, for legitimate variations and adaptations to different groups, regions, and peoples, especially in mission lands, provided the substantial unity of the Roman Rite is preserved; this should be borne in mind when rites are drawn up and rubrics devised" (*SC* 38).

THE CONTEMPORARY CAPACITY FOR LITURGY

Closely connected with the symbolic character of the liturgy is the question whether the men and women of our technological age are any longer at all capable of celebrating the liturgy. Are they any longer able to understand the signs and symbolic actions of the liturgy and to communicate, in and through these, with God and the community?

Romano Guardini, a pioneer in litugical reform and education, raised this question once again a few months after the publication of the Constitution on the Liturgy. In a letter to the Third German Liturgical Congress at Mainz in April 1964[57] he called attention to that which is at the very heart of any liturgical renewal, namely, the proper accomplishment of the liturgical act:

". . . the symbolic action is 'performed' by the relevant agent as a liturgical act, and is'read' by those who perceive it in an analogous act that intuits the inner meaning in the external form. . . . Symbols are by their nature something corporeo-spiritual; they are expressions of the interior in the exterior and, if they are to exercise their full expressive power, must be accomplished in a serious and recollected manner and be co-accomplished in an act of intuition" (328). (Even in his early years Guardini had felt this to be a key problem.)[58]

At the end of his letter Guardini asked this disquieting question:

"Is liturgical action, and with it everything we call 'liturgy,' so historically conditioned—so linked to the ancient or the medieval world—that we must in all honesty cease to practice it? Ought we perhaps force ourselves to admit that men and women living in the industrial and technological age and conditioned by the psychological and sociological structures which this age has created are simply no longer capable of liturgical action?" (331-32).

It is clear from the context that Guardini was not in principle rejecting the liturgy as the mystery of the application of salvation and the glorification of God. Rather he was focusing essentially on "liturgical actions" which men and women accomplish in a symbolic-corporeal manner and with "insight" and into which they must pour their entire personalities.

From the wealth of contributions to the discussion started by Guardini's letter I select one which begins by shifting the question to another area but which nonetheless seems quite helpful:

"Are the men and women of today capable of 'seeing' a work of art, listening to a symphony, marveling at a landscape, celebrating a feast, and of doing so not as mere passive spectators but with active participation and interior appropriation, with hearts deeply moved, in enthusiasm, with true participation in the festivity, and with the power and capacity to give their feelings an appropriate expression of noble festiveness, of praise and honor, and this in communion with others of the same mind?" [59]

Just as we may not in principle deny this faculty to the men and women of today, even though it is in many ways submerged and needs to be brought back to life, neither may we utterly deny the capacity for liturgy. In the secular sphere our contemporaries not infrequently display an understanding of and desire for a degree of cermonial and show themselves interiorly moved by it.[60] At the same time, however, the conscious, active accomplishment of liturgical "actions" depends on certain presuppositions; I must briefly mention the most important of these.

In the first place, there is need of a living *faith* that in the liturgy God himself, in Christ, is acting for our salvation and that we need this salvation. This faith includes, of course, the fundamental belief in a personal God. Back in 1944-45 Alfred Delp spoke of the "lack of capacity for God" that many people display; in the age of the "Second Enlightenment" this phenomenon has become even more marked, especially since the religious and Christian socialization of children and young people has been so neglected in recent decades.

A turnaround in this area will require an effort along the entire pastoral front and not simply in liturgical formation.

Another presupposition of proper participation in the liturgical celebration is a certain measure of interior *silence*, concentration, and spiritual alertness. These virtues are lacking in many people of our technological age with its numerous stressful situations but also its intrusive, limitless supply of light entertainment in the mass media. "Stillness must not be superficial . . . our thoughts, our feelings, our hearts must also find rest. . . . Stillness is the tranquility of the inner life; the quiet at the depths of its hidden stream. It is a collected, total presence, a being 'all there,' receptive, alert, ready."[61]

Finally, celebration of the liturgy presupposes the participants' *capacity for community*. A community is more than the sum of assembled individuals. It is the banding together of mature human beings for joint action in mutual affirmation and respect. It requires the renunciation of isolating individualism and self-centeredness. "A great deal that divides must be overcome, especially the isolation of the modern individual; in addition, all the interior stirrings of aversion and hostility toward the neighbor; the indifference to the many who 'are no concern of mine,' but who are in fact members of the same community; a lethargic sense of oppressiveness; and so on."[62]

Many Christians of our time will certainly not find it easy to create these conditions within themselves. Their attainment requires not only appropriate instruction but ongoing education and formation; nonetheless this attainment seems possible in principle even today. The occasional celebration of the liturgy with a small group can be a valuable help here .

Chapter Five

Music in the Liturgy

In order to prevent ambiguities and misunderstandings in dealing with this many-faceted subject it will be helpful to agree on a clear terminology. The expression *musica sacra* ("sacred music") of the Roman documents is usually a comprehensive term that includes both vocal and instrumental music. Thus the *Instruction on Music in the Liturgy* which was published by the Consilium and the Congregation of Rites on March 5, 1967, says: "The term 'sacred music' here includes: Gregorian chant, the several styles of polyphony, both ancient and modern; sacred music for organ and for other permitted instruments, and the sacred, i.e., liturgical or religious, music of the people."[1]

On the other hand, the International Study Group on Song and Music in the Liturgy (founded under the name "Universa Laus" in 1966) prefers the term "liturgical music" (see "Universa Laus Document '80"). By this it understands "all forms of vocal and instrumental music that are used in the liturgy."[2] This terminology will be used in the ensuing discussion; I shall distinguish between singing in its various forms and instrumental music.

HISTORICAL SURVEY

The primitive community of Jerusalem had its origins in Judaism and was quite familiar with the singing and instrumental music of the temple liturgies. It is very likely, on the other hand, that no musical instruments were used in the synagogues. The readings and prayers were delivered in a kind of chant, and the psalms were sung. In the accounts of the Last Supper of Jesus we are told that "when they had sung a hymn, they went out to the Mount of Olives" (Mt. 26:30; Mk 14:26); that is, the disciples and Jesus sang the "great Hallel" (Ps 112-17), which was part of the Passover ritual.

The Pauline letters exhort the communities to let "psalms and hymns and spiritual songs" be heard in their midst and to rejoice and sing the Lord's praises with full hearts (Eph 5:19; Col 3:16). In addition, the New Testament contains many texts of hymns, especially hymns to Christ: for example, Jn 1:1-18; Eph 1:4-14; 5:14; Phil 2:6-11; Col 1:15-20; Heb 1:3; 1 Tim 3:16. The "heavenly liturgy" in the Apocalypse frequently cites hymns in honor of God and the "Lamb": for example, 1:4-7; 4:8, 11; 5:9f.; 7:10, 12; 11:15, 17f.; 12:10-12; 14:3; 15:3f.; 19:1-8; 21:3f. It is therefore legitimate to conclude:

"The early Christian communities accepted and used singing as an element in their litugical life. . . . It can be assumed with a good deal of confidence that in addition to the spontaneous songs of Spirit-filled individuals there were set liturgical texts for the community. In the course of subsequent development the balance between the two forms of liturgical music shifted increasingly in favor of communal singing."[3]

The psalms in particular served as the "hymnal" of the early Christian communities.[4] Alongside the psalms, however, there were many hymns inspired by the Christian faith (*psalmi idiotici*, i.e., "homemade" psalms), the character of which is still attested by the *Gloria* and the older part of the *Te Deum*. On the other hand, early Christianity did not develop a taste for instrumental music in the liturgy.

It is understandable that since there was no liturgical centralization regional influences should have made their appearance in liturgical music. In what follows I shall concentrate solely on the development in the West, and even there I must be very brief.[5]

The Constantinian revolution and the erection of magnificent basilicas strengthened the tendency to greater solemnity in the liturgy. This may already be seen in the manner of singing the psalms. Initially the singing was responsorial, that is, a choir or cantor alone sang the ongoing text, while the community took part by singing an unchanging and often repeated *responsorium* (refrain), which , in the beginning, might be such short formulas as "Amen" or "Alleluia" or "Glory be to the Father. . . ." At a later period, however, antiphonal psalmody (two alternating choirs) came into use.

In the fourth century Antioch and Milan (Ambrose) were the centers of this antiphonal psalmody. Part of the repertory of song from the fourth century on was the *Jubilus*, a wordless melody that served to express profound emotion, a melody "in which the heart voices what cannot be put into words."[6] The *Jubilus* found a home especially in the Kyrie and at the Alleluia (here in the form of a continuation of the final syllable). In the early Middle Ages the addition of texts to the *Jubilus* gave rise to tropes (especially at the Kyrie) and to sequences, which were joined to the Alleluia. We owe forty sequences to a single monk, Notker Balbulus of St. Gall (840-912). The many sequences of the Middle Ages were reduced to four at the Tridentine reform.

From the fourth century on, *hymns* too, which in early Christianity usually had quite simple texts and melodies, showed an advance in textual and musical quality. In the West, chiefly due to the influence of Ambrose, hymns became popular in character (this after Hilary of Poitiers had brought numerous Eastern hymns with him from Asia Minor). Their chief outward characteristic was repetition of the same strophaic structure, each stanza having the same number of syllables and the same melody (the stanzas were isostrophic and isosyllabic). It is estimated that about 35,000 hymns in all were composed.[7]

Gregorian chant acquired a position of special importance. According to a tradition that goes back to the eighth century Pope Gregory I (590-604) collected the melodies sung in the Mass and Office at the papal court and reorganized them. To him too is attributed the Roman *schola cantorum*, which substantially influenced singing in the West. As the Roman liturgy spread, so to a large extent did the Roman manner of singing. This was especially true of the Frankish kingdom under King Pepin and Emperor Charlemagne. In the past not only had regionally influenced liturgies developed, but so had many varied forms of singing. Now both Pepin and Charlemagne demanded an unqualified acceptance of the Roman manner of singing (their decision was to some extent politically motivated). The school of chant which Pepin founded at Metz was a great help in this process. Even then, however, Germanic versions of choral singing persisted for centuries; in fact, one is used even today in the parish church of Kiedrich near Mainz.

From the mid-ninth century on, *polyphonic Church song* developed North of the Alps (it was called *diaphonia* and, in the beginning, *organum* as well). It was closely associated with the development of the musical notation known as neumes. The latter, however, did not clearly indicate the pitch; it was therefore replaced, around the year 1000 (Guido of Arezzo), by a system of lines with the line notes a third apart and with prefixed letters for the pitch; these later became the clefs. Beginning in the twelfth century, the types of notation were developed that would ultimately survive: the German "horseshoe-nail" notation and the square notation which in its late medieval form has remained the notation used in Gregorian chant down to the present time.[8]

Polyphony "with its harmonic and melodic sweetness"[9] underwent a further refinement in the fourteenth century. The term *Ars nova* ("new art") was now used; the former manner of singing was described as *Ars antiqua* ("old art"). The links between polyphony, on the one hand, and Gregorian chant and the liturgy, on the other, were gradually weakened, and the "new art" found increasing favor at worldly celebrations. For this reason, in 1524 (during the exile in Avignon) Pope John XXII published the Constitution *Docta Sanctorum Patrum,* in which he condemned excesses and called for a return to the original liturgical music.

During the thirteenth and fourteenth centuries France was the leader in the world of music. The fifteenth century, however, brought a shift to England and the Netherlands. Under the influence of Franko-Flemish composers and musicians "classical vocal polyphony" developed at the leading royal courts and finally at the papal court; Filippo de Monte, Orlando de Lasso, and Giovanni Perluigi da Palestrina (known simply as Palestrina) may be regarded as the chief representatives of this new form.

In its decrees on church music the Council of Trent (1545-1563) concerned itself mainly with the elimination of abuses and gave no stylistic directives.[10] In its *Decretum de observandis et evitandis in celebratione Missae* (Session 22; September 17, 1562) it exhorted bishops to rid their churches of those types of music that introduced "anything unbridled or impure" (*lascivum aut impurum*) into the playing of the organ or the singing. In its Session 24 (March 22, 1563) the council included "effeminate music" in the condemnation.[11] The commission of cardinals that was charged with implementing the Tridentine decrees focused especially on the balance between text and music and on the comprehensibility of the texts.

The "Roman School" under Palestrina made a special effort to satisfy these requirements. "At the beginning of the seventeenth century the style of the Roman School became the 'serious style' (*stylus gravis*) which propagated itself through the following centuries; it was often expanded by the addition of new affective elements which served to interpret the text; most importantly, through the introduction of several choirs it became 'Roman Epic Baroque.'"[12] The new style of the Baroque period may be descibed as "concerto church music," the way for which had been prepared by the "Venetian School"; it was characterized by the use of several choirs, alternation between choir and soloists, and the inclusion of instrumental voices. Less and less attention was paid to the structure of the liturgy; liturgical music ceased to be a maidservant in the house of God and became a mistress filled with the spirit of triumphalism. The Mass became a musical work of art to which people "listened" with deep emotion. This was true especially of liturgies in the cathedrals of the (prince-) bishops and in the royal chapels of the great princely houses. This was the "vital setting" (*Sitz im Leben*) for the "Masses" of the great classical composers, Mozart, Haydn, and Beethoven.

Baroque exuberance came to an end in the nineteenth-century Church, impoverished as this was by the French Revolution and the loss of ecclesiastical properties in Germany (1803). There were timid attempts at reforming Church music so as to associate it more closely with the liturgy; in the second half of the century these attempts drew support from the endeavors of Abbot Gueranger (Gregorian chant). In this context mention must be made of F. X. Witt and the "Cecilian Association," which "sought new forms through imitation of early classical polyphony" but "for the most part did not get beyond an unartistic superficiality."[13]

An event of major importance was the publication of Pius X's Motu

Proprio *Tra le sollecitudini* (1903), which presented itself as a new code of law for liturgical music and to which reference would repeatedly be made in subsequent papal directives. The document calls liturgical music "a necessary part of the solemn liturgy," although its ministerial role is strongly emphasized and it is termed a "simple handmaiden of the liturgy" (no. 23). Indispensable characteristics of this music are said to be holiness, which excludes all "worldliness," and artistic quality (no. 2). The supreme model for all liturgical music is Gregorian Chant (no. 3), in close association with the classical polyphony of the "Roman School" under Palestrina. More recent music is acceptable in principle, "for it includes works of such high quality, seriousness, and nobility that they are by no means unworthy of the liturgical action" (no. 5).

At the end of this short survey some remarks on German liturgical song are in order. (Although these next few paragraphs speak of the history of German liturgical song, they have been retained because of their concise value. *Ed.*) There is evidence even from the early Middle Ages for the existence of accalmations and songs (*Leisen*, from "Kyrie *eleison*") that were sung by the liturgical assembly.[15] The evidence becomes much more plentiful in the high and late Middle Ages. Many of these German hymns are free renderings of Latin texts and at times display a mingling of Latin and German verses.

"Most of the references to German songs concern the elaborate liturgies on the major feastdays . . . [and] processions . . . [and in association with] sermons. . . . The sources justify the assumption that in the fifteenth and early sixteenth centuries German hymns were widely and enthusiastically used in the life of the communities. In the ritual accompanying the sermon and in the blessings on the major feasts and during pilgrimages specific hymns had an established place in the course of the liturgy." [16]

Ph. Harnoncourt brings out the importance of hymns in the Reformation communities under these rubrics: "Spread and consolidation of the faith," "Use in the liturgy in place of Latin hymns," "Development of hymns based on the psalms," "The introduction of hymnals."[17] The first Protestant hymnal, the *Achtliderbuch*, appeared in 1524; the first Catholic hymnal, that of Michael Vehe, was published at Leipzig in 1537. The number of hymnals and printed songs increased greatly toward the end of the sixteenth century and the beginning of the seventeenth. The first diocesan hymnals were introduced as early as the sixteenth century.[18]

In the seventeenth and eighteenth centuries it was still the rule that the Mass songs proper (*Kyrie*, etc.) were to take the form of Gregorian chant, but the German hymn gradually made its way even into this hitherto closed realm, especially in places that lacked trained singers or choirs. It was thus that the "German sung Mass" had its beginnings. This trend to a "German solemn Mass" intensified in the period of the Enlightenment. "In almost all dioceses, diocesan hymnals and prayerbooks, which included many 'hymns for Mass,' now made their appearance. . . . The novelty here was not the form but the type of hymn, for rhymed instructions and sung Mass devotions now replaced the former paraphrases of the Ordinary and the festal hymns for the Proper."[19] This type of hymnal was hardly to be found anywhere outside the German-speaking world.

In the second half of the nineteenth century the Cecilianist movement, which strongly supported Rome in its increasing trend to complete liturgical centralization, set itself against the use of German hymns at Mass. In the twentieth century, and especially in connection with the liturgical movement, there were strong disagreements over the use of German hymns in the context of the "German solemn Mass" and the German sung Masses of various kinds.[20] After Vatican II an important role in the development of German Catholic hymns was played by the Catholic Hymnal of Switzerland (1966) and by *Gotteslob*, the Catholic prayerbook and hymnal published in 1975 by the bishops of Germany and Austria and of the sees of Bolzano-Bressanone and Liege (for their German-speaking populations), with appendixes for Austria and the various German dioceses.[21]

LITURGICAL MUSIC AFTER VATICAN II

Vatican II devoted a special chapter (Chapter VI) to "sacred music" in its Constitution on the Liturgy. On March 5, 1967, the Consilium and the Congregation of Rites published an *Instruction on Music in the Liturgy*,[22] which set itself the task of concretizing what had been said in the Constitution and of resolving some problems. The *Gen-*

eral Instruction of the Roman Missal applies these prinicples to the Mass (*passim*). I shall bring together here the most important guidelines given in these several documennts.

Vatican II considers liturgical music or, more precisely, "sacred song closely bound to the text," to be "a necessary or integral part of the solemn liturgy" (*SC* 112). This means that in the liturgy music is not simply an ornamental setting, "not simply the laurel tree that is set up as a decoration on festive occasions,"[23] but *is itself liturgy*. "In the sung reponses to the readings and in the Sanctus and Gloria music itself becomes a liturgical action; it becomes liturgy which the community accomplishes by singing or listening and with a participation that is interior and not merely exterior."[24]

In addition, because of its sign character music in the liturgy is able to intensify the active participation of the faithful and to promote the states of soul which make human beings receptive to God's word and to sacramental grace. It sheds light on the mystery of Christ, promotes awareness of community and communication among the faithful, and gives the liturgy a befitting solemnity. "Instrumental and organ music continue as it were the wordless music of the early Chritian Alleluia-*Jubilus*. For there are realities that can be experienced and expressed only in the medium of art."[25]

Music must play the part of a *servant* in worship. It must be integrated into the liturgy and subordinated to it, rather than the other way around. Important parts of the liturgy must not be obscured, nor the several ministers hindered in their liturgical action for the sake of a magnificant musical display. Musical performances must not be allowed to prevent the active participation of the community or unduly prolong the celebration as a whole (*Instruction* 11). To take an example from the preconciliar era: the polyphonic singing of the Sanctus before the words of institution and of the Benedictus after them are no longer permitted to obscure the structure of the Eucharistic prayer and prevent its being heard.

The principle that "those parts which of their nature call for singing are in fact sung and in the style and form demanded by the parts themselves" is to be observed *especially in the celebration of the Eucharist (Instruction* 6). Most important in this context is what is known as "cantillation," that is, "the musical recitation of the celebrant's presidential prayers, the Our Father and the intercessions, the acclamations of the people, and the readings."[26] This enables the readings, prayers, and answers of the people to be expressed in such a way that word and text remain the essential element but gain in intensity and solemnity by being uttered in a rhythmic and melodious manner.[27] The *tonus rectus* that was common not too long ago in "community Masses" completely eliminated the rhythm and melodiousness of natural speech and therefore seemed "unnatural"; cantillation, on the contrary, heightens both, to the advantage of the text.

The conditions required by the solemn form of sung Mass are not present in every community. The *Instruction* points out, however, that gradations are possible. "For the choice of parts to be sung, those should be first that of their nature are more important and particularly those sung by the priest or other ministers and answered by the congregation or sung by the priest and congregation together. Later other parts, for the congregation alone or the choir alone, may be added gradually" (no. 7). Special emphasis is laid on the singing of the responsorial psalm and the congregational Our Father.

When the liturgy is celebrated in Latin, *Gregorian chant* takes precedence over all other forms of singing. The council speaks of Gregorian chant as "distinctive of the Roman liturgy" (*SC* 116). "But other kinds of sacred music, especially polyphony, are by no means excluded from liturgical celebrations, provided they accord with the spirit of the liturgical service" (ibid.). This is true, in particular, of the people's own religious songs, that is of hymns and other songs in the vernacular (*SC* 118).

The *peculiar music tradition* of each people is also to be esteemed and promoted (*SC* 119; see 123).

"The Christian tradition has at times and in many places excluded musical instruments from the liturgy. Even today there are reservations with regard to certain instruments, because they are regarded as embodying a musical culture that is incompatible with the liturgy. On the other hand, the instrumental music of many cultures represents a human and spiritual value whose inclusion in the music of the Christian liturgy can be a gain." [28]

Many (rhythmical) songs and musical instruments are not to be excluded in principle, provided they can serve a ministerial function.

The introduction of the vernacular into the liturgy inaugurated a difficult process of adjustment and adaptation for church composers and musicians; it was especially difficult in countries that had hitherto known nothing, apart from Gregorian chant, but polyphonic choral singing in Latin. The use of Latin melodies with vernacular texts proved on the whole to be the wrong approach, even if the effort was occasionally successful. A point made in the Instruction on the translation of liturgical texts applies here as well: new creations are needed.[29]

All this will require time and a good deal of patience on the part of the faithful.

"Compositions cannot be conjured up out of thin air, or at least good ones cannot, nor can enthusiastic singing be had by command. God grant that works may soon be composed and given to us which will strike the faithful as being contemporary and vital and will stir their enthusiasm and in which they can truly express themselves. Then their voices will not fall silent but rather fill the earthly liturgy with something of the heavenly jubilation which awaits us at the end of our pilgrim journey and which we cannot imagine apart from music and song." [30]

Chapter Six

Liturgy and Popular Piety

Alongside the official worship of the Church as set down in liturgical books and regulated by papal or diocesan law, there are many and varied expressions of Christian piety to be found in broad strata of the people or in municipalities, communities, and families; these expressions are summed up in the term "popular piety" or "popular religion," which includes religious customs. Many customs reach back to the time of the pagan religions and were later christianized to a greater or lesser extent. Although popular piety and Christian custom, and the problems they bring, play a substantially greater role in the Romance countries and among the peoples which these countries colonized and christianized, namely, those of Central and South America, the Phillipines, and so on,[1] the following exposition will be limited primarily to the situation in German-speaking areas.

Many forms of popular piety have their roots in the Middle Ages and the Baroque period, which had a quite different attitude to life and lived the faith in a different way; furthermore, these devotional forms presuppose social structures that are agrarian or characteristic of a society of artisans. Understandably, therefore, the men and women of our present-day industrial society, whose mentality has been shaped by the Second Enlightenment, take a very critical view of these devotional forms and have thrown many of them overboard. This is especially the case where traditional customs have been infiltrated by magical notions or have been the occasion for magical practices.[2]

Other, less questionable religious customs have also been affected, however, and for several reasons. First, broad levels of society now lack a living faith in the transcendent world and in suprasensible "principalities and powers." In addition, the consciousness of community and tradition has been weakened, as has the attachment to tradition; this development has been hastened by the prevalence of the nuclear family. Nor may we overlook the fact that in the lives of many the time available apart from work is largely devoted to the entertainment provided by the mass media or to exploitation of the possibilities afforded by increasing mobility. As a result, people have for decades been talking of a crisis in popular piety and popular devotional customs. This includes the bishops of the German-speaking world, who in 1980 had this to say in answer to a questionnaire of the Roman Congregation for Divine Worship concerning the reception of the liturgical reform: "Popular piety has long been on the wane. The liturgical reform has not halted but hastened the decline."[3]

Despite all this, it would be an error to describe popular piety as simply a "product of religious degeneracy" and to consider it a thing of the past. It may well be that the liturgical movement with its joyous rediscovery of the beauty and importance of the liturgy has somewhat overshadowed the kind of prayer and custom produced by popular piety. "No one can deny the weaknesses of popular Catholicism, its darker side, and its susceptibility to debasement. On the other hand, as Paul VI insisted in his Apostolic Exhortation *Evangelii nuntiandi,* it can also help many to an 'authentic encounter with God in Jesus Christ.'"[4]

Even ordinary common sense would suggest that we not indiscriminately discard "the old ways" without first inquiring into their real value. Thus at the General Congress of German Catholics (Katholikentag) at Trier in 1971 Balthasar Fischer urged that we "not blindly throw away whatever seems outdated but rather first ask whether the forms in question can be purified and deepened so as to justify their continued existence in a new world."[5]

It is therefore a pastoral obligation to separate the wheat from the chaff: that is, to rediscover the worthwhile good in the manifestations of popular piety, remove all the coats of paint, as it were, and the incrustations, and thus let the communities see that the old customs are meaningful and attractive. If the realization that "*ecclesia semper reformanda est*" applies to the liturgy, it applies much more to many manifestations of popular piety. What the Constitution on the Liturgy requires of the religious devotions of the Christian people and of the devotions proper to particular Churches is required also of popular piety: these manifestations "should be so fashioned that they harmonize with the liturgical seasons, accord with the sacred liturgy, are in some way derived from it, and lead the people to it" (*SC* 13). A reformed popular piety can complement and enrich the official liturgy, and its innate power of Christian socialization can provide a valuable service to a life of faith.[6]

New forms of popular devotion and religious customs that speak to the people need time to develop. They will develop more easily in the degree that the faith grows stronger and that a liturgy in touch with life yields authentic impulses and emotional support. A healthy popular piety will then in turn contribute to the deepening of the faith and the enrichment of the liturgy.[7]

Chapter Seven

Liturgy and Ecumenism

DIVIDED CHRISTIANITY AND THE ECUMENICAL MOVEMENT

The fact that Christianity is made up of over three hundred autonomous "Churches" or faith communities and thus presents a picture of division "contradicts the will of Christ, scandalizes the world, and damages that most holy cause, the preaching of the Gospel to every creature."[1] The first decades of the twentieth century saw the rise in the Protestant world of two movements, "Faith and Order" and "Life and Work" (the latter focusing on practical Christianity), which had for their goal to eliminate this disorder. The two movements combined, provisionally in 1938 and definitively in 1948 at their plenary meeting in Amsterdam, to form the "World Council of Churches." "The World Council of Churches is a fellowship of churches which confess the Lord Jesus Christ as God and Savior according to the Scriptures and therefore seek to fulfill together their common calling to the glory of the one God, Father, Son, and Holy Spirit."[2] The Faith and Order Commission, now part of the World Council, was commissioned to study the possibility of a rapprochement of the various traditions at the theological level.

On the Catholic side, John XXIII established the "Secretariat for Promoting the Union of Christians," under the presidency of Cardinal Bea, and thus inaugurated an intensified effort at unification and a closer collaboration with the World Council. The end of 1964 brought the publication of the Decree of Vatican II on Ecumenism. *Ecumenical Directory*, Part I, was published in 1967 and *Ecumenical Directory*, Part II, in 1970.[3] On the basis of these Roman documents episcopal conferences and individual dioceses issued further guidelines.

The efforts made by the Christian Churches to achieve unity have manifested themselves in numerous bilateral or multilateral study groups both at the international level and at the regional and district levels. A high point in these efforts at the international level has certainly been the Lima Report and the "Lima Liturgy," which was based on the report; I shall come back to these in the final section of the present chapter.

Of the numerous bilateral statements mention may be made of the reports issued by the Joint Lutheran-Roman Catholic Study Commission: *The Gospel and the Church* (the "Malta Report" of 1972),[4] *The Eucharist* (1978),[5] *The Ministry in the Church* (1981),[6] and *Unity Ahead. Models, Forms, and Stages of Catholic-Lutheran Ecclesial Communion* (1985).[7] Of equal importance are the reports of the International Anglican-Roman Catholic Study Commission on the Eucharist (1971 and 1979) Ministry and Ordination (1973 and 1979) and Authority in the Church (1976, 1981). Among documents of a regional kind I may mention The American Roman Catholic dialogue with the Episcopal Church and with the Lutheran Churches.[7a]

These documents are enough to show the extent and intensity of ecumenical efforts in our day. Nor may the accompanying ventures of local communities be overlooked. At this level, however, it must be remembered that impatience is a bad adviser and that the anticipatory steps taken by individuals, groups, and communities represent no small danger for the ecumenical movement as a whole. The reason is that this kind of behavior can easily lead to the formation of a new confession and thus cause further division and intra=ecclesial strife.[8] What we need is unwavering perseverance in efforts at unity, along with the realization that "differences which in the course of four hundred years have affected even our everyday behavior, cannot be eliminated in ten, fifteen, or twenty years. Any social psychologist would laugh at us, were we to approach him with such extravagant expectations."[9]

JOINT EFFORTS IN THE AREA OF LITURGY

Ecumenical efforts have not been restricted to scientific theological discussion but have had concrete effects in the liturgical realm. Of these steps, some short, some longer, toward unity I may mention the following:

a) In 1987 the representatives of the Christian Churches of the German-speaking countries agreed on a common version of the Our Father; the governing bodies of the Churches introduced it in 1968 or recommended it to the synods and communities.[10]

b) 1971 saw a new ecumenical translation of these texts which are spoken by the worshipping community: the Apostolic and Nicene Creeds, the Gloria, Sanctus, Agnus Dei and "Glory to the Father."[11]

c) The *Arbeitsgemeinschaft für ökumenisches Liedgut im deutschen Sprachgebiet* (Task Force for an Ecumenical German Hymnody) has been working since 1969 to develop common songs for the liturgy. The group has thus far produced the following collections: *Gemeinsame Kirchenlieder* (Common Hymns; 1973); *Gesänge zur Bastattung* (Hymns for Funerals; 1978; a children's hymnal: *Leuchte, bunter Regenbogen* (Shine, Mulitcolored Rainbow!; 1983); and "*Gesange zur Trauung*" (Wedding Hymns; not yet published). The Catholic hymnal, *Gotteslob*, of 1975, took over many hymns from the first of these collections (these are distinguished by an *ö—for "ökumenisch" = "ecumenical"*—under the number of the hymn), and there is a good chance that such ecumenical hymns will be incorporated into the new hymnals now being prepared for the Evangelical Church in Germany, the Evangelical Reformed Churches of German-speaking Switzerland, and the "Catholic Diocese of the Old Catholics in Germany."[12]

d) There are various rituals for the ecumenically celebrated wedding of spouses from different confessions, with ministers from both confessions taking part.[13]

e) In almost all communities ecumenical liturgies are celebrated in which officials of the participating Churches take part. These are liturgies of the Word without any Eucharist. All the governing bodies of the Churches desire that such liturgies become a regular part of ecclesial life. To be recommended as especially appropriate are the Week of Prayer for Christian Unity (January 18-25), the week before Pentecost, the Women's World Day of Prayer (first Friday in March), the ecumenical Way of the Cross for young people (Friday before Palm Sunday), liturgies on days of penance and prayer, and liturgies in schools.

There is disagreement with regard to shared Eucharists (intercommunion). The Evangelical Churches welcome Christians of other confessions to their celebrations of the Lord's Supper, but the Catholic Church is convinced that joint Eucharists are not possible because there is as yet no communion in faith and Church. Only in cases of necessity and under certain conditions are Evangelical Christians allowed to receive communion at the Catholic Eucharist.—In the view of the Catholic Church the faithful are obliged to attend Sunday Mass, and this attendance must not be made more difficult for them; they are therefore instructed not to schedule ecumenical liturgies on Saturday evening and Sunday morning.

f) In 1980 a new translation of the Bible was published with the collaboration of Evangelical exegetes. The translation of the New Testament and the Psalms was accepted and recommended as ecumenical by the Evangelical Church of Germany and the Evangelical Bible Society. On the Catholic side this new translation has already been accepted into the German Book of Hours and the new lectionaries for Mass, as well as into other liturgical books of more recent date.[14]

g) Ecumenical collaboration is also to be seen in various joint statements which touch at least in part on the liturgy. See, for example, the declaration *Den Sonntag feiern* (The Celebration of Sunday), which was published on the first Sunday of Advent, 1984, as a "joint statement of the German Episcopal Conference and the council of the Evangelical Church in Germany."

These various steps have created a broad area of common prayer and song. Not only have they led to reciprocal union and a renunciation of unloving prejudices, but they are the most tenacious expression of a determination to achieve unity in faith and in a life based on faith.

THE LIMA REPORT AND THE LIMA LITURGY

Among the loftiest achievements of the ecumenical quest for unity are undoubtedly to be numbered the statements of the Faith and

Order Commission of the World Council on consensus in the areas of Baptism, Eucharist, and Ministry. These received their finishing touches in January, 1982, at the plenary meeting of the World Council in Lima, Peru, and are therefore known collectively as the "Lima Report."[15] The three statements are the fruit of a 50-year process of study stretching back to the first Faith and Order Conference at Lausanne in 1927. The material has been discussed and revised by the Faith and Order Commission at Accra (1974), Bangalore (1978), and Lima (1982). Between the Plenary Commission meetings, a steering group on Baptism, Eucharist and Ministry has worked further on the drafting, especially after September 1979 under the presidency of Frère Max Thurian of the Taizé Community."[16]

Since 1968 theologians of the Roman Catholic Church and of other Churches not belonging to the World Council have contributed their share as full members of the Faith and Order Commission. In the final vote taken at the Lima meeting the question to be voted on was not whether the members agreed with what was said in every part of the three statements, but rather: "Is the text, in your opinion, sufficiently developed that it can be sent to the member Churches of the Faith and Order Commission for their comments?"[17]

These statements of convergence were sent to all the Churches, along with a request that they study them and take an official stand on them by the end of 1984. An answer was sought especially to several questions: To what extent could the individual Churches recognize in the text the faith of the Church down through the centuries? What consequences could the Churches draw for their relations with the other Churches? What help would the text provide the individual Churches for their worship, education, and ethical and spiritual life and witness? What suggestions could the Churches make for the ongoing work toward unity both in the areas discussed and generally?[18] The results of the replies were to be published and "the ecumenical implications for the Churches were to be analyzed at a future World Conference on Faith and Order."[19] In the intention of the authors the Churches would in this way be given an opportunity to accept the Lima Report while suggesting various changes and additions.

We can legitimately feel great excitement as we await the results of the process of reception. The text is capable of doing away with numerous misunderstandings, bringing the thought and language of the various traditions into closer line with the Church of the beginning, and thus effecting a mutual rapprochement of the Churches as they seek the goal of unity in truth and love, liturgy and life. The unity we seek is not a uniformity in every detail. Just as the Churches of the East and West were united during the first millennium despite many differences in theological method, modes of expression, liturgy, and vital manifestations, it is also conceivable that we may today achieve a consensus on all essential points without the individual Churches being compelled to surrender their special characteristics and independent existence. The goal is *unity in multiplicity*.

Within a short time numerous commentaries and aids have appeared that are intended to facilitate the study of the Lima document by individuals and groups.[20] As regards reception of the document, the response in Catholic circles has thus far been mainly positive.

"With regard to baptism it is possible to speak on the whole of a consensus. With regard to the Eucharist we can agree with everything positive that is said; other questions, however, are left open, which for the Catholic Church are not open, especially the question of the perduring presence of Jesus Christ in the Eucharist and the question of presidency (ministry) at the Eucharist. The existence of open questions is clearest in the statement on ministry, despite the many very positive things that are said there. Especially obvious is the question of apostolic succession. The question of the Petrine office is left aside completely. In summary: a very gratifying and far-reaching convergence and a clear step forward, but not a consensus."[21]

On the Evangelical side more and more criticism is being heard, especially of the third statement (ministry). The statement of eucharistic convergence is also regarded by many as heavily tilted to Catholicism.

By any accounting it can be said that the Lima Report has instilled new life into the ecumenical dialogue and given all ecclesial communities a valuable stimulus to reconsideration of their teaching and practice. It would be a shame if, as seems to be happening here and there, anxiety over possible changes in the received tradition, rather than the question of truth, were allowed to take priority and inflect the process of reception.

Taking the Lima Report as his basis M. Thurian composed a eucharistic liturgy (the "Lima Liturgy"), which was celebrated for the first time on the next to last day of the Lima Conference (January 3-15, 1982); it was celebrated again on July 28, 1982, in the chapel of the Ecumenical Center in Geneva, and in solemn fashion at the sixth plenary meeting of the World Council in Vancouver, 1983. The intention was to translate, as it were, the statements of convergence into the form of a celebration and thus make them concrete. In composing the liturgy M. Thurian took as his primary guide the main liturgical traditions of East and West. Since the Roman Missal of 1970 adopted the same approach, it is not surprising that the Lima Liturgy and the Roman Eucharist show extensive similarities. Thurian distinguishes three parts in the eucharistic liturgy:

"The introductory part unites the people of God in confession, supplication and praise (confession of sins, litany of the *Kyrie*, and the *Gloria*). The second part, the liturgy of the Word, begins with a prayer of preparation. It includes the three proclamations: of a prophet (first lesson), an apostle (second lesson), and Christ (the Gospel). Then the voice of the Church is heard in the sermon, making the eternal word contemporary and living. The sermon is followed by silent meditation. The faith of the Church is then summarized in the Creed and all human needs presented to God in the intercession. The third part, the liturgy of the eucharist, consists essentially of the great eucharistic prayer, preceded by a short preparation and followed by the Lord's Prayer, the sign of peace, and communion."[22]

Like Vatican II, Thurian strives to facilitate an extensive participation by the congregation, while at the same time not allowing the leadership of the official minister to be obscured. We should not overlook some deliberate assimilations, even in the text, to the Roman Missal. Conversely, some parts of Thurian's text could be used to enrich the Catholic eucharistic celebration (e.g., the preparation of the gifts).

The thing that prevents Catholic Christians from joining fully in an ecumenical eucharistic liturgy (including the reception of communion) are some as yet unclarified questions regarding the minister or leader of the eucharistic celebration and the divergences in belief about the eucharistic presence. As long as there is not a real communion in faith and Church, there cannot be communion in the Eucharist, because this is a sign of union with Christ and his Church.[23]

Part II

The Areas of Liturgy

Chapter Eight

Nature and Importance of the Sacraments

An essential part of the liturgy is the celebration of the seven sacraments. In this area theology has discovered new facets and created new emphases in recent decades. "Because full advantage has been taken of anthropology (sociology), ecclesiology, and, above all, a christology that emphasizes soteriology and pneumatology, this theological treatise now displays a multiplicity of new expressions and points of reference, shifts in emphasis, and new approaches."[1]

The Latin word *sacramentum* was originally a translation of the biblical Greek word *mysterion*, which in the New Testament does not mean simply "mystery" but refers to the unfathomable saving action of God in Christ (see Eph 1:9ff.) and, more specifically, to Christ himself, who is "the mystery of our faith" (1 Tim 3:16). The theologians of the first Christian centuries ultimately gave the name *mysteria* to all the words and actions of Jesus because these were spoken and accomplished for our salvation. The Church later on went even further and designated her teaching, worship, prayers, blessings, and rites as *mysteria = sacrament*.

Our current concept of a "sacrament" did not develop until the twelfth century, when the early Scholastics distinguished between greater or major and lesser or minor sacraments (*sacramenta maiora et minora*). The major sacraments included baptism, confirmation, Eucharist, penance, anointing of the sick, orders, and marriage; the remaining minor sacraments became known collectively as "sacramentals."[2]

It is possible, of course, to ignore the theological history of the word "sacrament," use the term in the broad sense of a sign of something valuable or significant (subjectively and objectively), and end up calling every vehicle of meaning, be it person or thing, a sacrament.[3] But such a use of the term would cause confusion nowadays and hinder rather than promote an understanding of the "seven sacraments." We ought therefore to maintain the meaning which "sacrament" has acquired over the centuries and reserve the name for the seven sacraments.

THE SACRAMENTS AS THE ONGOING SAVING ACTIONS OF CHRIST

The most important approach to an understanding of the sacraments is from the vantage point of Jesus Christ. His person, mission, and activity are the basis of Christian faith and the source that nourishes the Church in the activity by which it communicates salvation. The New Testament and the Church's Spirit-inspired faith makes the following key statements about Christ:

a) He is truly a human being and at the same time the eternally existing Son of God; in other words, he is God-man.

b) He is conscious of being called by the Father to bring the human race a new glad tidings and bestow upon it deliverance and salvation (see Lk 4:16-19).

c) His life is one of service and self-dedication to humankind and reaches its climax in his passion and resurrection, wherein he overcomes our death and gives us life in abundance (Jn 10:10 and elsewhere).

d) He promises to bestow the Holy Spirit, and in the Spirit his own abiding presence, on the community of disciples which we call the Church (Mt 18:20; 28:20).

e) He commissions his disciples, and gives them authority to continue his salvific service through preaching of the Word and administration of the sacraments. In doing so he identifies himself with them in so close a solidarity that he takes acceptance or rejection of them as acceptance or rejection of himself (for example, Lk 10:16).

This set of facts yields wide-ranging conclusions regarding the activity of the Church. Whenever the Church proclaims his word, worships the Father in Spirit and in truth, celebrates the liturgy, and administers the sacraments, he himself is present and acts through the Church. Vatican II shows a keen appreciation of this ongoing activity of Christ (*SC* 6-7) and calls the liturgy "an exercise of the priestly office of Jesus Christ" (7). The sacraments, being an essential sector of the liturgy, are thus actions of both Christ and his Church. Not only do they have their foundation (in a manner still to be specified) in his will for our salvation; in addition, he as well as the Church is the agent who accomplishes them and he fills them with saving power. We shall return to this basic idea of a sacrament as we deal with each of the seven.

THE INCARNATIONAL STRUCTURE OF THE CHURCH AND THE SACRAMENTS

In his incarnation the Son of God became part of the human race and made our nature his own. As a result we encounter in Jesus Christ both God and man, omnipotence and weakness, divine riches and human poverty, divine triumph and human suffering unto death. If we understand a sacrament as defined abstractly by traditional theology, that is, as a visible sign of invisible grace, then we can appropriately describe Christ himself as the "primordial sacrament." For his human life and activity and, above all, his self-giving for us on the cross are a visible, efficacious sign of his divine saving will that operates "for us human beings and our salvation." As primordial sacrament Christ became the dynamic center of a saving activity which seeks to apprehend and transform the entire human race via the Church and its liturgy.

In a certain sense and measure Jesus communicates his own divine-human constitution to the Church, insofar as he unites himself to it and makes it his mystical body. The Church thus has a visible, human side: it is a "Church of sinners" which is not unacquainted with wretched failure and knows that it is continually called to conversion and repentance. But as body of Christ it is also filled with God and called, in the Spirit and power of Christ, to collaborate in the salvation of the world. The Church thus becomes a visible sign of salvation among the nations; it has a sacramental structure and function. It stands between Christ, the primordial sacrament, and the particular sacraments which it administers at his command. Vatican II calls the Church the "universal sacrament of salvation" that has been established by the Spirit of Christ.[4] Many theologians speak of the Church as "sacrament of Christ," or "foundational and root sacrament," or "principal or comprehensive sacrament."

The seven sacraments likewise display the incarnational structure proper to Christ and his Church. They are at first glance inconspicuous occurrences in the visible world; simple human activities, made up of words and signs, that as such cannot have any far-reaching significance or effects: a little water poured on the head; oil used to anoint forehead or hands; bread and wine over which a prayer of thanksgiving is spoken; the laying of hands—accompanied by a prayer—on the sick and on candidates for orders.

But behind these simple, everyday occurrences stands the omnipotent saving will of God who communicates himself to human beings through Christ and his Spirit and thus brings into existence the new creation of the New Testament covenant. Christ, the high priest who seeks our salvation, stoops to human beings and lifts them up to the Father; like the Samaritan of the parable he pours oil and wine into the wounds of human beings and carries them to the inn where they are restored to health. Those who are unaware of the saving power that God exercises in the sacraments must view them as evidence of superstition and magic. Those, on the other hand, who approach the sacraments with faith are filled with wonder as they contemplate them.

As far as the concrete form of the individual sacraments (the actions with their interpretative words and prayers) is concerned, present-day theologians (and the present-day *magisterium*) no longer share the view of earlier centuries that each sacrament in all its details was established by Christ himself. *Christ, the primordial sacrament, makes his saving will effective through the Church as universal sacrament*. The Church's role is to render the saving work of Christ present to every generation and apply it to them. It was enough for Christ to have established and clarified the purpose served by the salvific effects of each sacrament. The function of the Church, on the other hand, is to determine the concrete form (sign and words) by which the saving will of Christ achieves its goal, or, in other words, to determine the concrete sacramental rite.

This makes it understandable that in the history of the Church there have been some differences in the outward form of the sacraments in East and West and that even in the history of the Western Church itself there have been changes in signs and words or "matter and form." This is true not least of our own postconciliar period, now that Vatican II has given the order "to undertake with great care a general reform of the liturgy itself." The council gives the following basis for the order: "For the liturgy is made up of immutable elements, divinely instituted, and of elements subject to change. These not only may but ought to be changed with the passage of time if they have suffered from the intrusion of anything out of harmony with the inner nature of the liturgy or have become pointless" (*SC* 21).

This theological conception of the sacraments as having their ultimate origin in the saving will of Christ and of the Church as commissioned to give the sacraments their concrete form protects us against a narrowly biblicist outlook that accepts as sacramental only what is expressly mentioned in the New Testament, and also against a narrow view of tradition that seeks to show the sacraments as having acquired a definitive outward form in the more or less distant past and that therefore rejects any change.

THE SACRAMENTS AS COLLABORATIVE ENCOUNTERS WITH CHRIST

The sacraments owe their existence to the saving will of God as this operates in Christ. In them Christ, the Savior of the world and the high priest of the new covenant, comes to meet human beings in need of salvation. In so doing, Christ, the primordial sacrament, makes use of the Church, the universal sacrament.

If we look upon these saving sacramental actions as *encounters with Christ* and, in and through him, with the Father, we have a concept that makes an important point. For "encounter" between partners who are intellectual beings requires reciprocal openness and reciprocal self-giving. Christ takes human freedom seriously and therefore refuses to impose his offer of grace on human beings, much less simply force it upon them. He wants a personal encounter between partners. The "share" which human beings must contribute is faith in Jesus as the exalted Lord and Savior of the world and in the Father as the one who sent him to sanctify humankind.

"A sacrament is in a sense the extension of that infinite gift which the Father has given, to a world in need of redemption, in the person of his beloved Son, who chose to give himself up for us on the cross. In giving himself, however, the Word appeals to free human beings. If they are to share in the gift of salvation, they must have faith; they must humbly and gratefully open themselves to the message of salvation and surrender themselves in faith to God who gives his gifts to them." [5]

"Faith," in this context, is to be understood in its full New Testament sense: faith as acknowledgement and confession and as trust and unreserved readiness for surrender to the Father. This is faith that is inspired by love (*fides caritate formata*) and reaches its completion and perfection in love. This kind of faith excludes every form of self-satisfaction, complacency, arrogance, domineeringness, and inconsiderateness. Jesus himself says that this kind of faith is a prerequisite for justification, and he expressly requires it of those who come to him for help and healing. He finds it only too often lacking in the spiritual and religious leaders of the Jewish people, and especially in his fellow-townsmen at Nazareth; he finds it chiefly among the lowly and despised members of his people, among tax collectors and sinners, and among foreigners. In the parable of the Pharisee and the tax collector he castigates the spiritual pride that insists on its own merits, while he promises divine favor (justification) to the tax collector with his humble, trusting openness. The evangelist even notes on one occasion that Jesus "could do no mighty work" in his home town, because the unbelief there was so great as to make him marvel (Mk 6:5f.; Mt 13:58).

Faith, then, and the desire for salvation and readiness for self-surrender which faith implies, is a necessary condition in the recipient if Christ is to effect salvation sacramentally and the sacrament is to be received fruitfully. In addition, every sacrament, being God's firm promise of salvation and his concretized saving word, is like a seed that is sown within the human being and that will not develop apart from the faith and love of the recipient. In this sense, every sacrament is a God-given beginning that must be followed up and brought to completion. Thus the sacramental gift brings its recipient a task and duty that cannot be fulfilled without persevering faith.

The basic importance of faith is further underscored by the fact that neither the promise of salvation contained in the sacramental gifts nor the meaning of the sacramental signs can be grasped without faith. The sacraments can be celebrated , in the full and proper sense, only in faith. On the other hand, one of the special effects of the sacraments is precisely to nourish and strengthen this faith in the recipients. It is correct, then, to speak of the "sacraments of faith," as Vatican II (*SC* 59) does.

THE SACRAMENTS AS RADICAL SELF-REALIZATIONS OF THE CHURCH

When the sacraments are described as personal, collaborative encounters of human beings with Christ, the impression may be given that these encounters take place solely in the private sphere of individuals who seek and find their God and the salvation he offers. Vatican II already rejects this view:

"Liturgical services are not private functions, but are celebrations belonging to the Church, which is the 'sacrament of unity,' namely, the holy people united and ordered under their bishops.

Therefore liturgical services involve the whole Body of the Church; they manifest it and have effects upon it, but they also concern the individual members of the Church in different ways, according to their different orders, offices, and actual participation (*SC* 26)."

This ecclesiological side of the sacraments is to be seen first of all in the fact that they are administered in and by the Church. As we saw, the Church is the universal sacrament, which brings the divine saving will to fruition by commission of Christ, the primordial sacrament. It is an instrument in the hands of Christ; it is his arm, as it were, that is extended and visible to all human beings; it is the abiding sign of his nearness and his helping love. The administration of the sacraments is, of course, not the only task God has given to the Church, but it is certainly one of the essential and important ones. It is one of the radical self-realizations of the Church and is comparable, in this respect, to the proclamation of the word of God.

Just as the Church must preserve the word of God as a priceless legacy and, in season and out of season, translate it and proclaim it to each successive age, thereby at the same time building itself up, so with the sacraments. These are in the final analysis *the paschal mystery of the Church's Lord made present* and applied to human beings in need of salvation, and the Church may not withhold them. Just as the Church may never fall silent in its proclamation of the good news, neither may it grow weary of administering the sacraments, even when a totalitarian government threatens punishment for this ministry. Paul cried out on one occasion: "Woe to me if I do not preach the gospel!" (1 Cor 9:16). In like manner, the Church must think of itself as betraying its most specific mission if it tires of administering the sacraments or allows itself to be dissuaded therefrom by external influences.

In all this the Church is not simply being faithful to a mandate; it is also building itself up in and through the Holy Spirit. Every sacrament that is administered and received *serves the building up of the mystical body of Christ*; it extends that body and gives it new life. For the sacraments, each according to its special purpose and gift of grace, bring new members into the communion of the Church or initiate new, lifegiving ties with the Church and its head. This, however, is something that decisively affects not simply the mystical body as a totality but all of its members as well. The Church thus actualizes itself in the measure that it sacramentally sanctifies human beings, and it has ever new reasons for thanking God and interceding for its members, whether new or more intensely graced or called to new powers and tasks (in orders and marriage).

This ecclesial dimension of the sacraments also makes it clear that their administration can never be a purely private matter, but must *by its nature be a liturgical celebration* and have a form that corresponds to this character. Thus there cannot be, in the strict sense of the word, a "private" Mass or baptism. This fact helps us understand the efforts of Vatican II to have all liturgical celebrations include the presence and active participation of some community, however small. "This applies with special force to the celebration of Mass and the administration of the sacraments" (SC 27). In describing the individual sacraments I shall lay special emphasis on this ecclesiological and litugical aspect of their celebration. It is clear from the outset, of course, that the possible measure of communal participation differs from sacrament to sacrament.

THE EFFICACY OF THE SACRAMENTS

What has been said thus far makes it clear that Christ is the ultimate source of the efficacy of the sacraments. He is the real giver; the individuals commissioned by the Church are as it were instruments in his hands. Even in Christian antiquity the question was already raised, in connection with the dispute over baptism by heretics, whether the sacraments are efficacious even when the human minister is unworthy (for example, because he is a heretic or has committed a serious sin and thus lost the grace of God). Theologians have always insisted that the salvific activity of Christ occurs whenever the human minister, even if personally unworthy, performs the essential rite with the intention of doing what the Church intends to do in the sacrament.

With this situation in mind the Scholastic theologians at the beginning of the thirteenth century developed the concept of *ex opere operato*: literally, "by reason of the work performed," that is, by reason of the properly performed rite. This conception, along with the phrase itself, was expressly sanctioned by the Council of Trent.[6] Lest the phrase lead to a misunderstanding of the sacraments as exercises in magic, it must be clearly understood that the rite is only a means by which Christ himself effects the interior sanctification of the recipient. At the same time, be it noted, the minister has an obligation to strive for that personal interior worthiness that is required by cooperation with Christ in communicating salvation.

As far as the recipients are concerned, the effect of the sacrament is always a gift, never something merited. What is required of them is that they open themselves, by faith and interior self-surrender, to the Lord who comes to them in the sacrament. The sacraments can produce no effect in those who by deliberate unbelief and interior rejection place an "obstacle" (Latin: *obex*) in the way of Christ's communication of grace. They go away empty and are even guilty of sacrilege. No less important a figure than Paul himself urgently warns against the unworthy reception of the body and blood of Christ (1 Cor 11:27-29).

SEQUENCE, HIERARCHY, AND INTERCONNECTION OF THE SACRAMENTS

In the Western Church theologians reflecting on the practice of the

Church came to the conclusion that there are seven sacraments, even though during the first millennium the name "sacrament" was given to other "mysteries" of the Church, such as the dedication of a church, monastic consecration, and funeral rites (at times over thirty "sacraments" were listed).

Since the Scholastic period the seven sacraments thus singled out have been presented in a set order that represents primarily the order of reception. Baptism, confirmation, and the Eucharist had already been regarded since antiquity as sacraments of "initiation" (sacraments whereby one becomes a Christian), and were usually administered during the Easter Vigil, after one or more years of preparation (catechumenate). The sacrament of reconciliation, looked upon as "the plank that rescues us after the shipwreck of [serious] sin," was originally administered only rarely, in some instances only once in a lifetime. The anointing of the sick was meant to serve bodily and spiritual recovery in the difficult situation of serious illness. The two sacraments of orders and matrimony, which were placed at the end of the list and were also known as "sacraments of states of life," have a special socio-ecclesiological funtion: ordination as the bestowal of office that ensures the promotion of salvation through proclamation of the faith, liturgy, and active love (martyria, leitourgia, diakonia); and matrimony which leads to the establishment and sanctification of the family and the building up of what have been called "little Churches" or "domestic Churches."

As far as the hierarchy or ranking of the sacraments among themselves is concerned, the Eucharist, being the memorial and actualization of the paschal mystery, is the center and summit of all sacramental activity; the other sacraments are in a greater or lesser degree ordered to it and derive their power from it. The same holds for the rich crown of sacramentals—the consecrations and blessings—and for all other forms of Christian liturgy. Even Lutheran theologians acknowledge this centrality of the Eucharist: "The Holy Communion worship service is the hidden, vibrant center of all worship services. If these detach themselves from this center, if the Holy Communion worship service is no longer preserved as the center supporting the entire worship life, then these detached services will necessarily become stunted and dwarfed.[7]

Baptism may be assigned a special place alongside the Eucharist, because, being the entranceway to all the other sacraments, it incorporates human beings into the mystery of Christ.[8] There are good reasons for saying, too, that confirmation and the sacrament of reconciliation—the gift of the Spirit and the forgiveness of sins—are in a way developments of the sacrament of baptism.

The Church maintains that three sacraments imprint a special mark on the recipient: the "sacramental character" (the Greek word *charaktêr* originally meant a die or stamp), which is permanent and therefore bars any repeated reception of these sacraments. The three are baptism, confirmation, and orders.[9] According to Augustine, the character is an abiding consecration that makes the recipient a permanent possession of Christ.[10] Thomas Aquinas interprets this consecration as a participation in the priesthood of Christ and an "appointment to worship of God" (deputatio ad cultum divinum), that is: "each of the faithful is destined to receive what is connected with worship of God or to communicate it to others."[11]

It is often said that the seven sacraments give divine strength and aid to human beings at the "nodal points" or decisive situations of their lives and are thus in profound harmony with human nature. "The seven sacraments bring out the implications of life's supreme moments and sublimate these."[12] Even Johann Wolfgang von Goethe, a Protestant, found the world of the seven Catholic sacraments deserving of praise and esteem from this point of view.[13] Thomas Aquinas had already developed this parallel between bodily life and the role of the sacraments in the spiritual life: conception and birth correspond to baptism, maturation to confirmation, nourishment to the Eucharist, healing from sicknesses to penance and anointing of the sick; authority for leadership in the life of the community corresponds to the sacrament of orders, while the sacrament of matrimony serves the natural and spiritual building up of the community.[14] In applying this analogy with natural human life, however, we must not overlook the truth of faith that the sacraments have as their supreme goal the incorporation of believers into the paschal mystery and, ultimately, eternal communion with the triune God. In the ensuing chapters I shall follow this same order as I discuss, in a necessarily brief way, the meaning and liturgical form of the individual sacraments.[15]

Chapter Nine

Baptism

THE IMPORTANCE OF BAPTISM

In the view of all the confessions baptism is the most important and basic event of Christian life; it is an ecumenical sacrament. Faith on this point is based on the clear testimony of the New Testament writings and an unbroken subsequent tradition. The New Testament testimonies regarding baptism vary in accordance with the theological stance of their authors and their intention in writing. Taken together, they give an impressive picture of the great importance attributed to this sacrament by the primitive community. It is to be observed, however, that the New Testament testimonies are concerned primarily with the baptism of adults, since the baptism of children became predominant only in later centuries.

In what follows I shall bring out the importance and significance of baptism rather in the form of theses than in the form of an exegetical or theological treatise. The subsequent explanation of the baptismal rites will afford an opportunity to develop some statements in greater detail.

a) Christian baptism has its origin in a directive of the Lord (see Mt 28:19; Lk 16:16). This fact is indirectly confirmed by the universal and undisputed baptismal practice of the primitive community. In this context, a prominent Protestant exegete remarks that the origin of the Christian custom of baptism remains a mystery unless we decide to take seriously the traditions regarding the missionary mandate of the risen Christ.[1]

b) The conditions a person must meet in order to receive baptism are an interior change of ways (conversion) and faith in Jesus and his message. But this human contribution is not to be interpreted as an independent achievement, as a meritorious act calling for a recompense, but rather as itself dependent on the prevenient grace of God. For "no one can come to me unless the Father . . . draws him" (Jn 6:44).

c) Baptism incorporates human beings into the Church as God's people of the new covenant; it is therefore the sign of a call and of salvation, just as circumcision had been the covenantal sign under the old covenant (see Col 2:11). Incorporation into the Church simultaneously brings membership in the mystical body of Christ and fills the baptized with the Holy Spirit (1 Cor 12:13). "Understood in this manner, incorporation into the Church is the primary basic effect of baptism. . . . At the same time . . . it is likewise the means by which we attain the fullness of baptismal grace."[2]

d) The union with Christ is so profound and interior that the baptized are drawn into the saving mystery of the death and resurrection of Christ; they share in his paschal mystery. "We were buried . . . with him by baptism into death, so that as Christ was raised from the dead by the glory of the Father, we too might walk in newness of life" (Rom 6:4; see also vv. 3 and 5; similarly Col 2:12ff.).

e) Baptism is the gateway to new life; it is a rebirth, as Jesus says in words reported in the Gospel of John: "Unless one is born of water and the Spirit, he cannot enter the kingdom of God" (Jn 3:5).

f) It is a new creation in which divine omnipotence is at work: "If any one is in Christ, he is a new creation; the old has passed away, behold, the new has come" (2 Cor 5:17).

g) The saving action of baptism does away with the separation of human beings from God; in other words, it brings forgiveness of all sin, including original sin. God bestows the love which he has for his "beloved Son" on the baptized as well, because they have become members of Christ's body and brothers and sisters of his Son. "See what love the Father has given us, that we should be called the children of God; and so we are" (1 Jn 3:1).

h) Baptism gives human life a new fullness of meaning and the hope of an eternal life in communion with God (see Rom 8:17).

Baptism is thus not simply an external rite of acceptance into a human organization. Looked at from God's side it is a proof of his mercy and saving will; for human beings it means a new life, in and with Christ, that is ordered to participation in his glory.

THE NEW RITE OF BAPTISM FOR CHILDREN

With the New Testament proclamation of baptism as the starting point, the first centuries developed an entire rite for becoming a Christian; this became known as the rite of Christian "initiation" (consecration, incorporation). It included in a single complex of actions all that we today distinguish as baptism, confirmation, and the Eucharist. For this reason these three sacraments are known as the sacraments of initiation or the foundational sacraments. Historical developments in the Western Church led to a clearer division between the three and to their reception on separate occasions.[3] But when infant baptism did become predominant from the fourth century on, no proper rite of child baptism was created that would take due account of the situation of the immature child. The rite of baptism for children was and remained an inadequately adapted rite of baptism for adults.

Vatican II performed a great service by introducing a radical change in this area; it decreed that "the rite for the baptism of infants is to be revised and it should be suited to the fact that those to be baptized are infants" (*SC* 67). In response to this directive the Roman Congregation for Divine Worship published a new rite for the baptism of children in 1969. The following reflections and explanations are based on (1) the General Introduction, *Christian Initiation,* to the rites of baptism for adults and for children; (2) the Introduction to the rite of baptism for children; and (3) the rite itself.[4]

The Legitimacy of Baptism for Children

This problem is not a new one. The history of the Church tells of efforts by various groups to have infant or child baptism declared illegitimate and invalid and to replace it by the baptism exclusively of adults. The exegetes give differing answers to the question of whether the New Testament is familiar with and approves the practice of the baptism of children or (to put it less ambiguously) of infants. Origen spoke in favor of the position that it had been practiced from the beginning: "The Church has received from the apostles the tradition of baptizing children no less than adults."[5]

Ever since Protestant theologian Karl Barth attacked it in 1943 ("a profoundly disordered practice"), the question of its legitimacy or, as the case may be, its appropriateness has once again been the subject of discussion.[6] The new rite adopts the following position in its introduction:

"From the earliest times, the Church, to which the mission of preaching the Gospel and of baptizing was entrusted, has baptized not only adults but children as well. Our Lord said: 'Unless a man is reborn in water and the Holy Spirit, he cannot enter the kingdom of God.' The Church has always understood these words to mean that children should not be deprived of baptism, because they are baptized in the faith of the Church, a faith proclaimed for them by their parents and godparents, who represent both the local Church and the whole society of saints and believers: 'The whole Church is the mother of all and the mother of each'" (Introduction to the Rite of Baptism for Children, 2).

Dialogue on Baptism and Postponement of Baptism
According to the new rite of baptism for children, an effort must be made to impress on adults presenting their children for baptism the obligation they have of raising these children as Christians. This is to be done primarily in preliminary meetings with the parents.[7] "When the parents are not yet prepared to profess the faith or to undertake the duty of bringing up their children as Christians, it is for the parish priest (pastor), keeping in mind whatever regulations may have been laid down by the conference of bishops, to determine the time for the baptism of infants" (Introduction to the Rite of Baptism for Children, 8, 4).

Such a postponement of baptism—which is not a definitive refusal of the sacrament—shows how seriously the Church takes the consequences of infant baptism. Everything must be done to keep baptism from becoming an empty show, a sowing of seed that is then not cultivated and has no chance of survival. At the same time, this attitude to infant baptism counters the ugly accusation that the Church's primary reason for clinging to infant baptism is increased membership, the greater external power that numbers bring, and, in some European countries, the larger number of people paying the Church tax.[8]

Child Baptism and the Community

Although the parents have the primary right and responsibility for the baptism and Christian rearing of their children, the local community, as visible representative of the universal Church, also has a significant duty and responsibility. The manner in which baptism was administered to children in many places until a few decades ago was such as to obscure the fact that the baptism of a child not only affects the salvation of an individual but is also an event of profound significance to the community of believers.

The new ritual highlights the relation of the event to the community and emphasizes the latter's responsibility. Baptism is, after all, an incorporation into the people of God. The latter must therefore make a continuing effort to see to it that in accordance with God's will as many human beings as possible are baptized and that this initial acquisition of salvation is organically continued by a life of faith with the ecclesial community. "Therefore it is most important that catechists and other lay people should work with priests and deacons in preparing for baptism" (*Christian Initiation* 7). The reference is evidently to dialogues with parents who are undecided because their faith is weak, but also to participation in the already mentioned dialogues on baptism which are meant to make parents more conscious of the gift and responsibility given them in the baptism of their children and to strengthen them in their faith.

"In the actual celebration, the people of God (represented not only by the parents, godparents, and relatives, but also, as far as possible, by friends, neighbors, and some members of the local Church) should take an active part. Thus they will show their common faith and express their joy as the newly baptized are received into the community of the Church" (*Christian Initiation* 7).

"In this way it is clear that the faith in which the children are baptized is not the private possession of the individual family, but the common treasure of the whole Church of Christ" (Introduction to the Rite of Baptism for Children, 4). In order to facilitate this participation of the community in the celebration baptism should normally be administered in the parish church; hospitals and private homes are acceptable venues only for reasons of health or other compelling pastoral need.

"As far as possible, all recently born babies should be baptized at a common celebration on the same day" (*Christian Initiation* 27). This practice will help ensure a larger attendance of the community at the baptism. Furthermore, baptism should occasionally be celebrated during Sunday Mass, so that the entire community may participate and the close connection between baptism and the Eucharist may be clearly seen (Introduction to the Rite of Baptism for Children, 9). Finally, baptism as an independent liturgical ceremony may also replace afternoon devotions or be celebrated as part of a Sunday liturgy of the word.

Even after baptism has been administered the community continues to have a responsibility. "The Church in the form of the local community and the believing family renders possible, fosters, and supports the decision of the individual to believe, for it is only in the community of the faithful that the individual is able to persevere."[9]

The Office of Sponsor

Those who accept the office of sponsor render a special personal service to the child and its parents. The practice of having sponsors (godparents) came into being in the first Christian centuries in connection with adult baptism and the period of preparation for it (the catechumenate). The duty of sponsors was to be guarantors to the community of the serious intentions and authentic conversion of the catechumens. They were to introduce those entrusted to their care into the life of the community, strengthen them by word and example in faith and the following of Christ, and stand by them as helpers during the prepartory rites and the administration of the sacrament. Afterwards they were to retain close ties to the new members of the community and help them as needed.

Historical developments (the entrance of the masses into the Church as a result of the Constantinian Revolution; the frequent postponement of baptism, often into old age; the increasing practice of infant baptism; and the general superficialization of the Christian consciousness) gradually eroded the catechumenate and with it the office of sponsor. At the end of antiquity, when infant baptism was already the usual thing in the Roman Empire, provision was indeed still made for sponsors, and in the beginning there was still an awareness that the parents were primarily responsible for the baptism and Christian rearing of their children.

Within the rite of infant baptism, however, the sponsors increasingly tended to replace the parents until finally the latter were completely excluded. The sponsors, and no longer the parents, were now regarded as guarantors and mediators of the faith. This serious misunderstanding of the relation of the parents to the child in the latter's spiritual and religious development was conditioned above all by an excessive theory of spiritual affinity.[10] The point was finally reached where parents absented themselves from the baptism of their children.

The new 1969 rite of baptism for children finally put a stop to these erroneous developments and restored the correct relation between parents and sponsors: "Because of the natural relationships, parents have a ministry and a responsibility in the baptism of infants more important than those of the godparents" (Introduction to the *Rite of Baptism for Children* 5).

But this primacy of the parental role in liturgy and life does not prevent the sponsors from playing an important, even if subsidiary part. The sponsor is as it were the permanent representative of the entire Church and a visible link with the community. Moreover, should the parents suffer a lengthy illness or die an early death, the sponsor can look after the child; he or she can assist the parents in difficult questions of the child's rearing and vocational direction and can directly encourage and guide the child. Sponsors can thus help counter the harmful results of a certain isolation that not infrequently affects the contemporary nuclear family.

The new rite of baptism sets down the following requirements for sponsors (*Christian Initiation* 10):

"They must have the maturity in faith and Christian living that the office of sponsor requires; their age should be such that, humanly speaking, it will allow them to exercise the responsibility of sponsorship for a fairly lengthy period.

"They must themselves have already received the sacraments of baptism, confirmation, and the Eucharist.

"They must belong to the Catholic Church and not be excluded from the office of sponsor by any canonical hindrance.

"A baptized person who is a believing Christian but a member of a Church separated from Rome can, however, be permitted to serve as sponsor or Christian witness along with a Catholic godparent, if the parents so desire.

"If the parents have difficulty in finding among their acquaintances a sponsor who possesses the desired qualifications, the parish community (parish council) should go to work. In an emergency the parents may also do without a sponsor, if no suitable one can be found in time (see Code of Canon Law [1983], can. 872). Better no sponsor than one who is not up to the task and, being a mere supernumerary, diminishes rather than increases respect for the office of sponsor."[11]

The Proper Time for Baptism

Until well into the Middle Ages the Vigils of Easter and Pentecost and, in many regions, the night before Epiphany were the preferred times for baptism. This choice was motivated by a desire to make clear the close connection between baptism and the great saving actions of Christ. But the high rate of infant mortality in past times and a concern for the child's salvation (the view was widespread that unbaptized children were lost) led to the custom and law that children were to be baptized as soon as possible. The words *quam primum* ("as soon as possible") in canon 770 of the 1917 Code of Canon Law were interpreted to mean that a child was to be baptized in the first few days after its birth. As a result the mother was in practice excluded from participation in the ceremony.

In order to facilitate the mother's participation and to allow enough time for preparing the parents (dialogue on baptism) and the ceremony itself, the new rite of baptism prescribes that the sacrament is to be administered during the first weeks after birth. Only if the child is in danger of death is it to be baptized without delay. For these emergencies an abbreviated rite is provided that may be celebrated by a layperson. If the danger of death is imminent it is enough to pour some water and at the same time pronounce the baptismal formula ("I baptize you in the name . . ."). In order to bring out clearly the paschal character of baptism it is desirable to celebrate it during the Easter Vigil or on a Sunday, which is the day of the weekly celebration of the paschal mystery. In any case, every baptism should have a clearly paschal character.

THE RITE OF BAPTISM FOR CHILDREN, *STRUCTURE:*

Introductory Rites
Greeting of the community assembled for the baptism
Dialogue with the parents
Dialogue with the godparents
Signing of the child with the cross

Liturgy of the Word
Reading(s) and homily
Intercessions
Prayer of Exorcism
Anointing with the oil of catechumens or imposition of hands

Celebration of the Sacrament
Blessing of the baptismal water
Renunciation and profession of faith
Baptism

Explanatory Rites
Anointing with chrism
Clothing with baptismal garment
Giving of the baptismal candle
Rite of the Ephpheta

Concluding Rites
Concluding address
The Lord's Prayer
Blessing and closing hymn

Introductory Rites
After donning liturgical vestments of a festive color, the baptizing priest or deacon (= celebrant) stations himself at the entrance to the church or in the part of the church where the community is assembled for the baptism, and greets them in his own words. The parents are asked what name they are giving their child. To the further

question of what they are asking of the Church they reply: "Baptism." Neither celebrant nor parents are obliged to use this precise formula; the questions and answers can be in other words, provided the meaning is the same. Already evident here is a certain flexibility that will show itself at numerous other points and that is sanctioned for the rest of the liturgy as well, but especially the liturgy of the sacraments. The hope behind this allowance for variation is that the ceremony will take on a greater vitality and be better adapted to the situation of the moment. The celebrant now reminds the parents of their obligation to raise their child in the Christian faith; he gives them the opportunity to express their readiness to do so. The godparents are asked whether they intend to aid the parents in their task.

The celebrant, parents, and sponsors next make the sign of the cross on the child's forehead. This signing or sealing is meant to attest that the child belongs to Christ; it is also a renunciation of Satan, who is conquered by this sign.

Liturgy of the Word

The purpose of this part of the liturgy is to strengthen the faith of the parents and other participants, deepen their understanding of baptism, and intercede for the fruit of the sacrament. During the reading(s) and homily the children may, if necessary, be brought to a nearby room (the cry-room), where their crying will not distract the assembly. This part of the ceremony begins with one or two readings, one at least of which should be from the New Testament. An appendix to the ritual contains numerous suggestions. The wishes and situation of the parents should be taken into account in making the selection. Between the readings psalm verses and appropriate refrains may be sung. Here again the ritual offers a wide selection. The celebrant now delivers a short address on the gift of baptism and the task it entails. A song may be added, but a time for silent prayer may be chosen instead.

The intercessions (four additional formularies are given in an appendix) are not only for the baptizands but for the parents, sponsors, and participating members of the community. They end with an invocation of the saints, to which the names of other saints may be added (for example, the patron saints of the baptizands and of the church). If the congregation is prepared to do so, members may add their own petitions to those formulated by the celebrant.

The celebrant now utters one of the two prayers of exorcism provided, asking that God would deliver the children from the bonds of sin and make them a dwelling for his Holy Spirit.

The anointing of each child on the breast with the oil of catechumens is introduced by a prayer that Christ would strengthen them. In antiquity, anointing with oil was thought to give health and strength (for example, in wrestling matches). Since this notion has largely disappeared and the practical use of the rite is difficult in the case of infants, the anointing may be omitted. If it is, the celebrant places his hand silently on each child. This laying on of the hand can be understood as it was in the ancient Roman rite of baptism: as a sign that the child is to be rescued from Satan's domination and made over to Christ.

Celebration of the Sacrament

The community now moves to the font or the baptistry where the celebrant speaks a few words in preparation for the blessing of the baptismal water. Only during the Easter season does he use the water that was solemnly consecrated during the Easter Vigil; at other times he blesses water for each celebration of baptism. An advantage of the new practice is that celebrants need no longer use for an entire year the water that was mixed with oil at the Easter Vigil and has in time grown stale—a condition certainly not desirable from the hygienic and esthetic standpoints. The rule to be followed now is enunciated in the general introduction to the several rites of baptism: "The water to be used in baptism should be true water and clean, both for the sake of the authentic sacramental symbolism and for hygienic reasons" (*Christian Initiation* 18).

It is explicitly allowed that the water may be "living" water, that is, water flowing into and out of the font (see *ibid.*, 21). The original form of baptism (still used as late as the high Middle Ages), namely, immersion rather than infusion, thus becomes possible once more, especially since there is today no difficulty in piping warm water to the font.

The celebrant may choose among three prayers for the blessing.

These contain a remembrance of God's past saving deeds (anamnesis) and a petition for the grace of baptism (epiclesis). At baptisms during the Easter season, at which the water blessed during the Easter Vigil is used, two of the prayers may be modified to recall that earlier blessing.

A further, immediate preparation for the administration of the sacrament is the parents' and sponsors' renunciation of Satan and profession of faith. It is the parents and sponsors, and no longer the children, who are questioned and placed under an obligation. In his introductory address the celebrant speaks of the parents' unconditional obligation to rear their children as believers. Two formulas are given for the renunciation of Satan. The three questions asked in the profession of faith make use of the Apostles' Creed, which was originally the baptismal profession of faith in the West (in the East the longer creed of Nicea and Constantinople—our present Mass creed—was used at baptism).

The celebrant and the congregation then give their assent to the profession of faith. Some other formula besides the one in the ritual may be used, or even a suitable song.

These preparatory rites are followed by the sacramental action proper: a threefold immersion or infusion with water on the head, while the celebrant speaks the words: "N., I baptize you in the name of the Father, and of the Son, and of the Holy Spirit." This is the crucial rite of baptism and suffices for a valid baptism in an emergency. The salvific action of God in the baptizand is symbolized by the use of water, for in the Bible water is a sign of purification and life.

After the baptism the faithful present may sing a short acclamation (a large number of texts are provided). In contrast to older custom it is desirable that if at all possible the parents should themselves hold the child during its baptism or, in case of immersion, "lift the child out of the font," while the godparents simply place their right hand on the child.

Explanatory Rites

After a prayer that prepares for and explains his action, the celebrant anoints the crown of the child's head with chrism. This rite is modeled on the anointing of priests and kings in the Old Testament and is intended to show that as a member of the people of God the baptized person shares in the royal priesthood of Christ, as we are told in 1 Peter 2:9.

The clothing of the child in a white garment not only recalls the early days of the Church when the newly baptized donned white garments which they then wore at the celebration of the Eucharist during Easter week. The white garment also symbolizes that the baptized are a "new creation" and "have put on Christ" (see Rom 13:14; Gal 3:27). The ritual expresses the wish that the families would themselves prepare the white garment; it should not be put on the child, however, before the baptism proper.

As the accompanying prayer indicates, the giving of a baptismal candle (which the father or godfather then lights from the Easter candle) is intended as a sign that the newly baptized have become children of the light and are to walk as such (Eph 5:8), so that they may one day, lamp of faith in hand, hasten to meet their returning Lord (see the parable of the ten virgins).

The (optional) Ephpheta rite is inspired by Jesus' miraculous healing of a deaf mute (Mk 7:32-37). The celebrant touches the ears and mouth of the child with his thumb and prays that Jesus will soon enable it to hear his word and confess the faith.

Conclusion of the Rite

If the spatial layout of the church allows, the entire congregation processes from the font to the altar as a baptismal song is being sung. The celebrant briefly recalls the baptism just administered and looks ahead to the sacraments of confirmation and Eucharist that are still to be received; then all join in the Lord's Prayer.

The celebrant then blesses the mothers of the newly baptized children, their fathers, the godparents, and the other faithful (four formulas are given). Finally, an Easter song or the Magnificat is sung. "Where there is the practice of bringing baptized infants to the altar of the Blessed Virgin Mary, this custom is observed if appropriate" (Rite of Baptism for Children 71).

To sum up: this new rite of baptism for children may be regarded as a considerable improvement upon the old. For the first time, it takes seriously the fact that the one to be baptized is at best an immature child. There is no artificial dialogue with a child that is still unable to think or speak; instead, the celebrant addresses the parents and godparents, asks them about *their* desire for the baptism, *their* rejection of Satan and sin, and *their* profession of faith. True enough, he still addresses the child at several points in the rite (the words of baptism, the anointing with chrism, the giving of the baptismal garment, the Ephpheta rite). There is, however, no pretense at a dialogue but simply words addressed to the child because the Church takes it seriously as a person, just as the mother does, whose behavior nonetheless we do not regard as irrational.

A further merit of the new rite is one that I have already alluded to several times: because the child is baptized in the faith of its parents, the latter are the real partners in the dialogue that elicits the desire for baptism, the renunciation of Satan, and the profession of faith. The parents are here called upon to be faithful to their own baptism and to render the necessary service of faith to their children as the latter grow. By comparison with the parents, the godparents (as I remarked in connection with the opening rites) withdraw to second place; theirs is a subsidiary role.

Not least because of the options allowed and the possibilities of varying its form, this rite of baptism can become an impressive and gripping communal celebration that does justice to the intrinsic meaning of the event. For the child being baptized, it becomes the beginning of a journey of faith which needs the continued help of the community if it is to reach its goal.[12]

THE INCORPORATION OF ADULTS INTO THE COMMUNITY

Historical Survey

The Christian community realized at a very early date that the way of an adult to faith and the Church is a process of growth that takes some time and usually needs help from the institution. Christian life requires a training and protection which as a rule can be provided only by the concrete local community. The result was the establishment, by the end of the second century, of the institution of the catechumenate for those seeking baptism. Hippolytus of Rome in his *Apostolic Tradition* (beginning of the third century) gives us a detailed picture of the structure of the catechumenate at the center of the Western Church.

The average length of the catechumenate was three years. During this time the applicants for baptism received instruction in the faith (catechesis) that closed on each occasion with a prayer and an impostion of hands. Some weeks (usually at the beginning of Lent) before the administration of baptism at the Easter Vigil they began a period of more intense preparation; they now became known as *competentes* or "candidates" (literally: "seekers"; at Rome they were also called *electi*, "chosen ones").

This period began with an examination of the candidates' manner of life. It was also marked by frequent attendance at liturgies of the word and by numerous other liturgical actions such as exorcisms, impositions of hands, signings with the cross, reception of the creed and the Lord's Prayer, the giving of blessed salt, and so on. The reception of the three "sacraments of initiation" (baptism, confirmation, Eucharist) took place during the Easter Vigil. The neophytes ("newborn") then entered upon a time of mystagogical instruction that occupied the whole of Easter week; during these days they were drawn deeper into the mystery of Christ and his community and were instructed more fully in the significance of the sacraments of initiation.

Once the masses began to enter the Church in the post-Constantinian period, the catechumenate with its several stages gradually lost its meaning and finally fell into disuse. Most of the liturgical components and texts of the catechumenate were retained, however, and crowded together into a single baptismal rite without any intervals of time between them. After various complaints about this unsuitable rite the Congregation of Rites gave permission in 1962 to break it up into seven stages, but it made no changes in the content. Vatican II tackled the problem in a more radical way and ordered the restoration of a multistage catechumenate for adults and children of school age (*SC* 64-66; Decree on the Missionary Activity of the Church 14). The new rite appeared on January 6, 1972, and a second, revised edition in 1974.

The new ritual published by Rome as a model (an *editio typica*) includes a rite for a multistage catechumenate, a simplified rite of adult initiation, an abbreviated rite for use in danger of death, instructions on preparing uncatechized adults for confirmation and the Eucharist, and a rite of initiation for children of school age. The following summary deals only with the full catechumenate and solemn initiation.

The Organization of the Catechumenate and Initiation

The Roman rite gives the name "precatechumenate" to the time during which individuals experience their first interest in the Christian faith, establish contact with believers or Christian groups, and slowly develop an initial faith and a readiness for conversion. The decisive factor here is that these "sympathizers" feel accepted by the Christians around them and experience an openness and heartfelt love on the part of the Christian community. No formal liturgical celebration is connected with the precatechumenate and the period of evangelization.

The catechumenate proper—understood here as the period of remote preparation for initiation—begins with a rite of acceptance into the order of catechumens. If the attraction to the Christian faith has grown strong enough that one can speak of the beginnings of faith in Christ and if the person is determined to ask for acceptance into the Church, then he or she can certainly be accepted among the catechumens. The applicants, along with the friends and acquaintances who have accompanied them thus far on their journey, gather in the vestibule of the church or in some other suitable place; here they are presented to the local community or its representatives, and the celebrant asks them about their resolve. Those who have helped the applicants come this far attest to their readiness to seek and follow Christ. These witnesses are therefore called "sponsors" and are asked to continue helping and guiding the applicants.

After a prayer of thanksgiving the celebrant (and, if desired, the sponsors and others) signs the applicants on the forehead with the cross and, if desired, their other senses, and leads them into the church. After a liturgy of the word the applicants are given a copy of the New Testament (and a cross). In the ensuing intercessions the catechumens are especially commended to the favor of God. The names of the applicants, who already belong to the Church in a certain degree ("the Church embraces the catechumens as its own with a mother's love and concern": Introduction to the Rite of Christian Initiation for Adults 47), are placed in the list of catechumens.

The following period is meant to be one of growth in faith and Christian life. Of decisive importance here are personal contacts and conversations within the circle of catechumens. This circle is also the venue for special instructions which, together with the conversations on the faith, are to help the growth of faith. These instructions, as well as the liturgies of the word at the Sunday Eucharist, may be followed by "prayers for deliverance" (exorcisms) and blessings. During this period, too, the candidates should try to find suitable godparents.

"The length of the catechumenate depends entirely on the situation of the catechumen. As a rule, it should take at least a year. When the time comes to ask for admission to baptism, the community providing the catechumenate should come to a decision together with the catechumen. From this community the latter should then choose as a sponsor someone who has been of special assistance in the practice of a Christian life and who can now bear witness to the lived faith of the applicant. Communal sponsorship is also possible and is especially appropriate when the catechumen has had his or her first experiences of the faith in a youth group or the family circle or a family that has befriended him or her." [13]

The period of proximate preparation for baptism usually begins on the first Sunday of Lent, the period of penitential preparation for Easter. Admission to the group of candidates for baptism presupposes that the candidate has undergone a genuine conversion, has an adequate knowledge of the Christian faith, and is firm in faith and love. Those involved in the work of the catechumenate must pass judgment on these points. Admission to candidacy occurs in a liturgical ceremony known as the "rite of election" or "enrollment of names." The candidates are now known as "the elect" ("chosen ones") or *competentes* ("seekers").

The "rite of election" begins with the presentation of the candidates and the testimony of their godparents. After the candidates have been questioned and have solemnly pledged that they desire to receive the three sacraments of initiation, they confirm this resolution by writing their names in a special book. As a sign that the godparents in turn are ready to accept their responsibilities, they are invited "to place their hand on the shoulder of the candidate whom they are presenting" (Rite of Christian Initiation of Adults 133). The rite of election or enrollment of names closes with intercessions, at the end of which the celebrant extends his hands in blessing over the catechumens.

The six weeks ending in the Easter Vigil are a "period of purification and enlightenment" and are marked by rites implementing this purpose. These include, first of all, the "scrutinies" or major exorcisms. In these, by means of silent prayer and intercessions accompanied by the imposition of hands, the candidates are to be strengthened in their efforts to renounce the Evil One and follow Christ more closely. The experience of the community must determine how many of the three scheduled scrutinies (after the homily on the third, fourth, and fifth Sundays of Lent) are actually celebrated.

Other rites of this period are the presentation of the Creed and the Lord's Prayer to the candidates. These two rites may take place during a weekday Mass after the third and fifth Sundays of Lent. They came into existence in Christian antiquity at a time when the "discipline of secrecy" was still practiced. Nowadays the ceremony might emphasize a meditation on the two texts.

The Rite of Christian Initiation of Adults provides for a special liturgy of the word for Holy Saturday morning; the recitation of the creed; the Ephpheta rite; and choosing of a baptismal name.

The actual "celebration of initiation" or incorporation takes place during the Easter Vigil; the community should be prepared for it by suitable sermons and dialogues. It begins, after the presentation of the candidates and a brief instruction by the celebrant, with the litany of the saints. This is followed by the blessing of the baptismal water, the renunciation of Satan and sin, the profession of faith, and the act of baptizing. The anointing of the crown of the head that follows upon the act of baptizing is normally omitted since confirmation is administered during the Vigil. Since the anointing is omitted here, then the only two remaining explanatory rites are the clothing with the baptismal garment and the giving of the baptismal candle. The baptizing priest is the minister of confirmation which then follows.

The ritual of initiation reaches its climax and completion in the ensuing celebration of the Eucharist. During this celebration special attention is given to the newly baptized and their sponsors: they, together with their relatives, receive communion in both kinds.

During the time between Easter and Pentecost the neophytes are to exercise the new life given to them during the catechumenate and Easter Vigil; they are also to achieve a deeper understanding of it. This period of postbaptismal catechesis is therefore also called a period of "mystagogy," that is, of being "led" (*agogé*: a "leading toward" or "guiding") more deeply into the "mystery" of Christ. It is at the same time a period of growing closeness to the community. The new rite provides that at the end of this "great Easter octave" (the seven weeks between Easter and Pentecost) there be a celebration; depending on circumstances this may be accompanied by external festivities. The bishop should make an effort to remain in close contact with these new members of the Church and also to celebrate the Eucharist with them at least once a year, especially if he himself was unable to preside at their initiation.

From time to time the effort to restore the multistage catechumenate for adults has been disparaged as an exercise in archeologism and as simply a hobby of historians of the liturgy. It is true, of course, that the old is not automatically better than the new. In this instance, however, the preparation for the sacraments of initiation involves more than intellecual learning; it must also be a training in the faith and in a life of faith. This, however, requires a period long enough for testing and probation, lest we return once again to the superficial Christianity that characterized the Constantinian age. Furthermore, the sacraments of initiation contain a wealth of theology and spirituality that can be assimilated only with time and in stages.[14]

Chapter Ten

The Sacrament of Confirmation

According to the Church's tradition, there is a second sacrament of initiation, known as "confirmation." The name is derived from the Latin *confirmatio*, which is to be understood as meaning "a strengthening." The medieval theologians also used the name "imposition of the hand" (*manus impositio*). The Eastern Churches call this sacrament *Myron* (that is, anointing with *myron* or chrism) and describes its effect as a "strengthening" (*bebaiōsis*) and a "completion" (*teleiōsis*).

ORIGIN AND MEANING OF CONFIRMATION

Confirmation must be viewed as very closely connected with baptism. The bath of water, accompanied by invocation of the name of Jesus or of the entire Trinity, effects an incorporation into Christ and his body, the Church. The action has its effect through the Holy Spirit and it also bestows the Holy Spirit. At a very early time, nonetheless, the baptismal action seems already to have included an imposition of the hand (see Acts 19:5f.). The schisms and heresies that sprang up in the first century apparently brought a growing danger that despite a shared baptism the connection with the apostolic Church and with the ongoing transmission of the word of God that was carried on therein might be weakened or entirely abandoned. It seemed desirable, therefore, to lay special emphasis on the imposition of the hand at baptism (as we find being done as early as Acts 8:14-17) and to reserve this imposition to the true leader of the community, namely, the bishop as successor to the apostles. This imposition became an effective sign of communion with the apostolic Church and of the resultant duty of Spirit-inspired service.

This hypothesis is confirmed by the first extensive accounts of initiation in Tertullian and Hippolytus of Rome. Both writers speak not only of a postbaptismal anointing by the baptizing priest but also of an imposition of the bishop's hand that communicates the Holy Spirit, and a signing of the forehead. Hippolytus includes, in addition, an episcopal anointing of the head.[1] The imposition of the hand and anointing by the bishop, together with the prayer of the community, thus become efficacious signs that the baptized person has by the power of the Holy Spirit become a complete member of the Church; he or she has all the rights of a Christian but is also obligated to share in the Church's work (see the biblical charisms that are forms of service to the Church).

The description of this part of the total rite of initiation as a "giving of the Holy Spirit" has, however, fostered the mistaken idea that the previous rite of water baptism does not bestow the Holy Spirit. This is an erroneous interpretation. For the New Testament, and especially the Pauline writings, make it perfectly clear that the Holy Spirit is also received in connection with baptism. In Paul's eyes, "to be in Christ" means equivalently "to be in the Spirit" (see 1 Cor 6:11, 19). The Gospel of John, too, presupposes that rebirth "from water and the Spirit" (Jn 3:5) is a single event (Jn 7:37-39). It is therefore preferable to speak of a special gift of the Spirit in confirmation.

This interpretation agrees with what is said in the documents of Vatican II. The Council says, among other things: "By the sacrament of confirmation they [the faithful] are more fully bound to the Church and the Holy Spirit endows them with special strength, so that they are more strictly obliged to spread and defend the faith, both by word and by deed, as true witnesses of Christ."[2] This passage is cited in the Apostolic Constitution *Divinae consortium naturae* of August 15, 1971, in which Paul VI promulgated and approved the new rite of confirmation. The meaning of confirmation is described in similar terms in the Introduction to the new rite of confirmation: "This giving of the Holy Spirit conforms believers more fully to Christ and strengthens them so that they may bear witness to Christ for the building up of his Body in faith and love."[3]

From the fourth century on, the importance given to the episcopal imposition of the hand and anointing and to the special gift of the Spirit therein received was significantly heightened by the fact that in many areas external circumstances caused confirmation and baptism to be separated in time and place. Thus St. Jerome wrote around 380: "I do not deny that it is ecclesiastical custom for the bishop to travel to those who have been baptized by priests and deacons in places far distant from the large cities, in order that he may impose hands on them and invoke the Holy Spirit upon them." He sees justification for these "confirmation journeys" in Acts 8:14-17, and adds: "Even if the authority of scripture did not support the practice, the agreement of the universal Church would have the force of a command."[4] This separation of the parts of the initiation rite was certainly not an ideal. It is therefore expressly provided in the new rite of Confirmation that when adults or children of school age are baptized the baptizing priest himself can, if the bishop is not present, administer confirmation before the ensuing celebration of the Eucharist.[5]

THE NEW RITE OF CONFIRMATION

The revised rite of confirmation commissioned by Vatican II appeared in the summer of 1971 as a fascicle of the Roman Pontifical. The new rite emphasizes the intrinsic connection of confirmation with Christian initiation as a whole and provides that as a rule it is to be administered within the celebration of the Eucharist, the third sacrament of initiation (no. 13). The sacred action is to have a festive character and, in view of its ecclesiological significance, is to be celebrated as far as possible with the participation of the entire community (no. 4).

The bishop is called the "primary minister"[6] of confirmation; the law also gives the faculty to confirm to territorial prelates and territorial abbots, vicars and prefects apostolic, apostolic administrators and diocesan administrators within the limits of their territory and while they hold office (no. 7a). In addition, any priest can confirm when he is baptizing adults or children of catechetical age in the absence of the bishop or when he is receiving those already baptized into full communion with the Church. In danger of death any priest can validly confirm. Furthermore, bishops and the above named officials and dignitaries can coopt priests for confirmation when the number of those being confirmed is large. According to the new Code of Canon Law (can. 884, 1) the diocesan bishop can, in case of necessity, give one or more priests the faculty to confirm.

With regard to the age for confirmation: by the end of the thirteenth century it had become the established custom to postpone confirmation to the seventh year.[7] According to the new rite bishops may for pastoral reasons set an age that seems more suitable (and that may therefore be more advanced).[8] One such reason may be "to implant deeply in the lives of the faithful complete obedience to Christ the Lord and a firm witnessing to him."[9] The revised Code of 1983 recommends the traditional "age of discretion" but also gives episcopal conferences the right to determine a different age (Can. 891).[10] Unfortunately, the later the age, the looser becomes the intrinsic connection between confirmation and baptism, and the more difficult it is to preserve the original sequence of baptism, confirmation, and Eucharist.

The institution of sponsorship is maintained in principle. Can. 796, 1, of the old Code has been repealed, and it is recommended instead that the godparents at baptism be also the sponsors at confirmation, thus making clearer the close connection of these two sacraments (Introduction, no. 5). The necessity of having a sponsor for confirmation is not absolute ("as far as possible," says Can. 892 of the new Code). The role of the sponsor is to see to it, along with the parents, that the confirmed person fulfills the obligations accepted with the sacrament (*ibid.*).

Confirmation is usually to be administered during the celebration of Mass. If in special cases it is administered outside of Mass, it must be preceded by a liturgy of the word that is modeled on that of the Mass. Except on the Sundays of Advent, Lent, and Easter, other solemnities, Ash Wednesday, and Holy Week, the formulary of one of the two Ritual Masses of Confirmation contained in the Sacramentary may be used. Chapter V of the Rite of Confirmation gives numerous suggestions for the biblical readings.

When confirmation is administered during Mass, it takes place after the gospel and contains the following parts:

Presentation of the candidates and homily of the bishop.
Renewal of baptismal promises (renunciation of Satan and sin and profession of faith).
Invitation to the community to pray in silence.

Prayer of the bishop for the gifts of the Holy Spirit (he and the other ministers of the sacrament extend their hands over the candidates).

Anointing of the forehead with Chrism in the form of a cross (which is the imposition of the hand[11]), and words of administration: "N., be sealed with the Gift of the Holy Spirit." This new formula was chosen for its similarity to the one used in the Byzantine Church; it replaces the older formula: "N., I sign you with the sign of the cross, and I confirm you with the chrism of salvation, in the name of the Father. . . ." The newly confirmed accepts the administration with an "Amen."

Intercessions for the newly confirmed, their parents and sponsors, and the entire Church follow.

During the ensuing celebration of the Eucharist the newly confirmed may take part in the preparation of the gifts. A solemn blessing or a prayer over the people may replace the usual blessing at the end of Mass.

The new rite omits the older custom (in use since the thirteenth century) of the "slap on the cheek," which had acquired a unique and distracting prominence in the minds of confirmands.[12]

CONFIRMATION OUTSIDE THE ROMAN RITE

The Eastern rites, unlike the Western, have always preserved the temporal connection of the three rites of initiation. In the Byzantine rite, after donning their clothing and after a prayer by the priest, the newly baptized are anointed with *myron* on forehead, eyes, nose, mouth, ears, breast, and feet; each anointing is accompanied by the formula: "Seal of the Gift of the Holy Spirit. Amen." After a Eucharistic liturgy of the word the confirmed (including infants) are immediately given communion.

In the other Eastern rites the newly baptized likewise receive several anointings, but these are done before they put on their clothing; they are "crowned" with a headband, and, in many rites, are also "girded"; only among the Eastern Syrians is the emphasis put on the imposition of hands.[13]

The Reformers rejected the traditional sacrament of confirmation, claiming that it denied the power and efficacy of baptism. In its place they developed, in their catechetical practice, a liturgical act by which at a certain age (about 12 to 14) the baptized are "consecrated" as full members of the community and are admitted to the Lord's Supper. This act was also given the name "confirmation." Understanding of this rite has undergone many changes, and even today there is not full agreement on it. Confirmation often includes an imposition of the hand. Each confirmand usually receives a biblical text that is to serve as a guide for the years ahead.[14]

The "Order of Confirmation or Imposition of the Hand" among the Anglicans closely follows the Roman rite (but without the anointing or signing of the forehead). The rite is regarded as signifying a personal ratification of the baptismal promises; the Church joins the confirmands with its intercession.[15] In contemporary Anglican rites the sacramental aspects of confirmation (imposition of hands with or without anointing with Chrism) now immediately follow baptism.

Chapter Eleven

The Celebration of the Eucharist

"Eucharist" (which in Greek originally signified an attitude of gratefulness, or thanksgiving) is the name of the sacrament which the Catholic Church usually calls the "Mass" or the "Sacrifice of the Mass," and which the Reformers call the "Lord's Supper." So much has been thought and written about this sacrament that an "outline," such as this book provides, cannot examine in detail all the aspects developed by exegesis, dogma and the history of dogma, and liturgical science.

ORIGIN, BASIC CONTENT, MAIN LINES OF EVOLUTION

There are five passages in the New Testament that deal extensively with this sacrament as a legacy left us by Jesus Christ. I am referring, first of all, to the four "accounts of institution," which in turn developed out of two streams of tradition: one represented by Mark 14:22-25 and Matthew 26:26-29, the other by Luke 22:15-20 and 1 Corinthians 11:23-25. "Careful investigation shows that the Lukan account is not simply a copy and development of the Pauline version, but that each of the two goes back to a version of the text that must have originated in Greek-speaking Antioch and been formulated around the year 40."[1] The source of the Markan account (and of the Matthean, which is dependent on the Markan) must have been even older, with its roots in a very early Semitic tradition and its origins in the first decade after the death of Jesus.[2]

The original form of the account of institution must have been something like this: "And he took bread, spoke the blessing over it, broke it, and gave it to them. And he said: 'This is my body, which is given for the many. Do this in memory of me!' In like manner also the cup after the meal, with the words: 'This cup is the new covenant in my blood.'"[3]

The fifth passage to which I referred is John 6:48-59; when taken in conjunction with the other four passages this sheds further theological light on the eucharistic mystery.[4]

Johannes Betz, a professor of dogmatics who died in 1984 and one of the most eminent students of the Eucharist in recent decades, sums up as follows the content of the biblical passages just cited:

"If we take a comprehensive view of the biblical message concerning the Eucharist, the lines of continuity and the sustaining ideas emerge all the more clearly. Such an overview yields the following synthesis: The more the New Testament speaks of the subject, the more clearly it proclaims the identity of the eucharistic gifts with the corporeal person of Jesus, who surrenders himself to a bloody expiatory death on the cross, for us and our salvation—and who gives himself in the sacrament as our food in order to apply to us the redemption wrought by his death. This redemption is therefore essentially identical with himself, with his person: incarnated, giving himself as a sacrifice of expiation, and in all things acting for our salvation. The presence of this person's past saving act is therefore closely bound up with his real presence, and the Eucharist is the sacramental presence of the entire saving event known as 'Jesus,' in which the person and his work form an indivisible unity. This is the faith which all of the New Testament witnesses attest."[5]

The two terms which J. Betz constantly uses—*real or personal presence* and *presence of the act* —are intended to bring out the point that in the eucharistic celebration not only is Jesus himself present, but so is his saving action that culminated in his self-giving on the cross for us and our salvation.

"The gift which Jesus has left us is not simply an idea that is to be proclaimed in words and rendered sensible in a sacrament; it is not simply an existential state that is to be realized by faith and the ethical following of Jesus. The final, supreme gift of Jesus, and thus the essence of Christianty as such, is he himself, Jesus Christ. This person means us not only to apprehend him through faith but to receive him in his corporality."[6]

The Last Supper of Jesus evolved into the eucharistic celebration of the primitive community in several stages. Initially, the words of blessing over the bread and wine were spoken after a regular meal. They were then completely separated from such a meal and combined with the liturgy of prayer on Sunday mornings. One of Justin Martyr's writings shows that around the middle of the second century the celebration of the Eucharist was preceded by a liturgy of the word such as was customary in the Jewish synagogues of the day.[7] The two liturgies fused to form a single celebration. The first complete wording of an early Christian Eucharist that has come down to us is in the *Apostolic Tradition* of Hippolytus, a priest of Rome; his treatise dates from about 215.[8] This document, like subsequent ones, offers texts intended simply as models that could be adapted by celebrants.

The continued spread of the Church led to the rise of a number of liturgical centers, each with its own organization of the liturgy and especially of the Eucharist. I cannot here go into the peculiarities of each of these centers. We saw in Chapter II that certain lines of development were in fact followed; further historical details will be given below in the exposition of the Mass liturgy. At this point I simply call attention to a dogmatic statement of the Council of Trent: the Mass is the rendering-present (*repraesentatio*), the memorial, and the application of the once-for-all sacrifice of Christ on the cross (DS 1740; Neuner-Dupuis 1546). With this statement the Council clearly reasserted at the beginning of the modern period the basic ideas we saw to be present in the New Testament sources.

In view of the numerous and not always felicitous forms taken by the celebration of the Mass the Council of Trent also commissioned a reform of the Roman Missal. The new Missal was promulgated by Pius V seven years after the close of the Council (1570), and remained in effect for almost four hundred years without major changes.[9]

In the second chapter of its Constitution on the Liturgy the Second Vatican Council deals extensively with "the most sacred mystery of the Eucharist." Its chief concern is that Christ's faithful, when present at this mystery of faith, should not be there as strangers or silent spectators; on the contrary, through a good understanding of the rites and prayers they should take part in the sacred service conscious of what they are doing, with devotion and full involvement.

They should be instructed by God's word and be nourished at the table of the Lord's body; they should give thanks to God (no. 480).

That this goal might be reached, the Council decreed that the Order of Mass be revised in a way "that will bring out more clearly the intrinsic nature and purpose of its several parts, and also the connection between them, and will more readily achieve the devout, active participation of the faithful.

"For this purpose the rites are to be simplified, due care being taken to preserve their substance; elements that, with the passage of time, came to be duplicated or were added with but little advantage are now to be discarded; other elements that have suffered injury through accident of history are now, as may seem useful or necessary, to be restored to the vigor they had in the tradition of the Fathers" (no. 50).

In accordance with these directives the Roman liturgical commission worked first on the unchanging part of the Missal, namely, the "Order of Mass." After a few changes made by the highest authority, Paul VI approved and promulgated the new Order on Holy Thursday (April 3), 1969, in his Apostolic Constitution *Missale Romanum*. A year later the entire new Missal was published. It contains, in addition to the text, a *General Instruction of the Roman Missal (GIRM)* and *General Norms for the Liturgical Year and the Calendar*. Unlike earlier introductions to the Missal the *GIRM* gives not only rubrial directives but also explanations of the contents of the celebration.

After years of preparation the American edition of the *Roman Missal* (*The Sacramentary*) was ready in 1974. On November 13, 1973 it was approved by the National Conference of Catholic Bishops; its use was then allowed by the Congregation for Divine Worship on February 4, 1974. The new Missal appeared in 1974 and became obligatory on December 1, 1974. Certain changes and additions had long since been considered; the Congregation for Divine Worship approved these on September 3, 1974, for insertion into a second edition of the Missal. These included, for example, a description of the functions of the newly established ministries of acolyte and lector (replacing the description of the subdeacon's functions: *GIRM* 142-

52). A few Mass formularies were also expanded or added. A second election of the American *Sacramentary* which incorporated these changes was published in 1985.

With regard to the Latin texts to be included in this Missal: the rule in effect since November 10, 1969, was that Missals in the vernacular should include a Latin appendix. A year later, Rome published a *Missale parvum* containing additional Latin texts. The Sacramentary incorporated this *Missale parvum.*

STRUCTURE AND INDIVIDUAL PARTS OF THE MASS

The liturgical reform has brought a transparent clarity to the overall structure of the Mass. "The Mass is made up as it were of the liturgy of the word and the liturgy of the Eucharist, two parts so closely connected that they form but one single act of worship. For in the Mass the table of God's word and of Christ's body is laid for the people of God to receive from it instruction and food."[10] This statement undoubtedly represents a revaluation of the liturgy of the word, which in the past was usually called the "Fore-Mass"; neglect of it was regarded by earlier casuistic moral theology as only a "venial" sin because this was but an "insignificant part" (*pars exigua*) of the Mass.[11] The opening and concluding rites of the Mass form a setting for these two "principal parts."[12]

The linguistic usage of the Church allows both the Mass as a whole and the second main part by itself to be called "the Eucharist." In order to avoid misunderstanding, it would be better to speak of this second part as "the Eucharist in the narrower sense."

The following outline is intended to show this structure and facilitate a comprehensive view of it. Under "Eucharistic Prayer" the outline reflects primarily EP II and III; the special characteristics of the other eucharistic prayers will be discussed later on in the chapter.

ORGANIZATION OF THE EUCHARISTIC CELEBRATION

a) *Introductory Rites*

Entrance with song (Introit); veneration of the altar with kiss and incense; sign of the cross; greeting of the congregation; introduction to the Mass of the day; penitential rite; Kyrie; Gloria; opening prayer.

b) *Liturgy of the Word*
Readings; song between the readings; gospel; homily; profession of faith; general intercessions (prayer of the faithful).

c) *Eucharist* (in narrower sense)
Preparation of the altar and the gifts
Presentation of the gifts; prayers of preparation; incensation; washing of hands; prayer over the gifts.

Eucharistic Prayer
Preface with Sanctus; consecratory epiclesis; words of institution; anamnesis; prayer of offering (anamnesis); communion epiclesis and prayer for unity; intercessions with commemoration of the saints; doxology.

Communion Rite
Our Father with embolism and doxology; sign of peace; breaking of the bread, commingling, and Agnus Dei; private prayer of preparation for the priest; reception of communion; period of silence or song of praise; prayer after communion.

d) *Concluding Rite*
Brief parish announcements; blessing; dismissal; kissing of altar; departure.

Introductory Rites
The purpose of these is to meld the congregation into a conscious community and prepare it for the proclamation of God's word and the worthy celebration of the Eucharist.

The entrance song (Latin: *antiphona ad introitum*) of the priest and other ministers has for its purpose "to open the celebration, intensify the unity of the gathered people, lead their thoughts to the mystery of the season or feast, and accompany the procession of the priest. . ." (*GIRM* 25). There are many ways of handling the entrance song.[13] "The congregation should not be frequently condemned to being dumb listeners; particularly in the entrance song the cantors, choir, and congregation should each play a part and thus begin to form the community which the celebration calls for."[14] The playing of the organ may at times replace the singing. If the entrance antiphon is not sung, it is recommended that it be made part of the priest's introduction to the Mass of the day.[15]

The priest, concelebrants, and deacon then kiss the altar to signify their veneration for it as a symbol of Christ. This may be followed by an incensation of the altar, especially on feast days. Incense (a mixture of various resins and gums) was used in worship both in the Old Testament temple and in pagan antiquity generally. Christians initially rejected its use, but in the Constantinian period it made its way from the East into Christian worship. It was understood here as a symbol of prayer (see Ps 140:2) and as a sign of respect and of the Church's intercessory prayer. Eventually the practice arose of incensing the altar, the sacrificial gifts, the cross and images, and even the celebrant and congregation. It would be a mistake to interpret incense as a gift to God, a material offering.

The celebrant now goes to the presidential chair and from there presides over the further introductory rites and the liturgy of the word. The location and style of the presidential chair should make it clear that the priest is the leader of the liturgical gathering. The *GIRM* recommends the back of the sanctuary as a suitable place for it and insists that any suggestion of a throne is to be avoided (*GIRM* 271).[16]

By making the sign of the cross together priest and congregation place themselves under the cross of Christ and signify that to this cross they look for their salvation. They then greet one another with one of the formulas of greeting or blessing that are provided in the Sacramentary. It is quite permissible at this point for the priest to add his personal greetings and good wishes. To be avoided, however, is any excessive expression of subjective feelings, since in the long run the majority of the congregation would find this intolerable. The formulas provided in the Missal have as one of their functions to make the congregation conscious of "the mystery of the gathered Church."[17]

The introduction to the Mass of the day, which the priest or other qualified minister may give at this point, should be brief and not be expanded into a first sermon.

The ensuing penitential act replaces the old prayers at the foot of the altar, of which a confession of sins (the Confiteor) was a part. It may still take the form of a communal confession of guilt, using a Confiteor that has been shortened but that also now includes a reference to the failure to do good. Instead of the Confiteor two other ways of asking God's mercy are provided; in these priest (or another minister) and congregation speak alternately. These formulas make use of the Kyrie and thus help to shorten the somewhat lengthy introductory rites. The Kyrie and the penitential rite may also be replaced by a sprinkling of the faithful with holy water.[18] The prayers and songs given for use in this rite make it chiefly a recall and renewal of baptism.

The Kyrie acclamation was used even in pagan antiquity as a form of homage to the deity or to a ruler who was being honored as a god. In keeping with the writings of Paul the Church applied it to Christ as its divine Lord. In the East such acclamations originally had their place in litanies (*ektenies*) of petitions; to each petition the congregation joined in with a Kyrie acclamation. In the West these litanies were gradually moved forward from their original place at the end of the liturgy of the word and ultimately acquired their later form through omission of the petitions. The *GIRM* (30) is in accord with ancient custom when it allows the insertion of short verses (tropes) into the Kyrie. The Kyrie should, as far as possible, be sung by the entire congregation. As a rule, each acclamation is sung only twice. If the Kyrie acclamation has already been used in the penitential rite or in a litany that has replaced the entrance song, the usual Kyrie may be omitted.[19]

The *Gloria in excelsis Deo* ("Glory to God in the highest") is one of the many hymns composed and sung by the early Church in the days before the Psalter became the Church's real hymnal. The first stanza of the Gloria repeats the song of the angels at Bethlehem and then sings the praise of the Father and the Son; the second stanza is an enthusiastic hymn to Christ, in the final part of which ("For you alone . . .") we can still hear echoes of the sharp opposition to the emperor worship of antiquity. In the course of their ecumenical efforts, representatives of all the Christian Churches of the English-speaking world have published a uniform translation of the Gloria and other liturgical texts used by the congregation. In the Mass the

Gloria is now sung only on solemnities, feasts, special celebrations, and Sundays (except in Advent and Lent) (*GIRM* 31).[20]

The final action of the introductory rites is the opening prayer. The priest first invites the congregation to pray and then allows a brief pause for reflection and personal prayer. In the ensuing presidential prayer, the special character of this particular Mass finds expression, especially on feast days. The old Roman opening prayers ("orations") were always addressed to the Father through Christ the Mediator, in the Holy Spirit. At the conclusion of the prayer, which the priest speaks in the first person plural ("we . . ."), the community says "Amen," a Hebrew word that is left untranslated in most liturgies and means "Yes, so be it!" or "Yes, it is so!" The Amen thus signifies that the congregation makes the priest's prayer its own and, as it were, puts its signature to it.[21]

The Liturgy of the Word

In the first section of this chapter I mentioned that as early as the second century the eucharistic celebration proper was preceded by readings from Scripture. This part of the liturgy was modeled on the synagogue service of prayer and readings. Vatican II resolutely declared that "in sacred celebrations there is to be more reading from holy Scripture and it is to be more varied and apposite" (*SC* 35). With regard to the eucharistic celebration it decreed that "the treasures of the Bible are to be opened up more lavishly" (*SC* 51), and it anticipated that "in this way a more representative portion of holy Scripture will be read to the people in the course of a prescribed number of years" (*ibid.*). The desire for this more extensive reading of Scripture was inspired by the conviction that in the liturgy of the word too Christ unites himself with his Church and actively seeks its salvation (see *SC* 7).

"In the readings, explained by the homily, God is speaking to his people, opening up to them the mystery of redemption and salvation, and nourishing their spirit. . . . Through the chants the people make God's word their own and through the profession of faith affirm their adherence to it. Finally, having been fed by this word, they make their petitions in the general intercessions for the needs of the Church and for the salvation of the whole world" (*GIRM* 33).

The *Lectionary for Mass*, which implemented the conciliar decree, was published by the Roman Congregation for Divine Worship on May 25, 1969. A second official edition was published on January 21, 1981. The latter contains a greatly expanded pastoral introduction and uses the *Neo-Vulgate* for the Latin texts. The following rules are laid down:

On all Sundays and feast days there are to be three readings at every Mass: the first from the Old Testament, the second from an apostolic letter or Acts or Revelation, and the third from a gospel. In order to open the Scriptures more fully to the congregations the pericopes to be read (a pericope is a passage of holy Scripture) are organized to cover a three-year period; the three annual series are known as A, B, and C. The C series is for years divisible by 3; the other two then follow (C, A, B).

Two principles control the choice of readings: thematic agreement and selective continuous reading. The first of these principles comes into play in the liturgically important seasons of Christmas and Easter. On the Sundays of "Ordinary Time" the principle of selective continuous reading is applied: this means that a book of the Bible is read through, but omissions can be made for pastoral reasons. The principle of continuous reading applies, however, only to the second reading and the gospel; the Old Testament reading is chosen to harmonize with the gospel of the day. The intention in this arrangement is to avoid an excessive multiplicity of themes in a single Mass and to bring out better the unity of the two Testaments. In Year A the Gospel of Matthew is read, in Year B the Gospel of Mark, and in Year C the Gospel of Luke. The Gospel of John is reserved for the final weeks of Lent and the Easter season, it also supplements the Gospel of Mark in year B. The Acts of the Apostles supplies the first reading of the Easter season.

The Lectionary usually schedules only two readings for weekdays. For the first there are two annual series, Year I for uneven-numbered years, and Year II for even-numbered years. The series of gospels, on the other hand, is the same every year. The gospels are so arranged that in Weeks 1-9 of Ordinary Time Mark is read, in Weeks 10-21 Matthew, and in Weeks 22-34 Luke. For the special seasons a special selection has been made that takes into account the character of the season.

The Lectionary also contains readings for the feasts and memorials of the saints, for the celebration of the sacraments and sacramentals, and for Masses on special occasions and votive Masses. The Lectionary provides a wide selection of readings for these occasions.

The readings are delivered from a lectern that is also known as an "ambo" (from the Greek verb *anabainein,* to ascend). The *GIRM* explains the reason for having such a lectern: "The dignity of the word of God requires the church to have a place that is suitable for the proclamation of the word and is a natural focal point for the people during the liturgy of the word" (272). Depending on the spatial possibilities, the lectern is to be located at a point where the reader can easily be seen and heard by all. This lectern is the place not only for the readings but for the songs between the readings, the gospel, and , if applicable, the homily and prayer of the faithful.

In keeping with tradition, the reader of the passages from Scripture is not to be the celebrant but another minister. This makes it clear that the celebrating priest too places himself under the word of God and listens to it. While the nonevangelical readings can be done by a reader who is a layperson, the gospel is always to be read by a deacon or a priest (the celebrant, if necessary).

The reader marks the end of each of the first two readings by saying: "This is the word of the Lord!" (*Verbum Domini!*), to which the congregation replies: "Thanks be to God."

A meaningful tradition provides that each reading be followed by a song that rounds off what has been read and provides a time for meditation. The first reading is therefore followed by a responsorial psalm (formerly the Gradual). The *GIRM* speaks of this as an integral part of the liturgy of the word. Because its content links it with the reading, the lectionary gives it right after the reading. For the various seasons of the liturgical year, however, and for various groups of saints' feasts there are some common responsorial psalms that do not vary. The singing is responsorial; that is, only the cantor or psalmist sings the psalm, while the community sings an unchanging response after each verse or group of verses.

The second reading is followed by the Alleluia ("Praise the Lord") together with a verse, usually from the New Testament. This song, however, does not look back to the preceding reading but is a preparation for the gospel. It is an acclamation addressed to Christ and should therefore be sung by the standing community (Pastoral Introduction to the second edition of the Lectionary). The Alleluia is omitted during Lent; "the verse before the gospel," which replaces the Alleluia, is also called the "Tract."

If there is only one reading before the gospel, the two songs between readings may be used, or one of them may be selected.

Two solemnities, Easter and Pentecost, have an additional song between readings, namely, the sequence. Sequences were originally *Jubilus* melodies added to the Alleluia; they were later given texts of their own, and these in turn were expanded by means of identically structured stanzas and of rhymes. The popularity of these songs can be seen in the fact that about 5000 medieval sequences have come down to us. Because the genre displayed so much uncontrolled growth, the Missal of Pius V (1570) limited the liturgical sequences to four. In addition to the sequences for Easter and Pentecost, there are optional sequences for Corpus Christi and the Memorial of Our Lady of Sorrows. In the future, all sequences come before the Alleluia, since the latter is meant as an immediate preparation for the gospel.

From time immemorial, the proclamation of the gospel at Mass has been an especially solemn affair. Among the signs of respect are these:
a) the reader must be a deacon or priest;
b) he receives a special blessing; or recites a special preparatory prayer;
c) the book of the gospels is carried to the ambo in a procession that includes incense and candles (optional);
d) the deacon (priest) signs the book and himself with the sign of the cross;
e) he incenses the book before the reading (optional);
f) before and after the proclamation the faithful say (sing) special acclamations of homage ("Glory to you, Lord"; "Praise to you, Lord Jesus Christ");

g) although the faithful sit during the earlier readings, they stand as they listen to the gospel (sign of reverence and readiness);
h) when he has finished, the reader kisses the book and quietly prays: "May the words of the Gospel wipe away our sins."

This special reverence led in both East and West to the creation of elaborate, illuminated evangeliaries, that is, limited lectionaries containing only the gospels or the needed gospel pericopes. The introduction to the revised Lectionary urges the revival of this custom (no. 36), after similar wishes had been expressed earlier. As a result, several editions of the *Book of Gospels* have been published in English.[22]

The special respect shown for the gospel reading in comparison with the others should not lead to any depreciation of the latter. They too are inspired sacred writings, contain God's word, and, if they are from the New Testament, are to be regarded as "good news" (= "gospel"). Therefore *GIRM* 33, following the Constitution on the Liturgy, says of all the readings without distinction: "In the readings . . . God is speaking to his people, opening up to them the mystery of redemption and salvation, and nourishing their spirit; Christ is present to the faithful through his own word."

The traditional veneration for the gospel reading probably had its source in the conviction that the many words of Jesus transmitted in the four gospels are his own actual words, while the other New Testament writings are simply doctrinal and pastoral letters of the apostles. Even though we are aware today that all of the New Testament books contain theological interpretation and represent adaptations to pastoral needs, the reformed liturgy maintains the special signs of honor bestowed on the reading of the gospel at Mass. Rome evidently does not think there is any great danger of undervaluing the other Scriptures; furthermore, it sees support for the tradition in the parallel rites of the Eastern Churches. Abandonment of such a universal tradition could certainly lead to misunderstanding.

The gospel and other readings are not to be understood simply as historical documents that inform us about the past. Such an approach would in fact lead to boredom, since regular participants in the liturgy are familiar with a great many passages of the Bible. The important thing is rather to understand the Scriptures as conveying a message and a summons to present-day listeners and to open ourselves to this call.

The sermon or homily, understood as an interpretation of the sacred texts, is one of the oldest parts of the liturgy of the word. It was originally reserved to the bishop. In view of a certain neglect of the homily in many periods and countries Vatican II emphasized that it is a part of the liturgy and may not be omitted, especially on Sundays and feast days (*SC* 52). "By means of the homily the mysteries of the faith and the guiding principles of the Christian life are expounded from the sacred text" (*ibid.*). Following up on what is said in the First Instruction on the Implementation of the Constitution on the Liturgy (September 26, 1964), the *GIRM* expands this directive to include an explanation of other texts of the day's Mass from the viewpoint of "the mystery being celebrated and the needs proper to the listeners" (41). As a rule, the celebrating priest should give the homily.[23]

On solemnities and Sundays the homily is followed by the creed (profession of faith), either spoken or sung. It represents the assent of the community to the word of God that has been heard in the readings and homily and to the essential realities of the faith; at the same time, it is a praise of the Triune God who has wrought our salvation. Only about the year 1000 did it make its way into the Roman Mass, in the form of the lengthy Nicene-Constantinopolitan Creed. This was originally the baptismal creed of the East, whereas in the West the short "Apostles' Creed" was used at baptism. In the celebration of the Eucharist, then, the creed also serves as a reminder of baptism and a call to renewal of the promises made at that time.

The liturgy of the word ends with the general intercessions or prayer of the faithful. This is one of those parts of the Mass to which the Liturgy Constitution is referring when it says: "Other elements that have suffered injury through accident of history are now, as may seem useful or necessary, to be restored to the vigor they had in the tradition of the Fathers" (no. 50). The loss of the prayer of the faithful lasted over 1400 years. These intercessions broaden the horizon of the faithful, as the people of God exercises its priestly office in behalf of the whole human race. For the petitions offered are concerned not with the personal needs of the individual participants but rather with the worldwide needs of the entire Church and of the whole race, in accordance with 1 Timothy 2:1-3.

As a rule the following order is to be observed: a) for the needs of the Church; b) for public authorities and the salvation of the world; c) for all those oppressed by any need; d) for the local community. Within this general framework the content and form of the petitions can be freely modified. In this way it is possible to let "the warm breath of the present" have a place in the eucharistic celebration. The role of the celebrating priest is to supply a spoken or sung introduction and conclusion; the individual petitions are made by a deacon or cantor or by one or more of the laity. The community accompanies the petitions with general acclamations or with silent prayer, in which case the necessary pause must be allowed.[24]

The Celebration of the Eucharist (in the narrower sense)

This second main part of the Mass begins after the preparation of the altar or "holy table," as the Eastern Churches still call it. The Sacramentary is placed on the altar; a square linen cloth, the corporal, is spread out at the center; the chalice is placed on the altar and, alongside the chalice, the purificator. The location of the preparation at this point rather than before Mass, as in the past, is meant to make it clearer that the liturgy is now entering into its second main part: the part that in its structure reproduces the Last Supper of Jesus and renders the paschal mystery present.

Preparation of the Gifts

The "presentation" of the bread and wine originally consisted simply in placing on the altar the gifts that were to be consecrated. As time passed, the faithful began to add to the bread and wine their gifts for the support of the clergy and the church and for the poor. In many areas of the Church this development led to the "offertory procession" or procession with the gifts, in which not only bread and wine but other produce of nature and, later on, money and objects were given.

In the liturgy of the New Testament such gifts could not be called "sacrifices" except in a metaphorical sense, because apart from the sacrifice of Christ the new covenant does not acknowledge other visible, cultic sacrifices such as were to be found under the old covenant or in the pagan religions. It cannot be denied, however, that from the beginning of the Middle Ages on, especially in the Franko-Gallic world, these gifts were assigned an almost cultic sacrificial character which found expression in many prayers and ceremonies. Many prayers of older liturgies of the Mass spoke of the bread and wine in terms which suggested that the consecrated gifts, that is, the flesh and blood of Christ, already lay on the altar and that the priest was already offering a cultic sacrifice at this point. Such phrases as "Receive, O holy Father . . . this spotless host" at the presentation of the bread and "We offer to you, O Lord, the chalice of salvation" at the presentation of the wine were premature at this point and could at best be interpreted as expressions of imaginative anticipation.

It is legitimate, of course, to understand these gifts, which are the product of human toil and effort, as symbols of the self-giving of the faithful. The people of God must at all times be wholly surrendered to the Father in trustful obedience and thereby united to Christ in his spirit of self-giving and his redemptive sacrifice.

The revised rite for the preparation of the gifts takes these points very much into account. The *GIRM* says that it is meaningful and desirable for the faithful to present the bread and wine, which the priest or deacon takes from them at a convenient spot and places on the altar; the priest then recites the accompanying prayers. Even though nowadays the faithful no longer bring the bread and wine with them from home, as in the past, the liturgical action remains an expressive spiritual sign. Money and other gifts for the poor which the faithful bring from home or which are collected at the church can appropriately be brought to the altar in the procession with the gifts. These are all to be deposited in a suitable place, though not on the altar (*GIRM* 49).[25]

The prayers that accompany the presentation of the gifts to God resemble the Jewish prayer of blessing *(berakah)* in that they express thanksgiving and praise of God's goodness from which we receive the bread and wine. The gifts are also the fruit of earth and vine, and of human toil; they are intended to become "the bread of life" and "our spiritual drink" in the second phase of the eucharistic celebration.

With regard to the composition of the gifts: the bread is described in *GIRM* 282: "According to the tradition of the entire Church, the bread must be made from wheat; according to the tradition of the Latin Church, it must be unleavened." The Latin custom was first established in the period from the ninth to the eleventh century. From the eleventh century on it elicited strong objections from the Byzantine Church, and at the reunion Council of Florence in 1439 the two sides agreed that the body of Christ is truly present in both the unleavened and the leavened bread and that each priest is to follow the custom of his own rite.[26] Moreover, the host used by the priest "should be made in such a way that in a Mass with a congregation the priest is able actually to break the host into parts and distribute them to at least some of the faithful" (*GIRM* 283).

Of the wine it is required that it be "from the fruit of the vine (*vinum de vite*)" and "natural and pure, that is, not mixed with any foreign substance" (*GIRM* 284). Until the sixteenth century red wine was preferred; this is still the case in the Byzantine liturgy. But when purificators made their appearance in the West in the sixteenth century, there was a shift to white wine, because it left fewer traces.

The bread and wine must be kept in good condition: the wine must not be allowed to turn to vinegar, or the bread to "spoil or become too hard to be broken easily" (*GIRM* 185).

In the Palestine of Jesus' time bread and wine were the principal food and drink. Eating and drinking have a profound significance, for they make continued life possible. Those incapable of eating and drinking or lacking food and drink must die. Every meal is thus a tacit allusion to the dependence and frailty of our life. In addition, religious persons look upon food and drink as gifts of a creator who is not simply the maker and source of life but also its preserver. A meal thus becomes a reminder of God the creator. When we reflect on this we are led to thank him. But thanksgiving is a form of prayer. Prayer at table is thus a human custom of incalculable antiquity.

Meals as such, then, have a religious character; they are inherently sacred. At the same time, they are a symbol of communion and friendship with all who partake of them. As a result, Christ could make bread and wine the visible signs of a meal in which he himself is the food and by which he establishes a communion with himself and among all who participate in it. The prayers for the preparation of the gifts thus already make a profound statement about the meaning and purpose of the eucharistic meal.

Before the priest places the chalice on the corporal, he mixes a little water with the wine. This rite comes from the ancient custom (and therefore reflects the practice of Christ himself) of not drinking unmixed wine. In any case, Christianity saw a multiple symbolism in the usage: first, an allusion to the blood and water which flowed from the side of Christ and which were thought to symbolize the birth of the Church and the sacraments; second, an image of the intimate union of the divine and human natures in Christ; and, finally, the close union with Christ that is bestowed on us. The second and third of these interpretations are the background for the prayer that accompanies the mixing of the water and wine: "By the mystery of this water and wine may we come to share in the divinity of Christ, who humbled himself to share in our humanity."

The preparation of the cup is followed by a prayer of "self-offering" ("Lord God, we ask you to receive us and be pleased with the sacrifice we offer you with humble and contrite hearts"). An optional incensation of the gifts and the altar, the priest and the congregation may then follow. The prayers that accompanied the incensation in the past are omitted in the new Sacramentary.

The ensuing rite of washing of the hands is attested as early as the fourth century (in Jerusalem). For a long time, however, it preceded the preparation of the gifts and was a symbolic call to interior purification before the beginning of the Eucharist proper. Only in the high Middle Ages was it moved to its present position. The accompanying prayer makes it a symbol of longing for purity.

The preparation of the gifts ends with the prayer over the gifts. This is preceded by an invitation to the congregation to join in the prayer: "Pray, brethren, that our sacrifice may be acceptable to God, the almighty Father." The congregation then expresses its participation by saying: "May the Lord accept. . . ." Both this exchange and many formulations of the following prayer over the gifts (known in the past as the "Secret") have not infrequently fostered the mistaken idea that the presentation of the gifts is itself already the real sacrifice of Christ and the Church by which we obtain forgiveness and salvation.[27]

The Eucharistic Prayer

The part of the Mass that begins at this point and is a first climax of the entire celebration consists of a block of prayers and rites known as the "Eucharistic Prayer" (*prex eucharistica*). It starts with the preface and ends with the great doxology before the Our Father. In the Roman liturgy it, or rather the first Eucharistic Prayer, is also known as the "canon," a term that signifies "fixed part" and promotes the idea that not the slightest change may be made in it. In fact, however, a survey of the oldest traditions, especially in the Eastern Churches (which call the Eucharistic Prayer "anaphora" = "offering"), shows that there are many possible ways of organizing the memorial of Christ, the re-presentation of the paschal mystery.

In the Western Church of the early Middle Ages the reverence felt for the Roman Canon led to the questionable custom, later made a law, that except for the preface and Sanctus the Canon was to be said in a low voice. The Canon thus had as it were a double veil thrown over it: congregations could not hear it nor, because it was in Latin, could they understand it. Only since 1965 has it been possible to say the Eucharistic Prayer aloud, only since 1967 to say it in the vernacular.

The many insertions made in the Roman Canon (prayers of self-offering, remembrances of the saints, and intercessions—before as well as after the words of institution) show that efforts to reform this, the only Eucharistic Prayer allowed in the West, could get nowhere. Therefore Pope Paul VI ordered that the Roman Canon should, apart from minor modifications, be left in its traditional form, and that a selection of three new Eucharistic Prayers be added to it. This new system went into effect in 1968. Since that time the Roman Canon has also been known as Eucharistic Prayer (EP) I.

EP II is a revision of the Eucharistic Prayer found in the *Apostolic Tradition* of Hippolytus, a Roman priest and martyr at the beginning of the third century. It may therefore be described as a Eucharistic Prayer from the age of the martyrs. EP III is a new composition in which an effort was made to organize the structural elements in a clearer way. EP IV contains important parts of the Eastern liturgy of St. Basil. Because it praises in detail all the saving acts of God it is also known as the "EP of salvation-history." Some of the peculiarities of each of the four Eucharistic Prayers will be mentioned when I come to describe the several parts of the structure. At this point I mention only the fact that EP II and IV have their own preface.[28]

The Eucharistic Prayer is introduced by three exhortations and responses in which we find ancient Jewish and Christian tradition ("The Lord be with you . . .," "Lift up your hearts . . .," "Let us give thanks to the Lord our God . . ."). This introductory prayer-dialogue makes it clear that even the Eucharistic Prayer is not an affair of the celebrant alone but a prayer of the entire people of God. The dialogue is a summons to, and the beginning of, the great prayer of thanksgiving (Greek: *eucharistia*) and therefore introduces not only the preface but the entire Eucharistic Prayer.

The Latin word *praefatio* should not be understood and translated as "foreword." The Latin prefix *prae-* is to be understood here not as temporal ("prior to") but as spatial ("before; in the presence of"): in the presence of God and the congregation" the priest praises the Father and gives thanks to him for the whole work of salvation or for some special aspect of it that corresponds to the day, feast, or season" (*GIRM* 55a). The traditional Roman prefaces, of which there were well over 200 by late antiquity but which were reduced to six at the end of the sixth century, for the most part speak only of a particular aspect of the work of redemption. In the many new prefaces there are those that praise and thank God for the entire saving work of Christ and even for the entire history of salvation from creation to the second coming of Christ.[29]

Every preface has a tripartite structure: an introduction, a laudatory description of the saving action, and a transition to the communal singing of the Sanctus. The second part shows that the prefaces are also authentic proclamations.

Of the ensuing Sanctus the *GIRM* (55b) says that it is part of the Eucharistic Prayer and should be sung or recited by priest and congregation together. The text of the Sanctus is derived from two passages of Scripture: the angelic hymn of praise in Isaiah's vision (Is 6:2f.) and the acclamations of the crowd at Jesus' entry into Jerusalem (Mt 21:9). The Sanctus is one of the oldest parts in almost all the liturgies; its first part was probably taken over from the Jewish liturgy of prayer. Hosanna is a Hebrew word that originally meant "Help" or "Save, I pray," and later became a triuphant cry in honor of God and the king.[30]

In the old Roman Missal there was a palpable break after the Sanctus; typography and illumination brought this out very clearly. The widespread and prevailing opinion was that only now did the Canon begin. The new Eucharistic Prayers, on the contrary, have introduced an organic transition, the postsanctus.

In EP II and III this transition is followed by the *epiclesis,* while in EP IV the *epiclesis* comes only after further lengthy praise of God's work in the history of salvation. In the *epiclesis* ("invocation") the Holy Spirit is called down for the purpose of transforming the bread and wine into the flesh and blood of Jesus. Even in EP I the prayer immediately preceding the words of institution can be called an *epiclesis,* although unfortunately it does not expressly mention the Holy Spirit. In the Eastern liturgies this *epiclesis* comes only after the words of institution. This discrepancy led to a bitter controversy in the early Middle Ages. The Western view was that the transformation of the gifts was effected by the words of institution, while the East attributed it to the *epiclesis.* The emphasis nowadays, as in the first four centuries, is on the Eucharistic Prayer as a single long prayer; as a result, this controversy seems to be losing its point, at least in the West. The final words of this consecratory *epiclesis* are underscored by two rites of blessing: the extension of the hands over the gifts and the blessing by the sign of the cross.

The words of institution in the Roman Canon are not identical with any of the four biblical accounts of institution. They probably go back to a liturgical tradition that was already fixed before the New

Testament documents received their written form. The decision was taken in the recent reform to make the words of Jesus the same in all of the Eucharistic Prayers. The phrase, "The mystery of faith," which had previously been inserted among the words of institution, were removed from there and turned into a transition to the newly introduced acclamation of the community (four acclamations are given in the Sacramentary).

In the Middle Ages the words of institution were highlighted by a number of solemn signs, among them genuflections expressive of adoration, incensation, and the ringing of bells. The elevation of the consecrated host (from about 1200) had its origin in the keen desire of medieval people to gaze upon it; the elevation of the chalice was added only later on.[31] The medieval theologians described the transformation of the gifts as a "transubstantiation." Theologians today speak also of a "transfinalization" and a "transignification," meaning thereby that the consecrated gifts have a new fullness of meaning and significance.[32]

The translation of the words of institution in the vernacular versions of the Missal has led in recent years to a heated dispute. The text in the Roman Missal says that the blood of Christ is "shed for you and for many" (as in Mt 26:28 and Mk 14:24). The English, German, Italian, and Spanish Missals, on the other hand, have "for you and for all." Many Catholics regarded this change as radical enough to endanger the validity of any Mass in which the words were used.

In response it may be said that the will of God to save the human race in and through Christ is universal and that consequently it was Christ's intention to shed his blood for all, as can be seen from: Rom 8:32; 2 Cor 5:14f.; 1 Tim 2:6; and 1 Jn 2:2. John 6:51 points in the same direction. When the Roman Missal uses the phrase "for many," it has in view rather the actual effect obtained; for according to Catholic teaching many human beings are in fact lost. To these considerations may be added the point made by the exegetes, namely, that Hebrew and Aramaic have no word for "all" and therefore use "many" in the sense of "all," a usage that can also be found in St. Paul (see Rom 5:12-18; 1 Cor 15:22).[33]

Until recently, only a priest might recite any of the prayers in the Roman Canon. Now, however, the congregation recites an acclamation after the words of institution. When, for example, the congregation says: "When we eat this bread and drink this cup, we proclaim your death, Lord Jesus, until you come in glory," it gratefully professes its faith in the Lord and his saving deeds, in accordance with 1 Corinthians 11:26. The ensuing *anamnesis* ("memorial") recalls the entire saving work of Christ, with each Eucharistic Prayer specifically naming some of the most important moments in that work; EP I: passion, resurrection, and ascension; EP II: death and resurrection; EP III: death, resurrection, ascension, and second coming; EP IV repeats III but adds the descent among the dead.

Closely connected with the *anamnesis* in all of the Eucharistic Prayers is a prayer of sacrificial offering. It refers primarily to the once-for-all sacrifice of Christ in which he is both sacrificial gift and sacrificing priest and which is sacramentally present in the eucharistic celebration (Betz' "presence of the act"). The Church as Christ's mystical body interiorly associates itself with his voluntary self-giving, linking its own self-giving to God with his sacrifice. The theme of the Church's "self-sacrifice" has already been sounded at the preparation of the gifts, but here it becomes especially relevant and effective. "The Church's intention is that the faithful not only offer this victim but also learn to offer themselves and so to surrender themselves, through Christ the Mediator, to an ever more complete union with the Father and with each other, so that at last God may be all in all" (*GIRM* 55f).[34]

The way to this goal leads through reception of the body and blood of Christ. Therefore the Eucharistic Prayer also contains a prayer for the fruitful reception of communion; this prayer is also called a "communion *epiclesis*." It asks at the time for the unity of the faithful, which is acknowledged to be a special work of the Holy Spirit.

The communion *epiclesis* is followed by the intercessions: for the entire Church, its officials, and the gathered community, but also "for all your children wherever they may be" (EP III). Commemoration is also made of the dead; in EP I-III provision is made for naming specific individuals. The intercession for the dead extends to "all the dead whose faith is known to you alone" (EP IV). Here again the universal salvific meaning of the sacrifice of the cross and of its sacramental re-presentation finds expression.[35]

All four Eucharistic Prayers also have a commemoration of the martyrs and saints, especially of the Mother of God and the Apostles. The commemoration is especially extensive in EP I, in which numerous saints are named both before and after the words of institution. The commemoration of the saints in EP III allows the addition of further names (saint or saints of the day and patron saints). There have certainly been periods in which an extravagant veneration of the saints has to some extent turned the eyes of Christians from Christ's mysteries of salvation. But the other extreme, a complete abandonment of veneration of the saints, would also be a loss of an element in the complete Christian faith and in the concrete clarity of lived faith.[36]

The final component of all four Eucharistic Prayers is the great doxology ("expression of praise; glorification"), which takes the same form in EP II-IV as in I. At this point the priest elevates the consecrated species above the altar and says or sings: "Through him, with him, in him, in the unity of the Holy Spirit, all glory and honor is yours, almighty Father, for ever and ever." It is in and through communion with Christ that our lives too glorify God and thus achieve their deepest meaning. The congregation makes this glorification its own with an "Amen." J. A. Jungmann considers this doxology to be a holdover from the earliest ecclesial tradition, a development of Ephesians 3:20f.[37]

In addition to the three new Eucharistic Prayers already discussed there are three for Masses with Children and two for Masses of Reconciliation. Since 1974 Switzerland has had a Eucharistic Prayer, with four variants, for use at its synods (this has now been adopted by Austria, Luxemburg, France, Italy, and Spain, among others). A Eucharistic Prayer for Masses with the Deaf was published as early as 1970.[38]

Since 1967 numerous Eucharistic Prayers composed by private individuals have made their appearance alongside the official Eucharistic Prayers. They originated especially in the Netherlands and became widely used. The bishops have frequently forbidden their use; on the other hand, they have also asked the Roman authorities for permission for new Eucharistic Prayers. But a circular letter of the Sacred Congregation for Divine Worship, dated April 27, 1973, granted the episcopal conferences permission only to approve new prefaces and insertions and to seek confirmation of these.

Every age must certainly be allowed to proclaim the praises of God in its own languages and in accordance with its living faith. On the other hand, approval by the government of the Church is a necessary aid to ensuring that "the center and summit" (*GIRM* 54) of the Christian liturgy is not distorted by imbalances and subjectivist leanings that reflect only the spirit of the age.[39]

The Reformers radically rejected the Roman Canon because of the idea of sacrifice expressed in it and in so doing abandoned the Eucharistic Prayer that is such a crucial part of the Christian liturgy. This realization, and regret at the mistake made, is growing today, although the road back will be a long one.[40]

Communion

The memorial of the paschal mystery, with its sacramental re-presentation of this mystery and the associated self-offering of the Church, is followed by communion, which is the memorial and sacrificial meal instituted by Christ and consisting of his own body and blood. Communion, which is an essential part of the celebration and its second climax, completes the Eucharist and active participation in it. The word "communion" (from Latin *communire*) originally meant "joint concern; joint possession." The early Church used it initially for the ecclesial community, from which sinners could be excluded (= ex-communicated). The word ultimately acquired its principal meaning, namely, union and communion with Christ through the sacred meal, in accordance with the words handed down from Christ himself: "Those who eat my flesh and drink my blood abide in me and I in them" (Jn 6:56).

In the oldest known descriptions of the eucharistic celebration the reception of the sacred gifts followed immediately upon the Amen of the doxology.[41] But some rites of preparation for the reception were introduced at an early date. The first and foremost of these was the recitation of the Our Father. The theological function of this prayer is "to complete the mystery of the sacrifice and prepare for communion," or "to be a connecting link between the sacrificial action and the shared meal with Christ which that action makes possible."[42] Gregory the Great is responsible for the fact that in the Roman Mass the Our Father no longer comes immediately before the reception of communion but is separated from it by the greeting of peace, the breaking of the bread, and the commingling.

The Our Father is introduced by a summons to prayer, for which the Sacramentary gives four forms.

By the middle of the third century, and perhaps even earlier, the petition for bread in the Our Father was understood as referring to the eucharistic bread.[43] Moreover, the request for forgiveness that follows in the Our Father was seen as referring to a necessary preparation of the soul for the sacred banquet (in accordance with Mt 5:23f.; 6:14f.). In the reformed liturgy the Our Father is recited (or sung) by priest and congregation together; previously the congregation said only the final petition ("but deliver us from evil").

The Our Father is followed by a prayer that develops the final petition for deliverance from evil. The priest here prays for peace, for God's merciful help, and for protection against confusion and sin, so that we may "wait in joyful hope for the coming of our Savior, Jesus Christ." This prayer, known since antiquity as the "embolism" (= insertion), has now been made less diffuse; it also ends in a way that allows the congregation to respond with the acclamation: "For the kingdon, the power, and the glory are yours, now and for ever."

The adoption of this encomium, which dates from the transitional period between the first and second centuries (*Didache* 9, 4), is also a small step toward ecumenical unity, since Evangelical Christians have added this acclamation to the Our Father ever since Luther introduced it into his translation of the Bible from the Greek manuscript of the New Testament which he was using. The Eastern Churches, too, have it in their eucharistic celebration, though in a somewhat modified form. This "prayer from the first hour" expresses the keen confidence of the first communities in the final victory of God's kingdom; it is comparable to the acclamations of homage to be found in the visions of the Apocalypse.

The ensuing greeting of peace is also to be understood as an immediate preparation for communion. Jesus says clearly, does he not, in his Sermon on the Mount, that reconciliation with the brethren must precede worship (Mt 5:23f.)? For this reason, in the Eastern liturgies the rite of peace precedes the Eucharistic Prayer; this was originally also the case in the West. The priest first recites a prayer that reflects Jesus' promise of peace (Jn 14:27). With outstretched hands he then says (or sings) the greeting of peace. Then, if the action is judged feasible, he exhorts the faithful to exchange a greeting of peace among themselves. The form this greeting is to take (for example, a kiss, a handshake, a bow) is left to the episcopal conferences to determine in accordance with the culture and customs of the people.

The priest now divides the large host into several pieces and drops a small piece into the chalice, meanwhile saying in a low voice: "May this mingling of the body and blood of our Lord Jesus Christ bring eternal life to us who receive it." This rite, known as the "fraction and commingling," is explicable only in the light of history. Before small, preformed hosts came into use (twelfth century), the large rounds of bread then used had to be broken into small pieces, as at the Last Supper of Jesus; it was this action that gave the eucharistic celebration its first name, the "breaking of bread."

Paul saw this practical necessity of breaking the bread as having a symbolic significance: the one bread which is Christ is shared by the many so that they become the one body of Christ (see 1 Cor 10:16f.). The *GIRM* makes this interpretation its own (56c; 283). The symbolism can be revitalized if large rounds of bread are used instead of small, preformed hosts; it must be acknowledged, however, that the traditional practice is better suited to large numbers of communicants. The *GIRM* (56h) expresses the desire that the hosts for the communion of the faithful be consecrated at each Mass; Pius XII, appealing to Benedict XIV, had already urged this.[44]

The dropping of a piece of the host into the chalice (the commingling) is not easily explained. The *GIRM*, which usually explains the rites, offers no explanation here. According to many scholars it goes back to the Roman custom according to which on certain feast days the pope sent a piece of the consecrated host to the priests of the neighboring churches. At their next Mass the priests put this piece, called the *fermentum*, into their own chalices as a sign of fraternal communion between the pope and the priests and as a way of signifying the oneness of the sacrifice of Christ.[45] Others think the practice was borrowed from a rite that arose in Syria and signified the resurrection of Christ and his presence on the altar.

Meanwhile, the choir or cantor sings the *Agnus Dei* ("Lamb of God") in responsorial fashion with the community. During this song the priest recites a prayer of personal preparation for a fruitful reception of communion. Then, after genuflecting, he raises the host somewhat above the altar and speaks the biblical words: "This is the Lamb of God who takes away the sins of the world. Happy are those who are called to his supper" (Jn 1:19; Rev 19:9). Then he and the congregation join in praying: "Lord, I am not worthy to receive you, but only say the word and I shall be healed" (Mt 8:8). The priest recites a short prayer and receives the body and blood of Christ first; he then gives the host to the faithful with the words, "The body of Christ," and the faithful answer: "Amen." Despite its brevity this "Amen" is a prayer of faith and adoration.

The faithful are free to choose between receiving communion in the hand (the original rite) and receiving it in the mouth (customary from the ninth century on). A third possibility—the faithful taking the host for themselves from the ciborium—is less commendable on several counts.[46]

The first point to be made with regard to communion from the cup is that it was customary even in the Western Church until well into the Middle Ages. Communion under both kinds is more in accord with the instructions of Christ and the example of the Last Supper. Although theologians have been convinced since the Middle Ages that the whole Christ, body and blood, is present in each of the eucharistic species, the fact remains that communion in one kind suffers from a defect of symbolic power. The gradual disappearance of communion from the cup since the thirteenth century was probably due to excessive anxiety lest the spilling of the sacred blood do great wrong to the sacrament and thus to Christ. Resistance to the

Hussites and Reformers then led to a broad prohibition against communion from the cup.

A first cautious return to the original practice came at Vatican II (*SC* 55). The *GIRM* (242) lists fourteen groups which may be allowed to receive under both kinds. Following upon an Instruction of the Roman Congregation for Divine Worship of June 29, 1970, the American bishops extended this permission to weekday Masses and Masses for other special occasions. In October of 1984 the congregation for Divine Worship authorized communion under both kinds on Sundays and Holy Days of obligation. In individual cases the celebrating priest, or in parish churches the pastor, must decide on pastoral and practical grounds whether use is to be made of these wide-ranging faculties. He should keep in mind that the *GIRM* (56h; 240) warmly recommends communion from the cup because of its fuller symbolism.

With regard to the manner of receiving communion from the chalice, the *GIRM* (243ff.) describes four possible ways: a) drinking from the chalice; b) dipping of the host into the chalice; c) use of a drinking tube; and d) use of a small spoon with which a small particle that has been dipped in the chalice is placed in the mouth. The Roman Instruction gives preference to drinking directly from the chalice because of its fuller symbolism. Before giving the chalice to the recipient the minister says: "The blood of Christ," and the recipient answers: "Amen." As a rule the recipients take the chalice, drink from it, and hand it back to the minister, who then cleans the lip of the cup with a small cloth. In a Mass at which communion is administered under both species the individual faithful are free to drink or not from the cup.

In the first millennium of Christianity it was customary in both East and West to stand while receiving communion; this was especially desirable in receiving from the cup. During the twelfth century the practice began of kneeling to receive. Since the recent council the old custom has again become widespread. The Instruction *Eucharisticum Mysterium* on worship of the Eucharist (no. 34) permits the faithful to receive communion in either the standing or the kneeling position.

The episcopal conferences, in accordance with Roman directives, may for pastoral reasons allow the laity to serve in the distribution of communion.[47]

The distribution of communion is accompanied by a communion song. "Its function is to express outwardly the communicants' union of spirit by means of the unity of their voices, to give evidence of joy of heart, and to make the procession to receive Christ's body more fully an act of community" (*GIRM* 56i). The text may be the communion antiphon, with or without the psalm, or some other appropriate song may be used. In general, the same rules apply here as for the singing of the Introit. If there is no singing, the antiphon should be read before or during the communion of the faithful.

In view of the high significance of communion, thanksgiving is appropriate and meaningful. It can find expression in silent prayer or in the singing of a hymn, psalm, or song. During this time the celebrant can sit in the presidential chair. The prayer after communion that follows is likewise a thanksgiving, but it is also a petition for the abiding fruit of the sacrament.

Conclusion

After the prayer after communion short announcements may be made of matters important to the parish. It would be a psychological error, however, to go into lengthy explanations at this point, since they would work against the continuing impression left by the eucharistic celebration. There is nothing to prohibit the priest from accompanying the announcements with his personal final word. He then greets the community with the traditional wish for God's blessings: "The Lord be with you," and adds the blessing proper.[48] Instead of the usual simple form of blessing the priest may use either a "solemn blessing" or a "prayer over the people." The *GIRM* does not say that the people are to kneel during the blessing (21); the Sacramentary says only that they are to bow their heads during the solemn blessing or the prayer over the people. The faithful are not said to make the sign of the cross on themselves at the blessing, but this is a meaningful gesture that should be kept.

The final Latin directive, *Ite, missa est*, really means: "Go, it is the dismissal" (from the Latin *dimissio*). In antiquity it was already customary to use these words to signal the end of an assembly. The addition of "Go in peace," to "The Mass is ended," is therefore to be understood as an extension of the meaning of the formula. It is to be noted that the name "Mass" originates in the Latin formula of dismissal. For since from an early time the dismissal was accompanied by a blessing, *missa* was interpreted as meaning the blessing which God gives to participants in the Eucharist. Furthermore, since every gift of God bestows a responsibility and obliges its recipient to a life of thanksgiving and to the passing on of the divine message and grace, the words *Ite, missa est* were sometimes interpreted (with the Latin word *missio* in mind) as signifying a mission: "Go, your mission is beginning."

As at the beginning, so now at the end the priest kisses the altar before returning to the sacristy.

THE FORMS OF EUCHARISTIC CELEBRATION

Although the basic structure of the eucharistic celebration is fixed, there are nonetheless varying expressions of it, which are called the "forms of celebration."

Mass with a Congregation

This is the normal form of celebration. "As far as possible, and especially on Sundays and holydays of obligation, this Mass [with the people taking part] should be celebrated with song and with a suitable number of ministers" (*GIRM* 77). The other ministers usually include an acolyte, a lector, and cantor or leader of song (78). In every form of celebration a deacon may assist the celebrant, should one be available. It is not permitted, on the other hand, for a priest to take the role of a deacon for the sake of greater solemnity, as was the practice in the past at "solemn Masses."

Among Masses with a congregation "first place should be given, because of its meaning, to the Mass at which the bishop presides surrounded by the college of presbyters and the ministers and in which the people take full and active part" (*GIRM* 74). The Constitution on the Liturgy had already focused attention on the public eucharistic celebrations of the bishop (traditionally called "pontifical Masses"), because in them the Church becomes visible in a preeminent way (*SC* 41).

Concelebrated Mass

The Mass takes an especially solemn form when it is celebrated by several priests simultaneously, with one of them acting as the principal celebrant. Historically, the early form of concelebration in the West was "silent concelebration" in which only the highest ranking celebrant spoke the Eucharistic Prayer. In thirteenth-century Rome "explicit concelebration" developed, with each concelebrant speaking the entire Canon along with the pope and holding his own host in his hand. Toward the end of the medieval period this form of concelebration was extended to Masses at the ordination of bishops and priests.

Vatican II reaffirmed the value of concelebration as manifesting the unity of the priesthood and the sacrifice. At the same time, it broadened the range of occasions for its use and decreed that a new rite of concelebration should be composed (*SC* 57ff.). This new rite was published on March 7, 1965,[49] and was further justified and recommended in the Instruction *Eucharisticum mysterium* of May 25, 1967.[50] The new Missal of 1970 contained a revised rite (*GIRM* 153-208) and again extended the occasions for its use. Concelebration "effectively brings out the unity of the priesthood, of the sacrifice, and of the whole people of God" (*GIRM* 153).[51]

The Conventual Mass

In the past the Mass daily celebrated in religious communities in conjunction with the choral office was highly esteemed, because people saw in it "the model of proper liturgical celebration."[52] "Vatican II, however, and the reforms emerging from it rightly emphasize the obligation of religious communities to (as far as possible) daily (con)celebration of the Eucharist, according to the possibilities in each situation."[53]

Mass with Children

Vatican II had come to the realization that uniformity in liturgical celebrations cannot be made the ideal (*SC* 38). Accordingly, the *GIRM* states that "each conference of bishops has the power to lay down norms for its own territory that are suited to the traditions and character of peoples, regions, and various communities" (6). This kind of adaptation seemed especially urgent in Masses for children. On November 1, 1973 the Congregation for Divine Worship published a *Directory for Masses with Children*.[54] In 1974 the earlier-mentioned three Eucharistic Prayers for Masses with Children were published.

The various documents mentioned keep the basic structure of the celebration but allow for some simplification in order to facilitate understanding and participation by children. It is important that children "as far as possible take physical part in the liturgy through participation in processions. . . . [and] vivid presentations. . . . But even a children's liturgy must have spaces for silence. . . . The Directory gives the priest certain liberties in the choice of readings."[55] The homily can, if need be, be given by a competent layperson (for example, a teacher or catechist).[56]

In 1970 Rome gave its approval to an "Order of Mass with Deaf Children" for the German-speaking countries: *Gottesdienst mit Gehorlosen* (Liturgy for the Deaf) (Einsiedeln-Freiburg).[57] The Pastoral Commission of Austria also issued texts under the title of "Pastoral Care of the Handicapped in the Parish."[58]

Mass with the Young

The religious situation of many young people is an object of great concern today. Many have been estranged from the Christian faith and therefore from the Sunday Eucharist. The causes of this can be stated here only in the form of sloganlike headings that do not apply in the same measure to all of the young: decline of Christian socialization and Christian tradition due to the de-christianization of many families; defective forms of religious instruction; spread of an "anti-authority" outlook and consequently a distancing from and skepticism toward the "institution"; the lack of awareness of transcendence and an exclusive attention to material things (the Second Enlightement). In consequence of these influences many young people lack motivation for participation in liturgies which they regard as boring and remote from life. "Many say: We no longer find in the liturgy the real problems of the world and the questions of contemporary men and women, especially since the liturgy in its usual form no longer allows a personal contribution of the participants."[59]

All this explains the effort being made in pastoral care of the young to take the faith-situation and psychological state of the young into consideration as far as possible in organizing the liturgy.[60] This effort is backed and encouraged by the Constitution on the Liturgy when it says that in liturgical instruction heed must be given to age, conditions, way of life, degree of religious development, and power of comprehension (*SC* 19; 34), and that "provisions shall also be made. . . for legitimate variations and adaptations to different groups. . . provided the substantial unity of the Roman Rite is preserved" (*SC* 38).

Mass with Special Groups

Because of the average size of present-day parishes and the steady shifts in the population (new housing developments; satellite towns), those who attend the community's liturgies are usually strangers to one another. This anonymity certainly makes it more difficult to experience the communal dimension of the Eucharist and thereby achieve a deeper understanding of this sacrament. For this reason, in September, 1970, the German bishops issued guidelines for the celebration of the Eucharist with special groups. The guidelines were based on the already mentioned general regulations set down in Vatican II and the *GIRM*, and on the Instruction *Actio pastoralis* of the Congregation for Divine Worship (May 15, 1969; revised: December, 1970), but also on the conclusions reached by various commissions in the German-speaking countries.[61]

"Special groups" can refer to various congregations: families, neighborhoods, apostolic groups, youth groups, participants and guests at conferences, people attending marriages or jubilees or funeral services, classes in schools, and, finally, even small groups gathered around a sick person. In these celebrations, also known (according to circumstances) as Masses with small groups and Masses in the home, the structure of the community Mass is to be retained. Care is also to be taken that the practice does not lead to isolation from the larger community but rather facilitates participation in its life.

"At a Mass with a small group it is possible to experience the basic structure of the eucharistic celebration in a direct way; the result can be a deeper understanding of the celebration when the congregation is much larger, for example, at the Sunday liturgy. The anonymity that is perhaps attendant upon a larger gathering will then not be felt as so oppressive. The celebration of Mass with a small group should help individuals to fit more easily into the larger community."[62]

It is desirable that these Masses be celebrated either in a small liturgical space (for example, a chapel or a church used just on weekdays) or a suitably prepared dwelling or place of assembly. A sickroom or a home for the aged can be such a setting. In nonliturgical venues a festively prepared table can serve as an altar. Liturgical vessels—a paten for the hosts and a chalice—should be provided. It should be taken for granted among believers that the dress and behavior of the participants will be suited to the dignity of the celebration. The priest should be recognizable as representative of Christ and leader of the eucharistic community and should therefore not celebrate without the liturgical garments. "In exceptional cases, the dress prescribed for the priest in the administration of other sacraments can be regarded as sufficient here; obviously, the stole should always be worn."[63]

As far as the organization of the celebration itself is concerned, the guidelines call for a careful selection of readings, prayers, and songs that will be suited to the particular situation and the capacity of the participants (see *GIRM* 313). A dialogue on spiritual things may replace the homily. In the General Intercessions the participants may add personal petitions; the rubrics allow only the priest to do this in community Masses.[64] Communion in both kinds is allowed, its distribution in such small groups being an easy matter.

The existing guidelines were taken over by the episcopal conferences of the German-speaking countries, except for Switzerland. The bishops of the latter country issued their own directives which were published in 1971 along with instruction from the Swiss Liturgical Commission.[65]

Mass without a Congregation

The most complete form of eucharistic celebration is one in which a community takes part (Mass with "the gathered people"; *GIRM* 25). The presence of a community is explicitly emphasized in the documents of Vatican II and those of the postconciliar reform. The assumption that a community is present explains that during many periods in many rites the Mass has been known simply as "the assembly" (for example; *collecta, synaxis*). The Mass is an activity of the Church (of the *ecclesia,* that is, the assembly of those who have been called) and not a "private ritual of the priest" (J. Ratzinger).

In extreme cases, nonetheless, the Church allows the celebration of Mass with but a single assistant who represents the community (though the sign is minimal) and gives the responses of the community in the several dialogues (*GIRM* 210).

In the Tridentine Missal the failure to have at least this single assistant, or server, was declared to be a *defectus Missae* (a defect in the Mass) and rendered the celebration illicit though not invalid (*De defectibus* X, 1). According to the new Order of Mass, however, in case of "serious necessity" Mass may be celebrated without even a server; in this case, the greetings and the blessing are omitted (*GIRM* 211).

The theological justification for saying that a Mass without a congregation retains "its effectiveness and worth" is that "it is the action of Christ and the Church, in which the priest always acts on behalf of the people's salvation."[66]

With regard to the ritual of a Mass without a congregation I shall simply point out the most salient difference from a Mass with a congregation: after kissing the altar the priest "goes to the missal at the left side of the altar, and remains there until the end of the general intercessions" (*GIRM* 214).[67]

FORMS OF EUCHARISTIC DEVOTION OUTSIDE MASS

Historical Retrospect

The real eucharistic presence of the glorified Lord in the consecrated gifts of bread and wine caused special attention and reverence to be paid to these even outside of Mass. Even in Christian antiquity some of this eucharistic bread was sent to the absent (the sick) or was given to the faithful to take home with them so that they would be able to receive it on days when the Eucharist was not celebrated. Above all, some of the eucharistic bread was kept so that it could be given to the dying as food for their journey (viaticum). This administration of the Eucharist as viaticum was the original and specific purpose of reservation.

In the early centuries the place of reservation was the priest's residence; from the eighth century on a sideroom in the church (the *pastophorion* or *diakonikon* in the East; the sacristy, or its predecessor, the *sacrarium* or *secretarium,* in the West) served as the repository.

A further reason for reservation arose with the practice of distributing communion on nonliturgical days in the liturgy of the Presanctified, which developed in the East from the sixth century on but which in the West found acceptance only on Good Friday. Generally speaking, however, an effort was made to consecrate only as much as would be needed for the next liturgy of the Presanctified.

The practice, first attested for Jerusalem in the eleventh century, of distributing the remaining pieces of eucharistic bread at the next Mass met initially with resistance in the West. Then, however, it spread gradually until the end of the sixteenth century. At that point it became common practice to consecrate enough "to have some in reserve." Despite numerous ecclesiastical warnings against this bad practice[68] it has still not been completely eradicated.

From the thirteenth century on, the veneration of the consecrated gifts outside the time of Mass grew rapidly; it was promoted especially by St. Francis of Assisi and his Order. This new devotional outlook found expression in, among other things, the elevation of the consecrated host after the words of institution (a practice first attested for Paris at the beginning of the thirteenth century), visits to the Blessed Sacrament, the institution of the feast of Corpus Christi with its procession (soon followed by other processions with the Blessed Sacrament), exposition of the sacrament outside and soon even during Mass (contrary to the wishes of Rome), and the custom of the "Forty Hours Devotion."[69] In the devotions of the many popular associations and confraternities adoration of the Lord present in the host likewise came to have an importance that was augmented by the incorporation of "Devotions and Prayers to the Blessed Sacrament" into the diocesan hymnals and prayerbooks.

These and similar forms of eucharistic devotion and worship are of course licit in principle. They do, however, bring with them the danger that their connection with the celebration of Mass will be obscured, that the liturgy of the word, the Eucharistic Prayer, and the reception of communion will no longer be experienced as forming a single whole, and that the reception of communion during Mass will no longer be perceived as the normative and highest form of eucharistic devotion.

The New Rite

The liturgical reform has cut away many (well-intentioned) excesses and reasserted the primacy of the eucharistic celebration as a unitary whole. In this context reference must be made first of all to the Roman Instruction *Eucharisticum mysterium* (May 25, 1967) and to the section of the Roman Ritual that the Congregation for Divine Worship published on June 21, 1973 under the title *Holy Communion and Worship of the Eucharist Outside Mass.*[70] Since the latter to a large extent repeats the directives of the Instruction, I shall refer to it alone in the following discussion.

The General Introduction to the document begins by stating that the celebration of the Eucharist is the origin and purpose even of the worship given to the sacrament on the altar outside Mass (2). "No one therefore may doubt 'that all the faithful show this holy sacrament the veneration and adoration that is due to God himself, as has always been the practice recognized in the Catholic Church'" (3). The primary and original reason for reserving the Eucharist is the administration of viaticum; a secondary purpose is the reception of communion outside Mass and the adoration of the Lord who is present in the Eucharist (5). Since the eucharistic presence of Christ is the fruit of the consecration, the Eucharist should not be on the altar of celebration at the beginning of Mass (6). In order to make adoration before the Blessed Sacrament possible during the day, churches should be open for at least a few hours each day (8).

If the faithful are unable to take part in the celebration of the Mass they have the right to receive communion outside Mass, although the pastor should make clear the intrinsic connection of communion with the sacrifice of the Mass (14f.). On Holy Thursday and Good Friday, however, communion is available outside Mass only to the sick. On Holy Saturday communion may be received only in the form of viaticum (16). Communion outside Mass should be given only in the setting of a liturgy of the word, whether brief or longer (17-53). The new rite then goes on to describe the administration of communion to the sick by an "extraordinary" minister (54-

78). The final chapter (III) strongly urges "devotion, both private and public, toward the Eucharist even outside Mass," but in conformity with the norms presently in force (79). In practicing such devotion the faithful should be aware that the sacramental presence of the Lord arises from the sacrifice and has communion for its purpose (80).

In connection with exposition of the Blessed Sacrament in a ciborium, pyx, or monstrance care must be taken to avoid everything "that could in any way obscure Christ's intention of instituting the Eucharist above all to be near us to feed, to heal, and to comfort us" (82). It is therefore forbidden to celebrate Mass while the Blessed Sacrament is exposed in the same church. In addition to the reasons already given for this in no. 6 (above), it is said here that "the celebration of the eucharistic mystery includes in a higher way that inner communion to which exposition is meant to lead the faithful" (83). A liturgy of the word should precede even a brief exposition; "exposition merely for the purpose of giving benediction is prohibited" (89). This means that the practice hitherto widespread of giving the final blessing with the Blessed Sacrament, for example, at the end of devotions, is no longer allowable.

"The ordinary minister for exposition of the eucharist is a priest or deacon"; if a priest or deacon is not available, an acolyte, an extraordinary minister of communion, or (by appointment of the Ordinary) a member of a religious community or pious association dedicated to eucharistic adoration may serve as minister. These exceptional ministers may not, however, give the blessing with the sacrament (91).

The prayers, songs, and readings at an exposition of the Blessed Sacrament should be such that they focus the full attention of the faithful on Christ (95). "It is fitting that a eucharistic procession begin after the Mass and the host to be carried in the procession is consecrated at this Mass" (103).[71]

The Debate over the Administration of Communion at Priestless Liturgies on Sundays and Feastdays

The acute shortage of priests in wide areas of the world has led in many communities to priestless liturgies on Sundays and feastdays. Initially this meant "only" liturgies of the word, which had already been recommended by Vatican II (*SC* 35, 4) and for which directives were given in no. 37 of the Instruction *Inter oecumenici* on the orderly carrying out of the Constitution on the Liturgy (September 26, 1964). When Rome allowed the Berlin Conference of Ordinaries in 1965 to commission laypersons to distribute communion, the reception of communion was soon added to the liturgies of the word conducted by the laity. The rapid extension of distribution by laypersons ("extraordinary ministers of the Eucharist") soon led in other countries to the same form of priestless liturgies. The majority of bishops recommended the practice in their official gazettes and provided concrete directives that reflected in part, the decisions of the national synods of the sixties.[72]

Objections were soon raised, however, to the regular distribution of communion at these liturgies of the word,[73] on the grounds that the distribution of communion outside Mass could be viewed only as a stopgap measure and not as a praiseworthy permanent solution. In addition (it was said), there was danger of promoting a static or isolationist understanding of the Eucharist that focuses attention solely on the consecrated host (the real presence of Christ) and attaches less importance to the re-presentation of the paschal mystery (Betz's "presence of the saving act"). A further danger was that the constant association of liturgy of the word and communion would lead to decreased esteem of the liturgy of the word in the minds of the faithful.

The German Episcopal Conference intervened in the debate with a recommendation of September 20, 1983. It said: "The association of communion with the liturgy of the word should not be made the rule at priestless community liturgies on Sundays" (II, 3). The accompanying "Pastoral and Theological Clarifications" justified this on grounds of the nature of the Eucharist as a complex totality: "Its several dimensions or aspects may not be arbitrarily detached from one another and made independent." Also to be taken into account in this area is the ongoing ecumenical dialogue, which sees the Eucharist as a unitary whole and seeks an organization of it that is in accord with its nature. On the other hand, the bishops had no intention of denying the basic legitimacy of a liturgy of the word that is accompanied by the distribution of communion or, consequently, of forbidding it. But when communion is distributed in this context its connection with the Mass should be brought out clearly.[74]

On June 2, 1988 the Congregation for Divine Worship published a *Directory for Sunday Celebrations in the Absence of a Priest.*[75] The Committee on the Liturgy of the National Conference of Catholic Bishops of the United States, in keeping with the *Directory,* prepared a ritual for use in Sunday celebrations in the absence of a priest that provides for Morning and Evening prayer and a celebration of the Word of God. When it is pastorally appropriate communion may be distributed at these services. The Liturgy Committe also prepared a pastoral statement to assist bishops in the use of the ritual: *Gathered in Steadfast Faith.*[76]

Chapter Twelve

The Sacrament of Reconciliation

BIBLICAL FOUNDATIONS

A correct understanding of the sacrament of reconciliation or of penance requires a faith-based understanding of sin. Sin is a deliberate, free departure from the binding will of God; it is a self-willed, egocentric "No" to the creator and his commands. The English word "sin" is ultimately derived from a German word meaning to separate, to put a gulf between creature and creator. For Christians it is at the same time a betrayal of a divinely given vocation and of the authentic self-fulfillment that is achieved through the following of Christ.

Sin also has a social dimension, since it capriciously destroys the basic foundations and system of laws of human society and works injustice upon one's fellow human beings. This social aspect emerges even more strongly when we focus on the community of believers, the Church, which Christ calls to an obligatory holiness. Every serious sin of its members is a drag upon and an injury to the vitality and credibility of the Church and therefore to its missionary impact. Sin thus militates against the accomplishment of Jesus' purpose of which Ephesians 5:25 speaks when it says that he "loved the Church and gave himself up for her, that he might sanctify her, having cleansed her by the washing of water with the word." — In summary, then, it is possible to speak of a theological, an anthropological, and a social and ecclesial negative aspect of sin.

It is easy to see that these far-reaching claims apply only to the kind of sin which we call "mortal" (1 Jn 5:16): an act of complete, freely willed turning from God and the order he has established. Modern pastoral theology and pastoral psychology are inclined to regard real mortal sin as rare, because psychological conditions and milieu-conditioned entanglements often make a supposedly conscious basic decision against God seem in fact dubious. But even where there is not such a decision, there can be momentous incoherences of behavior and culpable failures that are not reducible to those "venial" sins of which we are all guilty (see James 3:2). It has therefore been suggested that we need a category of "serious" sin between "mortal" and "venial."[1]

According to the gospels, Jesus of Nazareth, whose food was to do the will of the one who had sent him (see Jn 4:34), took sin very seriously and had harsh words to say against it (for example, Mt 18:6-8; 23:13ff.). But he was not simply an uncompromising preacher of repentance; he also loved sinners, led them to reconciliation, and forgave their sins (see Mt 9:2 par.). The climax of his pity for sinful humanity was reached in his expiatory and reconciling suffering and death (see, e.g., Rom 5:8).

He gave permanence, as it were, to this once-for-all act of reconciliation by instituting the sacrament of his body that is given for us and his blood that is shed "for the forgiveness of sins." He also gave his disciples the commission and authority to preach "repentance and forgiveness of sin . . . in his name to all nations" (Lk 24:47) and to administer baptism for the forgiveness of sins. In addition, he made his Church a sign and instrument of reconciliation by bestowing upon it, through the power of the Holy Spirit, the authority to forgive sins (Jn 20:22f.; see 2 Cor 5:18).

HISTORICAL DEVELOPMENT OF PENANCE

In its concern for the conversion of sinners the Church has in different historical periods and regions exercised varying degrees of strictness and mildness and has developed a variety of forms for penance. The primitive community already had the practice of excluding (= excommunicating) sinners from the community of God's people for a certain period in order to urge them to conversion (see 1 Cor 5:1-13). Prayer, fasting, almsgiving, and other good works were regarded as adequate means of obtaining forgiveness of everyday faults.

In the following period the so-called capital sins, chief among which were apostasy, murder, and adultery, were made subject to public penance. If we allow for certain variations in different periods and regions, the process of public penance involved the following phases: private confession to the bishop or his representative; acceptance into the ranks of the penitents, with determination of the obligatory penance; exclusion from the celebration of the Eucharist and the reception of communion. The period of penance might last several years; in some regions it lasted until the person was dying. In Rome, readmittance into the Church (= reconciliation) usually took place on Holy Thursday; the rite consisted of an imposition of the hand and a prayer by the bishop.

As a general rule, the principle in force was that reconciling penance was possible only once in a lifetime. In many regions of the Church penitents were given lifelong penances that proved an often intolerable social and economic burden. The result was the widespread postponement of penance until the hour of death.

In the monastic communities of the East a divergent form of penance developed that might be characterized as "confession to a layman." A monk confessed his guilt to a fellow monk, who was usually not a priest, and asked for his prayers. The period of penance imposed for sins confessed in this manner was substantially shorter than in official ecclesiastical penance. When the period of penance was completed the penitent was again received into full communion with the other monks, and his sins was considered to have been forgiven.

Under the influence of Irish itinerant monks, almost all of whom were priests, a combination of the two forms of penance just described came into existence from the sixth century on. Individuals confessed their sins to a priest and received absolution. Their penance, which originally had to precede absolution, was now to be performed within a short time after it. Moreover the penance itself was calculated according to lists in penitential books ("tariff penance"). As early as the ninth century the demand was being heard that persons confess their sins once a year or perhaps three times a year. This development reached its end at the Fourth Lateran Council (1215), which prescibed that all sinners must confess their sins at least once a year.[2]

The modern period brought the development of "devotional confession" in which only venial sins were confessed; it served especially as a preparation for the reception of communion. The penances imposed became increasingly lighter and often consisted of only a short prayer. Penance almost completely lost its public and social element and character. It did so all the more when from the sixteenth century on confession was no longer made in the sanctuary but in an enclosed confessional in which the person was separated from the priest by a grill. This development meant that the original sign of forgiveness, the imposition of the hand, was reduced to a raising of the priest's hand in the direction of the penitent. The words of forgiveness which the priest spoke at this point had until the thirteenth century been in the form of a petition (the deprecative form) but now became a declarative sentence ("I absolve you . . .").[3]

The last-named development also led to the widespread use of the name "confession" for the sacrament of penance. It is a defective name because it places exclusive emphasis on what is only one of the actions of the penitent and does not refer to other personal conditions which the penitent must have: conversion and repentance, a firm resolution, and recompense for harm done. Above all, however, the name "confession" does not make it clear that the sacrament of reconciliation is a liturgical action in which the active agent is not simply the one confessing but also Christ, who through the Church is saving human beings and glorifying God. In addition, the much reduced form of the rite promoted the impression that the sacrament of penance was a purely private affair; hardly anything suggested its social and ecclesial character.

THE NEW POSTCONCILIAR RITE

The Fathers of Vatican II were aware of the inadequacies just decribed. They therefore decreed that "the rite and formularies for the sacrament of penance are to be revised so that they more clearly express both the nature and effect of the sacrament" (*SC* 72).

The new *Ordo paenitentiae* (Rite of Penance) appeared on December 2, 1973.[4] It was deliberately not entitled *Ordo sacramenti paenitentiae* because there are other forms of efficacious penance and because Christians are called to conversion and repentance as permanent attitudes even outside the sacrament.[5]

After an extensive theological and pastoral Introduction, the new Rite of Penance contains three forms for the administration of sacramental absolution, as well as examples of nonsacramental penitential celebration:

A. Rite for reconciliation of individual penitents.

B. Rite for reconciliation of several penitents with individual confession and absolution.

C. Rite for reconciliation of several penitents with general confession and absolution.

D. Penitential services without sacramental absolution (= Appendix II).

Rite for Reconciliation of Individual Penitents
With regard to the place for the administration of this sacrament the Introduction speaks simply of "the locations . . . and the place prescribed by law" (12). During the four hundred years preceding the council this place was the confessional with its grill. Since the council the law allows for a "reconciliation room" which better satisfies the desire of many for a more personal penitential dialogue.[6] With regard to the time of administration the new Rite excludes only times when Mass is being celebrated (13). The question of the minister's liturgical garb is left to the competent Ordinary. Almost everywhere in the German and English-speaking countries the stole is the only vestment required. We ought to ask, however, whether the wearing of liturgical vestments such as are customary in, for example, the administration of baptism (alb [or cassock and surplice] and stole) might not by reason of their greater symbolic power be more appropriate and helpful to the sacramental process.[7]

Short Description of Rite I:
The priest greets the penitent and, after the latter has made the sign of the cross, urges him (or her) to trust in God. The priest then has the option of reading (or reciting from memory) a short passage of Scripture on the mercy of God and human conversion. The point of such a reading is to make it clear that God's word and grace precede any and all human efforts. Next comes the personal confession of sins, which is followed by a dialogue of clarification, direction,

and encouragement, and by the assignment of an appropriate penance. This penance, which evidently does not do away with the obligation to make good any harm done by the person's sins, "may suitably take the form of prayer, self-denial, and especially service to neighbor and works of mercy. These will underline the fact that sin and its forgiveness have a social aspect" (18).

After a prayer of repentance by the penitent, the priest "extends his hands, or at least his right hand, over the head of the penitent and pronounces the formulary of absolution" (19). Given the theological context of the absolution, the new formula has advantages over the old. It reads:
"God, the Father of mercies,
through the death and resurrection of his Son
has reconciled the world to himself
and sent the Holy Spirit among us
for the forgiveness of sins;
through the ministry of the Church
may God give you pardon and peace,
and I absolve you from your sins
in the name of the Father, and of the Son,
and of the Holy Spirit."

During the final words ("I absolve you . . . Holy Spirit"), which suffice in danger of death, the priest makes the sign of the cross, thus showing the connection between Christ's death on the cross and this act of reconciliation. After the penitent's "Amen" the priest dismisses him or her; several formulas for this dismissal are provided.

Rite for Reconciliation of Several Penitents with Individual Confession and Absolution

The second form of reconciliation locates the personal confession and sacramental absolution of individual penitents in the setting of a liturgy of the word in which a congregation of believers takes part. This form offers no difficulties if the group is relatively small; as the group increases in size, however, it becomes desirable to have the services of several priests. A communal celebration certainly helps to bring out more clearly the liturgical and ecclesial character of the process of reconciliation.

Rite for Reconciliation of Penitents with General Confession and Absolution

This third form differs from the first two in that individual or personal confession is replaced by a general confession of all the penitents and that absolution is given to all as a group. The rite presupposes that the individual penitents are repentant, have a firm resolution to sin no more, and a readiness to make good the harm their sins have done. Form 3 is allowed only in danger of death or if there is a "serious need," that is, "a case in which , given the number of penitents, not enough confessors are available to hear the individual confessions properly within a reasonable time, with the result that, through no fault of their own, the faithful would be forced to be for a long time without the grace of the sacrament or without communion" (31). Except in urgent cases, the decision on whether the conditions needed for general absolution are verified is for the bishops to make. Before absolution is given, "some expiatory penance should be proposed for all to perform; individuals may add to this penance if they wish" (35a).

Those who have received such a general absolution remain obliged to confess their serious sins to a confessor within a year's time. The new Rite (34) justifies this obligation primarily by an appeal to the Council of Trent and to the Pastoral Norms *Sacramentum Paenitentiae* on general absolution (no. 7) which the Congregation for the Doctrine of the Faith issued on June 16, 1972.[8] The Swiss bishops adduced further arguments in the directives they published on the subject:

"Because the penitents being reconciled are ones who by their behavior have separated themselves from the Church, a practice dating back to the apostles and the uninterrupted custom of the Church require that they make a personal confession to a priest. When sinners present themselves to the authorized representative of the Church they give especially clear expression to their attitude of repentance. On the other hand, the act of personal confession helps them to distance themselves from their sins in a more decisive fashion and to deepen their readiness for penance" (2. 8. 1. 8).

It is necessary, of course, to be sure, and to make it sufficiently clear, that the "serious sins" needing to be confessed are indeed mortal sins that contain, subjectively as well as objectively, a radical decision against God.[9]

In response to the question when a "serious need" for general absolution existed outside the danger of death, the Swiss Bishops stated that "this situation can arise in our territory during the season of preparation for Christmas and Easter. The pastor or rector of the church must decide whether or not the situation indeed exists. Conscious of their responsibility, priests should act prudently and in agreement with their Ordinary. Deliberately to create a 'serious need' would go against the intention of the Church and its understanding of general absolution. Pastoral care requires the avoidance of arbitrary action and a unified practice" (*Directives* 2. 8. 1. 2 and 2. 8. 1. 3).

In taking this position, the Swiss Bishops, like their French confreres, have chosen a solution that magnanimously extends the framework preestablished by Rome and builds on the pastor's consciousness of his responsibility.[10]

Penitential Services without Sacramental Absolution

In addition to these three forms of sacramental reconciliation the new Rite of Penance also gives guidelines and examples of penitential liturgies at which sacramental absolution is not given. These originated in the Netherlands in the mid-sixties, but then spread through the German-speaking countries where they enjoyed considerable popularity in many parishes.

In the beginning, however, these services were accompanied by serious confusion, inasmuch as many looked upon them as a valid alternative to individual confession and many theologians allowed them a sacramental efficacy in relation to all sins, even though the services contained only a general confession of sins. The guidelines given in the document *Sacramentum Paenitentiae* of the Roman Congregation for the Doctrine of the Faith (June 16, 1972)[11] countered these views and expectations; the new Rite of Penance then contributed substantially to a clarification of the situation.

The new Rite explains that these services are "gatherings of the people of God to hear God's word as an invitation to conversion and renewal of life and as the message of our liberation from sin through

Christ's death and resurrection. The structure of these services is the same as that usually followed in celebrations of the word of God and given in the *Rite of Reconciliation for Several Penitents*" (36). The text then goes on to warn in 37 and again in Appendix II that "care must be taken to ensure that the faithful do not confuse these celebrations with the celebration of the sacrament of penance."

In what, then, is the chief value of these services to be found?

It is desirable to arrange them especially for these purposes:
—to foster the spirit of penance within the Christian community;
—to help the faithful to prepare for individual confession that can be made later at a convenient time;
—to help children gradually to form their conscience about sin in human life and about freedom from sin through Christ;
—to help catechumens during their conversion.

Penitential services, moreover, are very useful in places where no priest is available to give sacramental absolution. They offer help in reaching that perfect contrition that comes from charity and that enables the faithful to receive God's grace through desire for the sacrament of penance in the future (37).

The new Rite makes quite clear the line of demarcation between the "Rite for Reconciliation of Several Penitents with Individual Confession and Absolution" and the penitential services just described. This does not mean, however, that in these services penitents may not receive forgiveness of those "venial" sins which the Council of Trent itself says "can be expiated by many other remedies."[12] It does not even mean that at such services serious sins too may not be forgiven if a penitent is helped in and by the service to achieve a perfect repentance and an unreserved love of God. As everyone knows, forgiveness may be acquired in this way even outside any and all penitential services, as the theologians have taught for centuries. But according to the directives of the Church serious sins thus forgiven, like serious sins forgiven through general absolution, must be confessed in individual confession, if possible before the next reception of the Eucharist.

In its Appendix II the new Rite gives models for penitential services during Lent and Advent, for general penitential services, and for penitential services with children, the young, and the sick. In recent years there has been a vast number of publications giving patterns and models of such services, so that there is plenty of help available for organizing them.[13]

The documents discussed make it clear that the authorities of the Church are holding strictly to the principle enunciated by the Council of Trent, that in every case mortal sins must be individually confessed,[14] even if they have already been forgiven through general absolution and perfect contrition. On this point, however, widespread doubts have been raised which found expression even at the Sixth Synod of Bishops (Rome, September 27—October 29, 1983). There is no doubt that the practice of individual confession is presently in a state of crisis, as the empty confessionals and often crowded penitential services make clear. On the one hand, many of the faithful show a genuine readiness for conversion and reconciliation; on the other, for whatever reasons, they do not make their way to the confessional.

The question arises, therefore, whether the Church must hold immutably to the detailed confession of mortal sins as a condition for the exercises of its power to forgive sins and whether the assertion of Trent is really based on "divine law." "Hubert Jedin, one of the leading experts on Trent, came to the conclusion that neither the arguments from Scripture nor the argument from tradition justified the claim that this is an immutable precept of divine law."[15] F. Nokolasch, one of the leading scholars on this subject, is convinced that in the long run an open attitude will be unavoidable.

"A multiplicity of forms of sacramental penance can make people aware once again of the special value and dignity of individual confession, but it can also show quite clearly that Christian penance is not bound to a specific form. In the final analysis penance always requires a radical interior turning of the repentant Christian to Christ and God. Given human nature, this turning must also find an outward expression, as the history of the Church shows, but not a particular expression that is absolutely immutable."[16]

PENANCE AND RECONCILIATION AMONG THE SEPARATED CHRISTIANS

None of the Christian Churches can ignore the basic call of the gospels for conversion and penance (see, for example, Mk 1:15). For this reason all the Churches not only preach the need of penance but have more or less institutionalized forms of reconciliation.

The penitential rites of the several Eastern Churches today display a wide variety of forms. These are revisions and expansions of rites arising out of the early practice of ecclesial reconciliation. In many of the orthodox Eastern Churches, however, any rites corresponding to our sacrament of penance have fallen into disuse.

"In many locales in the present-day Churches of the Byzantine world a group of penitents, following ancient custom, join in reciting certain prayers, but in every case each individual approaches the priest and confesses his or her sins. As a rule, absolution is given only after the imposed penance has been performed. The same is true in the West Syrian Church. Among the Copts the practice of sacramental penance seems to have been forgotten for quite some time. In many Coptic communities one may hear the expression "To confess at the incense," that is, to make a silent confession during the incensation at the beginning of Mass, after which a solemn formula of absolution is uttered."[17]

The Churches of the Reformation continued to preach the need for a change of heart and for penance, but they abandoned the sacramentality of the process of reconciliation, on the grounds that there are no explicit words of institution by Christ in the New Testament (as there are for baptism and the Lord's Supper). Luther himself highly esteemed and practiced private confession and in the beginning was still prepared to regard it as a sacrament. In its liturgy[18] the United Evanglical Lutheran Church of Germany has "private confession" (with various suggestions on how to organize it), "communal confession" in two forms, and a "public penitential service." In communal confession there is a general confession of sins, after which absolution may be given to each individual as the "confessor" lays his hand on them or it may be given to all the penitents together without any imposition of the hand.[19]

In the United States, the 1979 *Book of Common Prayer* of the Episcopal Church provides a Penitential Order that may precede the celebration of the Eucharist or be used as a separate service. The Order includes a general confession of sins and a prayer of absolution. If the Penitential Order is not used, the general confession and absolution may conclude the intercessions at the end of the liturgy of the Word. The Prayerbook also provides two forms for the Reconciliation of a Penitent. Alternative prayers of absolution are provided in both forms, the first absolution is based on the revised Roman prayer of absolution. Provision is also made for confession to a deacon or lay person. In such case, the absolution is replaced by a declaration of forgiveness.[20]

The *Lutheran Book of Worship*[LBW] (1978) of the Evangelical Lutheran Church in America also has a Brief Order for Confession and Forgiveness that may be used before the celebration of the eucharist. In addition to the Brief Order the LBW provides a rite for Corporate Confession and Forgiveness which may include an individual imposition of hands and absolution. The LBW and the ritual or book of *Ocassional Services* provides a rite for individual confession and forgiveness including the imposition of hands and a prayer of absolution.[21]

The *Book of Worship*, (1986) of the United Church of Christ contains two orders for reconciliation: Order for Corporate Reconciliation and Order for Reconciliation of a Penitent Person. In the rite for the reconciliation of a penitent the minister declares:

In Christ's name,
and as one with you in the church,
I declare to you:
Your sins are forgiven.
Go in peace,
in the knowledge of God's mercy.

In the corporate rite the congregation declares to the minister that his sins are forgiven immediately after his declaration of pardon to them.[22]

The Presbyterian Church (USA) has recently published, as a part of it series of supplementary resources, a Service of Repentance and Forgiveness for use with a Penitent Individual. This brief service consists of invitation to confession, prayer of confession, declaration of pardon, sign of peace and a dismissal.[23]

The new rites of the United Church of Christ and the Presbyterian Church mark the first time these Churches have provided a form for individual confession and absolution.

Chapter Thirteen

The Sacrament of Anointing of the Sick

The difficult situation created by sickness that bows down both body and soul is an age-old human experience which I assume is familiar to my readers. Sickness makes human beings conscious of their finiteness and dependence and vividly reminds them of the often forgotten law that all human beings must die. Another element that makes sickness burdensome is the interpretation which many religions give of it: that it is a punishment for the guilt of the individual or of an entire group (nation, tribe, family), including even ancestors. This interpretation may cause the sick person's fellow human beings to look down on him or her.

BIBLICAL FOUNDATIONS, MEANING, HISTORICAL DEVELOPMENT

Jesus of Nazareth rejected the interpretation of sickness as a punishment (see Jn 9:1-3) when he pointed out that it can also have meaning derived from the future. In addition, Christian faith makes the suffering and resurrection of Jesus himself the foundation of a new understanding of Christian suffering and death (see Rom 8:17f.). Sickness can and must also be understood as a participation in the paschal mystery of Christ; this means that the suffering of Christians can even be fruitful for the community of believers (Col 1:24).

The gospels tell us in numerous passages that Jesus showed special concern for the sick and healed many of them in body and spirit. He showed solidarity with them as he did with others in distress; in fact, he even identified himself with them to the point that in his discourse on the final judgment (Mt 25:31-46) he interpreted all the help given or refused to those in need as help given or refused to himself. Furthermore, he commissioned and authorized his disciples to impose hands on the sick (Mk 16:18), anoint them with oil

(Mk 6:13), and heal them (*ibid.* and Lk 9:1ff.). The Acts of the Apostles report that after the death and resurrection of Jesus the apostles healed the sick in the name of Jesus and by his authority (see Acts 3:1; 5:15f.).

Of special importance in understanding the service given to the sick by the apostolic communities is the directive in the Letter of James 5:14-15. The reason is that it shows this healing activity as already taking an institutional form. "Is any among you sick? Let him call for the elders of the church, and let them pray over him, anointing him with oil in the name of the Lord; and the prayer of faith will save the sick man, and the Lord will raise him up, and if he has committed sins, he will be forgiven."

What the community or Church is here called upon to do is nothing less than to continue the commission which Jesus gave to his disciples. The prayer of faith, accompanied and given visible form by the anointing with oil (and by an imposition of hands: many thus interpret the Greek phrase *ep'auton* [= "over them" in the translation given above]), brings about bodily and psychic deliverance and restoration and, if needed, even the forgiveness of sins. It is to be noted that the persons thus aided are described not as dying but simply as sick; the service to be given them aims at life and health. Also important is the fact that the sick are referred to the "elders" (Greek: *presbyteroi*), that is, to the officials of the community, and not to charismatics of one or other kind. In the Bible, the service of the sick is an official activity of the Church.[1]

The data supplied by the Bible yield two important conclusions:

The first is that when the Church, acting in the name and by the power of its risen Lord, uses visible signs to secure the salvation of believers, we legitimately speak of it as administering a sacrament. But the service of the sick that is described in the Letter of James clearly corresponds to the intentions of Christ; moreover, when accompanied by the prayer of the faithful and the use of visible signs, it pledges supernatural saving effects. Therefore this service is a sacramental activity of the Church; it is a sacrament. This means that, like the other sacraments, the anointing of the sick is in the final analysis a saving action which the risen Christ performs for the sick, and that the human priest is as it were simply an instrument in his hand.

It is Christ who in the prayer and sign of anointing continues for the sick of our time the loving, beneficent service he began long ago in Palestine. As he gazes out on the countless throng of the sick he repeats today his words of sympathetic readiness to assist: "I have compassion on the crowd" (Mt 15:32; Mk 8:2). Full of pity, he stoops to them and raises them up; he gives them new strength and hope, and forgiveness if they have sinned; he becomes for them the compassionate Samaritan who looks after the prostrated sick. Anointing of the sick, then, has nothing to do with magic and superstition. It is a saving action of the Lord in behalf of human beings who are in need of salvation.

The second important conclusion has to do with the meaning of the anointing of the sick. Because this anointing continues the service of the sick begun by Jesus and his apostles, it may not be viewed as "the sacrament of consecration for death" and as a kind of official seal set upon the imminent passage through death. It is rather a sacrament of bodily and psychic restoration for the sick, a sacrament of assistance and healing.

This last sentence describes how the sacrament was understood by the Church, both Eastern and Western, in antiquity; the chief proof of this is the prayers used in the blessing of the oil of the sick from early times down to the present.[2] In, for example, the *Euchologion* (Prayer Book) of Serapion of Thmuis, a fourth-century Egyptian bishop, we read:

We call on you, who possess all authority and power, you who are "the Savior of all men". . . . We pray you to send from the height of heaven (where your) only-begotten Son (reigns) a power of healing into this oil. In those who receive anointing . . . let it put to flight "every disease and every infirmity"; . . . let it obtain good grace and forgiveness of sins, remedy of life and salvation, health and wholeness of soul, body, and spirit, and full vitality.[3]

The same thoughts are still to be found in the prayers with which the bishop blesses the oil of the sick on Holy Thursday. Even in the prayers which until recently accompanied and followed upon the anointing of the sick, bodily and psychic restoration and healing played a key role.

Beginning in the early Middle Ages, however, the emphasis in this sacrament was gradually misplaced, resulting in a questionable practice. At that period, people tended to postpone the sacrament of reconciliation to a point as close to death as possible, in order to avoid the harsh penances then imposed; as a result, the sacrament of anointing of the sick was also pushed back closer and closer to death, because it was thought that this sacrament could not be administered until after confession. The emphasis thus came to be placed less on the healing and restorative function of the anointing and more on the forgiveness of sins, despite the fact that it was immediately preceded by the real sacrament of reconciliation. The name "Last Anointing," which came into existence in the twelfth century, also contributed to the reinterpretation of the anointing of the sick as a sacrament of the dying. Thus it came to be feared rather than loved. (Originally "last anointing" meant only that the anointing of the sick is the last of the sacramental anointings, following as it does on those administered in baptism, confirmation, and ordination.)

The movement of liturgical and pastoral renewal in recent decades led to a rethinking of the situtation. Applying the ancient principle that liturgical prayer provides a norm for faith and the practice of faith (*lex orandi—lex credendi*), people came to realize that the sacrament of anointing is intended more as a help to life on earth than as a preparation for death. This gratifying change of outlook was reflected in a change of name, as "Last Anointing" was replaced by "Anointing of the Sick." Vatican II also welcomed the change, saying: "'Extreme Unction,' which may also and more properly be called 'anointing of the sick,' is not a sacrament for those only who are at the point of death" (*SC* 73).

It is, of course, not the intention or function of this sacrament to render medical attention to the sick superfluous and, as it were "to pray them into health," as we are told is done in many sects. Sacraments do not suspend the laws of nature and are not a kind of conveyor belt for spectacular miracles; they do not automatically restore health.

The existence of a sacrament of the sick is also not meant to suggest to the sick that they should put up no resistance to illness. On the contrary, the new Rite clearly says in its Introduction that divine providence intends human beings to be healthy and strong: "Part of the plan laid out by God's providence is that we should fight strenuously against all sickness and carefully seek the blessings of good health" (3; see 4 and 32).[4]

In summary, it can be said that according to the evidence in the Bible and the documents of the tradition the anointing of the sick is not a sacrament of "consecration to death" but is intended rather to promote bodily and psychic restoration. Like every sacrament, it brings the sick close to the Lord and assures them of his beneficent love. Thus it renews their faith and hope and gives them the strength to understand and accept their illness as a disposition of a God who is a loving Father. It preserves them from faintheartedness and doubt and gives them serenity and peace.

First of all, then, the anointing eases and heals the spiritual and psychic distress of the sick. In not a few cases, however, this first effect has a positive impact on the overall course of the sickness. A human being is, after all, a "psychosomatic entity," a union of body and spirit. Bodily affliction weighs down the spirit; spiritual distress often makes the body ill, and conversely spiritual restoration promotes bodily health.

In addition, Jesus repeatedly assures us that persevering, faith-filled prayer can "move mountains" (see Mt 21:21; Mk 11:23). Who then will dare set limits to the efficacy of the Church's sacramental prayer, in which Christ himself leads the prayer and prays with us, or deny that this prayer can promote and produce bodily healing?

The passage in the Letter of James should therefore be understood according to its maximal and hope-filled meaning. Chaplains and nurses can tell of many cases in which the sick have experienced a striking improvement, both bodily and psychic, after receiving the sacrament with faith.[5]

THE NEW RITE OF ANOINTING OF THE SICK

Vatican II commissioned a revision of the rite for this sacrament (*SC* 74), focusing its attention specifically on the number of the anointings and on the prayers accompanying the rite (*SC* 75). The new section of the Ritual was published on December 7, 1972, by the Congregation for Divine Worship, under the title *Ordo unctionis infirmorum eorumque pastoralis curae* (Rite of Anointing and Pastoral Care of the Sick). It was preceded by Paul VI's Apostolic Constitution *Sacram Unctionem infirmorum* of November 30, 1972.

The 1982 Englilsh edition of the Rite includes an extensive pastoral Introduction, chapters on visits to the sick, visits to a sick child, and communion of the sick, the rite of anointing of a sick person outside Mass, the rite of anointing within Mass, anointing in a hospital or institution; a chapter on viaticum, the continuous rite (called for in *SC* 74) of penance, anointing, and viaticum for those near death; a chapter on Christian initiation of the dying, commendation of the dying, the prayers for the dead, and texts for use in rites for the sick. In what follows I shall focus on the ordinary rite of anointing. The "continuous rite" will be described below in Chapter XVII.

The renewed understanding of the anointing of the sick affects especially the question of the recipient of this sacrament. Vatican II had already asserted that the sacrament is not reserved to those who are at the point of death but may be administered "as soon as any one of the faithful begins to be in danger of death from sickness or old age" (*SC* 73). The General Introduction to the new rite speaks of those "whose health is seriously impaired by sickness or old age [Latin: *periculose aegrotant*]" (8). In estimating the seriousness of the sickness "a prudently or reasonably sure judgment, without scruple, is sufficient . . . if necessary a doctor may be consulted" (*ibid.*). To be avoided, however, is the excessive zeal that would like to administer the sacrament even in mild illnesses or automatically from a certain age on.

A repetition of the sacrament is allowed "if the sick person recovers after being anointed or if during the same illness the person's condition becomes more serious" (Introduction, 9). The sacrament can also be received before surgery "whenever a serious illness is the reason for the surgery" (10). Administration to sick children is declared legitimate "if they have sufficient use of reason to be strengthened by this sacrament" (12). This last regulation is to be seen against the background of earlier regulations and practice, according to which children are capable of receiving this sacrament only once they have become capable of sin. Against this exclusion of children who have not reached the use of reason "is the ancient practice of the Western Church, still followed in the East, that takes seriously the potential bodily effect of which James speaks and to which the prayers of the rite and the Introduction to it refer."[6]

The sacrament of anointing may be conferred upon sick people who, although they have lost consciousness or the use of reason, would, as Christian believers, probably have asked for it were they in control of their faculties" (14). It is not to be administered to the dead unless there is doubt whether true death has already occurred; in this case the sacrament may be administered conditionally (15 and *Rites*, no. 166).

The new rite expressly condemns the wrongful practice of postponing the sacrament (13), since postponement brings with it the danger that the believer may, when the time comes, be unable to unite his own faith and prayer with the prayer of the Church, thus preventing a full reception. "If the sickness grows worse, the family and friends of the sick and those who take care of them have the responsibility of informing the parish priest (pastor) and by their kind words of prudently disposing the sick for the reception of the sacraments at the proper time" (34).

Like all liturgical actions, the anointing of the sick has a communal dimension that comes to light especially when it is administered during the celebration of the Eucharist (after the gospel). The Mass in question may be one celebrated in the sick room of an individual or one at which a number of the sick are anointed in a church or chapel (on days for the sick of the parish or during pilgrimages of the sick; in the hospitals or old-age homes).[7] But even when the sacrament is administered outside Mass, a little community should be assembled that will not only accompany the sacred action with their faith and prayer but even contribute to it. For the "prayer of faith" is an essential part of this sacrament[8] and should be offered by as many of the faithful as possible. These might include, in addition to the immediate family, other relatives, friends, and neighbors. If circumstances permit, the members of this little community may even play an active part in the liturgical celebration by, for example, doing the reading or sharing in the intercessions.

With regard to the minister of this sacrament, the General Introduction, referring back to the Council of Trent, says that a priest is the sole "proper" minster, and that "this office is ordinarily administered by bishops, parish priests (pastors) and their assistants, priests who are responsible for the sick or aged in hospitals, and superiors of clerical religious institutes" (16). Other priests can administer the sacrament with the permission (at least presumed) of the above-named; if they have in fact presumed this permission, they should afterwards inform the competent priest (18).

Since "in the practice at least of the West the blessing of the oil—and thus also the 'prayer of faith' (James 5:15)—was reserved to bishops and priests until the ninth century, but not the administration of the sacrament (as of the Eucharist) to the individual sick person through an anointing," E. J. Lengeling thinks it "dogmatically possible that deacons or even lay persons appointed by the bishop or the priest (for example, eucharistic ministers) could anoint the sick with the oil blessed by bishop or priest"[9]; the case would be similar to that of extraordinary eucharistic ministers bringing the already consecrated Eucharist to the sick. This new situation would evidently need a special authorization from the Church.

The oil used in the anointing must be olive oil, or some other oil derived from plants (20), that is blessed for the purpose by the bishop, usually at the Chrism Mass on Holy Thursday. In necessity any priest can bless it (21).

The New Rite

It is not difficult to see in the "ordinary rite" a structure similar to that found in the Mass and the other sacraments: opening and closing rites, a liturgy of the word consisting of a reading from Scripture and intercessions, and the essential part of the sacrament: imposition of the hand, blessing of the oil (or, as the case may be, a thanksgiving that looks back to the blessing), and the anointing with its accompanying formula.

The priest begins by greeting the sick person and all who are present; he may use one of the several formulas suggested or one of his own. In any case, "the minister should take into account the particular circumstances, needs, and desires of the sick and of other members of the faithful and should willingly use the various possibilities that the rites provide" (40).

The sprinkling of the sick person (and the room) with holy water ("according to circumstances") is one of the most fundamental symbolic actions in many religions. Water not only cleanses but refreshes and revives. For Christians it is also a reminder of their baptism. The situation of illness is thereby linked to the baptism whereby the person became a Christian and to the eschatological hope based on baptism. The accompanying (optional) texts make the link explicit.

The introductory instruction of the priest is offered as a model (it alludes to Mt 18:20 and cites James 5:14-15).

All sacraments require a proper disposition in the recipient. At this point, therefore, provision is made for sacramental confession if this is needed and if it has not already been made at an earlier time (certainly a desirable practice), or else for a penitential act in the form of the Confiteor or other confession of sinfulness (Rites, no. 118), followed by the priest's prayer for forgiveness. This marks the end of the opening rites.

The liturgy of the word begins with a reading from Scripture. The rite refers here to: Mt 11:25-30, Mk 2:1-12, and Lk 7:18b-23 but lists another thirty-two non-gospel readings and seventeen gospel passages, of which some are indicated as especially suitable for the dying. In providing such a lengthy list the new Ritual is heeding the call of Vatican II that in sacred celebrations "there is to be more reading from holy Scripture and it is to be more varied and apposite" (*SC* 35). "Depending on circumstances, the priest may give a brief explanation of the text" (Rite: no. 120).

The litany of intercession that follows is to be taken as a model and should be adapted to circumstances. The intercessions may be made after the anointing instead of before. They relate first and foremost to the sick, but they also include "all those dedicated to the care of the sick" (121).

The essential rite begins after the liturgy of the word; the Introduction (5) lists its parts and describes it as the rite that signifies and confers the grace of the sacrament.

The first part is the laying on of hands. This gesture, often attested in sacred Scripture, symbolizes, among other things, the outpouring of strength, authority, grace, spirit, aid, healing, and forgiveness. The laying on of hands in the anointing of the sick has its exemplar in Jesus and the apostles, who in turn inherited it as a gesture of healing from their Jewish background. The psychological power of the symbol derives from the fact that it directly expresses belongingness, a being accepted and made secure, a wordless comforting. The laying on of hands is "a fundamental gesture in the Church's ministry of healing" (B. Fischer) and a sign that is easily understood and accepted by the sick. Because the gesture is made in the name of Jesus and in imitation of him and because the priest who imposes his hands represents Christ and Christ acts through him, this gesture is able to awaken confidence and trust in the sick person.

The next step is the blessing of the oil, if the priest does not have with him any that has already been blessed by the bishop. The oil used need no longer be exclusively olive oil but may be any oil derived from plants.[10] In the ancient world oil played an important part as a nutrient, a healing agent, and a cosmetic (used also before and after bathing); it was also used to grease wrestlers and as a fuel in lamps. It was thought of as "the stored up power of the sun" (R. Berger) and therefore became a sign of abundant blessing and fruitfulness. In the symbolic world of the Christian sacraments it is a symbol of life, enlightenment (see *photismos* = enlightenment as an Eastern name for baptism), the gifts of the Spirit and spiritual powers, healing, hope, and joy.[11] If the priest uses oil already blessed by the bishop, he first utters a prayer of thanksgiving that is modeled on the Jewish *berakah*: praise of the three divine Persons is followed by a petition that through anointing with this oil the sick person may experience an alleviation of suffering and a strengthening in time of weakness.

In the new rite the anointing that is now administered is made on the forehead and hands. As "central *foci* of human expressivity,"[12] forehead and hands represent the entire human being, soul and body, thoughts and deeds, or, in short, "the whole human person as a thinking, acting being."[14] In the older rite used since the Middle Ages it was customary to anoint the five senses (eyes, ears, nose, mouth, hands, and if it seemed appropriate, feet). The formula accompanying each anointing referred, somewhat unfortunately, to the sins the person had committed through the particular sense organ. At an earlier time the minister also anointed those parts of the body at which the sick person experienced the greatest pain. In the future, too, it will be possible to increase the number of anointings and vary the places of anointing, if the mentality and tradition of the various peoples make this advisable (Introduction, 24 and Rite, no. 124). In case of necessity a single anointing suffices, which may be made on the forehead or some other spot (if, for example, the forehead is concealed by bandages).

During the anointing of forehead and hands the minister recites the accompanying sacramental formula, the two parts of which are geared to the two anointings. "Through this holy anointing may the Lord in his love and mercy help you with the grace of the Holy Spirit. — Amen. May the Lord who frees you from sin save you and raise you up. — Amen." A new element in this formula is the emphasis on the Holy Spirit (comparable to that found in the prayer for the blessing of the oil). The Spirit is seen, especially in Eastern theology, as the "finger of God"; he brings the work of Christ to completion and is the real efficient cause of all saving actions.

The sacramental effects named in the formula clearly reflect what is said in James 5:14-15: deliverance, health, raising up of the sick person, and, if needed, forgiveness of sins. The new formula thus avoids the rather one sided emphasis on the forgiveness of sins in the old sacramental formula, which read: "Through this holy anointing and his loving mercy may the Lord forgive whatever sins you have committed through your sight (hearing, etc.)."

The twofold "Amen" shows that the sick person and the others present are taking part in the "prayer of faith" and that this sacrament, like the others, involves the whole people of God.

The prayer that follows upon the anointing is not one of the concluding rites but rather sums up once more the effects prayed for and thus emphasizes the basic thrust of this sacrament: easing of body and mind and healing of soul and body by the power of the Holy Spirit. Several alternative prayers are given in view of the quite varied situations in which this sacrament may be administered (advanced age, extreme or terminal illness, before surgery, for a child or young person).

The concluding rites of the "ordinary form" consist of the Lord's Prayer, (holy communion), and a blessing.

If the anointing of the sick is conferred during Mass, the formulary of Mass for the anointing of the sick is used. The opening rites and liturgy of the word used in the ordinary form are omitted; the sacrament is conferred after the gospel.

In a communal celebration at which several sick persons are anointed—a celebration that requires the permission of the local Ordinary—care must be taken that "the priest lays hands on each one individually and anoints each one, using the appointed form. Everything else is done once for all, and the prayers are recited in the plural" (Rite, 110).[14]

THE ANOINTING OF THE SICK IN THE NONCATHOLIC CHURCHES

Except for the Eastern Syrian Church, all the Eastern Churches have (or had) rites for the anointing of the sick, although these have fallen into oblivion among the Ethiopians and the Armenians of Georgia. The rites have an especially distinctive form among the Orthodox, who speak of "the mystery of the holy oil" or "the liturgy of the lamp" (because the anointings are done with oil from a little lamp). If the sick person can be transported, the ceremony of anointing takes place in a church; otherwise it takes place in the home.

The rite is normally celebrated by seven priests. After the "consolation of the sick," which is a kind of votive office, the oil is blessed. Seven anointings follow, each done by one priest; each anointing is preceded by a reading (from the Apostles) and a gospel with an *ektenie* (litany) and rather lengthy prayer. The anointings, for which a twig dipped in the oil is used, are made in the form of a cross on forehead, nostrils, cheeks, mouth, breast, and both sides of the hands; each is followed by a prayer that is the same for all the anointings. The open book of the gospels is then laid on the sick person's head, and several prayers are recited. An abbreviated form is provided for one in danger of death.

The length of this rite has worked to the disadvantage of its frequency. The custom has developed of using the formulary as a penitential service, especially in Holy Week.[16]

In the Churches of the Reformation the anointing of the sick has been and is presently advocated only by a few theologians. In the twentieth century many local Churches of the Anglican Communion have reintroduced (as an option) a repeatable anointing for healing. In the United States the Episcopal Church, Evangelical Lutheran Church in America, Presbyterian Church (USA), and the United Church of Christ provide for the laying on of hands and the optional) anointing of the sick with oil. These Churches also have communal services for healing.

Chapter Fourteen

The Sacrament of Consecration (Orders)

In the list of the sacraments that has been customary since the high Middle Ages the sixth is the *sacramentum ordinis*. "Sacrament of orders" has often been misleadingly restated as "sacrament of priestly ordination"; in fact, however, the Catholic Church understands this sacrament to include three degrees of service, the representatives of which are known as bishops, priests, and deacons (for reasons to be given below, I prefer to call this sacrament of service "the sacrament of consecration"). To what extent do these offices reflect the intentions of Jesus Christ? How were they viewed and practiced in the apostolic communities? For an answer we must look to the New Testament writings.

NEW TESTAMENT FOUNDATIONS AND HISTORICAL DEVELOPMENT OF THE SACRAMENT OF ORDERS

The New Testament has numerous titles for Jesus that bring out the significance of his person and activity for his fellow human beings.

"In the view of the early Church Jesus is the bringer and giver of the Spirit, the sent and the sender, the servant and the one who calls to service. For this reason he is assigned many traditional names and titles that are meant to underscore his unique and utterly new mediatorship as the crucified and risen one who lives on both with God and in his Church. Thus he is the Holy One of God, the celebrant of liturgy, the mediator of the covenant, the priest who is both sacrificer and sacrificial gift, the final and only high priest. He is possessed of all power, and all authority has been given to him in heaven and on earth. He is the Son of David, the prophet, the Son of man, the Good Shepherd, the King of Israel, the Son of God. Jesus is the faithful witness, the pioneer of salvation for all of humanity."[1]

Of these titles those of prophet (teacher), pastor (king), and priest describe his activity in behalf of the human race in an especially concentrated way, and we speak therefore of the prophetic, kingly, and priestly offices of Jesus. As prophet he proclaims a new and joyous message from God. As pastor he gives unselfish, active, self-sacrificing service to human beings, who are "like sheep without a shepherd" (Mt 9:36; Mk 6:34), and he even gives his life for them (see Jn 10:1-18). He looks upon his own death on the cross as an act of unlimited obedience to his Father's will and gladly accepts it as a sacrifice for the salvation of the world, as the key words in the account of the Last Supper clearly show. But one who sacrifices himself in such a way for the salvation of the world is in fact also to be described as a priest and even a high priest.

The pastoral or kingly office of Jesus is thus completed by his priestly office. "In my view it is beyond doubt that the term 'pastor' most comprehensively describes the mission of Jesus but also that his priestly action is the climactic exercise of his pastoral office, because by his self-giving even to death Christ carried out his pastoral office to the full."[2] He is at one and the same time sacrificing priest and sacrificial gift.

But the divine will which Jesus serves is a *universal* salvific will of God. Therefore, as risen Lord and through his Spirit, he continues his saving service through all ages, remaining present to the human race as its teacher, pastor, and priest. He effects this presence by sending his disciples, who by the power of his Spirit proclaim his words (see, e.g., Mt 28:18; Acts 1:8), continue his pastoral service, and make his once-for-all high-priestly sacrifice present by celebrating it in a liturgy of commemoration.

When Christ thus sends his apostles and disciples to continue his threefold office, he also promises that he stands fully behind them, is in complete solidarity with them, and is even identical with them. Thus when he sends the 70 disciples on their mission he says: "He who hears you hears me, and he who rejects you rejects me, and he who rejects me rejects him who sent me" (Lk 10:16). He makes a similar promise after washing the feet of his disciples: "Truly, truly I say to you, he who receives any one whom I send receives me; and he who receives me receives him who sent me" (Jn 13:20).

A mission and authorization in which those sent are identified with Christ to such an extent carries with it a superhuman responsibility. The first concern of those sent must be to deal with human beings on every occasion as Christ would deal with them and to make themselves transparent as it were so that the person and saving intentions of Christ become visible in them. To fit them for the task Christ promises them his Holy Spirit and prays for them: "Sanctify them in the truth; thy word is truth. As thou didst send me into the world, so I have sent them into the world. And for their sake I consecrate myself, that they also may be consecrated in truth" (Jn 17:17-18). It is clear from this passage that the sending of the disciples does not simply bestow a commission (ordination) but also has a dimension of sanctification that justifies us in speaking of a "consecration." Those who receive the task of serving as prophet, pastor, and priest receive a corresponding consecration in the sense of being equipped by grace for their holy activity and not in the sense of being given a private halo.

The continuation of Christ's threefold office in those whom he sends refers directly to the narrow circle of disciples whose members the evangelists describe sometimes as apostles, sometimes as disciples. But in the apostolic community as described in the New Testament we also find a wide range of gifts of the Spirit, or charisms, which are meant to aid in building up the body of Christ (see 1 Cor 12:28). In that same chapter Paul expressly says that these gifts of the Spirit are not given primarily for personal sanctification but for the good of others. The charisms are another way in which the saving activity of Christ is to be made present to the human race by the power of the Spirit.

We must not so concentrate on the offices and charisms as to overlook the fact that all of the faithful are obliged, by their calling and sanctification, to collaborate in the building up of God's people. The "common priesthood of the faithful" (see 1 Pet 2:9) is communicated to them in baptism and confirmation; they too are in the service of Christ.

As a result of historical development, the manifold gifts of the Spirit lost their prominence in many communities around the end of the first century; the offices of service were reduced in number and concentrated in the hands of the leaders of the community.[3] These community leaders were called (without distinction in the beginning) pastors, overseers (*episkopoi*), and elders (presbyters); only later on were the offices given distinct functions and competencies. The Letters of St. Ignatius, the martyr-bishop of Antioch (d. after 110), already show the existence of a heirarchy of bishop, priest, and deacon, each having a well defined authority and relationships with the others.

This structured set of offices spread rather quickly throughout the entire Church and has lasted to the present. The basic ideas and initial implementations to be seen in the New Testament might indeed have developed along several lines; if history established and institutionalized one particular line of development, this was quite legitimate and by no means unbiblical. It is, after all, the very nature of historical development that not all potentialities can be simultaneously actuated but only a few at a time and that even these few cannot be fully actuated at once, so that there is room for future development. (We must of course take into account that the de facto development of the Church was due not only to temporally conditioned factors but also to the action of the Spirit whom Christ promised would be present to the Church as energizing force and helper.)

The de facto evolution of the Church, then, does not necessarily mean that it is bound exclusively and for all time to this concrete set of offices. We are seeing in our own time how pastoral needs and a new vision of the laity are giving rise to new activities and even to new offices of service that are comparable, in the areas they cover, to the New Testament charisms described in 1 Corinthians 12.

The acknowledgment of historical changes and of still unexhausted possibilities does not, however, remove the obligation of seeing and accepting the present organization with its three-stage sacramental office of service as a legitimate development that has its ultimate basis in the saving will of Christ. To call these official services "sacramental" means that bishops, priest, and deacons are signs and instruments, active representatives of Jesus Christ, the prophet, pastor, and priest who continues to work in and through his Church. Wherever these representatives proclaim the word, administer the sacraments, and perform for their fellow human beings the many works of love that serves and leadership that assists, he is present and working with them (see *SC* 7).

At many periods of Church history and in not a few of its representatives, the office of service unfortunately took forms that were out of keeping with its meaning and obscured the vision of Christ as high priest and pastor which it should have mediated. Official activity by order of Christ should never be linked to a sense of power or be distorted by a craving for domination. Christ himself urgently warned his disciples of these perversions. But, more effectively than any exhortations, the striking sign of the washing of the disciples' feet shows the attitude required by office in the Church. If historical development, especially since Constantine, has to some extent taken a different course, no one has been more deeply afflicted by it than those who love the Lord and his Church. On the other hand, it must be acknowledged that especiallly since Vatican II the Church has been making an honest effort to do away with many unfortunate legacies from the past.

ORDINATION OF A BISHOP

As I noted, above, the words *episkopos* ("overseer"; source of our word "bishop") and *presbyter* ("elder"; source of our word "priest") are used in the New Testament pretty much without distinction. But the beginning of the second century saw the rise in Syria and Asia Minor of the monarchical episcopate in which the bishop took precedence over priest and deacon. The earliest witnesses to this development are the letters of St. Ignatius, the martyr-bishop of Antioch. The authority attached to the episcopal office was augmented by the fact that from the middle of the second century on those holding that office met from time to time in synods in order to discuss ways of defending the Church against heresies, which were multiplying at an alarming rate.

The liturgical transmission of office by the laying on of hands and prayer, of which the New Testament already speaks (Acts 6:6; 1 Tim 4:14; 2 Tim 1:6), is described for the first time around 215 in the *Apostolic Tradition* of Hippolytus of Rome. The description refers explicitly, among other things, to the epicletic prayer of the community. The election of the new bishop by the community preceded his ordination.[4]

In the following centuries this simple rite gradually became longer and more luxuriant. An acknowledged liturgical scholar says of the process: "The sacramental sign has developed into a profusion of symbols that bring the liturgy to the threshold of sacred drama. The danger that the secondary would take precedence over the essential was very great, and the Church succumbed to it." [5]

Pius XII had already taken a step of epochal significance when he exercised his teaching office to decide, in his Apostolic Constitution *Sacramentum ordinis* of November 30, 1947, that the essential rite in all three stages of orders is the laying on of hands and the prayer of ordination.[6]

Vatican Council II was aware of the weak points not only in the rite of ordination but also in the theology of the episcopal office. The Constitution on the Liturgy, being the first conciliar document, clearly exercised restraint and called simply for a revision of the rite of episcopal ordination (in the process it allowed all bishops present to lay on hands, instead of only three, as previously). The Constitution on the Church, however, and the Decree on Bishops went more fully into the theological foundations of the office. Of episcopal ordination the Constitution on the Church teaches that it bestows "the fullness of the sacrament of orders" and that "bishops in an eminent and visible way carry on the roles of Christ himself as teacher, shepherd, and high priest and act in his person" (21).

It is also to be noted that the documents of Vatican II use the Latin terms *ordinatio* and *consecratio* without distinction, as is already clear in *SC* 76. The Council sets aside the unsatisfactory Scholastic theology of orders and no longer thinks of the sacraments as "a one-way, ascending ladder" and of episcopal ordination as "an addition of dignity but not substance to priestly ordination."[7] Instead, because bishops receive "the fullness of the sacrament of orders," they "have lawfully handed on to different individuals in the Church in varying degrees a participation in this ministry" (*LG* 28), so that the one ministry branches out as it were in a descending direction. For this reason the second typical edition of the rite of ordination begins with episcopal ordination.

The new rites of ordination that had been commissioned by Vatican II were approved by Paul VI in his Apostolic Constitution Pontificalis Romani of June 18, 1968, and published later that same year.8 All the ordinations take place during the celebration of the Eucharist, after the gospel, and, as far as possible, on a Sunday or feastday so that a large number of the faithful may participate. For pastoral reasons, however, another day can be chosen; for example, for an episcopal ordination, the feast of an apostle.

The rite of episcopal ordination provides that the principal consecrator have at least two other bishops as co-consecrators. But all other bishops present should, as far as possible ("it is fitting"), become co-consecrators by laying hands on the ordinand. The candidate, called a bishop-"elect" (*electus* = chosen) in the official texts, is assisted by two priests. All those mentioned concelebrate the Eucharist. The ordination begins after the gospel and is structured as follows:
a) Hymn, presentation, reading of the papal mandate;
b) Homily of the principal ordaining bishop;
c) Examination and promises of the candidate;
d) Prayer of the community (litany of the saints);
e) Laying on of hands and prayer of ordination while the book of the gospels is held on the candidate's head;
f) Explanatory rites: anointing of head with chrism; presentation of the book of the gospels; investiture with ring, miter, and pastoral staff; seating of the new bishop.
g) Kiss of peace;
h) Concluding rite at the end of Mass.

a) The hymn is the *Veni, Creator Spiritus* or a similar hymn. The candidate approaches the principal ordaining bishop. One of the priests assisting the candidate requests episcopal ordination for him. The papal mandate is then read and all answer "Thanks be to God."

b) In his homily the principal ordaining bishop takes as his starting point the sending of Christ by the Father, which is continued in Christ's own sending of the twelve apostles, who in turn communicate their mission to successors through the imposition of hands. By this laying on of hands, "the sacrament of orders in its fullness" is conferred, and "a succession of bishops" is maintained "unbroken from one generation to the next" and, with it, the continuation of the work of redemption. In the person of a bishop Christ himself continues to exercise his threefold office. It is for this reason that the faithful are exhorted to accept and honor the bishop as "a minister of Christ and a steward of the mysteries of God."

The candidate himself is expressly reminded that his new office is one of service: "The title of bishop is one not of honor but of function, and therefore a bishop should strive to serve rather than to rule." In his participation in the threefold office of Christ he should "always be mindful of the Good Shepherd." He is to love as a father and brother all those entrusted to his care, especially "the priests and deacons who share with you the ministry of Christ"; above all he must not forget the poor and the sick, the homeless and the stranger. He is to show love to those, too, who are far from the Church, since he is responsible for them as well. He must encourage the faithful to collaborate in the work of the apostolate and willingly listen to what they have to say. In addition, he must share the concern for all the Churches and assist Churches in need.

c) The examination by the principal ordaining bishop returns to these lofty obligations and develops them in the form of questions about the candidate's readiness to "maintain the deposit of faith, entire and incorrupt, as handed down" and to remain united to the pope in faithful obedience. In the presence of the entire community the candidate gives his consent by saying "I am."

d) The principal ordaining bishop, and after him all the bishops present, lays hands in silence on the candidate's head. The open book of the gospel is then laid on his head and held there by two deacons until the end of the prayer of ordination. This ceremony, in use as early as the fourth century in the East (West Syria), probably symbolized originally the descent of the Spirit "as gift from the Lord Jesus Christ who is present under the sign of the book of the gospels." [9]

The old prayer of ordination has been replaced by the prayer, slightly revised, of Hippolytus, a prayer also used in the patriarchates of Antioch and Alexandria in the Eastern Church. This change harks back to the earliest tradition and at the same time has an ecumenical value. On the other hand, a new composition would have made it possible to introduce the theology of ordination of Vatican II with its rich biblico-Christological statements. The Apostolic Constitution *Pontificalis Romani* singles out as the essential words: "So now pour out upon this chosen one that power which is from you, the governing Spirit whom you gave to your beloved Son, Jesus Christ, the Spirit given by him to the holy apostles, who founded the Church in every place to be your temple for the unceasing glory and praise of your name."

f) Since the laying on of hands and the prayer constitute the rite of ordination, the ensuing rites must be regarded as expressions of what has occurred at the moment of ordination. This is true even of the anointing of the head with chrism, which in the past was integrated with the prayer of ordination and was regarded as essential. It had been brought into the rite of ordination in the eighth century in the Franko-Gallic territories, and obviously was derived from the anointing of the high priest in the Old Testament (Lev 8:12). It is now an expression of the fact that the newly ordained participates in the high priesthood of Christ, as the accompanying words make clear.

The presentation of the book of the gospels refers to the bishop's participation in the teaching office of Christ. The giving of the episcopal ring (which, with the miter and staff, is no longer blessed during the Mass of ordination but at some earlier time) symbolizes the bishop's obligation of fidelity to the Church, especially the local Church, which is described in the accompanying words as "the bride of Christ."

The miter is placed on the bishop's head with a brief accompanying formula. The accompanying text in the older rite described the miter as the helmet of protection and salvation and linked it symbolically with the horns seen on the radiant head of Moses. This text was thought to be out of tune with modern sensibilities. The new text prays that the "splendor of holiness" may shine in the new bishop and that he may be worthy of the crown of glory when Christ appears.

The pastoral staff, used also in the Eastern Church, is an eloquent symbol of the pastoral office. The principal ordaining bishop gives it to the new bishop with words based on Paul's farewell address at Miletus (Acts 20:28): "Take this staff as a sign of your pastoral office: keep watch over the whole flock in which the Holy Spirit has appointed you to shepherd the Church of God."[10]

g) At the the conclusion of the rite of ordination the new bishop is led to his episcopal chair, if the ordination has taken place in his own church; there he receives the kiss of peace from all the bishops present and takes his place as the presiding concelebrant of the eucharist.

h) At the end of the prayer after communion the newly ordained is conducted through the church to the singing of *Te Deum;* as he goes he gives the faithful his first blessing as a bishop. After a few words from the altar he gives the solemn final blessing.

A review of the new, much more concise, and therefore shorter rite and a comparison of it with the older rite show that there has been a real improvement, even if all expectations have not been completely satisfied.

OFFICE AND ORDINATION OF A PRESBYTER

What was said in the first section of this chapter has already made clear that the ministry of presbysters must likewise be seen as a participation in the threefold office of Christ and thus as a development of the one ministry which Christ has given to his Church. Any derivation of the priestly ministry from the sacrificial priesthood in Israel and in pagan religions, or any likening of it to these, is erroneous. For this reason we can only regard as highly dubious the process by which textual elements crept into the rites of ordination at the end of antiquity, and increasingly in the Middle Ages, that presented the Old Testament priesthood and Levitical office as prefigurations and models of Christian priesthood.

The fundamental content and significance of the presbyteral office are stated chiefly in some doctrinal documents of Vatican II, in particular, the Constitution *Lumen gentium* on the Church (*LG*), the Decree *Christus Dominus* on the Pastoral Office of Bishop (*CD*), and the Decree *Presbyterorum ordinis* on the Ministry and Life of Priests (*PO*) of January 7, 1965.

"Even though they do not possess the fullness of the priesthood and in the exercise of their power [or better: authority!] are subordinate to the bishops, presbyters and nevertheless linked to the bishops in priestly dignity. By virtue of the sacrament of orders, in the image of Christ the eternal High Priest . . . they are consecrated to preach the Gospel, to shepherd the faithful, and to celebrate divine worship as true priests of the New Testament. Partakers of the function of Christ, the sole Mediator (see 1 Tim 2:5), at their own level of ministry they announce the divine word to all. They exercise their sacred function above all in the eucharistic worship or celebration of Mass, by which, acting in the person of Christ and proclaiming his mystery, they unite the prayers of the faithful with the sacrifice of their Head (*LG* 28)."

The same document goes on to speak of their ministry in reconciling sinners and alleviating the suffering of the sick. As participants in the pastoral office of Christ they lead their flock to the Father through Christ in the Spirit. "Presbyters, as prudent cooperators with the episcopal order, its aid and instrument . . . constitute one priestly college with their bishop, charged with different duties" (*ibid.*). In their several communities they as it were make their bishop present and at the same time make the universal Church visible.

These and similar doctrinal statements were of great help in revising the rite of priestly ordination. This rite, like that of episcopal ordination, had, under the influence especially of the Franko-Gallic Church, become a highly complex affair which for centuries obscured the vision of the essentials. As a result, there was for a long time confusion about what the essentials of the rite were (the "matter and form" of the Scholastics). Thus Thomas Aquinas (d. 1274) and the Decree for the Armenians (1494), which was heavily influenced by his writings (especially his *Summa contra gentiles*), held the view that the essential sign in priestly ordination was the bestowal of the paten with hosts on it and the chalice with wine in it, and the accompanying words. As we saw in the previous section of this chapter, in 1947 Pius XII corrected these and other errors and stated that the essential element of the rite at each stage of orders is the laying on of hands and the prayer of ordination. Outstanding studies in the history of the liturgy ultimately paved the way for a radical revision of the rite after Vatican II.[11]

The new rite closely resembles those of episcopal and deaconal ordination in its structure.[12] Like them, the ordination of presbyters takes place after the gospel of a Sunday or feastday Mass and is structured as follows:
a) Presentation of the candidates and election by the bishop;
b) Homily of the bishop;
c) Promises of the candidates and placing of their joined hands between those of the bishop;
d) Prayer of the community (litany of the saints);
e) Laying on of hands and prayer of ordination;
f) Explanatory rites: investiture with stole and chasuble; anointing of the hands; presentation of the gifts of bread and wine;
g) Kiss of peace.

a) The candidates, vested in amice, alb, cincture, and deacon's stole, are called by name. Each answers: "Adsum" ("Present") and goes to the bishop. In response to a question of the bishop, a priest designated by the bishop answers that "the people of Christ and . . . those concerned with his training" have been asked and that they regard the candidate as worthy. There is an echo here of Christian antiquity when the bestowal of orders depended on the preceding election or at least consent of the congregation. When this attestation of worthiness has been given, the bishop in turn responds: "We rely on the help of the Lord God and our Savior Jesus Christ, and we choose this man, our brother, for priesthood in the presbyteral order." The people give their assent with an "Amen."

b) The ensuing model for the bishop's homily leans heavily on what is said in *LG* 28 (see above).

c) The promises given by the candidate in response to questions of the bishop express his readiness to accept the duties of the office of pastor, priest, and preacher and to consecrate himself to God in an increasingly close union with Christ the High Priest for the salvation of humankind. After this each candidate kneels before the bishop, places his joined hands between those of the bishop, and promises "respect and obedience" to him and his successors. This gesture goes back to the ancient Germanic practice whereby a vassal receiving a fief placed his joined hands in those of the king and promised submission and allegiance.

d) In response to the bishop's invitation to prayer, the congregation sings a much abbreviated litany of the saints, into which the invocation of certain saints (patrons of the place, the church, and persons) can be inserted, as can topical petitions. In light of new knowledge of liturgical history this prayer of the community for the candidates must be regarded as an important element of the ordination ceremony and as linked to the bishop's prayer of ordination. "For a man is ordained by the laying on of hands and the prayer of the *ekklesia* assembled around the bishop."[13]

e) The bishop now silently lays his hands on the head of each candidate. The priests present do the same and then remain grouped around the bishop until the end of the ensuing prayer of ordination. This makes it clear that the newly ordained are being accepted as brothers into the presbyterium. The prayer of ordination unfortunately is still very much captive to the Old Testament parallels used in older prayers of ordination. However, the second edition of the ordination rite has added a new paragraph which speaks of Christ and the apostles. Unfortunately, the present prayer still does not reflect the depth and riches of a more recent theology of ordination and office. The Apostolic Constitution *Pontificalis Romani* says that the essential section of the prayer is this: "Almighty Father, grant to these servants of yours the dignity of the priesthood. Renew within them the Spirit of holiness. As co-workers with the order of bishops may they be faithful to the ministry that they receive from you, Lord God, and be to others a model of right conduct."

f) As a sign of the priestly ministry they have received, some of the presbyters present vest the newly ordained in the priestly stole (by rearranging the deacon's stole) and a chasuble. The bishop then anoints the palms of their hands with chrism, praying meanwhile that Christ, whom the Father anointed with the Holy Spirit and power, will protect and strengthen the newly ordained in their priestly ministry. A psalm or a song may be sung during this interpretive rite. The bishop next receives the bread and wine for the Eucharist from the people and, after the chalice has been prepared he gives each new priest the sacrificial gifts of bread and wine (on paten and in chalice) for the Eucharist that is to follow; as he presents them he says: "Accept from the holy people of God the gifts to be offered to him. Know what you are doing, and imitate the mystery you celebrate: model your life on the mystery of the Lord's cross." Thus the sign that was regarded in the past as essential has now become an explanatory symbol.

g) The rite of ordination ends with the bishop giving the kiss of peace to each of the new priests. Other priests present may do the same.

The newly ordained join the bishop in concelebrating the Eucharist that follows. A special intercession may be introduced into the eucharistic prayer.

If we compare the new rite with the old, it is impossible not to see a valuable improvement; we may nonetheless hope that a future edition will remove defects still to be found in it.[14]

OFFICE AND ORDINATION OF A DEACON

The office of deacon (from the Greek *diakonein* = to serve) is already mentioned in the New Testament (Phil 1:2; 1 Tim 3:8ff.). We may see a kind of forerunner of the deacons in the seven men whom, according to Acts 6:1-6, the first community in Jerusalem chose and whom the apostles appointed to be their helpers by praying over them and laying hands on them. For, although their first task was "to serve tables" (therefore a socio-caritative work), we soon find the seven also preaching, converting, and baptizing (Philip, Stephen).

1 Timothy 3:8-12 already sets down certain moral requirements for deacons. At the beginning of the second century deacons appear in the letters of Ignatius, the martyr bishop of Antioch, as a clearly defined office within the hierarchical government of the Church. Down to the present time the Eastern Church has had a deaconate that is a lifelong ministerial office; in the West, however, the deaconate was from the early Middle Ages on simply a stage on the way to priesthood. Men became deacons not in order to remain in that office but as a condition for ordination as priests.

The Council of Trent did attempt to reintroduce the permanent diaconate, but the resolution was never implemented.[15] Before World War II a similar effort was made; this gathered momentum after the War and led even before Vatican II to the formation of "diaconal circles." The breakthrough came, however, only at Vatican II. *LG* 29 described the role of deacons as follows:

"Insofar as competent authority assigns them, the duties of the deacon are to: adminster baptism solemnly; care for the Eucharist and give holy communion; assist at and bless marriages in the name of the Church; carry viaticum to the dying; read the Scriptures to the people and exhort and instruct them; preside over worship and prayer; administer sacramentals; officiate at funeral and burial rites. Dedicated to duties of charity and service. . . ."

The document then continues with this decisive statement:

"As the discipline of the Latin Church currently stands, these diaconal functions, supremely necessary to the Church's life, can be carried out in many places only with great difficulty. Henceforth, therefore, it will be permissible to restore the diaconate as a distinct and permanent rank of the hierarchy. To the various sorts of authorized territorial bodies of bishops it belongs to decide, with papal approval, whether and where it is advantageous to create permanent deacons for the care of souls. With the pope's consent, the permanent diaconate may be conferred on men of mature years, and even on married men, and upon qualified young men. For the latter, however, the law of celibacy must remain in force (*LG* 29).

The Decree *Ad gentes* on the Church's Missionary Activity (December 7, 1965) confirmed this decision and related it especially to men already doing diaconal work:

To make their ministry more effective through sacramental grace, it is advantageous to strengthen and bind closer to the altar through the apostolic tradition of the laying on of hands those men who are actually exercising diaconal fuctions: preaching God's word as catechists; presiding in the name of a pastor or bishop over scattered Christian communities; engaging in social or charitable works (*AG* 16).

After further intensive consultations these declarations of intention were followed by the official revival of the permanent diaconate in the Motu Proprio *Sacrum diaconatus* of Paul VI (June 18, 1967). In many Christian countries schools were established, under a head appointed by the bishop, to prepare men for diaconal ordination.

The papal documents of June 18, 1967 (*Sacrum diaconatus ordinem*) and August 15, 1972 (*Ad pascendum*)[16] set down some specific regulations. For example, in the case both of candidates for the presbyterate and of unmarried candidates for the permanent diaconate, ordination must be preceded by a rite in which the candidates accept celibacy. "In accordance with the traditional discipline of the Church, a married deacon who has lost his wife cannot enter a new marriage."[17] When candidates for the priesthood are ordained deacons they accept the obligation of the liturgy of the hours; of permanent deacons, on the other hand, it is said only that "it is most fitting that permanent deacons should each day recite at least a part of the liturgy of the hours, to be determined by the conference of bishops."[18]

The rite of ordination, which takes place after the gospel during a Mass, closely resembles that of the presbyterate in its structure.

a) Presentation of the candidates and election by the bishop;
b) Homily of the bishop;
c) Promises of the candidates, and the placing of their hands in those of the bishop;
d) Litany of the saints;
e) Laying on of hands and prayer of ordination;
f) Explanatory rites: vesting with diaconal stole and dalmatic; presentation of the book of the gospels;
g) Kiss of peace.

a) The presentation and election of the candidates, who wear amice, alb, and cincture, takes place as in the rite for the ordination of presbyters.

b) The model homily provided for the bishop begins by describing the position and functions of the deacon in a general way: "He will draw new strength from the gift of the Holy Spirit. He will help the bishop and his body of priests as a minister of the word, of the altar, and of charity. He will make himself a servant of all." The deacon's functions are then described in detail (see above, the passage fron *LG* 29). Different conclusions are provided depending on whether the candidates are married or not.

c) The deacon's promises and the placing of his hands in those of the bishop resemble the parallel actions in the rite for the ordination of presbyters. Unmarried candidates make their committment to celibacy in the course of the promise.

d) The same is true of the litany of the saints.

e) The laying of both hands by the bishop and the prayer of ordination are once again the essential nucleus of the rite. The prayer contains praise and petition but, most importantly, the epiclesis or call for the descent of the Holy Spirit, which the Apostolic Constitution *Pontificalis Romani* says is the essential passage: "Lord, send forth upon him the Holy Spirit, that he may be strengthened by the sevenfold grace to carry out faithfully the work of the ministry." The community backs the prayer with its "Amen."

f) Some deacons or presbyters vest the new deacons in their proper vestments. The bishop then gives the book of the gospels to each of the newly ordained, saying: "Receive the gospel of Christ, whose heralds you now are. Believe what you read, teach what you believe, and practice what you teach."

g) The rite ends with the kiss of peace from the bishop. The other deacons present may also give it thus signifying the acceptance of the newly ordained into their college.[19]

STEPS LEADING TO THE SACRAMENT OF ORDERS

In the course of the centuries a number of steps leading up to the sacrament of orders were developed; they might not be bypassed. A short description of the order earlier followed in the Roman Catholic Church will help us better to appreaciate the postconciliar reform.

The Older Arrangement

Tonsure

Reception into the clerical state (as into the monastic)was accompanied, as early as the end of Christian antiquity, by a partial shaving of the head, which subsequently developed into the rite of tonsure (from Latin *tondere* = cut). This was intended as a sign that the candidate gave himself (like a slave) to the service of God. In this rite of reception, which did not count as a minor order, a surplice was given to the candidate as a symbolic clerical garment.

The Four Minor Orders

In the Latin Church the functions of porter, lector (reader), exorcist, and acolyte were regarded as minor orders; in the Eastern Church only those of lector and subdeacon were so regarded. In antiquity the men in these orders performed specific services in the communities; later on these orders became simply transitional stages without concrete functions. In the West, too, the subdeaconate was regarded as a minor order until about 1200; Innocent III made it one of the major orders.

The function of porters (Latin: *ostiarius* from *ostium = door*) was to keep unauthorized persons out of the house of God and to see to the security of the building. In the old rite for this minor order the candidates were given a key to the church and had to open and close the doors and ring a bell. Their office is filled nowadays by sextons.

The task of lectors (readers) was to proclaim the scripture readings during liturgical celebrations. For this reason the lectionary was presented to them at their ordination. Today any member of the community is entitled to perform this service; only the gospel is reserved to a deacon or priest.

In antiquity the function of exorcists was to undertake exorcism, especially in connection with baptism. By "exorcism" is meant the effort to deliver human beings from the control of powers hostile to God by means of special prayers. The office of exorcist lost its real function before the end of antiquity and continued in existence only as a functionless minor order. The external sign for this rite in the old liturgy was the presentation of a book containing prayers for exorcisms (usually the Roman Ritual).

Acolytes (from Greek *akolouthos* = follower, attendant) performed certain services during liturgical celebrations. They may therefore be compared with present-day altar servers, who in fact have in large measure taken over their functions. In the rite of ordination they were presented with candle and cruets as their external symbol.

Ordination to the Subdeaconate

The subdeacon was originally a deacon's helper, especially during the Eucharist; among his other services there was the reading of the epistle. This step in orders was upgraded when celibacy and the recitation of the breviary were imposed on subdeacons (beginning of the thirteenth century) and the subdeaconate was accounted a major order. Yet the rite of ordination never included a laying on of hands; this shows that it was not to be regarded as a major order in the strict sense, that is, part of the sacrament of orders. In the rite the bishop presented the candidate with chalice and paten (without bread and wine), cruets, epistolary, and several liturgical vestments: amice, alb, maniple, and tunicle.

The Postoconciliar Reform

The reform, sought in many quarters before and during Vatican II, began with the two Motu Proprios, *Ministeria quaedam* and *Ad pascendum* which Paul VI issued on August 15, 1972.[20] The first of these decreed that the previous four minor orders were to be replaced by the two ministries of reader and acolyte. These two ministries also took over the tasks of the older subdeaconate, which now ceased to exist. Only by reception of the deaconate is a person now received into the clerical state. The two ministries of reader and acolyte are no longer reserved to candidates for orders, but can be given to laypersons (only to males, according to ecclesiastical tradition).

The second document, *Ad pascendum,* decrees that tonsure is no longer the rite of reception into the clerical state. It is replaced by a rite of admission to candidacy for diaconate and presbyterate. These candidates must in time be commissioned as readers and acolytes in order that they may prepare for the diaconate and presbyterate by exercising these ministries.

The Congregation for Divine Worship published special rites (December 3, 1972) for the institution of readers and acolytes, admission to candidacy for diaconate and presbyterate, and commitment to celibacy.[21]

LITURGICAL MINISTRIES FOR WOMEN

With regard to the ministries of lector or reader and acolyte (to which others may be added at the discretion of the episcopal conferences) the Motu Proprio *Ministeria quaedam* says that they are no longer to be thought of as "minor orders" and that those who exercise them remain laypersons. At the same time, the document says that these ministries are based on the common priesthood of the faithful, because they are a participation in Christ's priesthood, even if this participation be distinct from that found in the sacramental priesthood.[22]

All the more surprising, then, is the statement in no. VII: "In accordance with the ancient tradition of the Church, institution to the ministries of reader and acolyte is reserved to men."[23] This regulation was regarded by many as a painful form of discrimination against women, since they too participate in the common priesthood through their baptism and confirmation. In addition, it is difficult to harmonize it with other statements of the Roman authorities.

Thus the third Instruction *Liturgicae instaurationes* on the carrying out of the liturgical constitution (September 5, 1970) allows women to proclaim the readings (except for the gospel); the espiscopal conferences are to decide on the most suitable place for this reading.[24] There is a similar regulation in *GIRM* 70 in the second typical edition of the Roman Missal (1975).[25] And in the Instruction *Immensae caritatis* of the Congregation for the Sacraments (January 29, 1973) women are permitted to be extraordinary ministers of the Eucharist both during and outside Mass. [26]

The 1983 *Code of Canon Law* says, first, that laymen can be appointed on a stable basis and by means of the prescribed rite to the ministries of reader and acolyte (can. 230 n.1). Secondly, all laypersons can be temporarily appointed to the "function (*munus*) of reader" in liturgical celebrations; "likewise all lay persons can fulfill the functions of commentator or cantor or other functions, in accord with the norm of law" (*ibid.*, n.2). Thirdly, in case of necessity and if clerical ministers are lacking, laypersons, even if not readers of acolytes, can take over certain of their tasks, namely, to celebrate liturgies of the word, lead liturgical prayer, administer baptism, and distribute holy communion (*ibid.*, n.3).

But if women can in specified instances minister as readers and acolytes, the question arises: Why may they not be appointed by a liturgical rite? "The only argument given to justify this discrimination in the Church is an 'ancient tradition of the Church.' But in this context we must not forget that in all probability the early Church officially commissioned women for ecclesiastical services."[27] In Germany, the synod of Wurzburg petitioned the pope that "institution as readers and acolytes not be reserved to men."[28]

In many countries a question that has been and is still being debated even more hotly is whether girls and women may act as servers at Mass. In its Instruction *Inaestimabile donum* of April 3, 1980, the Congregation for the Sacraments and Divine Worship said that "women are not allowed to exercise the ministry of acolyte or altar server" (no. 18). On the other hand, as we saw above, in its Instruction *Immensae caritatis* of January 23, 1979, the Congregation for Divine Worship allowed women the far more important ministry of distributing communion.

There was thus great interest in seeing what position the new Code of 1983 would take. In canon 906 it drops the provision of the 1917 Code (can. 813 § 2) that a woman may not be an altar server, and does not replace it with anything specific. And instead of the old can. 813 § 1 which forbade the celebration of Mass "*sine ministro*," i.e., without a male server, can. 906 of the new Code says simply: "A priest may not celebrate without the participation of at least some member of the faithful, except for a just and reasonable cause" (or: "of at least one believer," *fidelis* being either masculine or feminine). To exclude any doubt Archbishop R. J. Castillo Lara, (Pro-) President of the Commission for the Revision of the Code, declared in an official lecture (February 14, 1983): "With regard to the distinction of men and women in the ecclesiastical realm: apart from exclusion from orders and the instituted ministries no distinction is made between the male and female sexes."[29]

In Rome itself the Pontifical Biblical Commission unanimously stated that the Scriptures cannot by themselves clearly and definitively decide the question of whether or not women may be ordained.[30] In contrast, the Congregation for the Doctrine of the Faith published a "Declaration on the Question of the Admission of

Women to the Ministerial Priesthood" (October 15, 1976), the key sentence of which reads: "The Church, in fidelity to the example of the Lord, does not consider itself authorized to admit women to priestly ordination."[31]

This statement does not mean a definitive "No" to the ordination of women as deacons; this questions is, it seems, still being studied by Rome. But a recent investigation by an acknowledged scholar leaves little prospect of an affirmative response.[32]

Chapter Fifteen

The Liturgy of Marriage

As the title of the chapter suggests, I shall not here discuss in detail the anthropological, sociological, and dogmatic aspects of marriage or questions relating to moral theology and canon law, even if one or other of these does influence my presentation. The focus will be on the liturgical celebration of marriage, which presupposes the sacramentality of Christian matrimony.

CHRISTIAN MARRIAGE AS INSTITUTION OF THE CREATED ORDER AND AS SACRAMENT

Marriage is in the first place part of created reality and is recognized and highly esteemed as such in both Testaments of sacred scripture. The will of the creator as expressed in the second story of creation (Gen 2:24) is fulfilled in the freely accepted communion of two human beings and in their mutual love and fidelity. In this being for and with one another the author of the Letter to the Ephesians sees a parable and sign of the relationship for and with one another of Christ and his Church.

In their communion and unity, Christ, who "loved the church and gave himself up for her, that he might sanctify her, having cleansed her by the washing of water with the word" (Eph 5:25-26), and the Church as his body which commits itself to him in reverence, readiness to serve, and love, are the great saving reality of the new covenant. Every baptized person stands within this reality and draws life from it. This is true in an even greater degree of the community formed by the two partners in a Christian marriage, who not only have a model for their own mutual relationship (of love, fidelity, service, self-sacrifice, forgiveness) in the unity and loving communion of Christ and the Church but also draw their life from this saving gift of God. To the extent that their own marital covenant allows the saving covenant between Christ and the Church to manifest itself, this saving covenant becomes reality in this small part of the created order.

The Christian couple thus form the smallest particular Church, a "Church of the household," as Vatican II calls it in one passage (*LG* 11). Marriage thus continues to be a secular reality but at the same time is the visible, empirical concretization of the decisive saving reality of the new covenant. The archetype is manifested in its image. Marriage is as it were the epiphany of the covenant between Christ and the Church. The communion of Christ with the Church becomes effective in the community of man and wife. The latter is filled with the life exchanged between Christ and the Church, with the grace and truth which Christ has bestowed on his bride, the Church, and with the power of the love that unites Christ and the Church.[1]

This view of the matter is also congenial to Protestant theology as Evangelical theologian H. Baltensweiler shows:

"The archtype-image schema, as usually applied in Protestant theology to describe what is really meant in Ephesians 5, is too weak. We need rather the concept of representation or making present. Just as the community as such represents Christ in this world, so the marriage of Christians renders the Christ-event present among human beings. That is why the unbelieving partner can be consecrated by the believing partner (1 Cor 7:14)." [2]

It follows from what has been said that marriage does not become a sacrament simply because the grace of God is bestowed on this covenant through an external rite, thus elevating it from outside. "The sacramentality of marriage consists of more than a blessing which the Church gives to its children at a decisive point of their journey, more than a ceremony that accompanies the contracting of a marriage and removes it from the sphere of the everyday and the ordinary. It is in fact the filling of the marital covenant with the glory of Christ."[3]

The establishment of Christian marriage as "an image of and participation in the covenant of love between Christ and the Church"[4] brings with it an imperative, a mission. Like the people of God in its entirety, Christian marriage must become in a special way a sign and empirical proclamation of Christ's love for human beings. The love of the couple for one another, their mutual service and self-sacrifice, their tolerance and forgiveness, their fidelity until death, are to show forth with clarity what Christ is and does, even now, for the human race and especially for his Church. Thus every Christian marriage can and ought to become a sign of Christ and a witness to him.

Since a marriage as a reality of the created order is established by the will of the partners to marry and since this marriage is really identical with what we call a sacrament, it follows that the will to marry is also the constitutive element in the sacrament of marriage. In other words, it is not the Church or the priest conducting the ceremony who administer this sacrament; the partners themselves administer it to one another when they express their consent in a form recognized by the Church.

According to the Church law presently in force this obligatory form (canonical form) has consisted since the Council of Trent (1545-46) in this: all marriages in which at least one partner is a Catholic, must be entered into in the presence of a competent Catholic cleric and two witnesses. This binding precept is meant to make the partners more clearly conscious that their expressed consent is a decision made also before God and the community of God's people and that their covenant of love and life must take its character from the faith of the Church and bear witness to this faith.

The obligation of form does not bind in danger of death if a competent cleric cannot be found, nor does it bind outside the danger of death if a competent cleric cannot be found for a lengthy period (a month). In addition, in his Motu Proprio *Matrimonia mixta* (no. 8) of March 31, 1970, Paul VI decreed that in mixed marriages the competent bishop can dispense from the obligation of form "when serious problems stand in the way of observing the canonical form."[5]

But even though consent is the constitutive element in a marriage, the liturgical celebration is of no small importance. The rites bring out the essential character of Christian marriage; they place the two partners and their covenant under the binding and guiding word of

God and strengthen their faith. In the presence of the Church of which they are members the couple themselves publicly attest their faith, by which alone the claims made on them by Christian marriage can be known and fulfilled. In the person of its official representative (a priest or deacon) the Church accepts and acknowledges their marital consent, makes it the object of its intercessory prayer, and bestows its blessing on it. Through word and symbol the Church deepens the awareness and readiness of the couple to bear witness by their love and fidelity to the all-embracing saving covenant of Christ with his Church. The liturgical celebration of a marriage is thus not meant to be simply a setting that elevates the mind and cheers the heart; on the contrary, it possesses a lofty functional value. The forms according to which a marriage is celebrated cannot, therefore, be a matter of indifference.

LINES OF DEVELOPMENT IN THE WESTERN RITE OF MARRIAGE

Only slowly and at a relatively late date did the liturgical celebration of Christian marriage develop the wealth of rites that we know today. It "has always derived its external character from the customs connected with the celebration of marriage in the various countries. In both East and West, the many and varied traditions of society and the prechristian symbolism, which until the Peace of Constantine had alone provided the framework of the marriage ceremony, played a part in the development, beginning in the fourth century, of the liturgical rite of marriage."[6]

There was agreement in Christian antiquity on the basic notion that Christians enter into marriage by mutual agreement and the blessing of the Church and that the reciprocal consent to marriage is the factor that brings the marriage into being. Only those traditional customs were excluded that were strictly pagan, such as sacrifices to the household gods and the querying of oracles; in addition, people were on guard against the many excesses that marked wedding celebrations.

At an early date (there is evidence from around 400) marriage was accompanied by the celebration of Mass; the salient ceremonies were the "veiling" of the bride in the West and the "crowning" of the couple in the East, together with the corresponding prayer of blessing. The blessing of the bride came after the Our Father of the Eucharist. In Roman antiquity there had been a separate ceremony of betrothal or engagement, comprising promises and the bestowal of a ring and other gifts on the bride. In the Church, however, these customs were subsumed into the marriage rite proper; as a result, the Roman liturgy had no separate rite of betrothal until the publication of the *Book of Blessings* in 1984, which contains a rite for blessing an engagement..

Until well into the Middle Ages the actual declaration of consent took place in the home of the bride and in the presence of the immediate family.

"Only when Carolingian domination collapsed in the ninth and tenth centuries did the Church feel obliged to concern itself with the legal acts that established a marriage, although this did not yet mean turning the domestic ritual into a liturgical rite. Even more than the state, the family was falling victim to a period of decline, social disorder, and civil wars in which the abduction of women was commonplace. The Church's first response to these abuses was to require that marriages be celebrated in public so as to ensure that the woman's consent was freely given. It was in Normandy that the exchange of consents was first given a liturgical blessing. In order to make the act as public as possible, it was no longer performed in the home of the bride but before the door of the church, in view of the house of God. The expression "*in facie ecclesiae*" ["before the face of the church"] must therefore be understood as having originally had a spatial meaning." [7]

According to a missal of Rennes (Northern France) from the beginning of the twelfth century, the rite of marriage conducted in these circumstances was structured as follows: The priest, vested in alb and stole, took his place in front of the church door, sprinkled the couple with holy water, questioned them about their intention to marry and their freedom from possible impediments of kinship, and instructed them on living their married life in accordance with the law of the Lord. He then called upon the parents of the bride to surrender their daughter to the groom. The latter then gave the bride her dowry (a documented statement about it was read), placed a blessed ring on her right hand, and honored her with gifts of gold or silver (depending on his means). After the blessing by the priest, the party entered the church, the couple carrying lighted candles which they would present as sacrificial gifts during the Mass. After the Our Father and the embolism the priest covered the bridal couple with a veil, blessed them, and gave the groom the kiss of peace, which he in turn gave to his bride.[8]

In like manner, a colorful variety of marriage customs developed in other countries and regions, often differing even from diocese to diocese. The Council of Trent not only approved these varied riches but even recommended their retention.[9] In contrast, the rite of marriage in the Roman Ritual of 1614 was extremely sketchy. It comprised only the question regarding consent, the joining of hands by the couple while the priest spoke the theologically ambiguous words, "I unite you in marriage," the blessing of the ring which the groom then placed on the bride's finger, and a concluding prayer.

The rite of marriage, for use in all German dioceses, that appeared in the German *Collectio rituum* of 1950 represented a successful attempt to reduce the multiplicity of German marriage rites and create a standard liturgy. It was a "new structure," "though composed, of course, of traditional materials that were tested, carefully chosen, cleared of superfluities, trimmed, and re-arranged";[10] a special effort was made to give prominence to the consent that establishes a marriage and to the free partnership of husband and wife. This German rite of marriage exerted a lasting influence on the postconciliar model rite promulgated by Rome. The rite contained in the American *Collectio rituum* (1954 and 1961) reflects the German-British marriage practices rather than the stark ritual of the *Roman Ritual.*

Vatican II commissioned a revision of the rite of marriage as found in the Roman Ritual; the intended aim was to give clearer expression to the grace of the sacrament and lay greater emphasis on the duties of the married couple. The Council also repeated the wish of the Council of Trent and the old Roman Ritual that the praiseworthy customs and ceremonies of various regions should by all means be kept. In addition, each episcopal conference was given authority "to draw up its own rite . . . suited to the usages of place and people" (*SC* 77). "Marriage is normally to be celebrated within Mass. . . . The prayer for the bride" was to be "duly emended to remind both spouses of their equal obligation to remain faithful to each other." Marriages outside a Mass were be celebrated in the setting of a liturgy of the word (*SC* 78).

The revised rite appeared on March 19, 1969, as a fascicle of the Roman Ritual, under the title *Ordo celebrandi matrimonium.*[11] This rite was translated into English by the International Commission on English in the Liturgy and published in 1969 under the title: *Rite of Marriage.*

CELEBRATION OF MARRIAGE

The Introduction begins by calling to mind the most important theological truths about the sacrament of marriage and giving pastoral suggestions for the preparation of the bridal couple. Catholic couples are normally to be married during a Mass so that by the reception of the Eucharist the bride and groom may be nourished in their love and be lifted up into communion with Christ and each other (6). If the marriage is of a Catholic and a baptized non-Catholic, the marriage is celebrated without a Mass. Exceptions are possible, however, with the permission of the bishop (8). There is no Mass at the marriage of a Catholic and an unbaptized person (8).

The formulary for the marriage Mass may be any one of the three provided in the Sacramentary (among the "Ritual Masses"), unless the marriage is celebrated at a community Mass on a Sunday or solemnity. The Mass of the day must always be celebrated from Holy Thursday to Easter, on the Sundays of Advent, Lent, and the Easter season, and on the solemnities of Christmas, Epiphany, Ascension, Pentecost, Corpus Christi, and holydays of obligation (11).

The celebration of marriage during a Mass is structured as follows:

a) Entrance rite, including reception of the couple and leading of them to the altar;
b) Liturgy of the word and homily;
c) Marriage: Questions regarding readiness for a Christian marriage;
Declaration of marital consent in one of four possible ways;
Attestation of the marriage by the priest (deacon);
Blessing and exchange of rings;
Intercessions;

d) Celebration of the Eucharist; nuptial blessing after the Lord's Prayer;
e) Concluding rites: Solemn blessing.

a) The priest (deacon) may greet the bridal couple (and their retinue) at the door of the church, and accompany them to their places near the altar or he may await them at the altar. The usual opening rites of Mass follow.

b) The readings may be chosen from the passages provided in the *Lectionary for Mass,* with the limitation that in Masses on Sundays and solemnities only one such reading may be included. The purpose of this provision is to ensure that the congregation will hear at least part of the proclamation proper to that day. The homily is to focus primarily on the meaning, purpose, and dignity of Christian marriage and is also to stress the duties of the married couple.

c) The questions regarding the readiness of the couple for a Christian marriage are to be understood as an immediate preparation for the declaration of consent that effects a marriage. The first three questions, which, being so personal, may be directed to each partner separately, have to do with their freedom in marrying, marital fidelity until death, and readiness to "accept children lovingly from God, and bring them up according to the law of Christ and his Church."

The declaration of consent may be made in one of two forms which are equally valid. The priest (deacon) first invites the couple to join their right hands and exchange their consent.

The first form of consent goes back to the Anglo-Saxon tradition. The groom and then the bride exchange their consent by repeating the text after the priest (deacon) or by saying it from memory or by reading it: "I, N., take you, N., to be my wife [my husband]. I promise to be true to you in good times and in bad, in sickness and in health. I will love you and honor you all the days of my life." The traditional English version of the vows may also be used.

The second form for declaring consent is simply the "I do" of each party in response to the question of the priest (deacon): "N., do you take N. to be your wife? Do you promise to be true to her in good times and in bad, in sickness and in health, to love, and honor her all the days of your life?" (Same question to the bride, with the necessary changes.) As in the first form, the traditional English wording of the questions may be used.

Since the exchange of consent effects the marriage, the declaration of the minister which follows can only serve as an attestation and a proclamation that a marriage has taken place. The priest (deacon) says: "You have declared your consent before the Church. May the Lord in his goodness strengthen your consent and fill you both with his blessings. What God has joined, men must not divide."

The blessing and exchange of the rings then follows. The texts make reference to the readiness of the couple for an exclusive love and for fidelity until death. The three blessings (one to be chosen) interpret the rings as symbols of true faith, and signs of love and fidelity.

The ancient Roman custom whereby only the groom gave the bride a ring at the betrothal was carried over into the Christian marriage ceremony; it was included in the Roman Ritual of 1614 and remained in use outside of any liturgical context. This "onesided" ring service did not give symbolic expression to the obligation of both partners to be faithful; in keeping with the ancient pagan idea of marriage, the groom bound the bride to himself and obliged her to fidelity, but not vice versa. In the Byzantine rite of betrothal and in the Mozarabic rite of marriage the reciprocal giving of rings was introduced as early as the eleventh century. By contrast, it was only due to the continued efforts of the Church that in the thirteenth century "the obligation of mutual fidelity was acknowledged in German civil law and, as a result, two rings were used as symbols of fidelity."[12] After the blessing, the couple exchange the rings each saying: "N., take this ring as a sign of love and fidelity. In the name of the Father, and of the Son, and of the Holy Spirit."

The exchange of rings is followed by the intercessory prayer of the community. The general intercessions should "as a rule not be limited to the newly married couple but include their parents, children, relatives, and friends." People present who are closely connected with the bridal couple may pronounce the intercessions, using a text which they have prepared or one taken from another source. In keeping with the universal rule the celebrant says the introduction and the concluding prayer.

d) During the ensuing celebration of the Eucharist the couple may take an active part in the presentation of the gifts. Each of three ritual Masses for marriage has its own preface (titles: "The dignity of the marriage bond"; "The great sacrament of marriage"; "Marriage, a sign of God's love"). In Eucharistic Prayers I-III special embolisms are provided.

The nuptial blessing follows (three formularies are provided) the Our Father. Because the prayer is partly epicletic in form, it has also been called a "consecratory prayer,"[13] for which the gesture of hands outstretched over the couple is appropriate. According to Vatican II (*SC* 78) the prayer is for both partners and not just for the bride. The first of the three forms is strongly reminiscent of the old "nuptial blessing," but the other two are new compositions, the third being distinguished by its brevity and concrete objectivity.

e) The couple and all present may receive communion under both kinds. The celebration of the marriage ends with the solemn concluding blessing. Four texts are provided for the blessing, each of which is taken from the 1965 American edition of the *Collectio Rituum.*

Marriage outside Mass

If the ideal—marriage during Mass (see Introduction 8)—is not possible or desirable, the rites already described take place during a liturgy of the word. Vatican II expressed a desire that in this case "the epistle and gospel from the nuptial Mass . . . be read" (*SC* 78); according to no. 40 of the *Rite of Marriage,* the beginning and the liturgy of the word may be organized with some freedom, and there may be three scripture readings, if desired. The exchange of consent and the blessing and exchange of rings follow the homily. The intercessions are concluded by the nuptial blessing and the Lord's Prayer. The marriage rite concludes with one of the Solemn blessings.

ECUMENICAL WEDDINGS

The number of mixed marriages has been constantly increasing during the second half of this century. In many cases these unions are by no means the result of religious indifferentism. In these cases, consequently, the partners in a mixed marriage feel all the more deeply the burden which the marriage law of the one partner's Church places on the conscience of the other; in addition, the law frequently causes disputes with members of the families.

The Motu Proprio *Matrimonia mixta* of Paul VI (March 31, 1970) sought to bring help in this difficulty by allowing the possibility of dispensing from the obligation of canonical form in case of "serious problems."[14] The dispensation is given by the bishop at the petition of the couple (forwarded by the competent pastor); as a result of the dispensation a public, legal exchange of consents in the city clerk's office constitute a valid marriage.

"[This marriage] is begun in God's presence and is a sacrament. It should be kept in mind that a religious form of marriage is more befitting the dignity of the sacrament than a simple civil ceremony. . . . The pastor of the partner from another confession can take part in the church celebration, whether this be held in a Catholic church or, after a dispensation from canonical form, in a non-Catholic church. For many this is a consoling assurance that they remain in the communion of their own Church even though the marriage is being celebrated in the Church of their partner. The authorities of the two Churches will endeavor jointly to prepare the texts for such a celebration." [15]

In consequence, the German episcopal conference and the Council of the Evangelical Church in Germany commissioned the composition of a double ritual, which appeared in 1971 under the title *Gemeinsame kirchliche Trauung. Ordnung der kirchlichen Trauung fur konfessionsverschiedene paare unter Beteiligung der pfarrer beider kirchen* (Joint Church Weddings. Rite of Church Wedding for Couples from Different Confessions, with Participation of the Pastors of Both Churches).[16] This ritual contained the rite for a Catholic wedding in a Catholic Church with participation of the Evangelical pastor and a rite for an Evangelical wedding in an Evangelical Church with participation of the Catholic priest. For the Catholic rite the ritual of 1950 was used with some elements from the Roman model rite of 1969. For the marriage rite in an Evangelical church the most widely used of the nine marriage rituals of the member Churches was taken as a basis, namely, that of the Evangelical Church of the Union and of the United Evangelical-Lutheran Church of Germany. In the United States the Consultation on Common Texts (CCT) has prepared an ecumenical marriage rite. The National Conference of Catholic Bishops approved use of this rite, but still awaits the confirmation of the Apostolic See.

It would certainly be inaccurate and premature to describe such a wedding as "ecumenical," since the latter concept presupposes a common theological understanding of Church weddings, and this unfortunately does not yet exist. In the German Protestant understanding the preceding, obligatory civil ceremony effects the real marriage, while the Church ceremony is simply a subsequent blessing of the already existing marriage; the Catholic Church, on the contrary, sees a marriage as coming to pass only in the Church wedding. In addition, there is, of course, a different view of the sacramentality of marriage.[17] For these reasons the German joint ritual carefully avoids using the term "ecumenical wedding."

Not so another ritual, entitled *Okumenische Trauung* (Ecumenical Wedding) and published by the Joint Evangelical-Catholic Task Force for the Pastoral Care of Couples in Mixed Marriages in German-speaking Switzerland.[18] This was an unofficial document. In justification of the title it was said that the concept is "in itself not yet unambiguous" and that it is used "because it is common throughout German-speaking Switzerland." The introduction ("Basic Considerations on Ecumenical Weddings") shows that the authors are using the concept in a broader sense: "An Evangelical or Catholic wedding ceremony . . . in which the pastor from the other confession takes part, or a ceremony in which only one pastor (Evangelical or Catholic) presides but which is so organized that the participants from both confessions have no trouble in understanding it, fully accepting it, and taking part in it" (11). The ritual presupposes that for wedding conducted by a Protestant pastor "the Catholic party must already have received a dispensation from canonical form" (13). This understanding also underlies the American ecumenical marriage rite.

It is not possible in this context to give a more detailed description and appraisal of these various rituals. B. Kleinheyer conducted this kind of detailed critical study in 1977.[19] According to an announcement by the Liturgical Institute of Trier in August, 1984, a revision both of the Roman *Ordo celebrandi Matrimonium* and (in dependence on this) of the German *Feier der Trauung* is imminent. This will in all likelihood be followed by the long desired revision of the *Gemeinsame Kirchliche Trauung* of 1971. In the revision of the last-named it is desirable that "the alternation of roles be determined more by the internal liturgical structure of the rite than by the desire to have a balanced distribution of parts among the two confessions. Furthermore, it is absolutely necessary that the practice of the community regularly celebrating in a given church should be the basic norm even for a celebration in which a pastor from another confession participates. It is desirable, in addition, that as far as possible there be no need to sacrifice any of the symbolic actions (handclasp of the spouses, rite of the stole and placing of celebrant's hand on the spouses' hands, exchange of rings) in a joint church wedding.[20]

CELEBRATION OF BETROTHALS AND WEDDING ANNIVERSARIES

Betrothals

The betrothal, or engagement, understood as "the expression of the firm intention of two people to enter into a marriage,"[21] has its roots in ancient Eastern, Greek, and Roman matrimonial law and the custom of pledge-betrothal (which had in turn developed out of the practice of bride-barter). In a pledge-betrothal the bridegroom gave the bride's father earnest money as security for the fulfillment of the contract by which the bride was eventually to be surrendered to him. This earnest money later took the form of a ring for the bride, who was now regarded as firmly bound to the bridegroom and obliged, even in the sight of the law, to remain faithful to her betrothed (*sponsolia de futuro*). The actual entrance into marriage (*sponsolia de praesenti*) took place at a later date when the girl's family surrendered her and the bridegroom took her into his home.

Christianity initially made no change in these domestic marriage customs. But in the West, beginning in the eleventh century, the rites of betrothal became part of the rite of marriage *in facie ecclesiae*. Some diocesan rituals of the Middle Ages and the modern period continued, however, to provide for the custom of betrothal or engagement in which the Church played a part, whereas the Roman Ritual of 1614 took no notice of such a practice.[22] The Code of 1917 dealt only with the legal side of betrothal (can. 1017); the Code of 1983 assigns the whole mattter to the area of particular law which is established by the episcopal conferences in the light of custom and civil law (can. 1062. 1). Nothing is said of a liturgical ceremony.

The Roman Book of Blessings that appeared in the autum of 1984 (as part of the Roman Ritual) also has an engagement service.[23] This can be conducted by a parent or other layperson or by a priest or deacon; if a priest or deacon presides, care must be taken that those present do not confuse this service with an actual marriage (196). This concern is probably behind the prohibition against combining the betrothal with a Mass (198). The rite may be adapted to circumstances, provided its structure and main elements are preserved. The ceremony consists of entrance rites, a liturgy of the word, the blessing of the rings or other engagement gifts, and a prayer of blessing with a concluding formula of blessing.

Liturgical Celebration of Wedding Anniversaries

In the early Middle Ages we already find liturgical texts for the thirtieth day after a wedding and for annual anniversaries. Only at the beginning of the Enlightenment period, however, do we find many diocesan rituals providing rites for golden and, later, silver jubilees. The Roman Ritual did not introduce such a rite until 1952.[24]

The *Sacramentary* recommends that on anniversaries, if the rubrics allow, the Mass of Thanksgiving (no. 39 among the Masses and Prayers for Various Needs and Occasions) be celebrated, with special presidential prayers for yearly anniversaries and for the twenty-fifth and fiftieth anniversaries (see "The Anniversaries of Marriage" among the Ritual Masses).

The *Book of Blessings* enriches these anniversary Masses with a special rite of blessing (after the homily). The celebrant may bless the wedding rings of the couple and they may renew the exchange of rings. The blessing follows the Lord's Prayer and is similar to the nuptial blessing of the marriage rite. A solemn blessing is provided for use at the end of Mass.[25]

Chapter Sixteen

Celebrations Peculiar to Religious Communities

Even in the early period of the Church's history many Christians felt called to an especially close following of Christ. This following was expressed particularly in observance of the "evangelical counsels" of consecrated virginity, poverty and obedience. Christ himself had lived "virginal and poor" (cf. Mt. 8:20; Lk. 9:58) and had "redeemed and sanctified men by obedience unto death on the cross" (cf. Phil. 2:8).[1] As a result, "from the God-given seed of the counsels a wonderful and widespreading tree has grown up in the field of the Lord, branching out into various forms of religious life lived in solitude or in community" and "different religious families have come into existence."[2]

The goal of these religious communities is not only personal perfection and sanctification but also service of God's kingdom and thus of the salvation of their fellow human beings.[3] Therefore, "let no one think either that their consecrated way of life alienates religious from other men or makes them useless for human society. . . . For this reason, then, this sacred council gives its praise and support to men and women, brothers and sisters, who in monasteries or in schools and hospitals or in missions adorn the bride of Christ by the humble and steadfast fidelity of their consecrated lives and give generous service of the most varied kinds to all manner of men."[4]

Vatican II looks upon life in the religious orders and congregations and in comparable communities as a sign of and a witness to the new life in Christ and the future resurrection. It is possible to speak of religious communities as having a christological, an ecclesial, and an eschatological aspect of character.[5]

At a relatively early date the acceptance and beginning of religious life found expression in a liturgical rite, as is clear from the Rule of St. Benedict of Nursia (d. 547). From the seventh century on such rites were connected with Mass and in the Middle Ages underwent a luxuriant and to some extent quite dubious development. Vatican II was concerned, therefore, that the rites be revised in the interests of "greater unity, simplicity, and dignity" (*SC* 80).

In response to this directive the Congregation for Divine Worship published a new rite of religious profession on February 2, 1970.[6] A short time later the revised rite for the consecration of virgins was also published (May 31, 1970).[7] I shall briefly describe these and other monastic rites.

THE RITES OF RELIGIOUS PROFESSION

Membership in a religious community is acquired in several stages, each of which is marked by a special rite.

Reception into the Novitiate

As was already the case in Benedict's time, religious life begins with a period of testing, known as the novitiate. The intention is to allow the novices to gain a better knowledge of the religious community and learn from experience whether or not they can meet its requirements. The reception consists of a simple rite that is celebrated apart from Mass and in the presence solely of the religious community (without relatives and friends). It takes the form of a liturgy of the word at which the superior of the community presides. The postulants are questioned and declare their resolve; this is followed by a prayer of the superior (confirmed by the community's "Amen"), a scripture reading and homily, a prayer of intercession, the Our Father, and a collect. Afterwards the community greets the novices.

First ("temporary") Profession

After the successful completion of the novitiate (the duration of which differs in various communities), the candidates consecrate themselves to the special service of God and the Church for a limited time (usually three years) and promise to live in accordance with the evangelical counsels. This first profession is usually made during a Mass for which there is a special formulary (Ritual Masses VI A). The faithful participate if feasible. The ceremony begins after the gospel and has the following parts: calling or request of the candidates; homily; examination of the candidates; prayer for God's grace; profession of vows; presentation of the insignia of religious professsion (habit, Rule); and general intercessions.

Some religious communities recently introduced a kind of preliminary commitment between novitiate and temporary profession, in the form of a promise for which there was a special rite. The ceremony took place during a liturgy of the word or in connection with an hour of the breviary. The candidates declared their readiness to belong to the community for a specified period; and intercessory prayer of the superior was followed by scripture readings and a homily and, finally, by the promise itself. The ceremony ended with intercessions and the Our Father, to which a further prayer for the candidate could be added. —The entire "Rite of a Religious Promise" was suppresed in the *Emendations in the Liturgical Books Following upon the New Code of Canon Law.*

Final Profession

In this rite the candidates bind themselves definitively and permanently to the religious community. The ceremony should take place on a Sunday or feastday so that many of the faithful may take part, since final religious professison is an extraordinary witness to Christ and discipleship and has significance for other Christians as well. In this ceremony, too, the rite begins after the gospel of the Mass, for which two formularies are given (Ritual Masses VI B 1 and 2). The rite is organized as follows: calling or request of the candidates, who ask for permanent membership in the community; homily of the celebrant; examination of the candidates; litany; profession of perpetual vows and deposition of the (signed) written profession on the altar; expression of the newly professed's self-surrender in song; solemn blessing or consecration; presentation of the insignia of profession in the religious community (for example, ring, choir mantle, breviary); statement of admission or sign of peace.

In the ensuing celebration of the Eucharist there is a proper preface, embolisms in the eucharistic prayers, and a solemn blessing at the end of Mass.

Renewal of Vows
In many religious communities vows are renewed at regular intervals according to the statutes of the order or congregation. The renewal may take place during Mass, but without solemnity, especially if it is an annual affair. A special liturgical rite is provided only if the renewal has juridical significance for the community in question. But a more solemn rite is also appropriate for renewals at special jubilees of members of the community. The renewal takes place after the gospel, a homily, and a prayer of the celebrant that God would assist the members of the community; in form it resembles the original profession. The rite ends with intercessions.[8]

CONSECRATION OF VIRGINS
Even in apostolic times there were people in the Church who professed celibacy "for the sake of the kingdom of heaven" (Mt 19:12) and a life of undivided love of God and others. Virginity as understood in the Bible thus means not simply celibacy and sexual continence as such but also an undivided interior availability to God and other human beings. It serves as a visible sign that the reign of God has begun and is approaching its eschatological completion.

Virgins in this sense of the term were to be found not only in religious communities but also in the world. In order, however, to bring out more clearly the fact that this way of life was an answer to a call and that it was accepted as a witness to Christ, the bishop in ancient times would present the woman in question with a bridal veil as a sign of her spousal union with Christ. The Roman-German Pontifical of the tenth century has already expanded this rite by including further elements taken from, among other sources, the rites of marriage. The Pontifical has one rite for virgins in religious communities, another for those outside them. Later on, further elements were introduced from the liturgy of ordination.

In response to the instruction of Vatican II that the rite for the consecration of virgins in the Roman Pontifical should be revised, the Congregation for Divine Worship published a new rite on May 31, 1970.[9] Both in the Introduction and in the liturgical action itself there is an emphasis on the twofold purpose of virginity: to develop a more fervent love of Christ and to serve others more readily and with greater self-sacrifice. There is one great novelty in the new rite: after the lapse of many centuries virgins living in the world may once more be candidates for this consecration. In the case of religious women the consecration can be linked to final profession.

The rite, at which the local Ordinary is the celebrant, begins after the gospel of the Mass and proceeds as follows: calling (sung or spoken) of the candidates, who enter the sanctuary carrying lighted candles; homily of the bishop, for which a (somewhat overly long) model is provided; examination of the candidates as to their resolve; litany; renewal of intention to remain virginal in the following of Christ; prayer of consecration during which the bishop extends his hands over the candidates; presentation of the insignia of consecration (veil, ring, book of the Hours).

After the final prayer of the Mass the newly consecrated virgins stand before the altar and receive a solemn blessing.

The days recommended for this rite are the octave of Easter, solemnities (especially those connected with the incarnation of Christ), Sundays, feasts of Mary or holy virgins or saints who are especially important in the life of the religious community. If possible, the Mass for "Consecration to a Life of Virginity" (Ritual Masses V) should be used. The Mass of the day must be celebrated on solemnities and the Sundays of Advent, Lent, and Eastertide, but with special texts during the eucharistic prayer and with a solemn final blessing.[10]

BLESSING OF AN ABBOT

In his *Rule* Benedict of Nursia describes in detail the difficult task of an abbot, but nowhere does he make any clear reference to a special liturgical rite for the entrance of an abbot into office. The first trace of such a rite is in a prayer in the *Regula Magistri* ("Rule of the Master") (93, 6). In the course of the Middle Ages, as abbots acquired a social status very much like that of bishops, the rite for the induction of an abbot became a solemn affair that increasingly resembled episcopal ordination. On November 9, 1970, the Congregation for Divine Worship published a new rite as a fascicle of the Roman Pontifical: *Ordo benedictionis abbatis et abbatissae*.[11]

In its decree of promulgation the Congregation speaks of the blessing as a traditional liturgical rite, the purpose of which is "to show that the whole religious community is praying for God's grace to come upon the person they have chosen to lead them along the way to perfection." The new rite therefore endeavors to bring out more clearly the role of the abbot as spiritual guide and to avoid as far as possible any similarities with episcopal ordination. The blessing of an abbot is, after all, precisely that: a blessing which is a sacramental, and not a degree of the sacrament of orders.

The blessing is to be given, if at all possible, on a Sunday or feast-day. The celebrant is usually the bishop of the place where the monastery is located, but he may allow another bishop or abbot to be celebrant. The Mass is to be concelebrated by the bishop, abbot-elect, and others, with two religious from the abbey of the future abbot assisting him. The rite begins after the gospel and comprises: the presentation of the abbot-elect and, in the case of abbots having their own territorial jurisdiction, the reading of the papal mandate; homily of the celebrant and examination of the candidate; litany and celebrant's prayer of blessing with hands extended (choice of four prayers); presentation of the Rule of the Order, presentation of the pontifical insignia (ring, staff, and, if need be, the miter); kiss of peace and, at the end of Mass, solemn blessing and *Te Deum*.

If the abbot has jurisdiction over a territory, the *Te Deum* is sung at the end of the prayer after communion, and during it the abbot processes through the church, blessing the faithful; he may then address the faithful briefly and give the final blessing.[12]

BLESSING OF AN ABBESS

This is given by a bishop or abbot and is the same in form as the blessing of an abbot. At the presentation of the insignia of office the Rule of the Order and the ring are given but not the pastoral staff. The presentation of the ring is omitted if the abbess has already received it on the day of her profession or her consecration as a virgin.[13]

Chapter Seventeen

The Liturgy of the Dying and of Funerals

The postconciliar liturgical reform included a revision of the liturgy of death and burial, in response to the call of Vatican II for a reorganized liturgy of the sick and of viaticum and in keeping with its instruction that "the rite of funerals should express more clearly the paschal character of Christian death" (*SC* 81). The new rite for the liturgy of the dying is to be found chiefly in chapters 3-6 of the *Ordo unctionis infirmorum eorumque pastoralis cura* (1972); the new rite of funerals is in the *Ordo exsequiarum* (1969); a new edition of the funeral rite was published in English in 1989 under the title: *Order of Christian Funerals.*[1]

THE LITURGY OF THE DYING

Viaticum

To the eyes of faith the dying of a baptized person is a "passover" or passage through death to everlasting life with God; it is thus the fullest embodiment of the paschal mystery of Christ in the life of the individual Christian. Care of the seriously ill and the dying has always been a pre-eminent pastoral concern of the Church. This concern finds its liturgical expression in the administration of the sacrament that is in the full sense the sacrament of the dying, namely the Eucharist given as viaticum or "provision for the journey." For, according to the Lord himself, the Eucharist is the pledge of resurrection (Jn 6:54). We find the first ecumenical council at Nicaea (325) already insisting on administering "the ultimate and most necessary viaticum" to the dying, in accordance with "the old canonical law."[2]

The ordinary ministers of viaticum are parish priests, hospital chaplains, and the superiors of religious communities; in case of necessity, another priest, a deacon, an acolyte, or an extraordinary minister of the Eucharist may administer the sacramemt. There is a special rite for use by the last two ministers named.[3]

The proper time for viaticum (unlike the anointing of the sick) is when death is close at hand. It may and ought, if possible, be received during the celebration of Mass. In this case, the ritual Mass for Viaticum or the Mass of the Holy Eucharist may be celebrated, if permitted (*Pastoral Care of the Sick* 184).

If the sacrament of reconciliation is to be received, it should be administered before Mass (185). The rites accompanying viaticum are celebrated after the gospel (and homily); viaticum itself is administered in both kinds at the time of communion.

Since viaticum is more often received outside Mass, I shall briefly describe this rite. After the greeting the priest sprinkles the sick person and the room with holy water (optional). Following a brief instruction he administers the sacrament of penance if this is requested; otherwise the penitential rite as at Mass follows. The sacrament of penance or the penitential rite may be followed by the bestowal of the apostolic pardon for the dying. If time and the condition of the sick person allow, a short passage from Scripture is read, and the sick person renews his or her baptismal profession of faith (202-4). After some intercessions (litany) and the Lord's Prayer, the priest shows the sacred host in the usual manner and says: "Jesus Christ is the food for our journey; he calls us to the heavenly table" or "This is the bread of life. Taste and see that the Lord is good," to which all present reply with the usual "Lord, I am not worthy. . . ." Communion may be administered under both kinds, and, at the end, the minister adds: "May Jesus Christ protect you and lead you to eternal life." The rite ends with a prayer and a blessing. "The minister and the others present may then give the sick person the sign of peace" (211).

The new ritual also provides for the not uncommon case in which a person is suddenly in danger of imminent death without having previously been able to receive the sacraments of penance, anointing, and possibly confirmation. This is the "continuous rite of penance, anointing, [confirmation], and viaticum" (232-74).

Commendation of the Dying

After the sacraments have been administered, the prayers (commendation) for the dying (212-22) are also to be said, if need be by relatives or other laypersons. They include "classical" prayers that go back in part to the eighth century: for example, the "paradigm prayer" ("Deliver your servant, O Lord, as you delivered Noah," Abraham, Job, and so on) and the *Proficiscere* ("Go forth, Christian soul. . .").[4] The prayer service known as the "Commendation of the Dying" was included in the Roman Ritual of 1614 and many diocesan rituals, and, in an enriched form, in the *Collectio rituum* of 1950. The new ritual also provides a number of short scriptural prayers and readings (217-18).

THE RITE OF FUNERALS

Historical Observations

The early Christian rite of funerals reflected in large measure the customs of pagan antiquity. In the Roman liturgy this was true especially of the funeral banquets that were celebrated on certain days (the third, seventh, and thirtieth days after death and the annual anniversary) at the grave or in the mausoleum, in order to remember the dead at a family meal. As early as the second century the Christians of Rome were already linking this meal to a celebration of the Eucharist at which the family felt especially close to the dead person because of their common union with Christ.

Christians did not mourn as others do who have no hope (1 Thess 4:13), but were filled with hope of the resurrection. This hope also found expression in their white garments, which contrasted with the black worn by bereaved pagans. Instead of the monotonous lamentations of the professional mourners, Christians sang psalms and hymns; in the East they even sang the Alleluia.[5] John Chrysostom (d. 407) provides an important testimony to the faith in the resurrection with which Christians faced death: "In the past there were demonstrations of grief and cries of sorrow in behalf of the dead; today there are psalms and hymns. . . . In the past, death was the end; now it is no longer so. People sing songs, prayers, and psalms, all as a sign that in their eyes death is a joyful event."[6]

In the Middle Ages Christians accepted expressions of mourning into their liturgy to such an extent that the hope of resurrection was seriously eclipsed. Anxiety and terror at the thought of the *Dies irae* of judgment largely determined the attitude of the faithful and shaped many liturgical texts as well. Intercessions for the dead acquired a predominant place. In the modern period, the introduction of extravagance and pomp led to a class system of funerals.

Vatican II forbade these mistaken practices with its general decree that, with certain exceptions, "no special honors are to be paid in the liturgy to any private person or classes of persons, whether in the ceremonies or by external display" (*SC* 32). It also decreed that "the rite of funerals should express more clearly the paschal character of Christian death and should correspond more closely to the circumstances and traditions of various regions. This applies also to the liturgical color to be used" (*SC* 81).

In fulfillment of this mandate, on August 15, 1969, the Congregation for Divine Worship published an *Ordo exsequiarum* (from Latin *exsequi* = "to go along with" in a funeral procession). The International Committee on English in the Liturgy prepared a version of this which included adaptations for the United States. A revised edition; the *Order of Christian Funerals* (1989), contains additional material for use before the funeral and a great variety of new prayer texts.

The Revised Funeral Liturgy

Because Christians are members of the body of Christ, their death concerns not only their families and relatives but the entire community of the local Church. During the days between death and burial the Church remembers them in the Eucharist and in the form of the vigil or wake. The community renders them the service of fraternal love and honors the body that had become a temple of the Holy Spirit through baptism. It is mindful of the death and resurrection of Christ and looks forward in faith and hope to his return and the resurrection of the dead. A Christian funeral thus becomes a proclamation of the Easter message (Introduction 1-3). The community also intercedes for the deceased and endeavors to console the bereaved by reminding them of Christian hope.

The Vigil or Wake

In many regions, the relatives, friends, and neighbors of the deceased gather on the days between death and burial, in the home or funeral parlor or even the church, to offer special prayers under the leadership of a priest or layperson. The prayers may take the form of a liturgy of the word, for which the rite provides a large selection of readings and intercessory prayers. If the rosary is recited, it is desirable that at least the first of the glorious mysteries (the resurrection) be added to the sorrowful mysteries and that the whole end with a suitable prayer. An appropriate reading from Scripture (for example, from the passion) or a short meditation may precede each mystery.[7]

The Celebration of the Eucharist

The Mass for the deceased is an especially important part of the rite, no matter at what point in the funeral liturgy it is to be celebrated. In many places it is still the practice to celebrate this Mass immediately before the burial and in the presence of the corpse; in other places it is becoming increasingly the custom to have the faithful gather in the Church for the Eucharist after the burial or cremation. In either case, the lighted Easter candle should be set in a place where it is visible to all (if the corpse is present, the Easter candle may be placed at the head of the coffin); it serves to symbolize and strengthen the hope of resurrection in Christ. For the same reason, an Easter song is appropriate at the end of Mass.

The introductory rite in the church can be omitted if the body was received at the Church, using the appropriate rites, sometime before the funeral. Where customary, the offertory procession of the faithful may be kept in funeral Masses.

Plans for the Funeral Rite

Since meaningful local customs are to be retained, the new ritual does not give a single rite for universal use but rather provides for a variety of practices. *The Order of Christian Funerals* provides for the Vigil and related rites and prayers before the Funeral, which may be celebrated in the home or funeral parlor; the funeral liturgy, which may take place during or outside Mass in the Church or annother suitable place; and the Committal at the cemetery or place of cremation, (actual burial). The rites are arranged so that in certain circumstances the committal rite might take place before the funeral liturgy.[8]

I shall not go into these three plans in detail but shall simply describe the rites at the grave and add some general observations.

As soon as the mourners have gathered at the grave, the celebrant says a brief invitation and a scripture verse, he then says a prayer over the place of committal, (which may be a blessing of the grave, if this is needed). While the body is being placed in the grave, or at another suitable moment, the celebrant says, the committal prayer. Intercessions are then offered and all pray the Lord's Prayer. After a final prayer, the minister gives a blessing and an appropriate song may be sung, according to local custom.

All these plans and rites are characterized by adaptation to the situation, friendly participation, and extensive use of sacred scripture, the influence of New Testament theology, and the possibility of incorporating worthwhile local customs. The new liturgy for funerals not only renders the deceased a worthy final service of burial and fraternal intercession; it is also such as to console the bereaved, strengthen those present in their Easter faith, and speak to the unchurched in a humanly attractive way.

As a rule, a priest or deacon conducts the service at the grave. In special circumstances, however, a lay person may conduct it. In the liturgy of burial preferential treatment should not be given to individuals. It is to be hoped that the class system of funerals, which until recently was prevalent in many areas, will be eliminated once and for all, in keeping with the directive of Vatican II (*SC* 32; repeated in the Introduction to the Rite of Funerals 20). The use of holy water and incense should be adapted to local custom and sensibilities; it can even be omitted completely if circumstances require. The faithful should be encouraged to avoid external pomp in funeral ceremony and grave trappings and contribute the money instead to charitable works.[9]

The Funeral of Children

From the fifteenth century of the Roman Ritual had a special rite for the funeral of a baptized child who dies before reaching the age of reason. The rite did not include intercessions for the child because it had not been capable of sinning and was therefore already enjoying the vision of God. For the same reason, Mass was not offered for such a child.

Vatican II ordered that this rite be revised (*SC* 82). According to the new *Order of Christian Funerals*, the same liturgy is to be used as for adults, but with special readings and prayers (including prayers for the parents).[10] The same regulations apply—but with some adaptations—to a child that has died before receiving baptism as its parents intended. The new Sacramentary has two formularies for the funeral Mass of a baptized child, one for an unbaptized child.[11] The liturgical color used is white.

The Funeral Liturgy for the Cremated

Arguments attacking the teaching of the Church often played a role in spreading the practice of cremation in the second half of the nineteenth century. For this reason, the Church prohibited cremation for its members and refused any liturgical cooperation in the practice and even in the deposition of the urn. During Vatican II, a new attitude found expression in an Instruction of the Holy Office (May 8, 1963),[12] which allowed the blessing of the body and the cooperation of a priest in the deposition of the urn, provided that the decision to cremate was not inspired by any hostility to the Church and its teaching. The new liturgy of funerals provides for a liturgical celebration either at the cremation itself or at the deposition of the urn. If a church service takes place at the cremation, the urn is later set in its place in a simple ceremony. The funeral liturgy may also be celebrated after the cremation has taken place.[13]

Chapter Eighteen

The Sacramentals (Blessings)

BASIC OBSERVATIONS

Since the Church is sacramental (incarnational) in its basic structure and since Christ acts in it as the high priest of the new covenant, the Church's entire saving activity is also sacramental, that is, it has a dimension that can be grasped by the senses and another that is suprasensible and divine. The "visible signs of invisible grace" which it accomplishes are not limited, however, to the seven sacraments, which are radical self-actualizations of the Church at the key points of human life. When the twelfth-century theologians of the Western Church began to distinguish the seven sacraments as having a place apart in the cosmos of visible liturgical signs and actions, they called them *sacramenta maiora* (major sacraments) and the remaining signs *sacramenta minora* (minor sacraments).[1] In that same century the second and larger group was also given the name "sacramentals" (Peter Lombard).

Sacramentals, too, are visible liturgical actions, "bearing a kind of resemblance to the sacraments: they signify effects, particularly of a spiritual kind, that are obtained through the Church's intercession" (*SC* 60). Liturgical signs of this kind occur in large numbers during the administration of the sacraments (in baptism, for example, there is the signing of the forehead, the blessing of the water, and so on). Their purpose is to shed light on the mystery and dispose the recipient to a fruitful reception.

The liturgical year is also marked by many sacramentals (for example, the blessings of candles and of palms; processions with candles and palms; the bestowal of ashes; the washing of feet; the veneration of the cross). It is thereby enriched by graphic illustrations and a variety of ways of communicating salvation during the various seasons and on the feasts of the Lord and his saints.

Finally, the life of the parish community and the private life of Christians and their families are likewise marked by blessings. Behind these there is always the prayer of the Church that is united with Christ and therefore efficacious in its action. Theologians have expressed this relationship by saying that the sacramentals draw their efficacy *ex opere operantis (=orantis) ecclesiae,* "from the action of the acting (= praying) church."

Common to all sacramentals, then, is prayer in the name of the church: acknowledging God's dominion over persons and objects, praising his wisdom and goodness, and asking for his varied help. If material things are made the subjects of these blessings, the intention is not somehow to change their nature or fill them with a divine power, but rather to give them a new direction and allow the Creator of all things and the Redeemer of the human race to make himself known through them. They thus become signs of God's presence in our world. The innate capacity of things to serve as symbols, the interpretive word, and the prayer of the Church make it possible for these things not only to represent faith visibly but also the strengthen it. "As actions of believers, they express human self-surrender to God."[2]

This view of the sacramentals, and especially of the blessings of material objects, precludes any magical notions and practices that regard blessed objects as infused with a power "that is unleashed simply by encountering or touching or using the object and thereby placed at the service of human beings. In this approach the blessed object is not seen in its relation to God who bestows the blessing. . . . Furthermore, such a view of sacramentals misinterprets the intercessory prayer of the Church and of individuals and looks upon it as operating without fail and coercing God. Nor is sufficient attention paid to the fact that human beings must be prepared if they are to receive God's blessing, and indeed must prepare themselves ever anew."[3]

If we prescind from the symbolic actions performed in the course of the liturgical year and from processions, the monastic celebrations already described, and the liturgy of death and burial, then "the sacramentals consist principally of blessings."[4] Until recently, the numerous blessings were divided into two groups: *consecrations* and simple *blessings.* Consecrations showed that a person or object was being dedicated to the special service of God or the Church (for example, the consecration of a monk or an abbot or of an altar, bell, or entire church). According to an old tradition, blessings in which anointings with chrism are performed were regarded as especially important and were therefore distinguished by a name: "consecrations." The simple term "blessing" was used for invocations of God that are accompanied by prayer for his help for persons and objects. Modern authors, however, as well as the new Benedictional and the new liturgical books in general, prefer to use the term "blessing" in all cases. The Latin distinction between *benedictiones constitutivae* (consecrations) and *benedictiones invocativae* (simple blessings), which was made in the 1917 Code of Canon Law (can. 1148 n.2), has not been taken over into the new Code of 1983 (see can. 1166-72).

The Latin verb *benedicere* ("to speak well of "; corresponding to the Hebrew *berek* and the Greek *eulogein*) makes it clear that in a blessing attention is not focused solely or primarily on the person or thing being blessed. Rather, a blessing involves praise of God, the real giver of the blessing.

"In utterances in which the term *benedictio* is used, the object may be God to whom the praise . . . of creatures is directed and who in this praise is acknowledged as Lord and source of all blessing. The concept of *benedictio* thus expresses both components of a liturgical event: God's blessing and the praise of God."[5]

These two aspects or components are regularly found in the Jewish *berakah* (plural: *berakoth*); they have also continued to play a vital role in the tradition of the Eastern Churches. By its nature, then, a blessing is both an anamnesis, i.e., a remembrance of the beneficent deeds of God, and an epiclesis, or invocation of his kindness and help for human beings. In the Western Church, however, the doxological and anamnetic element was in the course of time less and less emphasized, to the advantage of the epicletic or petitionary element.[6]

THE POSTCONCILIAR REORGANIZATION

Vatican II was conscious of many shortcomings in the area of the sacramentals; it therefore decreed that "the sacramentals are to be reviewed in the light of the primary criterion that the faithful participate intelligently, actively, and easily; the conditions of our own day must also be considered" (*SC* 79). If needed, new sacramentals might be added. Reserved blessings were to be few in number. The laity were to be allowed to administer some sacramentals (*ibid.*).

Since the new Roman *Book of Blessings* was long delayed, despite the fact that a new edition was felt to be urgently needed,[7] the bishops of the German-speaking world took steps to provide a special Benedictional for their people. Rome gave its permission, but demanded that certain guidelines be followed: a) the blessings were to be structured as communal celebrations; b) the word of God was to be given its due place; and c) in blessings of objects the prayer must also take into account the human beings who would use the object.[8]

With regard to the minister it is determined that baptized and confirmed laypersons, on the basis of the common priesthood and provided they were commissioned thereto, can bestow certain blessings. The decisive criterion in determining the minister is the relation of a particular blessing to the diocese, parish, or family; depending on this relation the bishop or a priest or a parent acts as minister (Introduction 18).

The long-awaited Benedictional appeared as part of the Roman Ritual, under the title *De benedictionibus* (*Book of Blessings*).[9] In the decree of promulgation published by the Congregation for Divine Worship (May 31, 1984) the blessings are described as "liturgical actions that stimulate the faithful to praise of God and dispose them both to receive the principal effects of the sacraments and to sanctify the various situations of life in a proper way." The sizeable volume (540 pages) begins with a "General Introduction" and is divided into five sections, each of which contains numerous introductory observations at the beginning of the section and before the individual blessings.[10]

It is important to note that the new *Book of Blessings* acknowledges the value of local traditions and customs; these are to be taken into account in the vernacular editions of the book (General Introduction 39).[11]

EXORCISMS

Revelation and experience show that in every age human beings are threatened by the power of evil and that their temporal and eternal salvation is thereby imperiled. Jesus himself teaches us to pray: "Deliver us from evil (or: the evil one)." In the past, Christians endeavoring to understand their faith took as their starting point the unquestioned assumption that "evil" referred ultimately to a personal, spiritual being whom the Bible calls "Satan" ("Adversary") or the "devil" (a word derived from the Greek *diabolos,* "slanderer"). Recently there have been attempts, even the in the Catholic Church, to see in the "evil (one)" simply evil as such and to regard "the devil" as simply another word for "sin."[12] Among responses to this view may be mentioned the study "Christian Faith and Belief in Demons," which was sponsored and recommended by the Roman Congregation for the Doctrine of the Faith.[13]

I cannot take up here the difficult questions of the existence, nature, and operation of demonic powers. There is no doubt (the exegetes of every school are in agreement on this) that many statements of the New Testament are conditioned by their times and culture and require careful analysis. Our concern here is with the prayers and actions of the Church that constitute a special form of sacramental in the liturgy of the Church.

The widespread view of early Christians that all pagans were under the domination of Satan led to the use of numerous exorcisms (from Greek *exorkizein,* to adjure; to drive out demons) in the celebration of the catechumenate and, in shorter form, even in the rite of infant baptism.[14] In addition, there were many exorcisms of objects.[15] A distinction was made between imprecatory exorcisms, in which the exorcist, invoking God, issued commands to the powers hostile to God, and deprecatory exorcisms or prayers for deliverance from the evil one.

The Roman Ritual of 1614 contains not only specific exorcisms for objects but also an imprecatory exorcism for those thought to be in the control of the evil powers (possessed).[16] Such an exorcism was not to be celebrated without authorization of the bishop. Because it is susceptible to misinterpretation and misuse,[17] this exorcism has been extremely controversial and requires a radical re-examination. "It is impossible not to wish that the Roman Ritual be withdrawn from circulation as quickly as possible so long as it contains these norms and practices and that it be no longer used until it has been radically revised."[18] The *editio typica* of the Roman Ritual of 1925 also contains a shorter "Exorcism for Use against Satan and the Fallen Angels," published in 1890 under Leo XIII.

The exorcisms still to be found in the new baptismal ritual have nothing in common with the old imprecatory exorcisms. They are simply prayers for deliverance, in which possession is neither mentioned nor suggested. Exorcisms of objects have likewise not been included in the new liturgical books.

The new Code of Canon Law says in canon 1172 that no one may perform exorcisms over the possessed unless he has received special and express permission from the local Ordinary.[19] It seems uncertain whether the prayer, now being composed, "for the Deliverance of a Person Overwhelmed by the Power of the Evil One," will in fact have a place in the Roman Ritual. One thing is certain: there will be no more imprecatory exorcisms.[20] All prayers for deliverance have their model in the final petition of the Our Father: "Deliver us from evil/the evil one."

Chapter Nineteen

The Celebration of the Liturgy of the Hours

Liturgy as the joint action of Christ and his Church also takes the form of the Church's daily worship of prayer: the prayer or liturgy of the hours. For here too Christ is present and active as high priest of the new covenant when the word of God is proclaimed in the readings from scripture and when he unites himself to the praying Church and its members in order to sanctify human beings and glorify the heavenly Father.

The celebration of the liturgy of the hours must be regarded as an important part of the liturgy as a whole. In keeping with the character of the present outline, I shall first describe briefly the origin and historical development of the prayer of the hours; I shall then go into its theological meaning, thereby bringing out its importance; finally I shall discuss its postconciliar reorganization. The entire chapter focuses on the liturgy of the hours in the Roman rite; there is space only for a few references to the prayer of the hours in the Eastern and Reformed Churches, and for some bibliographical suggestions to guide the reader's further study.

ORIGIN AND HISTORICAL DEVELOPMENT

The strongest impulse for the daily prayer of the first Christian community certainly came from Jesus himself. The Gospels often tell us that he was a man of intense prayer and that he taught his disciples to pray (Mt 6:9-13; Lk 11:2-4) and exhorted them "always to pray and not lose heart" (Lk 18:1). He frequently urged watchfulness: "Watch therefore—for you do not know when the master of house shall come, in the evening, or at midnght, or at cockcrow, or in the morning."[1]

The disciples of Jesus faithfully followed the example and exhortations of their Teacher, as the Acts of the Apostles and the apostolic letters often attest.[2] Jesus and his disciples alike lived within the Jewish tradition of prayer and worship, which provided for prayer in the temple and synagogues at specific times during the day. It is not surprising, then, that set hours of prayers emerged very early among Christians. The most important of these times were the morning and evening, but there was also prayer at the third, sixth, and ninth hours, calculated according to the twelve "hours of daylight," which in the Greco-Roman division of the day began at six in the morning.

The prayer of the first community was not solely familial, much less purely individual and private. Numerous passages of scripture make it clear that there was also common prayer, which as such required a certain organization (see, for example, Acts 2:46f; 1 Cor 4).

The same situation is evident at the beginning of the second century in the letter of St. Ignatius, bishop of Antioch and martyr, to the Magnesians (7, 1). About a hundred years later, Tertullian speaks of *orationes legitimae* (prescribed prayers), by which he means times of prayer in morning and evening that are prescribed by law and custom.[3] According to Hippolytus of Rome, deacons and priests are to gather every morning at a place appointed by the bishop and, together with the faithful, celebrate a liturgy of the word that includes teaching and prayer.[4] The *lucernarium* (lamplighting service), a religious rite which accompanied the lighting of lamps at nightfall and took different forms among the Jews, Greeks and Romans, served to some degree as a model for the evening prayer of Christians. The *Apostolic Constitutions* (end of the fourth century) describe a prayer whose structure already resembles that of our present-day Vespers.[5]

The monastic communities exerted a major influence on the further development of the liturgy of the hours. In addition to the hours of prayer already mentioned, these communities made a daily practice of the nocturnal vigil of prayer, which until then had been customary only duing the nights before Easter and a few other feasts.[6] They also introduced Prime, which was to be said immediately before beginning the work of the day, and Compline, which was to come immediately before retiring for the night.

The prayer practices of the Eastern monks reached the West by various channels. The liturgy of the hours received its final form in the West from Benedict of Nursia (d. 547), who adapted to his own purposes the monastic office already in use in Rome.[7] In his organization of it, which increasingly influenced the manner in which the liturgy of the hours was celebrated in nonmonastic settings (cathedrals and titular churches), the office comprised Matins (*hora matutina* = the nocturnal hour), Lauds (earlier called *laudes matutinae,* "morning Lauds"), Prime, Terce, Sext, None, Vespers, and Compline. The office retained this structure until the reoganization of 1870.

The totality of these various times of prayer has been given various names. "Prayer of the hours" and "canonical hours" indicate that the prayer is offered at set times and is intended to sanctify the entire day.

The name "breviary" goes back to the Middle Ages and is derived from the Latin word *breviaria* (plural of *breviarium:* short statement; summary; abridgment). These were short lists in which key words and brief references showed which texts were to be read from the several books used in communal recitation of the office in choir. Only in the eleventh century did the practice arise of copying all the texts into a single book to which the name of the previous lists of text (also called *tabellaria*) was still applied. Such a book was much handier for private recitation, especially while traveling. Others explain the name "breviary" as derived "from the abridgment that resulted when the books used by various participants (psalter, antiphonal, collectary, lectionary) were brought together into one book intended for individual recitation . . . and that affected the length of the readings."[8]

Another name often given to this prayer is "office," the term often being preceded in this context by "divine" or "canonical." The original meaning of *officium* in Christian use was "duty" (and "office" in the sense of duties imposed by a position or charge) and was applied to the liturgy in its entirety. Gradually, however, the name was limited to the prayer of the hours. Renewed awareness that the office, too, is part of the liturgy has given rise recently to the name *liturgia horarum,* "liturgy of the hours."[9]

As the Roman liturgy spread throughout most of the Western countries, so too did the Roman prayer of the hours. In the Middle Ages the tendency to expand the number and length of these hours soon led to great discontent and even caused neglect of the office. At the beginning of the sixteenth century the cry for radical reform became ever louder. The subtantially shorter reform breviary of Cardinal Quiñones (1535), also known as the "Cross Breviary" (from the cardinal's titular church of Santa Croce), was intended for individual recitation and received an enthusiastic welcome; within a few years it had gone through about a hundred printings, but then it was banned and replaced by the uniform breviary of Pius V (1568).[10]

This in turn, however, was the object of numerous authorized and unauthorized attempts at reform.[11] Especially deserving of mention are the attempts made under Pius X that led to, among other things, a reduction in the number of psalms at Matins from 18 (or 12, as the case might be) to 9.[12] Pius XII revived the unimplemented reform plans of Pius X and in 1948 appointed a commission to prepare for a radical reform of the liturgy; the studies produced by this commission appeared in five volumes between 1950 and 1957 and bore their first fruits in the rubrical reforms of 1955 and 1960.[13]

Vatican II paid a gread deal of attention to reform of the breviary and devoted a special chapter to it in its Constitution on the Liturgy (Chapter IV, containing 19 articles: 83-101).[14] The council has some important things to say about the theology and spirituality of the prayer of the hours; it stresses the communal aspect of this prayer and places a strong emphasis on the *veritas temporis*, that is, the idea that the various hours of the office should be recited at the times of day for which they are intended (88). The council also sets down some extremely important guidelines for the concrete carrying out of the reform:

" When the office is revised, these norms are to be observed:
a. By the venerable tradition of the universal Church, lauds as morning prayer and vespers as evening prayer are the two hinges on which the daily office turns; hence they are to be considered as the chief hours and celebrated as such.

b. Compline is to be so composed that it will be a suitable prayer for the end of the day.

c. The hour known as matins, although it should retain the character of nocturnal praise when celebrated in choir, shall be so adapted that it may be recited at any hour of the day; it shall be made up of fewer psalms and longer readings.

d. The hour of prime is to be suppressed.

e. In choir the minor hours of terce, sext, and none are to be observed. But outside choir it will be lawful to choose whichever of the three best suits the hour of the day (89)."

These and other directives set the course for exhaustive work on the new breviary. A Consilium task force with a number of subcommittees worked on the book for seven years; it was finally approved by Paul VI in his Apostolic Constitution *Laudis canticum* (November 1, 1970), and the first volume was published by the Congregation for Divine Worship on Easter, 1971. This volume contains the (previously published: February 2, 1971.) *General Instruction of the Liturgy of the Hours* with its 74 pages and 284 articles. This *Instruction,* like the *General Instruction of the Roman Missal,* is not limited to rubrical matters but provides enlightening comments on the content of the prayer of the hours. Three further volumes of the new office appeared in the following years.

In order to bridge the period until an official German-language breviary should appear, the Liturgical Institutes of Germany, Austria, and Switzerland, following the example of France,[15] published a *Neues Stundenbuch. Ausgewählte Studientexte für ein künftiges Brevier.*[16] The Congregation for Divine Worship gave permission for its optional use in place of the old breviary. In contrast to the Latin edition, volume 2 of this German breviary contained two annual cycles of scripture readings and, correspondingly, two annual cycles of patristic readings which were published as an experiment in sixteen supplementary fascicles. In the United States an interim breviary appeared in 1971 under the title, *Prayer of Christians.* The interior text was prepared by the National Federation of Diocesan Liturgical Commissions and had the support of the Bishops' Committe on the Liturgy. A series of booklets containing a two-year cycle of readings for the Office of Readings was also published to supplement the *Prayer of Christians.*[17]

The English translation of the Liturgy of the Hours was prepared by the International Commission on English in the Liturgy (ICEL) and was published in four volumes between 1975 and 1976 (I. Advent and the Christmas Season; II. Lent and the Easter Season; III. Ordinary Time: Weeks 1-17; IV. Ordinary Time: Weeks 18-34).[18]

UNDERSTANDING THE LITURGY OF THE HOURS

For the sake of clarity I shall schematize in thesis form the rich material available, especially in the liturgical constitution and the *General Instruction of the Liturgy of the Hours* (*GILH*), for an understanding of the office.

The Prayer of the Hours is Prayer in, with, and through Christ

"Prayer directed to God must be linked with Christ, the Lord of all, the one Mediator through whom alone we have access to God. . . . In Christ and in Christ alone human worship of God receives its redemptive value and attains its goal" (*GILH* 6). This union of praying men and women with Christ is ultimately made possible by their membership in his mystical body, for by their baptism and confirmation they share in his priesthood and thus in his continuing prayer.

St. Augustine gives concise expression to this idea with its rich implications and, at the same time, shows us that we are in touch here with an ancient Christian conviction: "It is the one Savior of his Body, the Lord Jesus Christ, who prays for us and in us and who is prayed to by us. He prays for us as our priest, in us as our Head; he is prayed to by us as our God. Recognize therefore our own voice in him and his voice in us!" [19] Thus Christ is present and exercising his saving action in the celebration not only of the Eucharist but of the office as well.

This presence also aids our turning to the Lord in prayer: "He is prayed to by us as our God" (St. Augustine). In the liturgy of the hours our prayer to Christ finds various kinds of expression, as the commentary on the individual hours will show. The liturgy of the hours thus becomes an intense encounter with Christ, so that Hippolytus could sum up the meaning and fruit of this prayer in a short formula: "To be always mindful of Christ" ("Semper Christum in memoria habere").[20]

The Prayer of the Hours is a Prayer of the Church

Because God has given himself to the human race in Christ, those who believe and are redeemed are able to form a community that is molded by the Holy Spirit; this community can be described as the people of God and, in the language of St. Paul, as the mystical body of Christ. Unfortunately, in the minds of many people the word "Church" hardly evokes the spiritual reality thus described, because only too often they think of the Church as simply a historical institution and an external organization. In fact, however, the word "Church," at least in its Greek and Latin form (*ekklesia, ecclesia*), means the community of those who are called and who live in a union with Christ, the depth of which we cannot fully conceptualize.

Since the days of the apostles, the Church thus understood has not only sought to respond to God with thankful praise in the celebration of the Eucharist; in keeping the universal saving will of God it has also never ceased from interceding for all human beings. From the beginning, then, it has been an *ecclesia orans,* a praying Church. In addition, it has taken the prayer of the hours as an essential expression of this intercessory posture. "When the Church unites itself to Jesus Christ in prayer, it acts in accordance with what it already is, and gains the strength to become what it ought to be but is not yet."[21] All who take part in this prayer as members of the Church, whether or not they are commissioned to do so, help in this self-actualization of the Church for the glorification of God and the salvation of the human race. "All who render this service are not only fulfilling a duty of the Church, but also are sharing in the greatest honor of Christ's Bride, for by offering these praises to God they are standing before God's throne in the name of the Church, their Mother."[22] This applies both to the solemn choral office of religious communities and to the simple prayer of the smallest groups and even of individual persons.

The Prayer of the Hours is Dialogical

Like all other liturgical actions, the prayer of the hours is dialogical in character: "Our sanctification is accomplished and worship is offered to God in the liturgy of the hours in such a way that an exchange or dialogue [*commercium seu dialogus*] is set up between God and us" (*GILH* 14). In the person of his Son God comes to human beings and sanctifies them; the praying Church responds with praise, self-surrender, and intercession. This last, being a service to our fellow human beings, also glorifies God.

The Prayer of the Hours is Primarily a Communal Prayer
Both the liturgical constitution and the *General Instruction* lay particular emphasis on the communal character of the prayer of the hours. Since this prayer is not private in nature but is the official prayer of the Church, its celebration in community deserves priority over its recitation by individuals, as is the case indeed with other liturgical actions (see *SC* 26f., 99). The *General Instruction* not only urges communal celebration upon priests and religious who are not obliged by law to the choral office, but also invites lay groups and parish communities, "wherever possible," to "celebrate the liturgy of the hours communally in church" (21). "When the people are invited to the liturgy of the hours and come together in unity of heart and voice, they show forth the Church in its celebration of the mystery of Christ" (22). The family, too, "the domestic sanctuary of the Church," is encouraged not only to pray together but also, as far as is feasible, "to celebrate some parts of the liturgy of the hours" and thus "enter more deeply into the life of the Church" (27).

The Prayer of the Hours Must Be True to the Times of the Day
This is a primary concern of the *General Instruction,* just as it had been of the liturgical constitution (88, 94). "The purpose of the liturgy of the hours is to sanctify the day and the whole range of human activity. Therefore its structure has been revised in such a way as to make each hour once more correspond as nearly as possible to natural time and to take account of the circumstances of life today" (*GILH* 11). It would therefore be absurd to recite Morning Prayer (Lauds) in the afternoon or to recite Evening Prayer (Vespers) in the morning. Only a few years ago it was in fact the custom of many priests to "anticipate" Matins and Lauds on the afternoon of the previous day and to pray Vespers and Compline in the early morning, because they were afraid that their pastoral obligations

would not leave them sufficient time to recite these evening prayers at the proper hours.[23]

Certain Persons and Communities are Obliged to Celebrate the Liturgy of the Hours

In order that this essential prayer may be said in every land and all times, the Church has commissioned those in sacramental orders and in religious communities to celebrate this liturgy of prayer (GILH 17, 28f.). It is fitting that permanent deacons recite at least part of the prayer of the hours, as determined by the episcopal conferences (*GILH* 30).

In regard to the degree of obligation attaching to this service of praise and intercession the *GILH* moderates previous juridical severity to some extent and also makes distinctions among the various hours. In the past, moral theologians held that it was a serious sin to omit, even once, a Little Hour or a section of similar length in the other hours.[24] Vatican II, on the other hand, allowed the substitution of other liturgical functions for the office and gave bishops and higher religious superiors authority, "in particular cases and for a just reason," to dispense wholly or in part from the obligation of the office or to commute it (*SC* 97). The council Fathers expressly abstained from requiring serious reasons for such dispensations.

The *GILH,* for its part, generally uses language that is to be understood as exhorting the Church to the faithful fulfillment of its commission; only when there is question of the principal hours, Lauds and Vespers, does it add that these hours "should not be omitted except for a serious reason" *(31).* This reduction in the degree of obligation seems to be opposed, however, in the *Emendations in the Liturgical Books Following upon the New Code of Canon Law:* here, in Section XIV, the words of *GILH* 29, "should recite the full sequence of hours each day," are changed to "are bound by the obligation of reciting the full sequence of hours each day."

The Prayer of the Hours Requires Personal Devotion for its Proper Celebration

Even when performed by men and women commissioned to represent the Church, this service of praise and intercession is not to be a merely external thing or done thoughtlessly. The liturgical constitution already "earnestly exhorts" all "to attune their minds to their voices when praying" the office (*SC* 90). This harmony is necessary "if this prayer is to be made their own by those taking part and to be a source of devotion, a means of gaining God's manifold grace, a deepening of personal prayer, and an incentive to the work of the apostolate. Seeking Christ, penetrating ever more deeply into his mystery through prayer, they should offer praise and petition to God with the same mind and heart as the divine Redeemer when he prayed" (*GILH* 19).

In order to promote this kind of interior participation the liturgical constitution exhorts those who pray the office "to improve their understanding of the liturgy and of the Bible, especially the psalms" (90). Another helpful practice would be the occasional meditative silences which the liturgical constitution recommends during other liturgical actions (30). The *General Instruction* picks up this recommendation as especially helpful in the prayer of the hours: "In order to receive in our hearts the full sound of the voice of the Holy Spirit and to unite our personal prayer more closely with the will of God and the public voice of the Church, it is permissible, as occasion offers and prudence suggests, to have an interval of silence" (202). "In individual recitation there is even greater freedom to pause in meditation on some text that moves the spirit; the office does not on this account lose its public character" (203).[25]

THE POSTCONCILIAR REFORM OF THE OFFICE

The Psalter

The psalms are still the most important part of the liturgy of the hours. The third chapter of the *General Instruction* has a lengthy section on them (100-35), in which it praises these poems and songs of the old covenant but also shows awareness of the difficulties attending their use in Christian prayer. It therefore offers some suggestions for the proper praying of the psalms.

First of all, since those praying do so in the name of the Church, they can rise above contradictions between the text and their present mood if they bear in mind that the Church as a whole always has reasons for joy or sorrow, as the case may be. St. Paul's exhortation (Rom 12:15) applies to them: "Rejoice with those who rejoice, weep with those who weep" (*GILH* 108).

Furthermore, in praying the psalms the Church must attend to their messianic meaning; indeed it was for the sake of this meaning that the Church took the psalter as its prayerbook (109). Adopting this christological perspective, the Fathers (and the same applies to the liturgy) heard "in the singing of the psalms the voice of Christ crying out to the Father or the Father conversing with the Son; indeed they also recognized in the psalms the voice of the Church, the apostles, and the martyrs. . . . A Christological meaning is by no means confined to the recognized Messianic psalms but is given also to many others. Some of these interpretations are doubtless Christological only in an accommodated sense, but they have the support of the Church's tradition" (*ibid.*).[26]

This is especially true of feastdays, when the antiphons, which are (usually) taken from the psalm, highlight the christological aspect of the latter and give it a tonality appropriate to the day. In the new breviary another help to a christological understanding of the psalms is the caption, which consists of a few words that indicate the literal meaning, and a sentence from the New Testament or the writings of the Fathers that brings out the Christian dimension.

As regards the manner of delivery, it is appropriate that since the psalms were originally songs of praise accompanied by the harp, the music be such as to promote their singing and bring out their full lyrical richness. This musical character should be kept in mind when the psalms are simply recited or even prayed silently (see *GILH* 103).

In contrast to earlier breviaries in which all 150 psalms were prayed in the course of a single week, the new liturgy of the hours follows a four-week cycle. "The psalms are distributed over a four-week cycle in such a way that very few psalms are omitted, while, some traditionally more important, occur more frequently then others; morning prayer and evening prayer as well as night prayer have been assigned psalms appropriate to these hours" (*GILH* 126). Among those omitted are the curse-psalms (58, 83, 109), as well as individual verses of the same kind in other psalms, because they are difficult to harmonize with Christian prayer (*GILH* 131). Details on the distribution of the psalter in relation to the liturgical year are given in *GILH* 132-35.

The Hymns
Special attention is also due to the hymns which introduce each hour and help particularly in bringing out the character of the hour or of the feast being celebrated. The liturgical constitution decreed that "to whatever extent may seem advisable, the hymns are to be restored to their original form and any allusion to mythology or anything that conflicts with Christian piety is to be dropped or changed. Also, as occasion arises, let other selections from the treasury of hymns be incorporated" (*SC* 93). The *General Instruction* goes a step further by giving the episcopal conferences authority to "adapt the Latin hymns to suit the character of their own language and introduce fresh compositions, provided these are in complete harmony with the spirit of the hour, season, or feast" (*GILH* 178).

The Hours in the New Breviary
The revised liturgy of the hours has the following parts: call to prayer (Invitatory); office of readings (*Officium lectionis*); morning prayer (Lauds); daytime prayer or little hours (Terce, Sext, None); evening prayer (Vespers); night prayer (Compline).

The Invitatory is always used before the first hour being celebrated (office of readings or morning prayer). It comprises a versicle, "Lord, open my lips. —And my mouth will proclaim your praise," and Psalm 95. This psalm calls the person praying to sing God's praises, listen to his voice, and seek "the rest of the Lord" (see Heb 3:11; 4:1). Psalm 95 may be replaced by Psalm 100, 67, or 24. The antiphon accompanying the psalm changes according to season and feast. The *General Instruction* recommends the responsorial singing or recitation of the psalm and its antiphon (*GILH* 34).

The office of readings, which replaces the former Matins, is to be a night office of praise of God when celebrated in choir, but it is adapted to be recited at any hour of the day (*GILH* 57), "even during the night hours of the previous day, after evening prayer has been said" (59). It is also meant to be a help in opening up the treasures contained in the Scriptures and the ecclesiastical writers, especially the Fathers of the Church. It comprises an introductory verse, a hymn, three psalms (or parts of psalms), a reading from the Scriptures and another from the ecclesiastical writers (or, as the case may be, a reading having to do with the saint of the day: a hagiographical reading), each of the two readings being preceded by a versicle and followed by a responsory, and, finally, after the second responsory, the prayer of the day.

The new Latin breviary has only a one-year cycle of readings,[27] though the *General Introduction* anticipated that there would be a further volume containing a two-year cycle of readings for optional use (*GILH* 145, 161).

Morning and evening prayer "are the two hinges on which the daily office turns; hence they are to be considered the chief hours and celebrated as such" (*SC* 89a; *GILH* 37). The earlier name for morning prayer, *Laudes matutinae,* shows that it, and not Matins, was the real hours of morning praise. In order to avoid a doubling of morning prayer, the old hour of Prime, which came into existence in monastic circles, has been suppressed (*SC* 89d). Morning prayer comprises an introductory verse, a hymn, psalmody (a morning psalm, and Old Testament canticle, and another psalm of praise), a short reading with a responsory, the Canticle of Zechariah (Lk 1:68-79) with its antiphon, intercessions for the sanctification of the day and its work (this had been the focus of the old hour of Prime), the Lord's Prayer, the prayer of the day, and a blessing. According to ancient tradition, morning prayer also commemorates the resurrection of Christ (see *GILH* 38).

Terce, Sext, and None—the "Little Hours" with which the Christians interrupted their work at the three daily times of Jewish custom—are "linked to a commemoration of the events of the Lord's passion and of the first preaching of the Gospel" (*GILH* 75). According to Hippolytus of Rome, prayer at the third hour (9:00 a.m.) commemorates the beginning of the passion (see Mk 15:25), prayer at the sixth hour commemorates the darkness that fell at the crucifixion (Mt 27:45 par.), and prayer at the ninth hour commemorates the death of Jesus.[28] This commemorative link is especially evident in the daytime hours of Friday.

As for the connection with "the first preaching of the Gospel," Terce recalls the descent of the Holy Spirit on Pentecost (Acts 2:15); Sext, the prayer of Peter at Joppa (Acts 10:9), which was followed by the acceptance of the first Gentiles into the Church; and None,

Peter's cure of the cripple when he and John "were going up to the temple at the hour of prayer, the ninth hour" (Acts 3:1ff.).

Outside choir only one of the three daytime hours needs to be recited; the one that corresponds most closely to the time of day is to be chosen. The structure of the hour is the same in all three: introductory verse, hymn (reflecting the time of day), psalmody (three psalms and their antiphons), short reading with responsory, and concluding prayer.

Evening prayer or Vespers (from Latin *Vesper* or *Vespera* = evening) is one of the cornerstones or, in the words of the liturgical constitution, one of the hinges, of the entire liturgy of the hours. Its purpose is to thank God for the day now coming to an end but also for the saving acts of Christ on Holy Thursday evening and his death on the cross on Good Friday afternoon (*GILH* 39). It is especially recommended that Vespers be recited with the parish community or other groups, in particular on Sundays and feastdays (*SC* 100; *GILH* 21, 40).

Evening prayer has the same structure as morning prayer: introductory verse, hymn, psalmody (two psalms or longish sections of psalms and a canticle from the letters of the apostles or the Apocalypse). At public Vespers the short reading may be replaced by a longer one and followed by a homily. Instead of the usual responsory an appropriate song may be sung. Next comes the Magnificat with its antiphon, intercessions,[29] Our Father, and, at public Vespers, the concluding rite familiar from Mass. In his Apostolic Constitution *Laudis Canticum* Paul VI describes the inclusion of the Our Father at the end of morning and evening prayer as effecting a return to the early Christian practice of praying the Our Father three times daily (the third time being at Mass).[30]

Night prayer or Compline (from Latin *completorium* = achievement, completion) is the prayer recited before retiring for the night and may therefore be recited even after midnight (*GILH* 84). After the introductory verse an examination of conscience is recommended: "In a celebration in common this takes place in silence or as part of a penitential rite based on the formularies in the Roman Missal" (86). A hymn follows, with an alternative text provided for each day. The psalmody consists of two psalms on Saturdays and Wednesdays and of one on other days; they are chosen as expressions of trust in God (*GILH* 88), although the psalm for Friday (Ps 88, a lament in time of affliction) fits less well into this category. Those wishing to pray Compline from memory may always use the psalms for Saturday or Sunday (*ibid.).*

After the short reading and responsory the Canticle of Simeon (Lk 2:29-32) is recited with an antiphon that is always the same; the concluding prayer and blessing follow. This hour ends with one of the Marian antiphons; except for the *Regina caeli* during the Easter season, there is no longer any obligation to say a particular antiphon during a particular season. The episcopal conferences have authority to approve other antiphons (*GILH* 92).

All in all, as Pius Parsch wrote, Compline is "in its construction, a masterpiece created by St. Benedict and may be described as the ideal night prayer."[31]

OTHER FORMS OF THE LITURGY OF THE HOURS WITHIN THE ROMAN RITE AND OUTSIDE IT

In addition to the Roman liturgy of the hours which I have been describing there are special monastic forms of this prayer; they have not remained unaffected by the reforms emerging from Vatican II. These monastic forms of the office "present a pluralistic picture at the present time."[32] The law governing the Benedictine Congregations and monasteries is now the *Thesaurus Liturgiae Horarum Monasticae* of 1977; the Cistercians follow the *Liturgia Horarum Ordinis Cisterciensis,* which appeared in 1978. All of these are influenced to a greater or lesser extent by the Roman liturgy of the hours.[33]

I. H. Dalmis has given us a short survey of the liturgy of the hours in the Eastern Churches.[34] In volume III of *Leitourgia* H. Goltzen provides an extensive study of the prayer of the hours in the Reformed Churches.[35] H. Reifenberg has a concise essay on the liturgy of the hours in the Anglican Church;[36] there is a more detailed study, in French, from the pen of D. Webb.[37]

Chapter Twenty

Liturgical Time (The Liturgical Year)

MEANING AND STRUCTURE OF THE LITURGICAL YEAR

The liturgical year is the commemorative celebration, over the course of a year, of the saving deeds which God has accomplished in Jesus Christ. A recent Church document described it thus: "By means of the yearly cycle the Church celebrates the whole mystery of Christ, from his incarnation until the day of Pentecost and the expectation of his coming again."[1]

The term "liturgical year" should not be interpreted as a kind of ecclesiastical competitor of the "civil year." Even the "secular time" of a calendar year is a gift of the creator which Christians must approve, live through, and try to shape. In addition, however, God the Savior is present in historical time in manifold ways; in Christ he has made himself part of it in an especially clear and intimate manner, so that all time is God's time and a time of salvation, for his offer of salvation extends to all periods and human beings and is therefore universal.

It is the Church's task to proclaim and make accessible to all the human beings of all time the saving work whose foundations Christ laid. The Church does this in the proclamation of God's word, the celebration of the sacraments, and the numerous pastoral services which are intended to smooth the way for faith, hope, and love and promote growth in grace.

The Christian celebration of feasts as thankful commemorations of the saving deeds of Jesus Christ is something that must be constantly repeated if the Church is to be faithful to its role of proclaiming salvation and making it present or actualizing it. In order to avoid arbitrariness, it seemed appropriate to take the cosmically determined cycle of a year's time and assign a fixed place in it to the individual commemorative celebrations, thus ensuring a cyclical repetition of these. The scheduling of the commemorations is suggested in part by the Scriptures and determined in part by conventions established in the course of history. The scheduling is not so binding, however, as to exclude corrections and reforms that may seem necessary.

From what has been said in the course of this book it is evident that the celebration of the liturgical year is not exclusively a looking back to salvation already accomplished. Rather, those who already believe and have been redeemed in baptism must endeavor to consolidate their always endangered salvation and to realize, in and through celebration of the liturgy, that they share a responsibility to bear witness to all human beings concerning the salvation intended for them and to help them attain to this salvation. Under both of these aspects the celebrations of the liturgical year look to the future as well as to the past. They have an eschatological dimension, inasmuch as they look forward to the return of the Lord with its completion of all aspects of salvation and also seek to prepare the way for this return.

The liturgical year is thus the sum total of all the liturgical feasts that have found their appointed place in the annual cycle. But it must also be kept in mind that wherever the liturgy is celebrated, Jesus Christ, the high priest of the new covenant, unites himself with the celebrating congregation in common action that has for its purpose the salvation of the faithful and the glorification of the heavenly Father (see *SC* 7). Christian faith is thus concretely actualized in the liturgical year, which becomes a comprehensive self-portrayal of the Church and the basis and sustenance of a Christian life.

The Paschal Mystery as Heart and Center of the Liturgical Year

The heart and center of the liturgical year is the passion and resurrection of Christ. Vatican II often speaks of this central saving deed as "the paschal mystery."[2] "Mystery" in the liturgical sense means the unfathomable saving act which God in Christ has accomplished for the human race. The Greek and Latin adjective "paschal" goes back to the Hebrew word *pesach*. This referred originally to the act of the avenging angel in passing by and sparing the homes of the Israelites who were living as slaves in Egypt. Later on, the scope of *pesach* was broadened to include the salutary passage through the Sea of Reeds and the perilous wilderness into the Promised Land. *Pesach* was subsequently the name given to the commemorative meal celebrated on the 14th of Nissan at which those saving events were remembered; on this occasion the *pesach*-lamb was eaten as a sacrificial victim.

The first Christian community found it easy to connect the ancient saving act of God with the redemptive Christ-event, especially since the crucifixion of Christ occurred on the day of preparation for the Jewish Passover feast (see Jn 19:14 par.). The crucifixion took place at the time when the Passover lambs were being slaughtered in the temple. Paul is therefore evidently distinguishing between a Jewish and a Christian Passover when he writes: "For Christ, *our* paschal lamb has been sacrificed" (1 Cor 5:7; see Jn 19:36; 1 Pet 1:19; Rev 5:6, 9). By passing through the self-emptying of suffering and death to his resurrection and glorification, Christ has led God's people of the new covenant to a redemptive communion of grace and life with God the Father (see Col 1:12 and elsewhere).

If we were to translate the doubly foreign phrase "paschal mystery" into plainer English, the best version might be "Easter mystery of salvation." In substituting this, however, we ought to think not only of the resurrection on Easter morning but also include the entire "sacred triduum of the crucified, buried, and risen Lord"[3] which runs from Holy Thursday evening to Easter Sunday inclusive. Or, since the other stages in the theandric life of Jesus from the incarnation to the ascension and sending of the Spirit also have meaning for salvation and are part of the paschal mystery in its extended sense, we might translate "paschal mystery" simply as "the Christ-event."

As an historical event, this heart and center of the liturgical year belongs to the past, but its innermost essence, which is the self-sacrifice of Christ and his obedience unto death, lives on and is operative in the glorified God-man. Because his saving will is universal, he, the high priest of the new covenant, enables the human beings of every age to participate in it as often as they gather for celebrations of the liturgy.[4]

This radiation of the central mystery out into the remainder of the liturgical year must not be misunderstood, however, as a kind of automatic bestowal of grace. Rather it is God's offer of his grace to free human beings, a collaborative encounter to which men and women must bring their faith in its full form. As understood by the New Testament, this means confession of belief but also trust and readiness to sacrifice oneself in order to do the Father's will. The faith required is the faith that is characterized by love and operative in love (see Gal 5:6). Whenever human beings open themselves in this way to God's offer of salvation, the paschal mystery is operative in a fruitful way.

Types and Classifications of Christian Feasts

Feasts are celebrations of events calling for remembrance and thanksgiving.[5] This description holds both for periodically recurring feasts based on the cycles of nature and for significant occurrences in the life of individuals, familes ("rites of passage"), communities, and more inclusive societies. In the Jewish festal calendar[6] the commemoration of the saving events in which Jahweh the covenant God had come to redeem his people Israel was increasingly superimposed on feasts that originally celebrated the cycles of nature. The primitive community in Jerusalem had, of course, a very detailed knowledge of these feasts celebrated by their fellow Jews, but once they had experienced the Christ-event it was quite natural for them to make his paschal mystery the central object of Christian festivity and celebration, especially since its recurring celebration could be traced back to Christ's own command (1 Cor 11:24; Lk 22:19).

I shall have to show in greater detail later on how in the beginning the paschal mystery was celebrated on Sunday as a weekly Passover, and how, by the beginning of the second century at the latest, the feast of Easter was added as an annual Passover. This first development was followed in historical sequence by a series of other commemorations of the Lord. The stages in the life of his Mother were also added, as were the commemorations of the martyrs and saints.

Since the Middle Ages there has existed a special group of feasts known as "feasts of ideas," which have for their object various truths and aspects of Christian teaching and devotion, as well as various titles of the Lord, his Mother, or a saint. These are also described as "devotion-feasts" or as dogmatic, thematic, and static feasts (in contrast to the "dynamic" feasts concerned with the redemptive acts of Christ). Among these are, for example, the feasts of the Trinity, Corpus Christi, the Sacred Heart of Jesus, and Christ the King, the feasts of the Precious Blood, the Holy Name of Jesus, and the Holy Family, as well as many feasts of Mary. It is easy to multiply such feasts without limit; many of them are needless repetitions. The highest authorities in the Church have opposed the many attempts made to reintroduce such feasts. The official Roman commentary on the new *General Norms for the Liturgical Year and the Calendar* regards it as one goal of the reform to reduce the number of these feasts or leave them for particular calendars.[7]

Even greater reserve is called for when the object of a celebration would be an event in the history of the Church, the importance of which is to be highlighted by means of a feast.

Since Christian feasts reach their climax in the celebration of the liturgy, and especially of the Eucharist, it follows that they do not simply commemorate the paschal mystery of Christ but also render it present and operative so that individuals and communities can enter into it. In this way the lives of these individuals and communities are increasingly stamped by configuration to Christ (see Rom 8:29). Inasmuch as the liturgical year thus has an inner dynamism for those who celebrate it, it may appropriately be compared not so much with a circle (cycle) as with a screw's thread that leads ever upward or with a spiral in which each turn leads one a bit higher "toward Christ."[8]

As liturgical feasts became more numerous and diversified in the course of the Church's history, there was a growing danger that the basic structure of the liturgical year might be obscured and that essentials might be lost from sight beneath peripheral special devotions. Many prescriptions of liturgical law were an effort to counter this tendency. In recent centuries, however, this very effort led to a complicated classification of feasts in which there were no less than six different ranks, with further subdivisions.

Thus from the time of Pius V, who, as instructed by the Council of Trent, published a new Breviary (1568) and Missal (1570), there were the ranks of double of the first class, double of the second class, major double, double, semi-double, and simple.[9] Many doubles had octaves, and these in turn were divided, according to the rank of the feast, into privileged, ordinary, and simple. Privileged octaves were further subdivided into octaves of the first, second, and third class. For example, Easter as the supreme feast was a double of the first class with a privileged octave of the first class, while Christmas had only a privileged octave of the third class.

Beginning with Benedict XIV attempts were made to simplify matters, as, for example, in 1955 and again in 1960 (*Codex rubricarum* of July 25). Only in 1969, however, did the reform commissioned by Vatican II (*SC* 107) bring about a substantial simplification that finds expression in the *General Norms for the Liturgical Year and the Calendar.* Feasts are here listed in the order of their importance as solemnities, feasts, and memorials; these last may be either obligatory or optional. Only the two solemnities of Easter and Christmas have octaves.

An Outline of the Structure of the Liturgical Year

Nowadays we regard the first Sunday of Advent as the beginning of the liturgical year. This was not always the case. In fact, Christian countries in the Middle Ages were not in agreement even on the beginning of the civil year. The Julian Calendar of Gaius Julius Caesar (introduced in 45 B.C.) had moved the beginning of the Roman year forward from March 1, the ancient date, to January 1. But although this calendar became universal in the West, there was for a long time a variety of dates for the beginning of the year: March 1 in the Frankish Empire until into the eighth century and in Venice until 1797; Easter, especially in France until the fifteenth century; Christmas, chiefly in Scandinavia and Germany (until the sixteenth century); March 25 (feast of the Annunciation as the day of the incarnation of Christ), especially in Italy but also in the ecclesiastical province of Trier; September 1, in the Byzantine Empire from the seventh century on and in the regions under its influence.[10]

Not only was there a descrepancy in locating the beginning of the civil year; in addition, the very concept of a liturgical year took a long time to appear. As the custom grew, however, of placing the texts for the first Sunday of Advent at the beginning of the liturgical books (tenth-eleventh century on), the idea gradually took hold that the annual cycle of liturgical feasts began with the first Sunday of Advent.

It is quite possible to multiply feasts until the human capacity for celebrating them is overtaxed. This truth has been forgotten at times, but as the local Churches and the religious Orders sought the introduction of new feasts, the Roman authorities not infrequently tried to apply the brakes. On the positive side, the multiplicity of liturgical feasts and memorials makes "it easier to bring out various aspects and accents of the one mystery of Christ and thus allow the faithful to encounter the manysided Christ" (A. A. Häussling) and the unlimited fullness of salvation. Even here, of course, care must be taken not to lose sight of the woods for the trees, that is, not to let partial aspects obscure the vision of the whole.

I have already said several times that the paschal mystery of Christ is the heart and center of the liturgical year. In the form of the weekly Passover that was celebrated every Sunday even in apostolic times, this mystery already permeated the entire annual cycle. An anual Passover soon followed and gradually developed into the Easter cycle of feasts with its period of preparation and festive continuation. According to the *General Norms* the Easter cycle begins on Ash Wednesday and ends on Pentecost Sunday, having lasted for thirteen and a half weeks. The annual commemoration of the birth of Christ likewise developed into a cycle of feasts with its period of preparation and its festive continuation (first Sunday of Advent to the Sunday after the Epiphany, that is, the feast of Christ's baptism). These two cycles of feasts are the supporting pillars of the liturgical year. The intervening thirty-three (or thirty-four) weeks, which "are devoted to the mystery of Christ in all its aspects," are known as "Ordinary Time" (*GNLYC* 43). This period begins on the Monday after the feast of the baptism of Jesus and ends on the Saturday before the first Sunday of Advent. The two cycles of feasts, Ordinary Time, and the other solemnities and feasts concerned with the mystery of redemption are also known as the *Temporal* (from *tempus* = time) or "Proper of Seasons" (*GNLYC* 50). This "must be kept intact and retain its rightful preeminence over particular celebrations" (*ibid.*).

The calendar of saints' feasts is known as the *Sanctoral* (from *sancti* = the saints). In this connection a distinction will be made further on between the General Roman Calendar and the "particular calendars" (national or regional calendars; diocesan calendars; calendars of religious orders), which must be approved by Rome.

SUNDAY AS THE ORIGINAL CELEBRATION OF THE PASCHAL MYSTERY

Biblical Foundation and Historical Development

In the New Testament the first day of the Jewish week—our Sunday—is already regarded as very important. It is the day of the Lord's resurrection, as all the evangelists agree; it is also the preferred day of his appearances (Mt 28:9; Lk 24:13ff., 36; Jn 20:19ff.) and the day on which the exalted Lord bestows the promised gift of the Spirit (Jn 20:22; Acts 2:1ff.). In the minds of the disciples it is "the day which the Lord has made" (Ps 118:24). As a result, it becomes the preferred day for gatherings of the community (Acts 20:7). It is on this day each week that the Christians of Corinth and Galatia are to contribute to a fund in aid of the Christians of Jerusalem (1 Cor 16: 1f.).

It is true that at this time there was no uniform ritual for the Sunday celebrations of the community,[11] but it is nonetheless noteworthy that Paul regards the celebration of the Lord's Supper as the focus of the assembly (1 Cor 11:17-34; see Acts 20:7). This centrality is confirmed by the earliest extrabiblical testimonies that have come down to us: the *Didache*,[12] Pliny the Younger's letter to Trajan,[13] and Justin Martyr.[14] According to Ignatius of Antioch the celebration of Sunday served precisely to distinguish Christians from those who still followed the old order and celebrated the sabbath (Saturday). Christians for their part are called to a new hope and "live in observance of the Lord's Day on which our life dawned through him and his death."[15]

Since Sunday was an ordinary workday at that time, Christians had to gather in the late evening or, after the banning of evening meetings by Emperor Trajan, in the early morning. This meant a great deal of inconvenience and demanded a high degree of self-sacrifice. It is not surprising, therefore, that exhortations to regular attendance were needed as early as the Letter to the Hebrews (10:25). The exhortations become still sharper in the *Didascalia of the Apostles* (mid-third century).[16] Shortly after 300 the Council of Elvira in Spain decreed that "if anyone living in the city fails to attend church on three Sundays, he is to be excommunicated for a short time, so that it will be clear he has been taken to task."[17]

The significance of Sunday in early Christianity is reflected in the names given to the day. The earliest name, "first day," did not refer simply to the beginning of the week but was also an allusion to the first day of the week of creation, the day on which light was created. Sunday marks the beginning of the "new creation" (see 2 Cor 5:17). A name that subsequently became widely used is already to be found in the Apocalypse (1:10): "the Lord's day." (The Latin form *dies dominica* is not only still used in the official language of the Church, but has also supplied the name for Sunday in the Romance languages.) The name "eighth day" signifies that after the seven days of the week of creation with its sabbath or day of rest the resurrection introduces the new creation that will reach its climax in the everlasting sabbath rest of fulfillment.

Tertullian and many Greek writers speak of "Resurrection day," a name that lives on in many Slavic languages. After initial hesitations Christians accepted the name "Sunday" (*dies solis*), which comes from the Greco-Roman week in which the days were named after the planets. They gave the term a new meaning, however, as St. Jerome indicates: "When pagans speak of it [the Lord's Day] as the day of the sun, we gladly agree, for on this day the light of the world, the sun of justice, arose and salvation is hidden in the shelter of his wings."[18]

The law promulgated by Emperor Constantine on March 3, 331, played an important part in the subsequent development of Sunday. It decreed that "the venerable day of the sun" was to be a day of rest for all judges, city folk, and business people. The rural populace was permitted to go about its work, lest they fail to take advantage of the hours of good weather.[19] A few weeks later the Emperor issued a further law saying that the manumission of slaves—a desirable action—did not fall under the law of Sunday rest.[20]

These edicts greatly facilitated the celebration of the Sunday liturgy. Gradually, however, "Sunday rest" became more and more the focus of the sanctification of Sunday and indeed its essential criterion. "Servile work" (*opera servilia*) on Sunday was regarded as a criminal offense, the strict Old Testament sabbath law being taken as the model here.[21] The Scholastics of the High Middle Ages once again made a clear distinction between Sunday and the Jewish sabbath and based the prohibition of servile work on the fact that it facilitated attendance of divine worship.[22] But in the following centuries the prohibition against work on Sunday was still too much to the fore and obscured the primarily christological significance of the day. In the late Middle Ages and modern times a stronger emphasis was placed on the obligation of Sunday Mass, and every violation of it was declared to be a serious sin.[23]

Sunday Today

In view of the widespread attacks on the Christian celebration of Sunday Vatican II made an effort to bring out the Christian significance of the day as the celebration of the paschal mystery. "On this day Christ's faithful must gather together so that, by hearing the word of God and taking part in the Eucharist, they may call to mind the passion, the resurrection, and the glorification of the Lord Jesus and may thank God" (*SC* 106). It is also to be a day of joy and freedom from work. Since it is "the foundation and core of the whole liturgical year," no other feast may take precedence over it, unless it be truly of the greatest importance (*ibid.*).

With this last directive in mind, the *General Norms for the Liturgical Year and the Calendar* (1969) decreed that only a solemnity or feast of the Lord may replace the Sunday liturgy and that on the Sundays of Advent, Lent, and the Easter season the liturgy of the day never gives way even to a solemnity or feast of the Lord (*GNLYC* 5). The danger has arisen in recent years that these regulations in defense of the Sunday liturgy may be frustrated by the tendency to give many Sundays a special theme and purpose alien to Sunday and by the fashion for "motif Masses."

The Sunday liturgy has been enriched by the introduction of eight prefaces for Sundays, which proclaim aspects of the paschal mystery.

The new code of Canon Law (1983) has, fortunately, taken over almost verbatim (can. 1246 n.1) the christological view of Sunday that is expressed in article 106 of the liturgical constitution. The Code also emphasizes the duty of attendance at Mass, but speaks of Sunday rest in a more nuanced way than did the old Code of 1917: the faithful "are also to abstain from those labors and business concerns which impede the worship to be rendered to God, the joy which is proper to the Lord's Day, or the proper relaxation of mind and body" (can. 1247). If the lack of a priest or some other cause makes the Sunday Eucharist impossible, participation in a liturgy of the word (see above, Chapter XI,) or some special time of prayer (private or familial) is highly recommended (can. 1248).

A regrettable break with Christian tradition is to be seen in recommendation R 2015 of the International Organization for Standardization (ISO), a subsidiary organization of the United Nations. This urged that beginning on January 1, 1976, Sunday be regarded as the last day of the week in the economic and technical sphere and thus in the whole public realm. It is to be feared that in the consciousness of the general public Sunday will be regarded even more as the final day of weekend leisure and lose still more of its religious value and that it will cease even more completely to be thought of as the day of Christ's resurrection which inaugurates a new age of the world.[24]

The Austrian Institute of Standards (*ONORM*) accepted the recommendation of the ISO but showed greater respect for Christian tradition when it added its own explanation: "Monday . . . will be regarded as the first day of the week solely for purposes of counting. The recommendation leaves untouched the Christian and Jewish numbering of Sunday as the first day of the week" (*ONORM A* 2740). In keeping with this approach, the Austrian calendar that serves as a normative model has used simple typographical devices to take the new regulation into account while not giving the impression of altering the traditional order.[25]

The danger to the Christian Sunday becomes especially clear in the frightening decline in attendance at the Sunday liturgy.

THE LITURGICAL CHARACTER OF THE WEEKDAYS

Unlike Sunday, it was only gradually and in nonuniform manner that the weekdays acquired a religious and liturgical character of their own. The emphasis on Sunday as resurrection day, on which redemption was completed, left the other days of the week initially disregarded. An early exception was Wednesday and Friday. Thus the *Didache* or *Teaching of the Twelve Apostles* contains the instruction that Christians are to fast, not on Mondays and Saturdays like the "hypocrites" (see Mt 1:16), but on Wednesdays and Fridays.[26] A reason for this fast (a practice known to Tertullian[27]) is given in the Syriac *Didascalia of the Apostles,* which dates from the first half of the third century. Here the Wednesday fast is connected with the betrayal of Judas, and the Friday fast with the death of Jesus on the cross.[28] Similarly the Saturday fast that began to be observed in Rome at a very early date was connected with the mourning of the apostles over the death of Jesus.[29]

It is clear from all this that the events of Holy Week played an important role in developing the liturgical character of the weekdays. Finally, in the Middle Ages, Thursday too was given an unmistakable Christian accent as memorial of the institution of the Eucharist at the Last Supper of Jesus and of the passion that began with the agony in the garden.[30] "Just as Sunday represented a weekly Easter, so the whole week appeared to be a faint copy of Holy Week. The great facts of the story of redemption were to be set before the eyes of the people, not only once a year, but in the couse of the weekly cycle as well."[31]

This characterization of most weekdays by giving them a reference to the events of salvation history was obscured for a time in the Middle Ages, beginning with Alcuin (d. 804), by the introduction of a series of votive Masses that followed a different inspiration. Especially prominent were veneration of the Blessed Trinity and the saints and a concern for perfection and the salvation of the soul. The attempt to link the incarnation, too, and the earthly life of Jesus with the days of the week had no lasting success.[32] Finally, due to the post-Tridentine unification and codification of the liturgy, especially as this took shape in the 1570 Missal of Pius V, the following set of votive Masses was developed and, with a few later additions, remained in effect for exactly four hundred years, until the 1970 Missal of Paul VI.

MONDAY Trinity
TUESDAY Angels (including Guardian Angels)
WEDNESDAY Apostles; from 1920 on, also St. Joseph and Sts. Peter and Paul
THURSDAY Holy Spirit; from 1604 on, also the Eucharist; from 1935 on, also the high priesthood of Christ
FRIDAY Cross; from 1604 on, also the passion of Christ
SATURDAY Mary

The new Missal of 1970 has sixteen votive Masses, among them all the ones just listed. The new Missal makes no effort, however, to associate them with particular days of the week. The individual pastor is left more or less free to decide whether or not he will continue to follow the essentially medieval practice of celebrating particular Masses on specified days of the week.[33]

EASTER AND ITS CYCLE OF FEASTS

The New Testament writings make no clear statement about the celebration of an annual commemoration of the paschal mystery, although a few texts suggest that the first Christian community gave the Jewish Passover a Christian meaning (see 1 Cor 5:7f.). Clear evidence has come down to us only beginning in the second century. In this context the "Easter controversy" of the second half of that century is especially important.

At that time, the Christians of Asia Minor and Syria celebrated the annual commemoration not on a specific day of the week but always on the fourteenth day of Nissan, that is, the first day of the full moon in the first month of spring (they were therefore known as "Quartodecimans"). The rest of Christendom, however, opted for the Sunday after the fourteenth of Nissan. The Council of Nicaea in 325 settled this domestic ecclesiastical dispute over the date of Easter by decreeing that Easter was always to be celebrated on the Sunday after the first full moon of Spring. By adopting this lunar regulation of the date (that is, making it dependent on the phases of the moon) the Fathers allowed that the date of Easter might vary by as much as five weeks (March 22 to April 25) in the solar calendar, thus turning a large part of the liturgical year into a set of movable feasts. Modern efforts to fix the date of Easter (within limits) have thus far been unsuccessful.[34]

The Latin Church took over the Greek name for Easter, *Pascha* (derived from Hebrew *pesach*), and passed it on to many modern languages.[35]

The Easter Triduum

The Church originally celebrated its Easter feast on a single day or, as the case might be, during the night between Holy Saturday and Easter Sunday.[36] From the fourth century on, however, "the most sacred triduum of the crucified, buried, and risen Lord"[37] developed as a result of a more historically oriented approach and a more representational type of presentation. Since that time the liturgical celebrations during these three days from Holy Thursday evening to Easter Sunday have been the real annual celebration of the paschal mystery.[38] The celebrations were in need of reform, and Pius XII ordered a radical revision (1951 and 1955) that anticipated in important ways the postconciliar reform found in the Roman Missal of 1970.

Holy Thursday

According to the thinking of Judaism and Western antiquity a day begins on the evening before. Thus the evening of Holy Thursday is already part of the three sacred days. There is also substantive justification for this view, since at the Last Supper Jesus sacramentally anticipated his sacrificial death on the cross and since the passion really began with the agony in the Garden.

The Mass commemorating the Last Supper is the only Mass allowed on this day (apart from the "Chrism Mass" celebrated in the morning by the bishop). Connected with it is the (optional) custom of the washing of feet (also known as the *mandatum* = "commandment") after the gospel. After the final prayer the presanctified gifts for the Good Friday liturgy are carried to the tabernacle at an altar in a separate chapel; the main altar is then stripped. Adoration of the reserved sacrament is to be retained as far as is practicable. The description of the repository as a "holy sepulcher" must be regarded as a not too happy one.[39] Mention may also be made of the longstanding custom of ringing the bells at the recitation or singing of the Gloria and then not ringing them again until the Gloria of the Easter Vigil. In many places wooden clappers are used in place of the altar bells.

Good Friday

In the first Christian centuries there was no special Good Friday liturgy to commemorate the death of Jesus; instead there was a strict mourning fast on this day as on Holy Saturday. Toward the middle of the fourth century the Christians of Jerusalem venerated the holy cross in the morning and, in the afternoon, celebrated a liturgy of the word, at which the passion narrative was read. Augustine also speaks of a liturgy of the word in North Africa. In addition, local Churches that possessed a relic of the cross (for example, Rome) developed celebrations for the veneration of the cross.

As the Roman liturgy spread through the Franko-Gallic world and took fresh shape in the Roman-German Pontifical the simple communion service of Good Friday gradually developed into the "Mass of the Presanctified" (a Mass without a eucharistic prayer). The reception of communion fell off in the Middle Ages until finally the priest alone received on Good Friday. It was in this form that the Tridentine Missal of 1570 accepted the Good Friday liturgy and kept it for almost four hundred years. The revised rite published in 1955 kept the traditional three parts—liturgy of the word, veneration of the cross, and communion service—but dropped a number of rites and rubrics, among them the prohibition against reception of communion by the faithful. The Roman Missal of 1970 took over the essentials of the revised rite.

As a rule, the rite begins around 3:00 p.m., and the liturgical color is red. The celebrant's prostration before the bare altar and the opening prayer of the day are followed by a liturgy of the word with two readings, the reading of the passion according to John, a homily, and the solemn intercessions. The intercessions have now been made more concise, and the prayers for the Jews and those earlier called "heretics" and "schismatics" have been more carefully formulated.

At the veneration of the cross there are now two ways of displaying (elevating) the cross (unveiling in three stages or a procession with the unveiled cross). While clergy and faithful venerate the cross (with a genuflection or bow and a kiss), the choir and (or) the congregation sing venerable texts about the cross, in which the joy of Easter can already be felt.

The simple communion service with the presanctified gifts is introduced by the Our Father with its embolism and acclamation. The concluding prayer and blessing bring out the unity of the paschal mystery of Christ's death and resurrection.

The Easter Vigil
As the day of Christ's repose in the tomb and of sorrowful fasting Holy Saturday has from time immemorial had no liturgy of its own. When darkness fell the community began "the mother of vigils" (Augustine), the holy nocturnal watch in memory of the Lord's death and resurrection. "The great antitheses of night and dawn, fasting and eucharistic meal, mourning and festal joy provided an awesome experience of the contrast between death and life, decease and resurrection, Satan and Kyrios, old eon and new eon."[40] Nowadays many still find it in incomprehensible that the Church could go so far astray from the fourteenth century on as to move the Easter Vigil liturgy forward to early Saturday morning.[41]

The reformed Easter Vigil liturgy comprises a service of light, a liturgy of the word, and a celebration of baptism and the Eucharist.

The service of light begins with the blessing of the new fire, the preparation and lighting of the Easter candle, which represents the "light of Christ," and the entrance with the candle into the dark church, which is then illumined by the tapers which the faithful light from the Easter candle. The Easter song of praise follows; this is also known as the *Exsultet* from the first word of the Latin text.[42] Because this song is a climactic moment in the Easter proclamation, the question may legitimately be asked whether it should not come after the gospel.

The liturgy of the word contains nine biblical readings, the last two from the New Testament (Rom 6:3-11 and a pericope from the Synoptic resurrection narratives, the selection depending on the year in the cycle). For pastoral reasons the number of Old Testament readings may be reduced to two. Each is followed by a responsorial psalm and a prayer. After the seventh prayer the priest intones the Gloria (the bells are rung). After the first New Testament reading the Alleluia is sung for the first time since the beginning of Lent.

Celebration of baptism: Since Easter has from time immemorial been a preferred date for baptism, it is desirable even in our time that baptism be conferred during the Vigil, if possible as the climax of the catechumenate. After the presentation of the candidates and the litany of the saints, the baptismal water is blessed with an epicletic prayer (during which the Easter candle may be dipped into the water). After the renunciation of Satan and the profession of faith baptism is administered; confirmation is likewise administered by the baptizing priest (if no bishop is present) if the newly baptized are adults or of school age. If baptism is not administered, there is simply a blessing of the water (holy water). Since the restoration of the Easter Vigil in 1951, the rite of baptism or the blessing, if baptism is not administered, is followed by a renewal of baptismal promises, after which the celebrant sprinkles the congregation with the newly blessed water. Next come the general intercessions.

In the ensuing celebration of the Eucharist special emphasis is laid on the paschal mystery in the preface, the text inserted into Eucharistic Prayer I (with a special prayer for the newly baptized), the tripartite concluding blessing, and the twofold Alleluia of the dismissal; the same is true, of course, of the presidential prayers.[43]

There was originally no further celebration of the Eucharist during the postdawn hours of Easter Sunday. The custom of saying additional Masses began toward the end of the sixth century when the real Mass of the Resurrection was already concluded before midnight. In recent centuries popular piety created a further substitute for the lost Easter Vigil in the form of a "celebration of the resurrection" or sunrise service early on Easter Sunday morning (before the "early Mass"). There have been countless efforts to revive this practice, which would surely detract from the restored Easter Vigil. Also questionable are efforts to introduce elements from the Vigil into the principal Mass on Easter, for the sake of those who did not attend the Vigil. Not everything that people might find pleasing can be approved by the (liturgically) wise. —Easter Vespers form a meaningful conclusion to the Easter triduum.

The Easter Seasons or Pentekoste

The experience that moments of profound festivity require a certain amount of time to run their course is already reflected in the Jewish festal calendar. Here, fifty days (=seven weeks) after the feast of *pesach* or Passover (which was also the feast of unleavened bread) a "feast of weeks" (*Shavuot*) was celebrated in thanksgiving for the wheat harvest and in commemoration of the conclusion of the covenant at Mt. Sinai. In a parallel development, the Christian Church of the second century was already celebrating an Easter season of fifty days (Greek: *pentekoste*) which, according to Acts 2:1ff. reached its climax in the visible outpouring of the promised Spirit, who is the real fruit of the paschal mystery. The *General Norms for the Liturgical Year and the Calendar* is thus in accord with earliest tradition when it says: "The fifty days from Easter Sunday are celebrated in joyful exultation as one feast day, or better as one 'great Sunday'" (22). This continuing festal joy finds symbolic expression in the prescription that during these fifty days the Easter Candle, a symbol of the risen Lord, is to stand near the altar where the community can see it, and is to be lit during the liturgy.

The first week after Easter is the Easter octave. The liturgy of this octave reflects not only the paschal mystery but also a concern for the newly baptized: in the daily celebrations of the Eucharist these are led more deeply into the mysteries contained in the sacraments of initiation which they have received ("mystagogical catecheses"[44]). This week used to be known as "White Week" from the white garments worn by the newly baptized, and the Sunday after Easter was known as *Dominica in albis* ("Sunday in white garments") or "White Sunday." The European custom of celebrating solemn first communion on this Sunday dates from the eighteenth century.[45]

In the seventh century there arose the custom of the *pascha annotinum* (from *annus* = year), or anniversary commemoration of the reception of baptism. Since the actual anniversary day not infrequently came before the current Easter due to the shifting date of this feast, the Monday after White Sunday was finally chosen as the memorial day.

In order to bring out the unity of the Easter season more clearly, its Sundays are henceforth to be known as "Sundays of Easter," with White Sunday as the second of them and Pentecost as the eighth. The liturgical texts for these Sundays bear the strong impress of the paschal mystery. The traditional "Good Shepherd Sunday" has been moved from the third to the fourth, in order not to interrupt the series of gospels dealing with the appearances of the risen Lord. Five Easter prefaces are now available for use during the season; only the first of them is for use on specific days (Easter Vigil, Easter Sunday, the octave of Easter).

The fourth century saw Christians celebrating the feast of Christ's Ascension on the fortieth day after Easter, a date chosen chiefly on the basis of Acts 1:3. "The weekdays after the Ascension until the Saturday before Pentecost inclusive are a preparation for the coming of the Spirit" (*GNLYC* 26). The novena for Pentecost, which grew out of popular devotion, is thus given a place in the official liturgy.

The fiftieth day after Easter, that is, Pentecost (from Greek *Pentekoste* = fiftieth), is the crowning close of the Easter season. Over the centuries, however, it was increasingly seen as an independent feast of the sending of the Spirit. It was given an octave of its own and, in many parts of the Church, a second and third festal day after the Sunday; in the end people spoke of a "Pentecost cycle of feasts." The postconciliar liturgical reformers endeavored to link Pentecost more closely with Easter once again. The Pentecost octave was therefore abolished, and in many of the liturgical texts (see the opening prayer and the preface) a stronger connection was established with Easter. The sequence *Veni, Sancte Spirit* ("Come, Holy Spirit") continues to be obligatory on Pentecost.

A striking exception to the joyous spirit of the Easter season is the Rogation Days with their processions. There used to be an "older Rogation procession" (*litania maior*) on April 25 and "more recent Rogation processions" (*litania minores*) on the three days before the feast of the Ascension. The former is of purely Roman origin and must have replaced a pagan procession through the fields (an *ambarvale*) in honor of the god Robigus or goddess Robigo ("rust"). There is no connection with the feast of St. Mark, which is celebrated on the same day. The revised calendar has suppressed this procession because it was based on a local Roman Custom.[46]

The *litaniae minores* owed their origin to Bishop Mamertus of Vienne, who when his city was struck with serious disasters in 469 decreed intercessory processions and fasting on the three days before the Ascension. Rome adopted these processions (but not the fast) under Leo III (d. 816). The *General Norms* has kept them and interpreted them in the same context as the Ember Days: "On rogation and ember days the practice of the Church is to offer prayers to the Lord for the needs of all people, especially for the productivity of the earth and for human labor, and to give him public thanks" (*GNLYC* 45). The time and plan of the celebration are left to the episcopal conferences. The Bishops of the United States have left it to the local bishop to determine days of prayer for the fruits of the earth, prayer for human rights and equality, prayer for world justice and peace, and for the penitential observance outside Lent. "In this way no arbitrary rule is imposed until it becomes evident that a pattern of such supplication is emerging from practice."[47]

The Easter Penitential Period (Lent)

The historical development started with the two-day fast of mourning on Good Friday and Holy Saturday; in the third century this was extended to the whole of Holy Week (even if not in the form of a complete fast). The Council of Nicaea in 325 was already familiar with a fast of forty days before the Easter triduum; in Rome this began on the sixth Sunday before Easter, that is, on the first Sunday of Lent. Then, since there was no fasting on Sundays and since it was desired to have a full forty days of fasting, the fast was begun four days prior to that Sunday and the forty days included Good Friday and Holy Saturday.

In the sixth century special importance was attached, for various reasons, to the three Sundays before Ash Wednesday and they were given the names (using round numbers) Quinquagesima (fiftieth day, counting back from Easter), Sexagesima (sixtieth), and Septuagesima (seventieth); these two and a half weeks before Ash Wednesday were called "Pre-Lent." Fasting was not required, but the violet color of the vestments used and the omission of the Gloria, Alleluia, and Te Deum gave the period a penitential character.[48]

In the early Church, fasting meant that people contented themselves with a single meal (in the evening) and abstained from meat and wine, and, later on, milk products (milk, butter, cheese) and eggs. The weeks of Lent derived their liturgical and ascetical character primarily from the institutions of the catechumenate (preparation for baptism) and from the Church's practices in the area of public penance. In the Middle Ages the passion motif (passion mysticism) became highly important throughout Lent.

The new organization of Lent is set down in the *General Norms* 27-31, which takes into account the directives of the liturgical constitution (109-10). The "Pre-Lent" has been suppressed, and greater emphasis is placed on the motifs that determine the content of the Lenten liturgy (baptism, conversion, penance) and on the orientation to the paschal mystery.

Ash Wednesday is still the entranceway into Lent. The rite of sprinkling with ashes was originally practiced only on public sinners; once the institution of public penance disappeared, the rite was extended to all of the faithful (tenth century). The regulation that the ashes are to be secured by burning the palm branches of the previous year dates from the twelfth century. The blessing of the ashes takes place after the gospel. The ensuing distribution of the ashes is accompanied by the words of Gen. 3:19 or (in the revised liturgy) Mk. 1:15b. The rite of the ashes can also be celebrated as a liturgy of the word outside Mass.

The six Sundays of Lent each have a special character that is impressed on them chiefly by the gospel of the Mass. The first, second, and sixth have prefaces of their own which relate to the gospel of the day; the same is true of the other Sundays of Lent only in Year A of the cycle. The fourth Sunday (Laetare Sunday) is set apart by the optional use of rose-colored Mass vestments (since the sixteenth century); the color befits not only the joyous character of the Mass but also the papal custom of blessing a "golden rose" on that day. This latter practice in turn probably goes back to a Roman feast of Spring, at which people brought flowers with them to Mass (tenth century). From the High Middle Ages on, the fifth Sunday of Lent ("Judica" Sunday, from the first word of the entrance antiphon) was also called "Passion Sunday" and distinguished by the veiling (until the Easter Vigil) of crucifixes and images, the use of the Preface of the Holy Cross, and the partial omission of the *Gloria Patri*. The new calendar has dropped the name "Passion Sunday", "in order to preserve the inherent unity of the entire Easter penitential season."[49]

The passion motif does come to the fore, however, in the name given to the sixth Sunday of Lent, which is now called "Passion Sunday (Palm Sunday)." Here the commemoration of Christ's entrance into Jerusalem is linked to the commemoration of his passion. Egeria, a fifth-century pilgrim, tells us that a procession with palms was being celebrated in Jerusalem around 400.[50] In the West such a procession first made its appearance toward the end of the eighth century and soon acquired elements of popular theatricality and playacting. The new Missal provides several forms for the "Commemoration of the Lord's Entrance into Jerusalem."[51] The Mass receives its stamp from the reading of the passion as told by each of the Synoptic Gospels (according to the year of the cycle).

The following days of Holy Week also derive their character entirely from the passion motif, although it is now permitted to drop the reading of the passion according to Mark (Tuesday) and Luke (Wednesday), since these are read in the three-year cycle for Palm Sunday.

Each of the other weekdays in the Easter penitential period has its own Mass formulary. The biblical readings are the same each year, with the first reading and the gospel forming a thematic unity. Beginning with Monday of the fourth week of Lent the gospel is a more or less continuous reading of John.

The evening of Holy Thursday is already part of the Easter triduum. On the morning of that day the bishop celebrates the Chrism Mass at which he blesses the holy oils that will be needed for the administration of baptism and confirmation during the Easter Vigil. For practical reasons this Mass may be celebrated instead on one of the earlier days of Holy Week, and in the form of a concelebration of the bishop and his priests, in the cathedral if possible. In keeping with the Latin tradition, the blessing of the oils follows this sequence: the oil of the sick before the final doxology of the eucharistic prayer, the oil of catechumens and the chrism after the concluding prayer of the Mass. For pastoral reasons the entire rite of blessing may be celebrated at the end of the liturgy of the word.[52]

At the Chrism Mass the priests present renew their pledge "to priestly service."[53]

CHRISTMAS AND ITS CYCLE OF FEASTS

Origin and Liturgy of Christmas

The calendar of F. D. Filocalus for 354, which lists the anniversaries of the deaths of the bishops of Rome (*depositio espiscoporum*) and the Roman martyrs (*depositio martyrum*) show that Christmas was already being celebrated on December 25 at Rome in the year 336.[54] The introduction of this feast of Christ in the city of Rome is explained, according to the apologetical and history-of-religions hypothesis, as a response of the Roman community to the pagan civic feast of the *Natale Solis invicti* (birthday of the unconquered sun-god), which Emperor Aurelian introduced in 274 in honor of the Syrian sun-god of Emesa and which he hoped would unify and strengthen his vast empire. According to the hypothesis, in order to immunize the Christians of Rome against this popular feast, the Roman Church introduced the feast of the birth of Christ as "Sun of justice" (Mal 3:20) and "Light of the world" (Jn 8:12).[55]

The calculation-hypothesis starts with the fact that as early as the third century Christian theologians were endeavoring to calculate the date of Christ's birth, which is not mentioned in the gospels. The widespread Christ-as-sun symbolism caused them to pay special attention to the equinoxes and solstices. One opinion was that John the Baptist had been born at the summer solstice. In keeping with Lk 1:26, therefore, Christ must have been born at the winter solstice.[56]

A comparison and evaluation of the arguments for the two hypotheses suggests that these efforts to calculate the date of Christ's birth, which strike us today as aprioristic and therefore mistaken, may have created a background and readiness for placing the feast on December 25, but that Aurelian's feast of the sun may have given the decisive impulse.

There was little centralization in the Church of that time, and yet the new feast had spread with astonishing rapidity throughout the

West and in many of the Eastern Churches before the fourth century was over. The reason is probably that the struggle against the Arian heresy focused greater attention on the person, and not simply on the work of the God-man and that a feast of Christ's birth would give a suitable liturgical expression to the profession of faith drawn up at Nicaea, which condemned this heresy (325). In most of the Eastern liturgies "the form of the feast was based on that of the Epiphany. As far as content was concerned, only the mystery of the birth was, in principle, separated out from the complex of ideas proper to the feast of the Manifestation. In fact, however, duplications of ideas arose here and there, even in the Roman liturgy."[57]

The old Roman custom of allowing every priest to celebrate three Masses on Christmas is retained in the new Roman Missal. The custom goes back to a special development that took place in the papal liturgy from the fourth to the sixth century and was subsequently imitated elsewhere as the Roman liturgical books spread throughout Europe.[58] The Missal still has Masses for midnight (*Missa in nocte*), at dawn (*Missa in aurora*), and during the day (*Missa in die*). Apart from the fact that in the new Roman Missal these Masses have an Old Testament reading, the formularies are essentially the same as in the past.

The Mass of the Vigil (celebrated before or after evening prayer or First Vespers) is also part of the festive Christmas liturgy. In the reformed liturgy such Masses on the eve of feasts are no longer vigils in the sense of nocturnal watches which are penitential and preparatory in character. "Except for the Easter Vigil, which is celebrated in the night before Easter Sunday, the name 'vigil Mass' is henceforth given to a Mass which can be celebrated as a festive Mass during the evening hours before or after First Vespers of a solemnity."[59] The new Christmas Vigil Mass has therefore only a few texts from the old Vigil Mass that used to be celebrated in violet vestments during the morning hours of December 24.

Many texts of the Christmas Masses make it clear that Christmas too is celebrated as a feast of our redemption, even though the focus of attention is on the incarnation (i.e., the conception and birth). For there are repeated references to the paschal mystery. In view of this content which Christmas and Easter have in common, the suggestion has been made that "we would do better to divide the year into an 'Easter celebration of redemption' and a 'Christmas celebration of redemption.'"[60]

Since the life of the Virgin Mary is inseparably linked to the mystery of the incarnation of Christ, her name is expressly mentioned in the insertion for Eucharistic Prayer I. More importantly, the octave day of Christmas is especially dedicated to commemoration of her.

The Christmas Season

Christmas is the only feast other than Easter to have an octave. The octave day coincides with the beginning of the civil year, which Gaius Julius Caesar moved from March 1 to January 1 in 45 B.C. Because pagans made the beginning of the new year a feast in honor of Janus, the god who faces in two directions, and celebrated it with boisterous joy and supertitious practices, the Church tried in many places to immunize the faithful by instituting penitential liturgies.[61] At Rome, the Anniversary (*Natale*) of the Mother of God was at times celebrated on this day, while in Spain and Gaul it became the feast of the Circumcision in accordance with Lk. 2:21. Only in the thirteenth/fourteenth century do we find also this feast at Rome where, until the liturgical reform of 1960 (*Codex rubricarum*), it was celebrated under the title of "Circumcision of the Lord and Octave of Christmas" and was oriented toward Mary and Christmas. The *General Norms* returned to the original Roman practice ("Solemnity of the Mother of God") and linked the commemoration of the naming of Jesus with the solemnity.

There are good reasons for regretting that the liturgy pays so little attention to the beginning of the new year, which almost all peoples celebrate with festivities. The "Masses for Various Public Occasions" do indeed have, in first place, a "Mass for the Beginning of the Civil Year," but it is preceded by a surprising rubric: "This Mass may not be celebrated on January 1, the solemnity of Mary the Mother of God." The obstacle here was evidently the general rule that votive Masses may not be celebrated on solemnities. A new regulation seems appropriate and needed.[62]

Even the earliest liturgical calendars already have a series of saints' feasts in direct proximity to Christmas. The Middle Ages looked upon these saints as an honor guard for the Christ-child and called them "Companions of Christ" (*Comites Christi*). In the Roman liturgy the group includes Stephen the First Martyr on December 26, John the Apostle and Martyr on the 27th, and the Holy Innocents of Bethlehem, slain by King Herod, on the 28th. The optional memorial of Thomas Becket, the martyr bishop of Canterbury, is celebrated on the 29th, and that of Pope Sylvester I on the 31st.

The feast of the Holy Family is celebrated on the Sunday within the octave. If, however, Christmas and its octave day fall on a Sunday, this feast is celebrated on December 30. This is a quite recent devotion-feast that spread around the world in the nineteenth century, with Canada as the main source of influence, and was promoted especially by Leo XIII (from 1920 on it was celebrated on the Sunday after Epiphany).

Solemnity of the Manifestation of the Lord

A very prominent feast of the Christmas season is the solemnity of the Manifestation of the Lord, or his Epiphany (after its Greek name), which is celebrated on January 6. The first traces of it are to be seen in Alexandria at the beginning of the third century. There is much to be said for the view that the choice of date was influenced by a pagan feast (birthday of the god Aion). In the Eastern Church this was the original feast of Christ's birth, to which at an early date were joined the commemoration of his baptism (so that the feast became an important occasion for baptisms) and the commemoration of his first miracle, at Cana.[63]

In the second half of the fourth century, as I noted above in connection with Christmas, the East and the West took over each other's birthday feasts of Jesus, with the result that the East celebrated the birth of Jesus and the coming of the wise men on December 25 and the commemoration of the baptism of Jesus and of his first miracle on January 6 (on which day it also administered baptism), while the West celebrated the coming of the wise men, the baptism of Jesus, and his first miracle on January 6 as clear signs of his self-manifestation. In the classification of feasts the Western Church made Epiphany the second most important feast of the liturgical year (a double of the first class, with a privileged octave of the second class). Today it is a solemnity without an octave; in countries where Epiphany is not a holyday of obligation, it is celebrated on the Sunday between January 2 and January 8 (*GNLYC* 37).

In the popular religion of the Middle Ages the "three holy kings" acquired such prominence that Epiphany was usually called "the feast of the Three Kings" and regarded almost as a saints' feast.

Many pious (and often not so pious) customs came to be associated with Epiphany (as with Christmas).

Since 1960 the commemoration of the baptism of Jesus, which had always been an important part of the feast of Epiphany, has been made an independent feast (celebrated initially on the octave day of Epiphany). The purpose was to call attention to the salvational significance of the baptism as a revelation of the divine sonship of Jesus, to the anointing of Jesus with the Holy Spirit for his messianic office at the beginning of his public ministry, and to the sanctification of the water as a sign of the forgiveness of sins in baptism. The *General Norms* assign the feast to the Sunday after Epiphany. If Epiphany itself is transferred to Sunday, January 7 or 8, the feast of the baptism of Jesus is celebrated on the following Monday.[64]

This feast marks the end of the Christmas cycle. The following week already counts as the first of the 33 or 34 weeks of Ordinary Time.

Advent as a Season of Preparation for Christmas

Like the Easter cycle, the Christmas cycle is preceded by a time of preparation which we call Advent (from Latin *adventus* = coming, i.e., of the Lord Jesus Christ). The first traces of this season are found in Gaul and Spain, where, because of close ties with Byzantium, Epiphany on January 6 was the earliest feast of the birth of Christ and, for a time, an important date for baptism. It was thought that this day for baptism, no less than the Easter Vigil, should be preceded by forty days of preparation. Since these countries followed the Eastern custom of not fasting on Saturday, the season of preparation occupied eight weeks and began on the day after November 11 (*Quadragesima sancti Martini*, "St. Martin's Lent").[65]

The Sacramentary of Gregory I, which was used in the city of Rome, had four Sunday Masses and three Ember Day Masses that bore the mark of Advent. The focus of attention was not on the final coming of Christ but on his coming in the flesh.

In Gaul the emphasis was quite different, for here, under the influence of Irish missionaries, eschatological expectation was accented, and Advent became a penitential season (violet vestments for Mass, omission of the Gloria, Alleluia, and Te Deum). Some of these penitential elements entered the Roman liturgy in the twelfth century, but by retaining the joyous Alleluia Rome showed that it did not regard Advent as properly a time of penance. The Roman solution to the length of the Advent season (four Sundays of Advent) won out only gradually; Milan still has six Sundays of Advent.

The *General Norms* interpret Advent as a time both of preparation for Christmas and of expectation of the Lord's final coming. From both points of view "Advent is thus a period for devout and joyous expectation" (*GNLYC* 39). Specifically, the *General Norms* distinguish two phases in Advent: the period from December 17 to December 24 is ordered more directly to Christmas, while the preceding days look more to the eschatological return of Christ.[66] Both aspects, however, are made explicit in both stages, and there is no question of a penitential season. The Code of Canon Law of 1917 had already dropped any obligatory Advent fast.

As for the beginning of Advent, the first Sunday of this season is the one "falling on or closest to 30 November" (*GNLYC* 40), that is, the Sunday between November 27 and December 3.

The liturgy of Mass for the four Sundays takes its tone and character essentially from the gospel, the themes of which are picked up, to a greater or lesser extent, by the other texts. The preferred readings are from Isaiah and the pericopes relating to John the Baptist: both Isaiah and John are regarded as "preachers of the advent," that is, the coming. The seasonal liturgy has been enriched by two Advent prefaces; in contrast, the liturgy of Pius V had no special Advent preface. The third Sunday of Advent (Gaudete Sunday) is distinguished by its joyful spirit and the optional use of rose-colored vestments, both of which make it a kind of parallel to the fourth Sunday of Lent (Laetare Sunday).

The Mass liturgy of the weekdays of Advent has likewise been enriched. Before the reform these days had no proper Mass formularies; now each day of the second phase of Advent has its own Proper. For the weekdays of the first phase there is a recurring weekly series; thus each Monday, for example, has the same Proper, except for the prayer of the day and the biblical readings, both of which change from day to day. The weekdays from December 17 to December 23 are further enriched by having the famous O-antiphons from the liturgy of the hours (the antiphons for the Magnificat) serve as Alleluia verses. Each of these antiphons contains a laudatory invocation of the awaited Messiah and a prayer for his coming as Savior.[67]

Advent customs are to some extent connected with the expectation of Christmas (Advent wreath, Advent calendar) and to some extent with prechristian custom practiced at the winter solstice.[68]

Two Christmas Feasts Outside the Cycle

There are two feastdays that occur outside the Christmas season but are connected thematically with the mystery of the incarnation. In the past they were considered to be Marian feasts but because of the events they celebrate they are to be regarded rather as feasts of Christ; for this reason they have received new names in the reformed liturgy.

The feast of the Presentation of the Lord (February 2), which occurs forty days after Christmas, is based on incidents, narrated in Lk. 2:22-39, in which the focus of attention is on Jesus rather than on his Mother. In the East this feast was reported long ago by Egeria the pilgrim (about 400) and is known as the "Feast of the Meeting" (Greek: *hypapante*, that is, the meeting of Jesus with the temple and, in the temple, with Simeon and Anna). It is attested at Rome as early as the fifth century; there it was soon linked to a procession of lights through the city; this procession supposedly replaced an ancient pagan procession of expiation that was celebrated every five years at the beginning of February in the form of a procession around the bounds of the city (an *amburbale*). The purple vestments prescribed for this Mass as late as 1960 recall the original penitential character of the feast (in Rome). The candles carried in the procession are a reminder that Simeon called Christ "a light for revelation to the Gentiles." The blessing of the candles was added before the year 1000 in Gaul.

The blessing of the candles and the carrying of them in procession led to the name "Candlemas," which gave little indication of the real theme of the feast. The name "Purification of Mary," officially given to the feast until 1969, must be regarded as misleading. The blessing of the candles before Mass may take either of two forms.[69]

The Solemnity of the Annunciation of the Lord (March 25), nine months before the birth of Christ, has for its subject the incarnation of the Son of God in the womb of Mary. It is first attested in the sixth century in the East, in the seventh in the West (if we prescind from some anticipations of it).[70] Since March 25 falls within the period of penitential preparation for Easter, it is not possible to give expression to the true spirit of this feast. If it falls in Holy Week or (rarely) in Easter week, it is celebrated on the Monday after the Easter octave. The *General Norms* prefer the name "Annunciation of the Lord" (which was also used in some calendars in the past), but the name "Annunciation of Mary" is fully justifiable in the light of Lk. 1:26-38. This feast is very important by reason of its theme, but we should not forget that the incarnation has at all times been already commemorated by the feast of Christmas.

ORDINARY TIME

The New Division of the Year

The periods of time between the two annual cycles of feasts are now known as Ordinary Time (Latin: *tempus per annum* = "time in the yearly cycle"). Together with the festal cycles these periods form the *temporale* or temporal cycle. Ordinary Time comprises 33 or 34 weeks which fall into two consecutively numbered sections: the first runs from the Monday after the feast of the Baptism of Jesus to Ash Wednesday, and the second from the Monday after Pentecost to Advent. In this sum of weeks the Sunday of the Baptism of Jesus and Pentecost Sunday figure (in a purely theoretical way) as Sundays of Ordinary Time. This ensures that the liturgical texts (of Mass and Office) for the thirty-third and thirty-fourth weeks, with their eschatological orientation, will never be omitted.

Prior to the reorganization of the liturgy a distinction was made between a period after the Epiphany of the Lord until Septuagesima, for which six Sundays were provided in Missal and Breviary, and a period after Pentecost with twenty-four Sunday formularies. If Easter came early, not all the Sundays after Epiphany could be celebrated (in the extreme case there would be room for only two), while there could be as many as twenty-eight Sundays after Pentecost. The rule governing this situation was that the omitted Sundays after Epiphany were intercalated (as postponed Sundays) between the twenty-third and twenty-fourth Sundays after Pentecost; this was certainly not an ideal solution.

The numbering of Sundays as postpentecostal occurs first in the Frankish liturgical books of the eighth century. The earlier practice had been to count these Sundays according to their relation to certain postpentecostal feasts. After the introduction of the feast of the Trinity (1334) it was also possible to count Sundays "after Trinity"; this practice was later taken over by the Churches of the Reformation and is still customary there.[71]

The Lectionary for Ordinary Time

The Sundays and weekdays of Ordinary Time derive their specific theological and liturgical complexion chiefly from the readings assigned them in the new *Lectionary for Mass* of May 25, 1969 (second edition: January 21, 1981). The general pattern followed in the new lectionary has already been explained in connection with the liturgy of the word at Mass (Chapter XI). For this reason I shall simply give two tables that provide a quick overview for the second reading on the Sundays of Ordinary Time and the first on weekdays. The tables show which books of the Bible are read (in a semi-continous manner) and in what order.

The Second Reading on the Sundays of Ordinary Time

	Year A	Year B	Year C
2	1 Corinthians 1-4	1 Corinthians 6-11	1 Corinthians 12-15
3	1 Corinthians 1-4	1 Corinthians 6-11	1 Corinthians 12-15
4	1 Corinthians 1-4	1 Corinthians 6-11	1 Corinthians 12-15
5	1 Corinthians 1-4	1 Corinthians 6-11	1 Corinthians 12-15
6	1 Corinthians 1-4	1 Corinthians 6-11	1 Corinthians 12-15
7	1 Corinthians 1-4	2 Corinthians	1 Corinthians 12-15
8	1 Corinthians 1-4	2 Corinthians	1 Corinthians 12-15

	Year A	Year B	Year C
9	Romans	2 Corinthians	Galatians
10	Romans	2 Corinthians	Galatians
11	Romans	2 Corinthians	Galatians
12	Romans	2 Corinthians	Galatians
13	Romans	2 Corinthians	Galatians
14	Romans	2 Corinthians	Galatians
15	Romans	Ephesians	Colossians
16	Romans	Ephesians	Colossians
17	Romans	Ephesians	Colossians
18	Romans	Ephesians	Colossians
19	Romans	Ephesians	Hebrews 11-12
20	Romans	Ephesians	Hebrews 11-12
21	Romans	Ephesians	Hebrews 11-12
22	Romans	James	Hebrews 11-12
23	Romans	James	Philemon
24	Romans	James	1 Timothy
25	Philippians	James	1 Timothy
26	Philippians	James	1 Timothy
27	Philippians	Hebrews 2-10	2 Timothy
28	Philippians	Hebrews 2-10	2 Timothy
29	1 Thessalonians	Hebrews 2-10	2 Timothy
30	1 Thessalonians	Hebrews 2-10	2 Timothy
31	1 Thessalonians	Hebrews 2-10	2 Thessalonians
32	1 Thessalonians	Hebrews 2-10	2 Thessalonians
33	1 Thessalonians	Hebrews 2-10	2 Thessalonians

The First Reading on the Weekdays of Ordinary Time

	First Cyle	Second Cycle
1	Hebrews	1 Samuel
2	Hebrews	1 Samuel
3	Hebrews	2 Samuel
4	Hebrews	2 Samuel; 1 Kings 1-16
5	Genesis 1-11	1 Kings 1-16
6	Genesis 1-11	James
7	Sirach	James
8	Sirach	1 Peter; Jude
9	Tobit	2 Peter; 2 Timothy
10	2 Corinthians	1 Kings 17—22

	First Cycle	Second Cycle
11	2 Corinthians	1 Kings 17-22; 2 Kings
12	Genesis 12-50	2 Kings; Lamentations
13	Genesis 12-50	Amos
14	Genesis 12-50	Hosea; Isaiah
15	Exodus	Isaiah; Micah
16	Exodus	Micah, Jeremiah
17	Exodus; Leviticus	Jeremiah
18	Numbers; Deuteronomy	Jeremiah; Nahum; Habakkuk
19	Deuteronomy; Joshua	Ezekiel
20	Judges; Ruth	Ezekiel
21	1 Thessalonians	2 Thessalonians; 1 Corinthians
22	1 Thessalonians; Colossians	1 Corinthians
23	Colossians; 1 Timothy	1 Corinthians
24	1 Timothy	1 Corinthians
25	Ezra; Haggai; Zechariah	Proverbs; Ecclesiastes
26	Zechariah; Nehemiah; Baruch	Job
27	Jonah; Malachi; Joel	Galatians
28	Romans	Galatians; Ephesians
29	Romans	Ephesians
30	Romans	Ephesians
31	Romans	Ephesians; Philippians
32	Wisdom	Titus; Philemon; 2 and 3 John
33	1 and 2 Maccabees	Revelation
34	Daniel	Revelation

Because an effort has been made to achieve continuity in the weekday readings, they are "in most cases . . . to be used on their assigned days, unless a solemnity, feast, or memorial with proper readings occurs."[72] If one or other reading has to be omitted, "with the plan of readings for the entire week in mind, the priest in that case arranges to omit the less significant sections or suitably combines them with other readings, if they contribute to an integral view of a particular theme."[73]

Movable Solemnities in Ordinary Time

During the second millennium of the Christian era four solemnities were established during Ordinary Time; their date depends on the date of Easter and thus they are movable feasts. The four are the solemnities of: the Trinity, the Body and Blood of Christ, the Sacred Heart of Jesus, and Christ the King. They have in common that they had their origin in a piety characteristic of the age that gave them birth and are to be regarded as devotion-feasts.

The Solemnity of the Trinity

The struggle against Arianism led to a special emphasis on faith in the Trinity both in preaching and in piety, particularly in Spain and Gaul; there is plenty of evidence for this in the sixth/seventh century. The middle of the eighth century saw the appearance, in the Old Gelesian Sacramentary, of the present-day Preface of the Trinity, which is a compendium of classical trinitarian theology. Around 800 a Mass of the Trinity is found as a votive Mass for Sundays, which, it was thought, should have a more trinitarian emphasis. In Frankish and Gallic Benedictine monasteries a feast of the Trinity was probably celebrated on the Sunday after Pentecost even before the year 1000. Rome stubbornly resisted such a feast, but Pope John XXII finally introduced it for the universal Church in 1334, during the Avignon Exile. The location of this feast on the Sunday after Pentecost can be interpreted as a grateful look back at the now completed mystery of salvation, which, according to the theology of the Fathers, is accomplished by the Father through the Son in the Holy Spirit.[74]

The Solemnity Of The Body And Blood Of Christ (corpus Christi)

This feast is celebrated on the Thursday after the feast of the Trinity. The traditional name in English—Corpus Christi—is derived directly from the Latin title *(festum corporis Christi).*

Its origin must be seen as connected with the intense cult of the Blessed Sacrament that developed during the twelfth century. In that cult the concern was less with the proper celebration of the Eucharist than with the abiding real presence of Christ in the consecrated bread. The worship of the eucharistic Christ was accompanied by an intense longing to see the host; this led, among other things, to the elevation of the host after the consecration (first attested for Paris about 1200).

In this situation a vision which Juliana of Liège, an Augustinian nun, received in 1209, and often afterwards, played an important role in the establishment of a special feast in honor of the Blessed Sacrament. Bishop Robert of Liège introduced such a feast into his diocese for the first time in 1246. In 1264 Pope Urban IV extended it to the entire Church. Thomas Aquinas is said to have written or compiled the texts for Mass and Breviary at the request of the same pope, but today there is doubt about his sole authorship of the splendid hymns of the office. The death of the pope in that same year delayed the spread of the feast, which became universally obligatory only under John XXII when he published Urban IV's Bull of Establishment in the Clementine Decretals.[75]

The new name of the feast, which now expressly mentions the Blood of Christ, rendered superfluous the Feast of the Precious Blood, which Pius IX introduced in 1849 in thanksgiving for his return from exile (it was most recently celebrated on July 1). That feast evidently duplicated the Feast of the Body and Blood of Christ.

A Corpus Christi procession is first attested for Cologne between 1274 and 1279. By the end of the fourteenth century it had been enthusiastically adopted in most countries and was celebrated with great solemnity and splendor. In the procession a consecrated host was carried in a monstrance. In Germany the Corpus Christi procession acquired to some extent the character of a procession through the fields and a rogation procession. There was a station at each of four outdoor altars; here the beginnings of the four gospels were sung toward the four quarters of the heavens, and a blessing was given with the Blessed Sacrament. Especially in the Baroque period the procession developed into a magnificent and triumphalistic public display. In 1959 the Roman Congregation of Rites stated that the Corpus Christi procession is not a liturgical act falling under Roman law but an "exercise of devotion" (*pium exercitium*) that comes under the jurisdiction of the bishops.[76]

In the decades after the council dissatisfaction with the traditional form of the Corpus Christi procession led to efforts to develop new forms. For example, a festive Mass might be celebrated in a public square, with the various parishes coming in procession from their churches (see the old Roman stational liturgies), "so that the Christian people might experience themselves as forming a great community, with Christ and one another, that has its source in the 'sacrament of unity.'"[77] Still more recently, however, a growing number of people are calling for the retention or restoration of the procession with the Blessed Sacrament.

Feast Of The Sacred Heart Of Jesus

This feast is celebrated on the third Friday after Pentecost, the day that used to follow upon the octave Corpus Christi. It is a typical feast of devotion, honoring the God-man for the love that is symbolized by his heart. The beginnings of such a devotion may be found in the Fathers, who appeal especially to passages in the Gospel of John (e.g., 7:37; 19:34). These passages were also the point of departure for the medieval theologians: a few isolated figures in the twelfth century, and then a large number in the thirteenth.

This cult received an especially strong impetus from the mystics of the thirteenth and fourteenth centuries, in the person of such individuals as Mechtild of Magdeburg, Gertrude of Helfta, and Heinrich Seuse. Later on, the representatives of the *Devotio moderna* and the Jesuits of the sixteenth century promoted the Sacred Heart devotion with special zeal. In the seventeenth century the French Oratorians of Pierre Bérulle (d. 1629) and John Eudes (d. 1680) brought the devotion to new heights. John Eudes, with the permission of his bishop, was also the first to celebrate a feast in honor of the Heart of Jesus in the churches of his community (October 20, 1672). Between 1673 and 1675 Margaret Mary Alacoque, a Visitation nun at Paray-le-Monial, had a series of visions in which Christ bade her work for the introduction of a feast of the Sacred Heart on the Friday after the octave of Corpus Christi and for the practice of Fridays in honor of the Heart of Jesus and of holy hours.

Rome resisted for almost a hundred years, and only in 1765 did Clement XIII allow the Polish bishops and the Roman Archconfraternity of the Sacred Heart to celebrate such a feast. In 1856 Pius IX made the feast obligatory for the universal Church; in 1899 Leo XIII raised it to a highter rank and ordered that the world should be consecrated to the Most Sacred Heart of Jesus for the coming century.[78] Pius XI revised the liturgy of the feast in 1927 and elevated it still further. On the first centenary of its introduction as a universal feast Pius XII issued the Encyclical Letter *Haurietis aquas.*[79]

The chief opposition to devotion to the Sacred Heart came from Jansenism and the theologians of the Enlightenment. Our century, too, brought more or less open reservations regarding it; Pius XII discusses these in his encyclical. Many of the objections are based on misunderstanding and prove groundless once the term "heart" is understood as a primordial word or primordial concept, as explained by Karl Rahner: "For Scripture and the teaching and practice of the Church assume, when they speak of the heart of Jesus, the self-same total-human primordial word 'heart' as the inmost original core of the body-soul totality of the person. The object of the Sacred Heart Devotion is consequently the Lord with respect to this his heart."[80]

Other forms of devotion to the Sacred Heart are the Fridays in honor of the Sacred Heart, that is, the first Friday of each month, and the holy hour on the eve of first Friday. Leo XIII approved (1899) a special votive Mass for first Fridays. The two devotions, when properly explained and celebrated, have long since proved their pastoral value in many parishes.[81]

Solemnity of Christ the King

The external occasion for the introduction of this most recent idea-feast by Pius XI in 1925 was the sixteenth centenary of the first ecumenical Council of Nicaea. In his Encyclical *Quas primas* of December 11, 1925, the pope develops the idea that the most effective weapon against the destructive forces of the age is the acknowledgment of the kingship of Christ.[82] The pope appointed the last Sunday of October as the day of the feast; he chose this day in view of the coming feast of All Saints. On this Sunday the annual consecration to the heart of the Redeemer was to take place.

Although the new feast was initially greeted with enthusiasm, a number of reservations were soon voiced on the grounds that the idea of this feast already finds expression, and indeed a more organic expression, in other seasons and on other days of the liturgical year: Advent, Christmas, Epiphany, Easter, the Ascension, and even on every Sunday since Sunday is the day that celebrates Christ as Kyrios or Lord. It is certainly fortunate that the new calendar transfers this "Solemnity of Our Lord Jesus Christ, King of the Universe" (its full name in the *Missale Romanum*) to the last Sunday of the liturgical year, since this Sunday with its eschatological tonality brings home more clearly the idea that the glorified Lord is the goal of the universe and Christian life.

Other Feastdays in Ordinary Time

Feast of the Transfiguration of the Lord (August 6)

The basis of the feast is the substantially indentical accounts in the Synoptic gospels (Mt 17:1-8 par.). Such a feast was known in the Eastern Churches as early as the fifth century; not until 1457, however, did it become universal in the Western Church under Calixtus III, who established it in grateful commemoration of the victory over the Turks in 1456.

Feast of the Triumph of the Cross (September 14)

The feast originated in Jerusalem. A double basilica comprising the church of the Martyrium and the church of the Resurrection was consecrated there on September 13, 335. On the following day the Bishop of Jerusalem elevated the great relic of the Cross and showed it to the people so that they might venerate it (the Latin name of the feast, *Exaltatio crucis* meant literally "the lifting up of the cross").

This feast soon became more important than the feast of the dedication, which it originally accompanied, and spread far and wide. In the West, however, its celebration was eventually a subject of confusion. The Gallic liturgy celebrated a feast of the cross on May 3 from the eighth century on; May 3 was the day on which in 628 Emperor Heraclius brought back to Jerusalem the relic of the cross which the Persians had removed. This feast, too, was taken into the Roman festal calendar, which however already had the feast of September 14 (because Rome too possessed a relic of the cross). By a reversal of historical fact the feast of May 3 was named the feast of the Finding of the Cross (tradition dates Helen's discovery of it to September 14, 320), and the feast of September 14, though still called the feast of the Lifting Up of the Cross, was made to commemorate Emperor Heraclius' restoration of the relic.

Under Pope John XXIII the feast of May 3 was suppressed (1960). The *General Norms for the Liturgical Year and the Calendar* approved the suppression and restored the original meaning of the feast of the Cross on September 14.[83]

Feasts of the Dedication of Churches

The stimulus to an annual commemoration of the dedication of a church certainly came both from 1 Maccabees 4:59 and from the pagan custom of celebrating a *Natale templi* (a "birthday of a temple"). The earliest witness to the dedication of a Christian church is Eusebius of Caesarea, Church historian and bishop, who in 314 helped to dedicate the cathedral of Tyre with a Mass and a sermon.[84] We know from Egeria's account (400) that the anniversary of the dedication of a church was also celebrated with a feast.[85] Originally, these feasts of dedication were celebrated only locally. Some exceptions, still acknowledged today, are the feasts of the dedication of the Roman Lateran Basilica (November 9) and the Basilicas of St. Peter (November 18), St. Paul Outside the Walls (same day), and St. Mary Major (August 5).

Of special significance for each diocese is the anniversary of the dedication of its cathedral church; this is celebrated in all the parishes as a special feast of the diocese, while in the cathedral it is celebrated as a solemnity. The anniversary of the date of any individual church, if known, is celebrated there on that date as a solemnity. For churches whose anniversary date is unknown, each diocese celebrates a common annual commemoration in the form of a solemnity.

Ember Days

"Ember Days" is the name given to the Wednesday, Friday, and Saturday of four weeks of the year; these come at approximately the beginning of the four seasons and since the eighth century have been known in Rome as the *quattuor Tempora,* "four seasons."

The Ember Days are a specifically Roman institution that is still unknown in the East. Their origin has not been explained with complete satisfaction.[86] Recent research has looked for it in corresponding Old Testament regulations on fasting; here Zechariah 8:19 and Joel 2:12-19, in particular, would have played an important role—a supposition that finds support especially in the Ember Day sermons of Pope Leo I.[87] Different parts of the West celebrated the Ember Days on different dates, until Pope Gregory VII decreed uniformity at the Roman synod of 1078. Since then it has been the rule that the Ember Days begin on the Wednesdays after the first Sunday of Lent, Pentecost, the Exaltation of the Cross, and the feast of St. Lucy.

If we wish to sum up the meaning of the Ember Days in the light of the various historical and liturgical sources, we may say that they represented a special ascetical effort at the beginning of each of the four seasons. This effort took the form especially of the triad of prayer, fasting, and almsgiving. The Ember Days were also days of thanksgiving for the various seasonal harvests and, from the fifth century on, also served as days of preparation for and conferral of holy orders. In our time they have been days of prayer for vocations to the priesthood and religious life.

In the reorganization of the liturgical year, the Ember Days have been retained in principle, but their dates and the form they are to take have been left to the episcopal conferences so that better account can be taken of local conditions (*GNLYC* 46). As far as their interpretation is concerned, the official commentary on the *General Norms* points out that the worldwide problems of peace, justice, and hunger in our day can give renewed meaning to these periodically recurring exercises of penance and Christian charity.

THE SANCTORAL CYCLE OF THE LITURGICAL YEAR

History of the Veneration of the Saints

The beginning of Christian veneration of saints may be dated to the middle of the second century. The first to be venerated were the martyrs, "witnesses to Christ" in the fullest sense of the term. Bishop Polycarp of Smyrna (d. ca. 155) was probably the first martyr to be given cultic honors by his community. Initially, the cult of a martyr was confined to the community in which his tomb was located. Only later on were many martyrs taken into the festal calendar of other communities as well. There was an effort to make up for lack of possession of the tomb by relics, including "contact relics" (*brandea*), or even by images.

Special veneration was also shown to the "confessors," that is, those who in time of persecution suffered torture, imprisonment, and exile. Once the great persecutions had come to an end, outstanding bishops like Gregory Thaumaturgus in the East and Martin of Tours in the West were also honored. Finally, the same honor was paid to ascetics and virgins because of their extraordinary following of Christ.

At an early date altars, chapels, and churches were built over the tombs of such martyrs and saints; the acts of the martyrs were read over them, and the Eucharist was celebrated. The veneration paid them consisted not only in commemorating the anniversary of their death (their *natale* or "birthday") and imitating their virtues, but also in asking their intercession (*invocatio*).[88]

There is no clear evidence of a cultic veneration of the Mother of God during the first three centuries, probably because attention was focused on the cult of the martyrs and apostles. In the fourth century, however, the situation suddenly changed, as I shall show further on.

In order to counteract an uncontrolled extension of veneration of the saints the Church developed a process of canonization. It also gradually developed certain criteria: the proven heroic following of Christ and the evidence of miracles in answer to prayers addressed to the person. The authoritative document governing canonizations today is the Motu Proprio *Sanctitas clarior* of Paul VI (March 19, 1969).[89]

The exaggerated medieval cult of the saints meant that in the liturgy the temporal cycle was largely obscured. The Missal and Breviary which Pius V promulgated after the Council of Trent reduced the number of saints' feasts to "only" 158, but by the beginning of the present century the number had climbed to 230 again, and this does not include feasts proper to dioceses, many of which had over a hundred of them. Before I come to the reorganization of the calendar, let me say a few words on the theology of veneration of the saints.

Theology of the Veneration of the Saints

Despite all the exaggerations and even erroneous practices connected with the veneration of the saints at many periods and in many countries, the official teaching of the Church has never lost sight of the principle enunciated in 1 Timothy 2:5f. (Christ is the sole mediator). When the Church venerates saints, it is proclaiming the victorious grace of the one redeemer and mediator, Christ, who acts in his saints. This aspect of the veneration of the saints finds expression especially in the Prefaces for Masses of the saints and also in many presidential prayers. Authoritative statements of the teaching Church are to be found in, for example, various documents of Vatican II (*SC* 103-4, 111; *LG*, chapter VII).

What I have been saying applies also to veneration of Mary, the Mother of God, "who is joined by an inseparable bond to the saving work of her Son. In her the Church holds up and admires the most excellent effect of the redemption and joyfully contemplates, as in a flawless image, that which the Church itself desires and hopes wholly to be" (*SC* 103).

Veneration of the saints does not include only an acknowledgment that by the grace of God these men and women have become signs, witnesses, and models of Christian life. It also includes confidence in approaching them as brothers and sisters in Christ, making our cares and needs known to them, and asking them to intercede with God, the giver of every good gift; this confidence is based on the fraternal solidarity of all who make up the mystical body of Christ.[90] Catholic veneration of the saints, when thus properly understood, is far removed from "worship" of a creature. —In the Churches of the Reformation there are signs that many groups are finding their way back to a veneration of the saints as thus understood.[91]

The New Roman General Calendar

The primary principle followed in the reform of the General Calendar was the priority of the temporal cycle over the sanctoral, "in order that the entire cycle of the mysteries of salvation may be celebrated in the measure due to them" (*SC* 108). To make this possible, a rather large number of saints' feasts had to be limited to local Churches or religious communities; "those only should be extended to the universal Church that commemorate saints of truly universal significance" (*SC* 111). A further guideline was the reduction in the number of idea-feasts or at least their reduction in rank.

With regard to the choice of saints' feasts, the test of historical truth had to be passed if a saint was to be included in the General Calendar. Only saints of greater significance were to be admitted. Care was also to be taken that all countries and historical periods were represented (geographical and chronological universality). Furthermore, every state of life and the most varied expressions of Christian piety were to be represented as far as this was possible. On March 21, 1969, the Congregation of Rites published the new Roman General Calendar, which was preceded by the *General Norms for the Liturgical Year and the Calendar* and the *Commentary* on this document.[92]

Although the reduction in the number of saints was extensive enough to elicit regrets in individual cases, it fell short of achieving the intended goal, namely, a substantial liberation of the General Calendar from saints' feasts in favor of the temporal cycle. For, even apart from the Marian feasts and memorials, there are still four solemnities (Joseph; Birth of John the Baptist; Peter and Paul; All Saints), 17 feasts, 59 obligatory and 88 optional memorials, or 168 in all. Critics have pointed out that of that number 89 are saints from the Romance-language countries and 63 are from the religious orders. There is one commemoration of a unique kind, that of all deceased Christians (All Souls' Day); this goes back to Abbot Odilo of Cluny in 998 and has the same rank as a solemnity. If it falls on a Sunday, its Mass takes precedence.

The large number of Marian feasts and memorials certainly bears witness to the loving, grateful esteem in which the Church holds the Mother of God. Most of the Marian feasts arose (from the fourth century on) in the East and were soon adopted in the West. In many periods of history, however, it seems to have been forgotten that there can be too many feasts, to the detriment of an authentic veneration of Mary. Some doublets have been removed from the new calendar, but there is still a surprisingly large number of Marian solemnities, feasts, and memorials. I must limit myself here to a list without commentary.[93] I should also remind the reader that the feasts previously known as the "Presentation of Mary" and the "Annunciation of Mary" have already been discussed in connection with the feasts of the Lord, as has the "Solemnity of the Mother of God" in connection with the octave of Christmas.

Marian solemnities and feasts (in order of their occurrence in the liturgical year): Solemnity of the Immaculate Conception on December 8; Feast of Visitation on July 2; Solemnity of the Assumption on August 15; Feast of the Nativity of Mary on September 8.

Marian memorials (o. = obligatory; otherwise optional): Our Lady of Lourdes on February 11; the Immaculate Heart of Mary on the Saturday after the feast of the Sacred Heart; Our Lady of Mount Carmel on July 16; Queenship of Mary (o.) on August 22; the Name of Mary on September 12; Our Lady of Sorrows (o.) on September 15; Our Lady of the Rosary (o.) on October 7; Presentation of Mary (o.) on November 21.

I should mention here the special veneration paid to the Mother of God in May ("Mary's Month") and October ("Rosary Month"),[94] as well as the votive Masses for Our Lady on Saturdays.

Calendars of Regions, Dioceses, and Religious Communities
The regional calendar for the German-speaking countries was based on the *General Norms* 48-59 and the Instruction *Calendaria particularia* of the Congregation of Rites (June 24, 1970),[95] and was approved by Rome on September 21, 1972.

In compiling the calendar an effort was also made, in collaboration with a representative of the Evangelical Churches (D. F. Schulz), to bring it into harmony with the Evangelical "Festund Nameskalendar" in regard to the naming and dating of the various feasts and memorials. "The Catholic regional calendar now has 110 feasts and memorials in common with the Evangelical calendar of feasts and names; only in 19 cases are there presently still notable discrepancies in dating."[96]

A remarkable ecumenical convergence has also been achieved by the Christian Churches in the United States. In general, the Roman Calendar has been followed, although the terminology of Sundays after Epiphany and Sundays after Pentecost has been retained.

The Proper Calendar for the Dioceses of the United States of America lists one feast (Our Lady of Guadalupe, December 12), 9 memorials of saints, 7 optional memorials of blesseds, Thanksgiving Day and Independence Day.

Those having a right to a religious calendar are "orders of men; their calendar must also be followed by any nuns and sisters belonging to the same order and by its tertiaries who live in community and make simple vows." as well as "religious congregations, societies, and institutes of pontifical rank, if they are in any way obliged to recite the divine office."[97] To be inserted into a religious calendar are, "beside celebrations of their title, founder, or patron, those saints and blesseds who were members of that religious family or had some special relationship with it."[98] In order to strengthen the ties between the religious communities and the local Churches all alike are to celebrate the anniversary of the dedication of the cathedral and the feasts of the principal patrons of the place and the larger region.

A saints' calendar of a special kind is the Roman Martyrology, which had its origin in the lists kept of feasts and martyrs in the early Church. The last radical revision of it was made in 1583; since that time it has gone through numerous editions and translations.[99] A new edition is still awaited.

Chapter Twenty One

Liturgical Space (The Church)

It is not an inherent requirement of the Christian religion that its adherents have a sacred edifice at their disposal. That much is obvious from the simple fact that during the first two centuries Christians had no places of worship specifically set aside for that purpose. In addition, the later history of the Church in many countries tell us that Christian communities were without any church buildings for decades and even centuries but did not die out on that account. On the other hand, liturgical assemblies are helped in important ways by having spaces whose arrangement and furnishings lend support to the proclamation of God's word and the celebration of the liturgy and thus contribute in a positive way to the *koinonia* or communion of the members with God and among themselves.

The present chapter will discuss the theology of the Christian church building, then briefly review its history, set forth guidelines and criteria for modern churches, explain the names and types of liturgical buildings, and say something about the essential furnishings of a church. The chapter will conclude with a section on the dedication of churches and altars.[1]

THEOLOGY OF THE CHRISTIAN LITURGICAL BUILDING

The New Testament writings speak from time to time of liturgical gatherings, but never describe the place of assembly as "house of God," "sanctuary," or even "temple." On the other hand, Christ himself is regarded as the true temple of the new covenant, and indeed he describes himself as a temple in Jn 2:13-22. This means that henceforth the exalted Lord, and not the temple of stone in Jerusalem, is the place of God's saving presence. "No longer is there any specific place on earth that is the sole legitimate locus for worship of God. Rather, God is to be adored wherever Christ is, that is, everywhere."[2] Jn. 7:37-38 must be interpreted along the same lines. According to the Apocalypse (22:22) the "Lamb," together with the Father, is the temple of the holy city, and there is no other.

At the death of Christ the veil of the temple in Jerusalem was torn from top to bottom; many of the Fathers of the Church interpret this as symbolizing the end of worship in the Old Testament temple and the beginning of a new order of salvation. By his death Christ dismantled the wall separating Jews and Gentiles (see Eph 2:14) and thus established the universal temple that is open to all peoples and gives them salvation and a home. As a result, a new temple cult begins with and in Jesus, a new era in worship of God, when human beings will worship him "in spirit and in truth" (Jn 4:23f.).

Since those who believe in Christ form his mystical body and the glory of God dwells in them (see Jn 14:23), it is understandable that they and the community they form should likewise be called temples of the living God (1 Cor 3:16-17; see also 6:19; 2 Cor 6:16). In the image of the mystical body Christians are called the members of the body; so too in the image of the temple they are called its living stones (1 Pet 2:4-6; see Eph 2:20-22). Christ is the irreplaceable foundation of the temple formed by Christians (1 Cor 3:11); at the same time he is the cornerstone in which the whole building is joined together (Eph 2:20-21). Christ himself, citing Is. 28:16, speaks of himself as a cornerstone (Mt 21:42 par.; see 1 Pet 2:6-8).

In contrast, the material place in which the community gathers plays a secondary role; it simply supplies a service. From the very beginnings of Christianity it has been clear that no building sanctifies the liturgical community and that, on the contrary, the place of assembly is ennobled by, and derives its dignity from, the community and the liturgy it celebrates therein. This principle applies also to later ages when artistic churches were built and an extravagant rite for the dedication of churches was developed and even when, around the year one thousand, the practice began of reserving consecrated hosts in the church. If the dignity of Christian churches were derived from the last two developments just named, one would have to deny any dignity to the churches of the first millenium. The view I am setting forth here is confirmed by the introductory remarks in the new rite for the dedication of a church (Chapter II, 1-2) and by the recommendation in the *General Instruction of the Roman Missal* that the Blessed Sacrament be reserved in a chapel separated from the main body of the church (276).

HISTORICAL SURVEY

In the early days, Christian communities used to assemble in the homes of their members,[3] but from the beginning of the third century we find houses owned by the communities and reserved for their liturgical assemblies. The house-church of Dura Europos on the Upper Euphrates is a vivid example.[4] Once Emperor Constantine issued his edict of religious toleration (Edict of Milan) in 313, numerous basilicas were built; these halls with their several naves and apses were dedicated to their Christian purpose by the first Eucharist which the bishop celebrated therein. Centrally planned edifices arose as assembly halls over especially venerated holy places and memorials (for example, the Church of the Sepulcher in Jerusalem; churches of the martyrs) and exerted a strong influence on Byzantine architecture with its domes. The architecture of Justinian's period sought to combine the rectangular shape of basilicas with the centrally oriented plan of a domed building.[5]

In the West the basilica form developed into the architectural style of the Carolingian and Ottonian periods, from which in turn emerged the Romanesque style.[6] Romanesque was succeeded by Gothic, which became the prevailing style in the period from about 1150 to 1500.[7] But in the fifteenth century there were already forces at work in Italy that were seeking to move beyond Gothic. The result was Renaissance architecture, which represented a return to antiquity. The most important requirement was harmonious proportions reminiscent of the ancient temples.[8]

At the end of the sixteenth century new forms made their appearance out of which the baroque developed around 1600. This style was initially practiced only by Italian architects, but by the end of the seventeenth century architects throughout Europe were building uniquely perfect monastic, cathedral, and pilgrimage churches.[9] The ultimate refinement or, depending on the viewpoint, exaggeration of the baroque style that developed around the middle of the eighteenth century has been given the name "rococo," but the name "late baroque" seems preferable. At the same period, meanwhile, especially in circles influenced by the English and French Enlightenments, the pendulum was swinging in the opposite direction. There was a new enthusiasm for antiquity with its "noble simplicity and quiet grandeur." The new style was named classicism or neoclassicism.[10]

In the first half of the nineteenth century the Romantic movement gave rise to a new enthusiasm for the Middle Ages and its architectural styles: Romanesque and especially Gothic. The result was historicism or an imitative return to the past, which the authorities both Catholic and Protestant explicitly supported and encouraged as late as the first decades of the twentieth century. The end of the nineteenth century, meanwhile, saw the rise of Art Nouveau which supplied new impetus for a contemporary art.[11] The slow break from historicism was also aided by the use of new building materials and techniques that had been discovered in the nineteenth century and had already been exploited for secular buildings. The result was a new breakthrough in ecclesiastical architecture; this movement is often simply called "modern church architecture," but this does not give an idea of the variety of new architectural forms. The new consciousness of the liturgy and its Christocentrism has played an important role in this development.[12]

GUIDELINES AND CRITERIA FOR CHURCH ARCHITECTURE

The following guidelines, for which a more than contemporary validity may well be claimed, are derived from a theological understanding of the Christian place of worship, from historical experience of church architecture, and from the conciliar and postconciliar statements issued by the Church.[13]

A Church Must Be Appropriate to the Congregation

The people of God is hierarchically organized and comprises clergy and laity, although both are united in the Holy Spirit to form a single mystical body of Christ. The unity of Christ's community ought to be illumined rather than obscured by the architectural character of the building. Therefore, on the one hand it is legitimate and mandatory to emphasize the distinction between the sanctuary and the place for the congregation, but on the other the unity of the one community that is engaged in the liturgical action should not be lessened by spatial arrangements.

This last is what happened in, for example, the Middle Ages (Romanesque period) when a *lectorium* or reading platform divided each church into a "church of the clergy" and a "church of the laity," each with its own liturgy. Nor can the iconstasis ("wall of images") of the Eastern Rites be regarded as an ideal, especially since even in the early Church there was no "discipline of the *arcanum*" for the faithful but only for the nonbaptized. Also unsuitable from the viewpoint of manifesting the unity of God's people are massive, lofty walls around the choir, a narrow, lengthy choir area, and high, stage-like altar areas, with the faithful sitting at a distance like mere spectators. Long, narrow naves that make the congregation seem like columns of marching soldiers and that have sometimes been recommended as being "journeying churches" (R. Schwarz), obscure the fact that the pilgriming community is here gathered around its Lord for a meal.

A Church Must Be Appropriate to the Liturgy
A church must be functional for liturgical actions; that is, it must facilitate the celebration of the liturgy as far as possible. Since the eucharistic celebration is the essential part of the liturgy, the position and shape of the altar are especially important. The Instruction *Inter Oecumenici* of September 26, 1964, requires that the altar be freestanding and easily circled. "Its location in the place of worship should be truly central so that the attention of the whole congregation naturally focuses there. . . . The sanctuary area is to be spacious enough to accommodate the sacred rites" (91; *DOL* 23 no. 383). Care must be taken not to let the congregation's field of vision of the altar be disturbed by bright windows behind it or to let confusing superstructures or distracting sculptures on the altar itself detract from its character as "holy table" (the name given to the altar in the Eastern Churches) and as symbol of the Christ who offers himself in sacrifice to the Father and gives himself to the faithful.

Furthermore, since the liturgy of the word is closely connected with the eucharistic liturgy, the ambo (lectern, pulpit) as place for proclamation of the word ("table of the word") must share in the central and centering position of the altar.

Because of the great importance of the sacrament of baptism, it is rightly required that the place of baptism (the baptistery) likewise be within the congregation's field of vision.

A Church Should Be Symbolic and Challenging

Since the eucharistic celebration is by its nature an Easter assembly of the community around its exalted Lord and since this community here receives the joy, consolation, and strength given by the divine promises, a church should be a festive and uplifting place. It ought to reflect the splendor of the divine promises and challenge those present to a faith based on hope; it should be *Sursum corda* in stone.

In an earlier time this complex of qualities was summed up as the "sacredness" of a church. Nowadays this word elicits strong objections from many people, because (they say) the distinction between sacred and secular has become untenable since the incarnation of Christ (which effected a *consecratio mundi*, a "consecration of the world"). This subject has occasioned a flood of writings in the last few decades,[14] but the divergent definitions used by various authors have led to many misunderstandings.

H. Muhlen, who has written several solid books and articles on the subject,[15] defines secularity as "the distinction of creation from God" and sacredness or sacrality as "ultimate relatedness to this God who alone is holy." If we adopt these definitions, the two concepts are not contradictory to one another but support each other. How do they apply to a church and its furnishings? As created realities these retain their secular character, but because they are closely related to God the Holy One they are at the same time sacred. The more transparent the relatedness, the more profound the sacredness will be and the more they will do justice to their task of being a sign of the divine vocation of human beings and a challenge to its fulfillment.

From this point of view, the interiors of many modern churches do not earn good marks, because they seem so inhospitable and unattractive, so depressing, cold, and empty. An unsuccessful arrangement of spaces, a bleak monotony in light and color, an artistic poverty in furnishings do not symbolize the dignity of the liturgical assembly nor do they invite and lead the congregation into the mystery. To say this is not, however, to opt for either a lavish and showy style of architecture or an obtrusive monumentality, both of which repel rather than attract people today.

In this context I may refer to the programmatic decoration of our churches with images (pictures, statues, stained glass). Images can be signs and proclamations and thus serve faith in their own manner. Like music, they can embody and communicate a spiritual content. When viewed thus, pictures and sculptures are more than ways of instructing the illiterate; they have an innate power to proclaim and a missionary importance. Yves Congar, the French theologian, confirms this when he writes: "There are certain churches that are famous for the way they fulfill this function of being signs of the existence and truth of that 'something else' [=another world]. Many conversions have taken place or begun at Chartres, and at Ronchamps too, simply through the sign of stone and glass."[16]

Multipurpose Buildings Are To Be Regarded As Stopgaps
Political difficulties or economic and financial straits have sometimes forced communities to do without a real church and be satisfied with a multipurpose building. The building serves not only for the celebration of the liturgy but for other community functions of the parish. Given the situation, the community will have to make do with such a building. People here and there, however, have appealed to the needs of the world and the "underutilization" of buildings set aside exclusively as churches as proof that the times call for multipurpose buildings. In response I point out that because first-rate liturgies are exceptionally important and cannot be replaced by anything else, communities must try to provide themselves with truly sacred buildings that symbolize the things of faith and call men and women to them. Multifunctional "churches" are usually in fact neutral and should therefore be regarded as a stopgap and not as a pastoral ideal.[17]

NAMES AND TYPES OF LITURGICAL BUILDINGS

The liturgical buildings and spaces that have developed in the course of history have been given many names. Some of these, which I shall list here, refer to specific functions.

Temple

The word "temple"(Latin: *templum*) is derived from the Greek verb *temnein,* which means "to cut; to cut off; separate," and originally referred to a piece of land that was set aside and dedicated to a divinity as a sacred grove or for the building of a sacred edifice. Christians initially used it only of Christ and the Christian community. In later liturgical texts it occurs only in the concluding prayer of the Mass for the dedication of a church and in the prayer of the day in the Mass for the anniversary of a church's dedication. The preface of the Mass of Dedication speaks of "the mystery of your true temple" (= the heavenly city) and of the body of Jesus as "a temple consecrated to your glory."

Ecclesia—Church—House of God

The first gathering places of Christians were called *domus ecclesiae,* "house of the *ecclesia,*" that is, of the believing community (Latin *ecclesia* from Greek *ekklesia,* "assembly called apart"). The name *ecclesia* was then applied also to the place of assembly, so that it could mean either the community or the place in which the community assembled.

The English word "church" is also derived from a Greek word. The Greek-speaking Christians of the early Church spoke of *oikia kyriake,* a "house belonging to the Lord (*Kyrios*)." Subsequently, they used an abbreviated form *kyriakon* (a neuter adjective meaning "of the Lord"; Latin *dominicum*). It is from this that the word "church" developed. Used first of the building, it was later applied to the community as well. *Kyriakon* is the origin of the word for "church" especially in English and in the Germanic and Slavic languages, whereas *ekklesia/ecclesia* has supplied the word for "church" in the Romance languages.

The term "house of God" has to be distinguished from the pagan and Judaic notion of a house which belongs to God and is reserved to him as his dwelling. In Christian use, the "house of God" is a house wherein Christians gather and celebrate the liturgy; as such it becomes a place of encounter with God, a place where he proclaims his word and communicates himself to the faithful in the Christian mysteries, and where his people offer him a sacrifice of praise and thanksgiving and become more closely united to him in faith. When thus understood, the name "house of Christ" is perfectly acceptable.

Basilica

In Greek, *basilika* (from *basileus* = king) meant "royal hall" and originally described the palace of a king or the headquarters of his high-ranking officials. In prechristian Rome the name was also applied to buildings used for various functions. Christians took over the name in connection with the churches built by Constantine; in this context it referred both to the architectural style (an oblong building divided by colonnades and having an apse) and to Christ the King. Nowadays we use the name for churches in the basilica style and for churches to which the supreme authority in the Church grants it as an honorary title. Canon law distinguishes patriarchal basilicas (*basilicae maiores*), which are directly under the pope and have a papal throne and papal altar, and *basilica minores* ("lesser basilicas"), which are especially important churches throughout the world to which the pope gives the honorary title of "basilica."

Cathedral

In Greek antiquity the word *kathedra* designated the chair of a judge, teacher, or governor, and also the chair reserved for a particular dead person at ancient funerary banquets. The name (Latin: *cathedra*) was then applied to the bishop's chair at the Christian liturgy, from which he presided over the service and delivered his homily. In the sixth century a bishop's church was already being called a "cathedral" (from his *cathedra).*[18]

In the European countries the name gained currency especially in Spain, France, and England, while the German-speaking countries opted for the name "Dom" and Italy for "Duomo" (see below). The cathedral of an archbishop is also known as the "metropolitan church." In the history of art "cathedral" is used chiefly for the principal churches in the Gothic style.

Dom/Duomo

This name is derived from *domus episcopalis* ("bishop's house") and referred originally to the bishop's domestic chapel, which was also used for the choral office of the cathedral canons and the adminstrative work of the archdeacon. In the high Middle Ages the name was then applied to the bishop's church. Some other churches were given it as an honorary title, even though they never had a bishop. The churches of the Reformation retained their ancient designations.

Minster

The word derives from Latin *monasterium;* it referred originally to the entire precincts of the monastery but eventually came to designate the monastery church (e.g., Westminster Abbey). It was later applied to certain cathedral churches (in Germany, England, and elsewhere) and to parish churches with a large number of ministering priests and of "altarists".

Crypt

In antiquity, the Latin *crypta* (derived from Greek *krypta*) meant a covered walkway or a vault or a cave. In early Christianity it was used for the passageways and niches of the catacombs. Later on it referred to the usually vaulted spaces under the apse, choir, and crossing (crypts might take the form of a tunnel or gallery, a ring, a chamber, or a hall). Crypts played a prominent part especially in Romanesque architecture; at times they were expanded into halls with several naves, and sometimes even had a surrounding ring of chapels. As a result of this subterranean development the choir area had to be elevated, so that it could be reached only by a flight of steps. There are few crypts in Gothic and Baroque churches. The reason for the existence of medieval crypts was in many cases the location of saints' graves and sepulchers containing relics, these often being directly under the main altar.

Chapel

The Latin word *cappela* is the diminutive of *cappa,* "cloak" (worn during the choral office). Beginning in the time of the Frankish kings of the early Middle Ages, *cappella* was the name given to the place where the legendary cloak of St. Martin, Bishop of Tours, was kept at the royal court in Paris (*La Sainte Chapelle*). The name was eventually given also to the places for divine service at the courts of secular and spiritual lords (domestic, palace, castle chapels). The name was later applied also (in the form *cappellani*) to the priests (chaplains) and choirs of such chapels. In the Middle Ages numerous side chapels were built in larger churches; at times these served liturgical functions (baptisms, confessions) or were assigned to various groups as places of liturgical assembly.

In modern usage, a chapel is any place for liturgical celebration that does not possess the full legal status of a parish church. Thus there are pilgrimage chapels, and chapels in seminaries, hospitals, cemeteries, and prisons. Under the new liturgical law the eucharistic bread may be reserved in a side chapel.[19] Side altars, if allowed at all, may be located only in such side chapels.[20]

Oratory

An "oratory" (from Latin *orare* = pray) is a room or house of prayer; since the early Middle Ages the name has been given to sacred spaces that are not legally parish churches for the general public but serve only particular communities and families. An "oratory" is thus to a large extent the same as a "chapel." The old Code of Canon Law distinguished between public, semi-public, and private oratories (can. 1188-1196). The Code of 1983 distinguishes only between oratories and private chapels (can. 1223-1229). —The name "oratory" as a musical genre was derived from the oratory of St. Philip Neri (1515-95) in Rome, because the devotions held there were accompanied by music and bore a certain resemblance to cantatas and, later, even operas.[21]

THE FURNISHINGS OF CHURCHES

Altar and Tabernacle

Latin has two synonyms meaning a place where fire consumes a sacrifical victim, namely, *altare* (from *adolere* = "burn") and *ara* (from *arere* = "burn"). The first of these two Latin words gives us our English word "altar" (which is not derived from Latin *altus* = "high," as is sometimes claimed). I shall say nothing here about altars in the history of religions and in the Old Testament[22] but shall turn directly to the Christian altar.

The altar was originally a movable table on which to place the bread and wine. Paul speaks of the "table of the Lord" (1 Cor 10:21); and the Eastern Churches have always called the altar the "holy table." The Greek language also used "table of sacrifice" (*thysiasterion*) as a designation for an altar. After the Constantinian Revolution fixed stone altars gradually became the norm. Their location in the church and their form differed. Originally, each church had but a single altar; this practice changed in the West toward the end of the sixth century.

The cult of the martyrs that began in the second century led to the erection of altars near or over their graves. In places that did not possess the grave, it became customary at a later date to deposit relics under or in the altar. A baldachin-like structure, known as a *ciborium,* was erected over many altars; this was regarded as a special mark of honor, after the fashion of pagan antiquity. Around the year 1000 the custom grew up of placing pictures or reliefs—retables, from Latin *retro + tabulum*—behind or even on the altar, which meanwhile was being moved closer and closer to the rear wall.

In Gothic architecture, the retable became a set of lofty panels; from the fifteenth century on these rested on a benchlike support, the predella (Italian: "foot-stool"), which was immediately above the altar. In Renaissance and Baroque architecture the predella supported a great "altarpiece," a large picture which in Baroque churches was not simply framed by columns, as in Renaissance churches, but surrounded by an entire architecture of pillars, cornices, pediments, and scroll-shaped ornaments, which in turn were richly decorated with the figures of angels and saints and even with reliquaries. The Renaissance even managed to give the altar the form of a sarcophagus. The liturgical reform of our century is pressing for a restoration of the table-altar and for its central location.

In Christian antiquity only the bread, wine, and liturgical texts might be placed on the "holy table," which was covered with a linen cloth. Beginning in the eighth century, reliquaries were also placed on the altar and, beginning in the eleventh, a cross and candles. From the early Middle Ages on, the front of the altar was decorated with sumptuous hangings, later known as antependiums.

Vatican II ordered that the regulations governing the altar be revised, and these now take their cue chiefly from the earliest tradition:[23] central location, separation from the rear wall, easily circled, fixed in place, and made of durable materials. The custom of enclosing relics in or under the altar (no longer in the *mensa* or table-top) is to be retained, provided that they are certainly authentic. The altar stone prescribed in the past for movable altars or ordinary tables used for celebration is no longer required. Three linen cloths on the altar are no longer required; one suffices. The cross and candles may be placed either on or near the altar. Pictures or statues of the saints may no longer be placed on the altar. Flowers are allowed. As far as possible, any side-altars are to be kept at a distance.[24]

The position of the celebrant at the altar was originally connected with the eastward position for prayer and also with the eastward position ("orientation") of the church itself (either the apse or the entrance to the church might be "oriented").[25] As a result of Vatican II, celebration facing the people is officially allowed once more,[26] after having fallen into disuse in the West for almost a thousand years (although it was never officially prohibited). The new practice has now spread throughout the entire area of the Roman Rite, because it has been recognized as being more meaningful and of greater pastoral value.

In the course of history, consecrated hosts have been reserved, primarily for communion of the sick and for viaticum, in a variety of locations and types of container: the residence of the clerics; a side room of the church; a movable container (pyx) on the altar; a vessel hanging over the altar (hanging tabernacle) often in the form of a eucharistic dove; a small cupboard on the wall near the altar; a free-standing tabernacle (Late Gothic). Only in fifteenth-century Italy and Spain did churches begin to attach the tabernacle securely to the main altar. Due especially to the efforts of St. Charles Borromeo, Cardinal of Milan, this practice was prescribed in many places as early as the sixteenth century and eventually became universal. Only in churches in which the choral office was sung and in much-visited pilgrimage churches was it the rule that the sacrament be reserved on a Blessed Sacrament Altar in a special Blessed Sacrament Chapel.

Since 1964 (Instruction *Inter oecumenici,* 95) bishops have been authorized to let the tabernacle be placed elsewhere than on the altar; for example, on a pillar or in a wall niche. The Instruction *Eucharisticum mysterium* on the Eucharist of May 25, 1967, recommends (no. 53) that the Blessed Sacrament be reserved in a chapel set apart from the main body of the church; the recommendation is repeated in *GIRM* 276 and in the section on "Holy Communion and Worship of the Eucharist Outside Mass" (no. 9) in the Roman Ritual. The new Code of Canon Law (1983) requires that the tabernacle be placed in a part of the church that is prominent, beautifully decorated, and suitable for prayer (can. 938 n.2). There are to be two signs in particular that the Blessed Sacrament is in the tabernacle: a veil covering the tabernacle itself and a lighted candle nearby.[27]

Bishop's Cathedra and Priest's Chair

In antiquity the Greek word *kathedra* designated the chair from which high ranking civic officials, judges, and teachers exercised their office. Late Judaism was also familiar with the idea of an official chair (see Mt 23:2). Christianity adopted the term *cathedra* for the chair from which the bishop presided at the liturgy and preached the homily. Initially, it was a movable chair placed at the center of the apse; the chairs (*sedilia*) of the priests were arranged on either side of it. In the fourth century it was distinguished from these other chairs by being set on a podium, with a baldachin over it, and being shaped like a throne, in keeping with the lofty civil status of bishops in the post-Constantinian period. Around the year 1000 the bishop's chair was moved to one side of the altar.

The Instruction *Pontificalis ritus* (June 21, 1968) on the simplification of pontifical rites and insignia[28] says that the bishop's chair is henceforth to be known by its traditional name of cathedra and not called a throne, and is not to be surmounted by a baldachin, although existing valuable works of art from the past are not to be removed. The *Caeremoniale Episcoporum* of 1984 makes the point that the cathedra, being a presidential chair, must be clearly visible to the congregation.

As parishes developed in the fourth century, a presidential chair was soon provided for the parish priest. It lost its function, however, from the early Middle Ages on, once the priest began to remain at the altar throughout Mass. Only during Vatican II did it recover its function (Instruction *Inter Oecumenici 92). The GIRM* says that the best place for it is at the back of the sanctuary, facing the people, provided the structure of the sanctuary or other circumstances are not an obstacle (*271*). It is from this presidential chair that the priest leads the liturgy of the word and the concluding part of the Mass; he may also preach and lead the prayer of the faithful from there (*GIRM* 97, 99). It should not resemble a throne and should be plain.[29]

The Ambo (Lectern) as Place of Proclamation

As I pointed out above, the earliest place for proclamation during the liturgy was the cathedra of the bishop or, for the readings, the nearby chairs of the priest and other clerics. As churches became larger, acoustical problems caused the place for the readings and sermon to be moved closer to the congregation. Reader and preacher eventually stood at the altar rail (*cancelli*), which was sometimes placed out in the transept. Then an elevated balustraded platform was erected at the altar rail, with several steps leading up to it; this was given the name *ambo* (from the Greek verb *anabainein* = "go up").

The twelfth century saw the development of a *lectorium* or platform for reading, which was erected between choir and nave; it now separated the "church of the clergy" from the "church of the people." On the side toward the nave an "altar of the cross" was erected; over it was a cross, with statues of Mary and John the Evangelist on either side. Here Mass was celebrated for the people. During the Baroque period most of these altar-platforms were removed as detracting from the inner space of the building.

In churches lacking such platforms movable wooden pulpits were erected during the high Middle Ages, so that the preacher could be closer to the congregation and be more easily heard and understood. From the fourteenth century on, pulpits also took the form of stone structures attached to a pillar or to the side-wall of the church; they were usually basket-shaped, with a sounding-board roof, and had (circular) stairs leading up to them. (*Kanzel,* the German name for "pulpit," is a reminder that the *cancelli,* or altar rails, were the original place for reading and preaching.) One drawback of this solution to the acoustical problem was that a section of the congregation had their backs to the preacher, especially once fixed seats became customary. A further disadvantage was the obscuring of the inner connection between the table of the word and the table of the sacrament.

Vatican II brought a restoration of the ambo (in the form of a lectern). The Instruction *Inter Oecumenici* (96) recommended it; a letter of the Roman Consilium (October 26, 1964) called for it as necessary to the reformed celebration of the liturgy. The *GIRM* requires a stationary ambo, which is to be of such a kind and so located that it is "a natural focal point for the people during the liturgy of the word" (272).[29a]

The Place of Baptism

Special places for baptism are not attested until the third century (for example, in the house-church at Dura Europos).[30] From the fourth century on, special buildings were erected for the administration of baptism, usually close to principal churches. In these "baptisteries" there was a pool sunk in the ground for the baptismal water; it was called a "piscina" (from Latin *piscina* = fish pond) and had three steps leading down into it. It was only 40-60 centimeters deep, so that a complete immersion of adult candidates was hardly possible. Scholars assume, therefore, that the candidates, standing in the pool, had water poured over them and were thus covered with a "garment of water."[31]

Once the authority to baptize was extended from the bishop to the parish priest toward the end of antiquity, churches were satisfied with a portable wooden or stone tub. In the Romanesque period stone fonts, shaped like cups or chalices, were erected in which to keep the baptismal water. These had covers that could be locked, not only for the sake of cleanliness but to prevent the baptismal water with its admixture of holy oils from being used in magical rites. Charles Borromeo and the provincial synod of Milan in 1586, which took its lead from him, required cathedrals and other principal churches to have a separate baptistery, and parish churches to have a font at the left of the entrance. These practices became a kind of unwritten law for large areas of the Western Church. In the first decades of the present century, there was a renewed call for special chapels for baptism.

On the other hand, the 1951 regulations for a reformed Easter Vigil pointed out that baptism ought to be administered within sight of the community that is participating in the liturgy and that separate baptismal chapels are unsuitable from this point of view.[32] This view of the matter was also adopted in the Instruction *Inter Oecumenici* (99) and in the new rites for the baptism of children and adults.[32a]

For the reason just given, fonts near the church door, which in any case usually served only as receptacles for storing the baptismal water, are now outmoded, especially since outside the Easter season the water is blessed new for each baptism and is to be stored there only during the Easter seasons "if feasible." The rite of baptism should be celebrated rather in the area between altar and congregation; the ambo should obviously be used for the liturgy of the word that is part of this rite. The act of baptizing can then be performed in front of the ambo and (or) the Easter candle; because churches differ so much in their arrangement, it is not possible to specify a precise spot. In churches that have sufficient and suitably organized space the portable font can be replaced by an artistic baptismal pool with running water. The Easter candle may be placed close to this pool, thus increasing its symbolic power.

The Place of Choir and Organ

In the beginning, the singing at the liturgy was done by a group of clerics and monks, to which boys were admitted later on (*chorus psallentium; schola cantorum*). They stood around or in front of the altar, out as far as the altar rails. As a result, the entire sanctuary area came to be known as the "choir." The medieval platform for reading and preaching (the *lectorium*) and, in the Baroque period, the gallery at the rear of the church were also places from which the choir sang. There were also tribunes, galleries, and recesses or bays ("swan's nests") near, behind, and above the altar.[33]

Vatican II regards the members of the choir as exercising "a genuine liturgical function" (*SC* 39). The *GIRM* includes the other faithful who contribute to the music of the liturgy, especially organists (63). The place occupied by singers and organists should make it clear that they are part of the united community of the faithful (Instruction *Inter Oecumenici* 97); it should also "readily allow each member complete, that is, sacramental participation in the Mass" (*GIRM*

274). These various prescriptions revived discussion at the highest level regarding the optimal location for the choir. In some "modern" churches built in the third and fourth decades of this century it was decided that the proper place for the choir was the immediate vicinity of the altar.[34] This arrangement is certainly possible in many recent churches with their spacious sanctuaries.

The problem of the optimal location of organ and organist is more difficult. Ever since the organ became known in the kingdom of the Franks through gifts from Byzantium (757 and 811), it has had an important place in the Western liturgy.[35] Only beginning with the late Middle Ages, however, do we have specific information on its location in the Church.[36] In the Catholic churches of the nineteenth century it was usually placed in the gallery at the rear of the church. Since Vatican II there has been a tendency to locate the organ, like the choir, near the altar, either in a side gallery or at floor level. In order, however, to allow choir and organ to be close to one another (since the organist is often the leader of song), it is often necessary to make do with a smaller (supplementary) organ. Organ experts have serious objections to placing the keyboard alone close to the altar, while leaving the organ itself in the rear gallery; they warn that the quality of the organ playing is adversely affected when an electronic keyboard is used.[37] Thus, in many churches the question of the optimal place for the organ and choir is still unanswered.

Door and Atrium

Carolingian and Ottonian architects, and especially the architects of the Romanesque and Gothic periods, devoted special attention and artistic care to the doors of churches. They regarded them as symbolizing the *porta caeli* ("door to heaven") that leads into the heavenly Jerusalem. The symbolism of Christ as door (Jn 10:9; 10:7) also played an important part, as can be seen from the many representations of Christ on the doors of medieval churches. Modern architects usually decorate church doors with unobtrusive biblical or liturgical symbols.

The crossing of the threshold into a church calls for interior purity; for this reason, not only have the faithful been sprinkled with holy water (since the eighth century), but the custom soon developed of also sprinkling, or crossing, oneself with holy water as one enters the house of God. For this purpose a basin of holy water was placed near the entrance. To the motif of purification was added that of remembrance of one's baptism.

Also to be interpreted as a call to a proper interior mood and to purification is the architectural practice in early Christian and early medieval times of having an atrium at the entrance to basilicas. This was a rectangular or square forecourt as wide as the nave and surrounded on three or even four sides by columned halls. With a fountain in the middle and evergreen trees and shrubs around it understandably gave rise to the name "garden of paradise" or simply "paradise." The columned halls were also meeting places for the faithful and, in many cases, places where the catechumens gathered. The building of atria gradually ceased in the high Middle Ages.

The correlative of the atrium in Byzantine architecture is the narthex, also called the pronaos (fore-nave), a forecourt leading to the nave where the faithful participate in the liturgy.

In recent times the important function of an atrium as place of recollection and interior purification has been rediscovered, and its inclusion has been urged for new churches.[38]

Church Towers and Bells

The churches of Christian antiquity did not have towers. The beginnings of medieval church towers go back to the kingdom of Charlemagne. It is thought that two factors played a part in their origin: the tombs of antiquity, which influenced the form of the early medieval towers over crossing and choir, and the need of fortification, which influenced especially the west front of cathedrals and monastery churches.[39] Gradually, even less important churches acquired a tower; these not only symbolized the fortified city of God but subsequently served to house bells. The stairways of the towers gave access to the galleries in churches that had these; the broad shallow steps in the circular stairways of many Romanesque towers also made it easier to carry up building materials and water for putting out fires ("donkey-towers").

The mendicant orders and reform groups (for example, the

Cistercians) regarded towers as an unnecessary expense. Bell towers (campaniles) in the form of structures separate from the church developed early in Italy. Most towers are crowned by a cross or else by a weathercock, which is not a distinctive confessional sign. As early as the ninth century, the weathercock on a church tower symbolized the call to repentance and vigilance and was thus also a symbol of Christ.

Bells probably originated in China, where small bells were in existence in the twelfth century B.C. In the Christian world bells first appeared in monasteries; in the West they reached other communities via itinerant Irish monks. Their function was to call the faithful to divine services and to announce events both joyous and sad. Since the twelfth century many churches have had a whole set of bells, each with its special function.

A blessing for bells developed first in Gaul. The blessing given in the Roman Pontifical of 1961 was a greatly simplified rite (chief elements: sprinkling with holy water, anointing with chrism in the form of a cross in four places). The celebrant was the bishop or a priest whom he delegated. The *Benedictional* of 1984 has a revised rite. It can be celebrated by a priest and includes: introduction, liturgy of the word (with many suggestions for readings), short homily and intercessions, prayer of blessing (two formularies are provided), sprinkling with holy water and incensation (during which Psalm 149 is sung), and solemn final blessing. The blessing of bells can also take place during a mass, after the homily.[40]

THE DEDICATION OF CHURCHES AND ALTARS

Historical Survey

The act of taking possession of a church has from the beginning been celebrated with great joy. It occurred during a solemn pontifical Mass at which the bishop himself preached.[41] At Rome there were no other rites before the seventh century. In the East, however, a rich ceremonial developed at an early date, with its focus chiefly on the altar. The (re)interment of martyrs or saints, or at a later time their relics, played an important part in the ceremony. Since the Second Council of Nicaea in 787 it has been prescribed that relics must be placed in or under every altar.

As early as the sixth century, the Eastern delight in ritual rubbed off on Spain and Gaul, where a varied and extensive set of ceremonies for the dedication of altar and church came into existence; many elements bore the mark less of the New Testament than of Jewish ceremonial law and the ancient pagan religious outlook. From the ninth century on there was a mutual exchange of Roman and Gallo-Frankish elements. Via the Roman-German Pontifical of about 960 two formularies for the new rite reached Rome and were there accepted as the Roman rite for the dedication of churches. Toward the end of the thirteenth century William Durandus, Bishop of Mende (Southern France), expanded the rite still further; it was used in substantially this form until our time. [42]

One fruit of the postconciliar liturgical reform was an *Ordo dedicationis ecclesiae et altaris* which appeared in 1977 as a fascicle of the Roman Pontifical.[43]

Laying of the Cornerstone(Celebration of the Start of Building)
This ceremony, which is the subject of Chapter I of the new rite, came into existence as long ago as the high Middle Ages. The appropriate celebrant is the bishop of the diocese, but he can delegate another bishop or, by way of exception, a priest. The bishop first explains the significance of the laying of the cornerstone and offers an introductory prayer. He then goes in procession with the faithful to the building site, where the place of the future main altar is marked by a wooden cross. A liturgy of the word follows: two readings (with responsorial psalms between) and a gospel, followed by a homily of the bishop. The document pertaining to the laying of the cornerstone and the start of building is then read and signed; the bishop sprinkles the site with holy water, blesses the cornerstone, and lays the stone, with the document, on the foundation. Intercessions, the Our Father, a prayer, and a blessing conclude the celebration.

The Celebration of the Dedication of a Church
A lenghty pastoral introduction at the beginning of Chapter II combines considerations on the "nature and dignity of churches" with suggestions of a more pastoral and rubrical kind. The dedication takes place entirely within the celebration of the Eucharist, which is

"the most important and the one necessary rite for the dedication of a church" (II, 15).

The entrance can take three forms. The first includes a procession to the new church. In the second, the faithful gather at the door of the new church. In the third, they are already inside, and the celebrants come from the sacristy. In all three forms the church is handed over by the builders to the bishop, and the bishop, having blessed water, sprinkles the people, the walls, and finally the altar with it. This opening part of the ceremony ends with the Gloria and the prayer of the day. If relics are to be enclosed in the altar, they are placed in the sanctuary at the beginning of the liturgy between two lighted candles .

The liturgy of the word has three readings. After the bishop's homily and the profession of faith, the litany of the saints is sung and the relics are deposited in or under the altar. The bishop then sings the prayer of dedication, which gives fine expression to what New Testament theology says about the church building. The altar table is now anointed with chrism, as are the walls of the church, the former in four places, the latter in twelve (or four). A brazier is then placed on the altar, and incense is burned in it; the altar, congregation, and church walls are incensed to the accompaniment of singing. After the altar has been cleaned, covered, and decorated with candles, flowers, and a cross, the church is festively lighted as a sign that Christ, the "light of the world," has taken possession of it.

In the ensuing eucharistic celebration Eucharistic Prayer I or III is used, with the insertions provided for this occasion. The special preface once again gives expression to the most important theological statements about the Church as made up of living stones; it does so in hymnic language. After communion, if a Blessed Sacrament chapel is to be inaugurated the bishop carries a pyx containing the Blessed Sacrament to that chapel and places it in the tabernacle there. The concluding prayer, blessing, and dismissal follow.

The Belated Dedication of a Church

Chapter III of the new rite—"Dedication of a Church Already in General Use for Sacred Celebrations"—gives rise to questions. Such a dedication must be regarded as an anomaly, since, as III, 1, says,

Mass ought not to be celebrated in a new church until it has been dedicated. On the other hand, due to adverse circumstances, the liturgy may have been celebrated in a church before an opportunity of dedicating it presents itself. But then one may ask: Has not such a church already been dedicated by the first Eucharist celebrated in it, since the celebration of the Eucharist is "the most important and the one necessary rite" (II, 15)? This is true especially of churches that have received "only" a blessing.[44]

The new rite has evidently made an effort to limit the number of belated blessings of churches, but in doing so it has not been consistent enough. Thus it sets down as one prerequisite that the altars of such churches may not yet have been dedicated. But here again, should not an altar be considered to have been dedicated by the first Eucharist celebrated on it? Or, if the altar is new, it is not enough to dedicate it without dedicating the church?

Another possible justification is that there has been a major change in the building. In this case there can be no objection to a dedication, provided the building is for practical purposes a new one. But can the same be said if the change is simply one of "status in law (for example, the church's being ranked as a parish church)" (III, 1)? Theological consistency is more important than satisfying the desire of a community for a festal dedication of its church.

The Separate Dedication of an Altar

A dedication of an altar alone is provided for cases in which an already dedicated church acquires a new altar; here again the bishop of the diocese is the appropriate celebrant, but he may, if prevented, delegate another bishop or, in special circumstances, a priest. The celebration begins with the opening rites of a special Mass for the occasion; the penitential act is replaced by the blessing of water and the sprinkling of congregation and altar. The three biblical readings are followed by the homily and profession of faith. The litany of the saints is sung instead of the general intercessions. As at the dedication of a church, relics are deposited beneath the altar. The wide-ranging prayer of dedication sings in hymnic language the meaning and importance of the altar for the faithful. Next come the anointing and incensation of the altar, which is then festively illumined. The eucharistic celebration (using Eucharistic Prayer I or III) has its own preface, which "is, as it were, an integral part of the rite of the dedication of an altar" (IV 23).

The Blessing of Churches and Altars

Liturgical use and canon law make a distinction, in dealing with the sacramentals, between *consecrare* ("consecrate, dedicate") and *benedicere* ("bless'). With regard to churches the Code of 1983 says: "As soon as its construction is properly completed, a new church is to be dedicated or at least blessed as soon as possible. . . .Churches, especially cathedral and parochial churches, are to be dedicated with a solemn rite" (can. 1217).[45] According to the *General Instruction of the Roman Missal* both fixed and movable altars are consecrated (dedicated), but movable altars may simply be blessed (265). The difference between dedication and blessing is in the degree of solemnity of prayers and rites. It is with this difference in mind that the new rite for the dedication of churches and altars has chapters on the blessing of a church (V) and an altar (VI).

The Introduction to Chaper V states that "private oratories, chapels, or other sacred edifices set aside only temporarily for divine worship because of special conditions, more properly receive a blessing," (V, 1) of which the bishop of the diocese or a priest delegated by him is the competent minister. The Mass of the day or the Mass of the titular of the church or oratory is used for the celebration. At the beginning, the faithful, the walls of the church or oratory, and the altar (if not yet blessed or dedicated) are sprinkled with holy water. After the intercessions the altar (if need be) is blessed with a short prayer of blessing and then incensed (as are congregation and the main body of the church). The eucharistic celebration ends with a solemn blessing and dismissal. The blessing of an altar applies only to a movable altar, since a fixed altar is always dedicated (VI, 1). The blessing is given during the Mass of the day. After the intercessions and a suitable song the celebrant recites the prayer of blessing (see above). The altar is sprinkled with holy water and incensed. It is then made ready, and the Eucharist is celebrated.

The new rite for the dedication (blessing) of churches and altars has introduced many improvements, both theological and practical. Unfortunately, the prayers whether of dedication or of blessing lack an epiclesis or invocation of the Spirit.[46]

Chapter Twenty-Two

The Liturgy of the Future

There can be no question here of sharply defined prophecies about the future. I shall simply draw some conclusions about the liturgy from the Christian faith and make some suggestions inspired by experience of the recent liturgical reform.

REFLECTIONS ON BASIC PRINCIPLES

An inquiry into the liturgy of the future supposes an affirmative answer to a more basic question: Will there be a liturgy in the future? This "Yes" is based on the belief that God's saving condescension to humanity in Christ will last as long as there are human beings on earth. The cross and resurrection of Christ, which is the cornerstone of this faith, retains its power to illumine and attract; it is the sun that never sets. In addition, the Church is promised uninterrupted continuance as the community of redeemed believers, because the Lord (Mt 28:20) and his Spirit (Jn 14:16, etc.) remain with it. Therefore there will always be human beings who open themselves to God's call and obey it; mindful of the saving acts of Christ in history they will look forward to the consummation of their salvation through, with, and in Christ.

Since the active agents in the liturgy are not only Christ the high priest but also changeable human beings, it is easy to see that the possibility of change in forms is inherent in the liturgy. The liturgical constitution notes that the liturgy contains elements that are divinely instituted and immutable but also "elements subject to change. These not only may but ought to be changed with the passage of time if they have suffered from the intrusion of anything out of harmony with the inner nature of the liturgy or have become pointless" (21). Anyone who reads with care A. L. Mayer's studies on the liturgy in the history of European thought[1] will learn how to look concretely at the liturgy. To some extent the sentence of F. W. Weber also applies here: "And since each new day builds on the rubble of the old, an untroubled eye can look back and see into the future."[2]

THE RECENT REFORM AND ITS RESULTS

Even the concise outline that I have given in this book shows that there exists an almost confusing multiplicity of forms and other data to be comprehended in connection with liturgical assemblies and functions. On the basis of the preliminary work done by the liturgical sciences and the liturgical movement Vatican II and the commissions which it called into existence in the liturgical constitution (no. 21) were able to revise and enrich the liturgy that had developed in the course of time (Jungmann's *Gewordene Liturgie*). The ultimate goal of the reform was "to impart an ever increasing vigor to the Christian life of the faithful" (*SC* 1) or, in other words, to renew the Church by renewing the liturgy. Did not the council expressly say that changes are justified only when "the good of the Church genuinely and certainly requires them" (*SC* 23)?

Anyone who possesses the necessary knowledge of the subject matter and its history and endeavors to assess a reform so unmatched in its extent and intensity must inevitably end with a positive judgment on it, even though many of the steps taken in the reform bear the marks of inevitable compromise. As everyone knows, a convoy can move only as fast as its slowest ship. It must nonetheless be acknowledged that the rites have become clearer and more comprehensible, the texts richer in biblical theology. The old "clerical liturgy" has to a large extent become a community liturgy that is open to active, conscious participation by the faithful. The flexibility of liturgical functions in terms of choice, substitution, and creativity is substantially greater than before.

Despite all this the reform has also elicited dissatisfaction and adverse judgments. These come from contrary quarters: for some the reform has fallen short, for others it has gone too far. This is a clear proof that it has in fact followed a middle course, where (according to the proverb) truth is to be found.

The liturgy after Vatican II has not exhausted its possibilities of improvement. We may think, for example, of the to some extent still unsatisfactory translation of the Latin texts, the often insipid and stereotyped content of many traditional prayers, the weaknesses in the Lectionary for Mass, the still unfulfilled task of creating new liturgical prayers and songs, and the many outdated signs and rubrics that belong in a museum rather than in contemporary life. It is as true of the liturgy as it is of the Church as a whole that it is *semper reformanda,* always in need of reform. At the same time, we must bear in mind that impatience is a poor adviser in matters of liturgical reform.

ASPECTS OF THE LITURGY OF THE FUTURE

The Problem of Freedom and Order in the Liturgy

In the liturgy of the future it will be necessary to strive for a harmonious balance of freedom and order, subjectivity and objectivity, creativity and pre-established forms. On the one hand, the modern science of communication shows us how important the subjective qualities of the celebrant (the "sender") are for his success in informing and appealing to the congregation and how only "messages" on the right wave-length will in fact reach their destination and be received. From this point of view, there is much to be said for the liturgical celebration being personal, creative and true to life. On the other hand, even in its changeable parts the liturgy must have a degree of objectivity and must therefore put limits on subjectivity.

Those who seek at any price to introduce the "streamlined forms" of the moment into the liturgy will usually find themselves limping along behind and trying to catch up with the rapidly changing styles of the moment; they will also repel more of the faithful than they attract. Furthermore, infatuation with the fruits of one's own creativity all too often blinds one to their weaknesses and deficiencies. Even so critical an observer as Karl Rahner, who set great value on personal activity as compared with a more rubricist regulation, warned against throwing the doors wide open to a subjective organization of the liturgy. "Nor is it my view that every theologian ought to compose new eucharistic prayers which no one can tolerate after hearing them for three weeks . . . that every priest should simply be appointed a creative liturgist in every situation and every community. That would lead to nonsense worse than anything we have had in the past or today."[3] In short, a liturgy with a more or less permanent framework and texts formulated in advance provides better conditions for an optimal liturgy.

Nor may we overlook the fact that in an age when human beings are easily manipulated, "creative liturgists" run the risk not only of subjective onesidedness but also of introducing ideological and doctrinal elements that shift the emphasis from where it ought to be and bring confusion into the community. Those who regard this statement as a piece of timorous pessimism will think twice if they attend to the experience of the early Christians in this area. From his prison at sea, Ignatius, the martyr-bishop of Antioch (d. before 117), pleaded with his congregations and exhorted them to unity in the liturgy: "That Eucharist alone must be regarded as trustworthy that is celebrated under the presidency of the bishop or his delegate. . . . Rather, that alone which has been tested is also pleasing to God, so that whatever is done is sure and trustworthy."[4] The history of the Church tells us of many critical periods in which the traditional liturgy was the most important means of preserving unity and served as the standard of orthodoxy.

These considerations do not imply that the competent authorities in the Church may not vary the degree to which free creativity may be exercised or, above all, that they should not allow qualified groups the room to try new forms. But these experiments must remain subject to review. Only then can they lead the way to a better liturgy.

Reducing the Number and Complexity of Texts and Rites

I can illustrate what I have in mind here by a quick glance at a Western celebration of the Eucharist around the year 400. Augustine, bishop of Hippo and a man highly esteemed by his contemporaries and all of later Christianity, began the Sunday Eucharist with the greeting *Dominus Vobiscum* ("The Lord be with you"), and went to his cathedra. The lector then immediately began the first reading. Thus the entire introductory rite, as far as the priest (bishop) was concerned, consisted of two words.

Compare that with our present practice and we will be struck by the profusion of rites and prayers: kissing of the altar, perhaps an incensation of the altar, sign of the cross, greeting (often quite longwinded) of the congregation, introduction to the Mass of the day (often a short sermon), penitential act (with its invitation to reflection and its moment of silence), Kyrie, Gloria, and prayer of the day. At that time, two words; today, with eight parts (some of them extensive). Every age thought it had to add something, and no one later on ever dared to delete any of the additions.

A comparison of the preparation of the gifts at that time and today yields similar results. After the homily and the dismissal of the catechumens Augustine left his cathedra, went to the freestanding altar in the main nave, and led the prayer of the faithful. The deacons then collected the gifts of the congregation and from these selected bread and wine for the Eucharist; meanwhile the choir sang a psalm. Augustine himself did not utter a single prayer at the preparation of the gifts. When the gifts were ready, he began the eucharistic prayer with the preface.[5] Readers can make their own comparison with the present-day preparation of the gifts.

One thing should be clear by now: if the practice of adding and expanding continues into the coming millennium, the two essential parts of the Mass—the liturgy of the word and the liturgy of the Eucharist (in the narrow sense of the term)—will become even more like overgrown gardens; the ratio of framework to essential parts will be even more out of line; and sheer quantity will endanger the quality of participation in the Eucharist.

The conclusion, for the liturgy of the future, is this: If clarifications of the text and rite of the essential parts are recognized to be meaningful and necessary, they are by all means to be accepted (for example, improvements of what we now have or the introduction of new eucharistic prayers). In no case, however, is the framework to be further inflated; the need is rather to eliminate present excess.

As far as the Mass is concerned, it is conceivable and desirable that alongside the full form there should be an abbreviated form, especially for celebration with small groups or on weekdays. When I say "abbreviated" I am not thinking of a shortening of the time taken but of the elimination of an unhealthy profusion. At Vatican II Bishop Duschak, a German bishop working in the missions, made the bold suggestion that alongside the existing form of Mass there is need of a new and simpler one based on the spirit of the New Testament and that both should be made equally valid. Romano Guardini, who was deeply moved by the suggestiion, agreed and, with his own long cherished ideas in mind, said simply: "Yes, that's what we need."[6]

In the intervening years the suggestion has won more and more adherents. When the Congregation for Divine Worship issued a questionnaire in preparation for the Congress of the Presidents and Secretaries of the National Liturgical Commissions (Rome, October 23-28, 1984), representatives expresssed the wish that the Congregation "should once again reflect on whether a single *Ordo Missae* is adequate for all situations."[7]

What I have been saying here of the Eucharist applies, with the necessary changes, to the other areas of the liturgy, namely, that "less is more": elimination and tightening up can lead to qualitative improvement in the form of a more active and, as I shall say in a moment, a more meditative participation in liturgical celebrations.

Promoting a Meditative Silence

Numerous inquiries have shown that many of the faithful (as many as 50 percent) want more periods of silence during the celebration of the liturgy. In not a few parishes emphasis on "active participation" has created an atmosphere of bustle that keeps individuals from an adequate interior recollection and reflection. Many complain about an excessive wordiness in the postconciliar liturgy that makes it difficult for them to utter a "personal kind of prayer."

Such declarations as these ought not to be too quickly dismissed as manifestations of an individualistic piety that has no place in the liturgy. After all, even in the liturgy individuals have the right to bring themselves and their personal concerns before God. Furthermore, texts and signs call for an interior appropriation that is best achieved amid external and interior silence. In addition, the personal dedication and surrender to God that is united to the self-sacrifice of Christ and is an essential element in the active celebration of the Eucharist becomes possible primarily in a period of interior recollection.

The silence of which I am speaking is therefore not simply a pause in the action, but "the tranquillity of the inner life; the quiet at the depths of its hidden stream. It is a collected, total presence, a being 'all there,' receptive, alert, ready."[8]

At this point we must ask to what extent the recent liturgical reform has done justice to this concern. The liturgical constitution does have an article (30) in which various forms of active participation are recommended. Then, in a somewhat disconnected way, comes this further sentence: "And at the proper times all should observe a reverent silence." As J. A. Jungmann has told us, this sentence was added only later on at the wish of the Fathers.[9] The *General Instruction of the Roman Missal* goes into a little greater detail: silence is to be observed "at the designated times as part of the celebration"; "thus at the penitential rite and again after the invitation to pray, all recollect themselves; at the conclusion of a reading or the homily, all meditate briefly on what has been heard; after communion, all praise God in silent prayer" (23).

The liturgy of the future will in all likelihood have to provide more numerous opportunities for meditative silence, for example, during the preparation of the gifts and after the intercessions for the living and for the dead.

It is obvious that such periods of recollected silence must occur within an overall atmosphere that excludes a hectic pace, agitation, and boredom.[10]

Abbreviations

AAS *Acta Apostolicae Sedis* (Rome, 1909ff.)
ALW *Archiv für Liturgiewissenschaft* (Regensburg, 1950ff.)
AÖL *Arbeitsgemeinschaft für ökumenisches Liedgut*
ASS *Acta Sanctae Sedis* (Rome, 1865-1908)
BiLi *Bibel und Liturgie* (Klosterneuburg, 1926ff.)
CCL Corpus Christianorum, Series Latina (Turnhout, 1954ff.)
CD *Christus Dominus:* Decree of Vatican Council II on the Pastoral Office of Bishops (October 28, 1965)
CommAli *Commentarius in Annum Liturgicum Instauratum* (published by the Consilium)
CommNC *Commentarius in Novum Calendarium* (published by the Consilium)
Conc *Concilium* (New York, 1965ff.)
CSEL Corpus Scriptorum Ecclesiasticorum Latinorum (Vienna, 1866ff.)
Diak *Diakonia* (Mainz-Vienna, 1970ff.)
DOL *Documents on the Liturgy 1963-1979. Conciliar, Papal, and Curial Texts,* ed. and trans. International Commission on English in the Liturgy (Collegeville, 1982)
DS Henry Denziger and Adolf Schönmetzer (eds.), *Enchiridion Symbolorum* (Barcelona—Freiburg, 1963^{32})
EL *Ephemerides Liturgicae* (Rome, 1887ff.)
Gd *Gottesdienst* (Trier—Zürich—Salzburg, 1967ff.)
GILH *General Instruction of the Liturgy of the Hours* (1971)
GIRM *General Instruction of the Roman Missal* (1969, 1975^{2})
GNLYC *General Norms for the Liturgical Year and the Calendar* (1969)
GS *Gaudium et spes:* Pastoral Constitution of Vatican Council II on the Church in the Modern World (December 7, 1965)
HK *Herder-Korrespondenz* (Freiburg, 1946ff.)
HLW *Handbuch der Liturgiewinssenschaft,* ed. H. B. Mayer *et al.*
HPTh(Regensburg, 1983ff.) *Handbuch der Pastoral theologie,* ed. F.X. Arnold *et al.* (5 vols.; Freiburg, 1964-72)
HTG *Handbuch theologischer Grundbegriffe,* ed. H. Fries (2 vols.; Munich, 1962f.)
JAC *Jahrbuch für Antike und Christentum,* ed. Th. Klauser and successors (Munster, 1958ff.)
JLH *Jahrbuch für Liturgie und Hymnologie* (Kassel, 1955ff.)

JLW *Jahrbuch für Liturgiewissenschaft* (Münster, 1921-41)
LG *Lumen gentium:* Dogmatic Constitution of Vatican Council II on the Church (November 21, 1964)
LJ *Liturgisches Jahrbuch* (Münster, 1951ff.)
LQF Liturgiegeschichtliche Quellen und Forschungen (Münster, 1908-40, 1957ff.)
LTK *Lexikon für Theologie und Kirche* (Freiburg, 1957ff.[2])
MS J.A. Jungmann, *The Mass of the Roman Rite: Its Origins and Development (Missarum Sollemnia),* tr. F. A. Brunner (2 vols.; New York, 1951-55)
MTZ *Münchener theologische Zeitschrift* (Munich, 1950ff.)
PG Patrologia Graeca, ed. J.-P. Migne (Paris, 1857-66)
PL Patrologia Latina, ed. J.-P. Migne (Paris, 1878-90)
PLHL *Pastoralliturgisches Handlexikon,* ed. A. Adam and R. Berger (Freiburg, 1983[3])
RAC *Reallexikon für Antike und Christentum,* ed. Th. Klauser (Stuttgart, 1941, 1950ff.)
RDK *Reallexikon zur deutschen Kunstgeschichte* VII (Munich, 1981)
REDMF Rerum eccesiasticarum documenta. Series maior: Fontes (Rome, 1955ff.)
RGG *Die Religion in Geschichte und Gegenwart* (6 vols.; Tubingen, 1956[3] to 1962)
RQ *Römische Quartalschrift* (Freiburg, 1887ff.)
SC *Sacrosanctum Concilium:* Constitution of Vatican Council II on the Liturgy (December 4, 1963)
SMGB *Studien und Mitteilungen aus dem Benediktiner- und Zisterzienserorden* (Munich, 1880ff.; Neue Folge since 1911)
SdZ *Stimmen der Zeit* (Freiburg, 1871ff.)
TDNT *Theological Dictionary of the New Testament,* ed. G. F. Bromiley (Grand Rapids)
ThGl *Theologie und Glaube* (Paderborn, 1909ff.)
TPQ *Theologisch-praktische Quartalschrift* (Linz, 1848ff.)
TRE *Theologische Realenzyklopädie* (Berlin-New York, 1977ff.)
TTZ *Trierer theolgische Zeitschrift* (Trier, 1888ff.)
WGL *Werkbuch zum Gotteslob,* ed. J. Seuffert (9 vols.; Freiburg, 1975-79)
ZKG *Zeitschrift für Kirchengeschichte* (Stuttgart, 1876ff.)
ZKT *Zeitschrift für katholische Theologie* (Innsbruck—Vienna, 1877ff.)

Chapter I

[1] See H. Strathmann and R. Meyer, "Leitourgeo," *TDNT* 4:215-31.; E. J. Lengeling, "Liturgie," *HTG* 2:75f.

[2] Among these are: *ministerium, officium, munus, opus, ritus, actio, celebratio, collecta, cultus, mysterium, sacramentum, sacrum, servitium,* and *solemnitas.* See E. J. Lengeling (note 1) 77.

[3] See E. Raitz von Frenz, "Der Weg des Wortes 'Liturgie' in der Geschichte," *EL* 55 (1941) 74-80.

[4] For further details on the presence of Christ in the liturgy see K. Rahner, "The Presence of the Lord in the Christian Community at Worship," in his *Theological Investigations*10, trans. D. Bourke (New York, 1973), 71-83; there is a more extensive treatment with a comprehensive bibliography in F. Eisenbach, *Die Gegenwart Jesu Christi im Gottesdienst* (Mainz, 1982).

[5] Thus, e.g., E. J. Lengeling, *Liturgie — Dialog zwischen Gott und Mensch,* ed. K. Richter (Freiburg, 1981).

[6] *Mediator Dei* 25, trans. in J. J. Megivern (ed.), *Worship and Liturgy: Official Catholic Teachings* (Wilmington, N.C., 1978), 71, no. 208.

[7] See M. Mezger, *Die Amtshandlungen der Kirche* I (Munich, 1963[2]), 91ff.

[8] A. Lorenzer, *Das Konzil der Buchhalter* (Frankfurt, 1981).

[9] *Mediator Dei* 20 (Megivern 68, no. 199).

[10] *Code of Canon Law (Latin-English Edition),* trans. under the auspices of the Canon Law Society of America (Washington, D.C., 1983), 315.

[11] E. Lohmeyer, *Lord of the Temple* (Edinburgh, 1961), 6.

[12] P. Brunner, *Worship in the Name of Jesus,* trans. M. H. Bertram (St. Louis, 1968), 109.

[13] *Ibid.*, 125. See F. Hahn, *The Worship of the Early Church,* trans. D. E. Green (Philadelphia, 1973), 105.

[14] Brunner (n. 12) 126ff. and 197ff.

[15] K. Barth, *Gotteserkenntnis und Gottesdienst nach reformatorischer Lehre* (Zollikon—Zurich, 1938), 190.

[16] Brunner (n. 12) 114.

[17] See Ph. Harnoncourt, *Gesamtkirchliche und teilkirchliche Liturgie* (Freiburg, 1974)

[18] For a quick introduction to the various ministries see *PLHL.*

[19] *Ibid,*, 325f.

Chapter II

[1] R. Stählin, "Die Geschichte des christlichen Gottesdienstes," in *Leitourgia* 1:2.

[2] See *ibid.*; Klauser, *Short History* 1; Jungmann, *MS 1:2.*

3. For more details see F. Hahn, *The Worship of the Early Church*, trans. D. E. Green (Philadelphia, 1973), 36.

4. See Acts 2:46a; 3:1, 5; 12:42; 22:17.

5. See below, Chapter XX, and Adam, *Liturgical Year* 58. for an important recent treatment, see T. J. Talley, *The Origins of the Liturgical Year*, NY, Pueblo, 1986, 1-37.

6. O. Knoch, "'Jeder trage etwas bei. . ." (1 Kor 14, 26,) in *Gemeinde in Herrenmahl* 66.

7. See B. Altaner and A. Stuiber, *Patrologie* (Freiburg, 1978^8), 81; the first half of the second century is regarded as the period of the document's origin.

8. See Hahn (n. 3) 99.

9. *Ad Smyrn.* 8 (Bihlmeyer 108).

10. *Ibid.*, 7.

11. *Ad Eph.* 13 (Bihlmeyer 86).

12. Jungmann, *MS* 1:18.

13. See Stählin (n. 1) 17.

14. Chapter 67; trans. In *MS* 1:23.

15. See *MS* 1:29-30. Critical edition: B. Botte, *La Tradition apostolique de saint Hippolyte. Essai de reconstitution* (LQF 39; Münster, 1963, 1966^3).

16. Stählin (n. 1) 24; see also W. Nagel, *Geschichte des christlichen Gottesdienstes* (Berlin, 1970), 88.

17. See *MS* 1:32.

18. See Adam, *Kirchenbau* 19-26.

19. Klauser, *Short History* 35; idem, *Der Ursprung der bischöflichen Insignien und Ehrenrechte* (Krefeld, n.d.).

20. Jungmann, *Early Liturgy* 124; see also J. Quasten, *Musik und Gesang in den Kulturen der hidnischen Antike und christlichen Frühzeit* (Munich, 1930).

21. Augustine, *Confessions*, trans. R. S. Pine-Coffin (Baltimore, 1961), 191.

22. Documentation and details in Adam, *Liturgical Year* 44-45.

23. For interpretation of the *mysterium tremendum* see R. Kaczynski, *Das Wort Gottes in Liturgie and Alltag der Gemeinden des Johannes Chrysostomus* (Freiburg, 1974), 246-49, especially note 866.

24. Nagel (n. 16) 56f.

25. *Serm.* 252, 4; see F. van der Meer, *Augustine the Bishop*, trans. B. Battershaw and G. R. Lamb (New York, 1961; Harper Torchbooks, 1965), 169-77; the citation from Augustine is on p. 171.

26. *Martyrium Polycarpi* 18 (Bihlmeyer 1:130); see Jungmann, *Early Liturgy* 177.

27. For details see T. Klauser, *Christlicher Märtyrerkult, heidnischer Heroenkult und*

spätjüdische Heiligenverehrung (Cologne—Opladen, 1960); B. Kötting, "Heiligenverehrung," *HTG* 1:633-41.

28. Jungmann, *Early Liturgy* 281.

29. Wegman 93.

30. See F. Chirayath, *Taufliturgie des Syro-Malabrarischen Ritus* (Das östliche Christentum, N.F. 32; Würzburgh, 1981).

31. For details on the Eastern rites see, among others, I.-H. Dalmais, *Eastern Liturgies*, trans. D. Attwater (20th Century Encyclopedia of Catholicism 112; New York, 1960); W. Nyssen, *et al.*, *Handbuch der Ostkirchenkunde* I (Düsseldorf, 1984); J. M. Hanssens, *Institutiones liturgicae de ritibus orientalibus* (Rome, 1930-32).

32. *Itinerarium Egeriae*, ed. A. Francheschini and R. Weber (Turnhout, 1968); *Egeria's Travels*, trans. J. Wilkinson 2nd ed. Warminster, 1981.

33. For an extensive treatment see H. -J. Schulz, *The Byzantine Liturgy*, trans. M. J. O'Connell (New York, 1986); S. Heitz, *Der orthodoxe Gottesdienst* (Mainz, 1968), is a kind of popular missal that includes the liturgy for the sacraments.

34. W. Rötzer, *Des hl. Augustinus Schriften als liturgiegeschichtliche Quelle* (Munich, 1930); see F. Van der Meer, *Augustine the Bishop* (n. 25).

35. See T. Klauser, "Der Übergang der römischen Kirche von der griechischen zur lateinischen Liturgiesprache," in *Miscellanea G. Mercati* I (Vatican City, 1946), 467-82; idem, *Short History* 18-24.

36. Can. 21 (Mansi 3 [1759] 922).

37. See Neunheuser, *Storia* 57.

38. Most important edition: L. C. Mohlberg, L. Eizenhöfer, and P. Siffrin, *Sacramentarium Veronense* (REDMF 1: Rome, 1956). On the *libelli* see A. Stuiber, *Libellli sacramentorum Romani* (Theophaneia 6; Bonn, 1950) and D. M. Hope, *The Leonine Sacramentary*, Oxford, 1971.

39. Edited by, among others, L. C. Mohlberg, P. Siffrin, and L. Eizenhöfer, *Liber sacramentorum Romanae aeclesiae ordinis anni circuli* (REDMF 4; Rome, 1960); see A. Chavasse, *Le sacramentaire gélasine* (Paris, 1958).

40. K. Gamber, *Codices litiurgici latini antiquiores* (Spicilegii Friburgensis Subsidia 1; Fribourg, 1968[2]). For a complete survey of the development of Sacramentaries in English, see, C. Vogel, *Medieval Liturgy*, trans, by William Starey and N. Rassmussen, Washington, D.C. 1986, 61-106.

41. E. Bishop, "The Liturgical Reforms of Charlemayne", *Domside Review* 38 (1919), 1-16. See his "Genius of the Roman Rite" in *Liturgica Historica*, Oxford, 1918, 1-19.

42. Jungmann, *Early Liturgy* 296-97.

43. Surveys of the topic in Radò 1:103-5; Righetti 1:144-53.

44. See *MS* 1:83.

45. *MS* 1:89

46. Examples in *MS* 1:130, note 20.

47. Wegman 201.

48. The classical critical edition is by M. Andrieu, *Les Ordines Romani du haut moyen-âge* (5 vols.; Spicilegium Sacrum Lovaniense 11, 23, 24, 28, 29; Louvain, 1931-61), see Vogel, *Medival Liturgy*, 135-154

49. Klauser, "Austauschbezienhungen," 149f.

50. See F. Kemp, *et al.*, *The Church in the Age of Feudalism*, trans. A. Biggs (Handbook of Church History 3, ed. H. Jedin and J. Dolan; New York, 1969), 300 (essay of J. A. Jungmann).

51. Details in Adam, *Kirchenbau* 29-40.

52. Mayer, *Liturgie* 70.

53. *Ibid.*, 73.

54. Adam, *Kirchenbau* 40-47.

55. See H. B. Meyer, "Die Elevation im deutschen Mittelalter und bei Luther," *ZKT* 85 (1963) 161-217.

56. Details in P. Browe, *Die Pflichtkommunion im Mittelalter* (Münster, 1940); idem, *Die häufige Kommunion im Mittelalter* (Münster, 1938); idem, *Die Verehrung der Eucharistie im Mittelalter* (Münster, 1933).

57. *MS* 1:130, note 20.

58. J. Lortz, *The Reformation in Germany*, trans. R. Wall (2 vols; New York, 1968), 1:97-98. The author gives appalling facts about the "clerical proletariat" of the prereformation period.

59. *MS* 1:131.

60. Jungmann, *Pastoral Liturgy* 79.

61. See Neunheuser, *Storia* 110.

62. G. Witzel's plans for the reformation of Fulda (1542), in G. Pfeilschifter (ed.), *Acta reformationis catholicae* IV/2 (Regensburg, 1971), 246, with a translation into modern German by the editor. See L. Pralle, "Die volksliturgischen Bestrebungen des G. Witzel," *Archiv für mittelrheinische Kirchengeschichte* 3 (1948) 224-42.

63. Görres-Gesellschaft (ed.), *Concilium Tridentinum* VIII (Freiburg, 1964), 916-21.

64. H. Jedin, "Das Konzil von Trient und die Reform des römischen Messbuches," *Liturgisches Leben* 6 (1939) 47.

65. J. A. Jungmann, "Das Konzil von Trient und die Erneuerung der Liturgie," in G. Schreiber (ed.), *Das Weltkonzil von Trient* I (Freiburg, 1951), 328.

66. *Ibid.*, 329f.

67. Sess. 22, cap. 8: DS 1749. English translation in: J. Neuner and J. Dupuis (eds.), *The Christian Faith in the Doctrinal Documents of the Catholic Church* (rev. ed.; Staten Island, N.Y., 1982), no. 1554 (p. 427).

68. Cited in *MS* 1:146, note 30.

69. Klauser, *Short History* 2.

70. P. Jounel, "From the Council of Trent to Vatican II," in Martimort (1), ET 1:44.

71. Details in H. Vehlen, "Geschichtliches zur Überstzung des Missale Romanum," *Liturgisches Leben* 3 (1936) 90-95.

72. Klauser, *Short History* 120.

73. Jungmann, *Pastoral Liturgy* 88. [I have re-translated the first sentence form the German. —Tr.]

74. DS 2600-2700.

75. H. Schotte, "Zur Geschichte des Emser Kongresses," *Historisches Jahrbuch der Görres-Gesellschaft* 35 (1914) 89-109, 319-48, 781-820.

76. There is a short survey in F. Kolbe, *Die liturgische Bewegung* (Aschaffenburg, 1964), 15-19. More detailed studies: W. Trapp, *Vorgeschichte und Ursprung der liturgichen Bewegung* (Regensburg, 1940); A. Vierbach, *Die liturgischen Anschauugen des V. A. Winter* (Munich, 1929); Mayer, *Liturgie* 185-245; M. Probst, *Gottesdienst in Geist und Wahrheit: Die liturgischen Ansichten und Bestrebungen Joh. Mich. Sailers* (Regensburg, 1976); H. Hollerweger, *Die Reform des Gottesdienstes zur Zeit des Josephinismus in Osterreich* (Regensburg, 1976); G. Duffrer, *Auf dem Weg zur liturgischen Frömmigkeit. Das Werk des Markus Adam Nickel* (Speyer, 1962); A. Steiner, *Liturgiereform in der Aufklärungszeit* (Freiburg, 1976); W. Muller, "Die liturgischen Bestrebungen des Konstanzer Generalvikars Wessenberg (1774-1860)," *LJ* 10 (1960) 232-38. See also L. Snidler.

77. Mayer, *Liturgie* 272ff.

78. The *Institutions liturgiques* was in three volumes (1st ed.: Paris, 1840-51); the *Année liturgique* was in nine volumes (1st ed.: Paris, 1841-66).

79. *Institutions liturgiques* 3:71.

80. *Ibid.*, 168.

81. *Ibid.*, 4:340 (published posthumously: Paris, 1978[2]).

82. *Ibid.*, 2:35.

83. See A. Heinz, "Im Banne der römischen Einheitsliturgie. Die Romanisierung der Trierer Bistumsliturgie in der zweiten Hälfte des 19. Jahrh.,' *RQ* 79 (1984) 1-2.

84. Mayer, *Liturgie* 385.

85. Thus, e.g., B. Neunheuser, "Die klassische Liturgische Bewegung 1909-1963 and die nachkonziliare Liturgiereform," in *Mélanges liturgiques offerts au R. P. Dom Botte* (Louvain, 1972); O. Rousseau, *The Progress of the Liturgy: An Historical Sketch* (Westminster, Md., 1951; French original, 1945); Th. Bogler (ed.), *Liturgische Erneuerung in aller Welt* (Maria Laach, 1950); idem (ed.), *Liturgische Bewegung nach 50 Jahren* (Maria Laach, 1959); H. A. P. Schmidt, *Intoductio in liturgiam occidentalem* (Rome, 1960), 164-208; F. Kolbe (n. 76, above), 33-36; B. Botte, *Le mouvement liturgique* (Paris, 1973); W. Birnbaum (Evangelical), *Das Kultusproblem un die liturgischen Bewegungen* I. *Die*

deutsche katholische liturgische Bewegung (Tübingen, 1966).

86. *ASS* 36 (1903-4) 330; trans. in J. J. Megivern (ed.), *Worship and Liturgy. Official Catholic Teachings* (Wilmington, N.C., 1978), 18, No. 28.

87. B. Fischer, "Das 'Mechelner Ereignis,'" *LJ* 9 (1959) 203-19; F. Kolbe (n. 76), 33-36; L. Bouyer, *Dom Lambert Beauduin, un homme d'Eglise* (Tournai, 1964).

88. *Vom Geist der Liturgie* (Freiburg, 1919). ET: *The Spirit of the Liturgy,* trans. A. Lane (London, 1930).

89. Münster, 1909-41; 1957ff.

90. Münster, 1921-41; now *Archiv für Liturgiewissenscaft* (Regensburg, 1950ff.)

91. ET: *The Sacramentary,* trans. A. Levelis-Marke and (for completion of vol. 5) W. Fairfax-Cholmeley (5 vols.; New York, 1924-30).

92. Casel's teaching did not go unchallenged, but on the whole it led to a deeper understanding of the liturgical celebration and of many cultic expressions and symbols. Most important works: *The Mystery of Christian Worship, and Other Writings* (Westminster, Md., 1962); *Das christliche Festmysterium* (Paderborn, 1941); other writings in *JLW,* especially in the volumes for 1926, 1933, and 1941. Recent evaluation: A. Schilson, *Theologie als Sakramententheologie. Die Mysterientheologie Odo Casels* (Mainz, 1982); idem., "Neue Wende zum Mysterium," *Gd* 18 (1984) 72-76.

93. See B. Neunheuser, "Die 'Krypta-Messe' in Maria Laach," *Liturgie und Mönchtum* 28 (1961) 70-82.

94. M. Kassiepe, *Irrwege und Umwege im Frömmigkeitsleben der Gegenwart* (Kevelaer, 1939); A. Doerner, *Sentire cum Ecclesia* (Munich-Gladbach, 1941).

95. Initially published for private circulation under the title "Ein Wort zur liturgischen Frage."

96. The foregoing remarks are based for the most part on inspection of the documents in the literary remains of Bishop A. Stohr. See also Th. Maass-Ewerd, *Die Krise der liturgischen Bewegung* (Regensburg, 1981).

97. See J. Wagner (ed.), *Erneuerung der Liturgie aus dem Geist der Seelsorge* (Trier, 1957).

98. In *The Assisi Papers* (Collegeville, 1957), 224. See the Constitution on the Liturgy 43.

99. H. A. P. Schmidt, *Die Konstitution über die heilige Liturgie. Text, Vorgeschichte, Kommentar* (Freiburg, 1965), 65f.

100. For commentaries in English see, e.g., J. A. Jungmann, in *Commentary on the Documents of Vatican II,* ed. H. Vorgrimler (New York, 1967), 1:1-87. There is a list of commentaries in *EL* 78 (1964) 562-72; 79 (1965) 465-80.

101. The documents connected with these various liturgical books, as well as new translation of the introductory material in many of them, are in *DOL.* The rites themselves are in: *The Rites of the Catholic Church* (2 vol.; New York, 1976 and 1980).

102. Still to come are, among others, the Roman Martyrology; volume 5 of the *Liturgia horarum* with a second annual cycle of biblical and patristic readings; a replacement for the "major exorcism." See International Commission on English in the Liturgy,

Emendations in the Liturgical Books Following Upon the New Code of Canon Law (Washington, D.C., 1984). For some other desiderata see E. J. Lengeling, "Zum 20. Jahrestag der Liturgiekonstitution," *LJ* 34 (1984) 122f.

[103.] See H. B. Meyer, "Una voce—Nunc et semper? Konservative Bewegungen nach dem Konzil," *SdZ* 180 (1967) 73-90.

[104.] The Indult is translated in *Origins* 14, no. 19 (October 25, 1984), 290. See also the commentary of K.-O. Nussbaum, "Die bedingte Wiederzulassung einer Messfeier nach dem Missale Romanum von 1962," *Pastoralblatt* 37 (1985) 130-43.

Chapter III

[1.] Examples of this fantasizing, improvisatory method, which Albert vehemently rejected, are given in *MS* I, 113-14.

[2.] Volumes I and II, Passau, 1832; volume III, 1833. There were further reprintings.

[3.] Bäumer in a review of V. Thalhofer, *Handbuch der katholischen Liturgik* I (Freiburg, 1883) in *ZKT* 13 (1889) 351.

[4.] R. Guardini, "Über die systematische Methode in der Liturgiewissenschaft," *JLW* 1 (1921) 97-108; reprinted in Guardini, *Auf dem Wege. Versuche* (Mainz, 1923) 95-110 (citation from 104).

[5.] A. Wintersig, "Pastoralliturgik. Ein Versuch über Wesen, Einteilung and Abgrenzung einer seelsorgwissenschaftlichen Behandlung der Liturgie," *JLW* 4 (1924) 153-67 at 166.

[6.] A. A. Häussling, "Liturgiewissenschaft zwei Jahrzehnte nach Konzilsbeginn," *ALW* 24 (1982) 1-18 at 4; see J. A. Jungmann, "Liturgy, IV. Study of Liturgy," in *Sacramentum Mundi* 3 (New York, 1969) 337-40.

[7.] On the origin of the term "pastoral liturgy" see H. Rennings, "The Goals and Tasks of Liturgical Science," *Concilium* no. (1969).

[8.] See H. W. Gartner and M. B. Merz, "Prolegomena für eine intergrative Methode in der Liturgiewissenschaft. Zugleich eim Versuch zur Gewinnung der empirischen Dimension," *ALW* 24 (1982) 165-89; see A. A. Haussling (n. 6), 8f.; F. Kohlschein, "Liturgiewissenchaft in Wandel," *LJ* 34 (1984) 32-49.

[9.] National Conference of Catholic Bishops, The program of Priestly Formation; 3rd ed. (Washington, 1981), nos. 396-399

[10.] K. Richter, *LJ* 32 (1982) 60; on the multiplicity of methods see H. Reifenberg, *Fundamentalliturgie* I (Klosterneuburg, 1978), 67.

[11.] E. Griese, "Perspektiven einer liturgischen Theologie," *Una sancta* 24 (1969) 102-13; see M. -J. Krahe, "'Psalmen, Hymnen und Lieder, wie der Geist es eingibt.' Doxologie als Ursprung und Ziel der Theologie," in H. Becker and R. Kaczynski (eds), *Liturgie und Dichtung* II (St. Ottilien, 1983), 923-58.

[12.] See A. A. Häussling, "Die kritische Funktion der Liturgiewissenschaft," in H. B. Meyer (ed.), *Liturgie und Gesselschaft* (Innsbruck, etc., 1970), 103-30.

[13.] *Ibid.*, 129f. Haussling seems to be modifying here a view expressed earlier in the same essay, namely, that liturgics must deal, among other things, with "the theological reappraisal of the problem of atheism" (123ff.).

[14.] On this relatively new concept see J. Sudbrack, "Spiritualität," in *HPTh* V, 533-37, with further bibliography.

[15.] See W. Dürig's valuable study, *Pietas liturgica* (Regensburg, 1958).

[16.] See also K. Richter, "Liturgische Frömmigkeit im Wandel," *Diak* 16 (1958) 99-106.

[17.] There is a valuable compilation in K. Gamber, *Codices liturgici latini antiquiores* (Spicilegium Friburgense, Subsidia 1; Fribourg, 1968[2]).

[18.] See the list of revised liturgical books above in Chapter II.

Chapter IV

[1.] F. Kohlschein, "Gekreuzigte Liturgie. . .," *Gd* (1982) 113.

[2.] There are numerous manuals and reference books on this subject; e.g., P. Watzlawick *et al.*, *Menschliche Kommunikation. Formen, Störungen, Paradoxien* (Bern, 1970[2]); H. Bühler *et al.*, "Einführung in die Grundlagen der sprachlichen Kommunikation," in *Linguistik* I (Tübingen, 1970); G. Meggle, *Grundbegriffe der Kommunikation* (Berlin, 1981).

[3.] Helpful, among others, are Ph. Harnoncourt, "Liturgie als kommunikatives Geschehen," *LJ* 25 (1975) 5-27; F. Kohlschein, "Die liturgische Feier als Kommukationsgeschehen," in: Katholische Fachhochschule Mainz (ed.), *Theorie für Praxis* (Mainz, 1982), or, in abridged form, in *Theologie der Gegenwart* 26 (1983) 1-13.

[4.] No. 23 (*DOL* 276 no. 2156).

[5.] *Sermo Frangipane* 2, 8, in G. Morin (ed.), *Miscellanea Agostiniana* I (Rome, 1930), 199.

[6.] For an appraisal see G. Schmidtchen, *Zwischen Kirche und Welt* (Freiburg, 1972); idem, *Priester in Deutschland* (Freiburg, 1983); see the commentary of K. Forster (ed.), *Befragte Katholiken—Zur Zukunft von Galube und Kirche* (Freiburg, 1973[7]).

[7.] L. Roos, "Erwartungen and die Predigt," *Oberrhein. Pastoralblatt* 75 (1974) 44.

[8.] As early as 1968 in an essay, "Ein erquickender Gottesdienst," *Gd* 2 (1968) 67f., 76, K. Tilmann formulated these three expectations: "One would like to achieve some interior repose," "get closer to God," and "take some good throught away for the remainder of the week." See B. Fischer, "Gottesdienst als Ort der Ruhe," *Gd* 8 (1974) 185ff.; 9 (1975) 4f.

[9.] Extensive documentation in C. Korolevsky, *Living Languages in Catholic Worship: An Historical Inquiry*, trans. D. Attwater (Westminster, Md., 1957). The French original was published in Paris in 1955 under the title *Liturgie en langue vivante.*

[10.] Martimort (1), ET 1:137-38. Some reservations apply to the Nestorian Syrian Church in its missionary activity east of the Euphrates (*ibid.*).

[11.] See Th. Klauser, "Der Übergang der römischen Kirche von der griechischen zur lateinischen Liturgiesprache," in *Miscellanea G. Mercati* I (Vatican City, 1946), 467-82;

G. Bardy, *La question des langues dans 1'Eglise ancienne* (Paris, 1948). Also, Klauer, *Short History.*

12. PL 17:255

13. PL 126:906B. Details on the mission of Cyril and Methodius to the Slavs in Korolevsky (n. 9) 72-90.

14. Mansi 20:296f.

15. J. Fischer, *Essai historique sur les idées reformatrices des cardinaux Gian Pietro Carafa et Réginald Pole* (dissertation; Paris, 1957), 83f.

16. Cited in L. A. Veit and L. Lenhart, *Kirche und Volksfrömmigkeit im Zeitalter des Barock* (Freiburg, 1956), 16.

17. Session 22, canon 6 (DS 1759); Neuner-Dupuis 1563.

18. Details in H. Vehlen, "Geschichtliches zur Übersetzung des Missale Romanum," *Liturgisches Leben* 3 (1936) 89-97. See also F. Ellen Weaver.

19. *AAS* 30 (1897-98) 39-53. Despite all the prohibitions a surprisingly large number of German translations of the Missal were published; see A. A. Häussling, *Das Missale deutsch. . .* (LQF 66; Münster, 1984).

20. A detailed appraisal of the arguments on both sides is given by, among others, P. Winninger, *Volkssprache und Liturgie* (Trier, 1961).

21. *DOL* 123 nos. 838-80; official French text in Kaczynski 421-30.

22. E. J. Lengeling, "Wort, Bild, Symbol in der Liturgie," *LJ* 30 (1980) 242.

23. Extensive discussion in H. Becker and R. Kaczynski (eds.), *Liturgie und Dichtung* (2 vols.; St. Ottilien, 1983); see K. Rahner, "Poetry and the Christian," in his *Theological Investigations* 4, trans. K. Smyth (Baltimore, 1966), 357-67.

24. Further considerations in P. Born, "Sprache und Sprechen im Gottesdienst," *LJ* 25 (1975) 28-46.

25. *Summa theologiae* III, q. 60, a. 4 c.

26. W. Jetter, *Symbol und Ritual. Anthropologische Elemente im Gottesdienst* (Göttingen, 1978), 28f. See also D. Powers, *Unsearchable Riches,* NY, Pueblo.

27. A. Verheul, *Introduction to the Liturgy: Towards a Theology of Worship,* trans. M. Clarke (Collegeville, 1968), 106.

28. *Ibid.*

29. For various other concepts of "symbol" see R. Fleischer, "Zeichen, Symbol und Transzendenz," in R. Volp (ed.), *Zeichen. Semiotik in Theologie und Gottesdienst* (Munich—Mainz, 1982), 175-77; also T. Todorov

30. The unsatisfactory character of the usual criteria used in distinguishing between sign and symbol is also pointed out by A. Wucherer-Huldenfeld, "Theologie des Symbols," in E. Hesse and E. Erharter (eds.), *Liturgie in der Gemeinde* (Vienna, 1966), 94: "The attempt of some to gain an experience of symbol on the basis of signs has not led to any satisfactory result but has rather brought them up against the prob-

lems inherent in the concept of sign itself." See also Ph. Harnoncourt, "Der Gebrauch von Zeichen und Symbolen in der Liturgie," *TPQ* 133 (1985) 114-24.

31. W. Jetter (n. 26) 74.

32. *Ibid.*, 24.

33. *Ibid.*, 25, note 4.

34. G. Schiwy *et al.*, Zeichen im Gottesdienst (Munich, 1976), 10. On 141, note 2, the editor gives a short survey of the numerous competing schools and systems of semiotics, which cannot as yet be shown to have any common denominatior.

35. G. Schiwy (n. 34) provides an easily understandable introduction to the most important technical terms and methods of semiotics; he endeavors to give the reader a practical initiation into the "outlook" of semiotics as applied especially to the liturgy. See also R. Volp (n. 29).

36. From a poem of Silja Walter, cited in I. Jorissen and H. B. Meyer, *Zeichen und Symbole im Gottesdienst* (Innsbruck, etc., 1977), 11.

37. *Serm.* 74, 1 (PL 54:398).

38. *Summa theologiae* III, q. 60, a. 3 c.

39. I may mention, among others, R. Guardini, *Sacred Signs,* trans. G. Branahan(St. Louis, 1956); H. Lubienska de Lenval, *The Whole Man at Worship: The Actions of Man before God,* trans. R. Attwater (New York, 1961); D. Forstner, *Die Welt der christlichen Symbole* (Innsbruck, etc., 1982[4]); A. Kirchgässner, *Die machtigen Zeichen* (Freiburg, 1959); B. Kleinheyer, *Heil erfahren im Zeichen* (Munich, 1980); A. Kuhne, *Zeichen und Symbole im Gottesdienst und Leben* (Paderborn, 1982); H. Kirchhoff, *Ursymbole und ihre Bedeutung fur die religiöse Erziehung* (Munich, 1982); B. Fischer, *Signs, Words and Gestures. Short Homilies on the Liturgy,* trans. M. J. O'Connell (New York, 1981).

40. S. Walter and J. Baumgartner, *Tanz vor dem Herrn* (Zurich, 1974); Ch. Bittner, *Der religiöse Ausdruckatanz* (Munich, 1982); see *Gd* 18 [1984] 13; T. Berger, *Liturgie und Tanz. . .* (St. Octilien, 1985); W. Schneider, *Getanztes Gebet* (Freiburg, 1986). Also, J.G. Davies.

41. See below, Chapter XXI. Detailed discussion in Adam, *Kirchenbau.*

42. See Clement of Alexandria (d. before 215), *Paed* .III, 11 (PG 8:657).

43. For the history of liturgical vestments: J. Braun, *Die liturgische Gewandung im Occident und Orient* (Freiburg, 1907); idem, *Die liturgischen Paramente in Gegenwart und Vergangenheit* (Freiburg, 1924); J. Wagner, "Die geschichtliche Entwicklung der liturgischen Gewandung. . .," *Das Münster* 32 (1979) 91-94 and C. E. Pocknee. For present-day practice see *GIRM* 297-306, and Lengeling, *Ordnung* 405-11.

44. See R. Kaczynski, "Über Sinn und Bedeutung liturgischer Gewander," *Das Munster* 32 (1979) 94-96; H. Rennings, "Liturgische Kleidung im Wandel," *Gd* 13 (1979) 113-15. Also, R. Hovda.

45. W. Schöeneis, "Antique Farbung und liturgische Farben," *LJ* 8 (1958) 140-43 (with further bibliography); T. Schnitzler, "Von Geschichte und Sinn der liturgischen Gewandung und Färbung," *Das Münster* 32 (1979) 97-99; R. Kroos and F. Kobler,

"Farbe, liturgisch in der kath. Kirche," *RDK* 7 (1981) 54-121; A. A. Häussling and E. Hofhansl "Farben—Farbensymbolik," *TRE* 11 (1983) 25-30.

46. Innocent III, *De sacro altaris mysterio* I, 65 (PL 217:799-802).

47. William Durandus of Mende, *Rationale divinorum officiorum* III, 18.

48. See J. Braun (n. 43), *Die liturgische Gewandung im Occident und Orient* 753f.

49. K. Goldammer, "Farbe, liturgisch (prot.)," *RDK* 7 (1981) 122f.

50. *Ibid.*, 128.

51. B. Ficher, "Reform der Zeichensprache bei der nachkonziliaren Erneuerung der katholischen Liturgie," *LJ* 35 (1985) 45-57, has shown conclusively that the indictment of the reformed liturgy for hostility to signs is groundless.

52. A. Verheul (n. 27) 116.

53. K. H. Bieritz, "Zeichen der Eröffnung," in R. Volp (n. 29) 209.

54. In a Berlin lecture, cited in *Leitourgia* I, 403f.

55. R. Schwarz, *Kirchenbau. Welt vor der Schwelle* (Heidelberg, 1960), 13.

56. See A. Adam, *Firmung und Seelsorge* (Dusseldorf, 1959), 235; for other examples, see A. Chupungco, *Cultural Adaptation of the Liturgy.*

57. R. Guardini, "Der Kultakt und die gegenwärtige Aufgabe der liturgischen Bildung," published in, among other sources, *LJ* 14 (1964) 101-6, and W. Becker (ed.), *Romano Guardini. Ein Gedenkbuch mit einer Auswahl aus seine werk* (Leipzig, n.d.; probably 1969-70), 323-33. In footnote 1 accompanying the text it is said that "for this printing, the original wording has at many points been made somewhat more accurate or has been somewhat expanded."

58. In the preface of his *Sacred Signs* , 10(n. 39) Guardini wrote: "The primary need is to learn that living act by which the believing person apprehends, receives, and accomplishes the holy 'visible signs of invisible grace'".

59. B. Nauheuser, "Liturgiefähigkeit. Mindestmass der Vorbedingungen," in Th. Bogler (ed.), *Ist der Mensch von heute noch liturgiefähig?* (Maria Laach, 1966).

60. This view is shared by the respected French liturgist and musicologist J. Gelineau, in his *Die Liturgie von morgen* (Regensburg, 1979), 95.

61. R. Guardini, *Mediations Before Mass,* trans. E. C. Briefs (Westsminster, Md., 1955), 4-5.

62. R. Guardini, *Besinnungen vor der Feier der heiligen Mess* (Mainz, 1949[4]), 329. On this problem, see also J. Pieper, *In Tune with the World: A Theory of Festivity,* Chicago, 1973.

Chapter V

1. Instruction *Musicam sacram,* 4b (*DOL* 508 no. 4125). Latin text in Kaczynski 276, no. 736.

2. A German version appeared as a supplement to *Gd* 14 (1980) no. 15.

3. O. Söhngen, "Theologische Grundlagen der Kirchenmusik," *Leitourgia* IV, 12.

4. See B. Fischer, *Die Psalmen als Stimme der Kirche*, ed. A. Heinz (Trier, 1982).

5. I am especially indebted in this survey to H. Musch, "Entwicklung und Entfaltung der christlichen Kultmusik des Abendlandes," in idem (ed.), *Musik im Gottesdienst* I (Regensburg, 1983[2]) 9-107. There is also a detailed exposition in K. G. Fellerer (ed.), *Geschichte der katholischen Kirchenmusik* (2 vols.; Kassel, 1972-76).

6. Augustine, *Enarr. in Ps.* 32, I, 8 (CCL 38:254).

7. There is an important collection of hymns in G. M. Dreves, *Ein Jahrtausend lateinischer Hymnesndichtung* (2 vols.; Leipzig, 1909); G. M. Dreves and C. Blume (ed.), *Analecta hymnica medii aevi* (56 vols.; Leipzig, 1886-1922).

8. H. Musch (n. 5) 25f.

9. *Ibid.*, 30.

10. See K. G. Fellerer, "Das Tridentinum und die Kirchenmusik," in G. Schreiber (ed.), *Das Weltkonzil von Trient. Sein Werden and Wirken* I (Freiburg, 1951), 447.

11. *Ibid.*, 449.

12. H. Musch (n. 5) 43.

13. K. G. Fellerer, "Kirchenmusik II," *LTK*[2] 6:236.

14. Translation in *Official Catholic Teachings: Worship and Liturgy*, ed. J. J. Megivern (Wilmington, N.C., 1976).

15. J. Janota, *Studien zu Funktion und Typen des geistlichen Liedes im Mittelalter* (Münchener Texte und Untersuchungen zur deutschen Literatur des MA 23; Munich, 1968); W. Lipphardt, "Das Kirchenlied im Mittelalter," *MGG* 8:783-96; Ph. Harnoncourt, *Gesamtkirchliche und teilkirchliche Liturgie. Studien zum liturgischen Heiligenkalender und zum Gesang im Gottesdienst* (Freiburg, 1974), 294-446.

16. Ph. Harnoncourt (n. 15) 299.

17. *Ibid.*, 306.

18. The first German diocesan hymnal appeared in 1576 at Dillingen for Bamberg; see B. Schmid, "Deutscher Liturgiegesang," in H. Musch (n. 5), 395f.

19. P. Harnoncourt (n. 15) 358. See also J. Hacker, *Die Messe in den deutschen Dozesan-Gesang- und Gebetbüchern von der Aufklärung bis zur Gegenwart* (Munich, 1951); M. Hofer, *Die Gesang- und Gebetbücher der schweizerischen Diözesen* (Fribourg, 1965).

20. Ph. Harnoncourt (n. 15), 358-66, provides extensive documentation for this wide-ranging and many-faceted controversy.

21. Further details with references to aids and bibliography in "Gotteslob," *PLHL*. On the contemporary importance of hymns see Ph. Harnoncourt, "Das Bleibende in Form, Inhalt und Funktion des deutschen Kirchenliedes," *ZKT* 107 (1985) 52-63.

22. Translation in *DOL* 508 nos. 4122-90.

23. H. Rennings, "Musikalische Elemente als Teil des gottesdienstlichen Handelns,"

in H. Hucke *et al.* (eds.), *Musik in der feiernden Gemeinde* (Eisiedeln—Freiburg, 1974), 55.

24. H. Musch (n. 5), first ed. (1975), 10.

25. *Ibid.*

26. Ph. Harnoncourt, "Erneuerte Kirchenmusik. . .," in E. Hesse and H. Erharter (eds.), *Liturgie in der Gemeinde* (Vienna, 1966), 121.

27. Further discussion in K. Amon, "Kleine Schonheiten. . .," *Gd* 14 (1980) 113f.

28. *Universa-Laus-Dokument-'80* 6, 2.

29. Instruction *Comme le prévoit* (January 25, 1969), no. 43 (*DOL* 123 no. 880).

30. Ph. Harnoncourt (n. 26) 145.

Chapter VI

1. I refer the reader to several studies in *Consilium* no. 102(1977), which is entitled: "Liturgy and Cultural Religious Traditions" and to the section "Volksreligiosität in eizelnen Regionen" in J. Baumgartner (ed)., *Wiederentdeckung der Volksreligiosität* (Regensburg, 1979), 125-248.

2. Moderns can no longer, for example, regard as reasonable the idea of warding off lightning and thunderstorms by burning blessed palm-branches or placing them in the rafters or by ringing a "storm-bell." *Fulgura frango* ("I shatter the lightning") used to be a common inscription on bells.

3. See *Gd* 18 (1984) 179.

4. J. Baumgartner (n. 1) 8.

5. B. Fischer, "Gottesdienst und Gemeinde," in *Gemeinde des Herrn. 83. Deutscher Katholikentag in Trier 1970,* ed. Zentralkomittee der deutschen Katholiken (Paderborn, 1970), 396.

6. Examples under these headings are given in B. Fischer, "Liturgie und Volksfrömmigkeit," *LJ* 17 (1967) 129-43; idem, "Das Kreuzzeichen—aufzugebender oder beizuhaltender katholischer Brauch?" in J. Baumgartner (n. 1) 251-61.

7. In addition to the literature already cited see: L. A. Veit, *Volksfrommes Brauchtum und Kirche im Mittelalter* (Freiburg, 1936); L. A. Veit and L. Lenhart, *Kirche und Volksfrömmigkeit im Zeitalter des Barock* (Freiburg, 1956); H. Schauerte, "Kirche and religiöses Brauchtum," *ThGl* 56 (1966) 401-21; A. Heinz, "Altes wieder new entdeckt," *Gd* 13 (1979) 81-83; W. Heim, *Volksbrauch im Kirchenjahr heute* (Schriften der Schweizerischen Gesellschaft für Volkskunde 67; Basel, 1983); idem, "Altes und neues religiöses Brauchtum," *Diak* 16 (1985) 107-11; Th. Schnitzler, *Kirchenjahr und Brauchtum neu entdeckt* (Leipzig, 1975; Freiburg, 1984[6]); H. Kirchhoff, *Christliches Brauchtum. Von Advent bis Ostern* (Munich, 1984).

Chapter VII

[1.] Vatican II, Decree on Ecumenism 1 (Flannery 452). For the prehistory and importance see W. Becker, "Introduction," in *Commentary on the Documents of Vatican II,* ed. H. Vorgrimler, trans. L. Adolphus, K. Smyth, and R. Strachan, 2 (New York, 1967). 1-56, and the commentary of J. Feiner, 57-104.

[2.] The Basic Statement as modified at the New Delhi Assembly, in W. A. Visser t'Hooft (ed.), *The New Delhi Report: The Third Assembly of the World Council of Churches, 1961* (New York, 1962), 426.

[3.] There is a translation of the two parts in T. E. Stransky and J. B. Sheerin (eds.), *Doing the Truth in Charity: Statements of Pope Paul VI, Popes John Paul I, John Paul II, and the Secretariat for Promoting Christian Unity, 1964-1980* (Ecumenical Documents I; New York, 1982), 41-57 and 59-74.

[4.] Text in H. Meyer and L. Vischer (eds.), *Growth in Agreement: Reports and Agreed Statements of Ecumenical Conversations on a World Level* (Ecumenical Documents II; New York, 1984), 168-89.

[5.] *Ibid.,* 190-214.

[6.] *Ibid.,* 248-75.

[7.] See H. Meyer and L. Vischer, eds. *Growth in Agreement, Ecumenical Documents II* (New York, 1984), 61-130.

[7a.] See J. Burgess and J. Gros, eds. Building Unity, Ecumenical Documents IV (New York, 1989), 11-34 and 83-290.

[8.] Important points are made in H. Fries and K. Rahner, *Unity of the Churches: An Actual Possibility,* trans. R. C. L. Gritsch and E. W. Gritsch (Philadelphia and New York, 1983). The German edition of 1985 contains an appraisal by H. Fries, "Zustimmung und Kritik." See also H. Fries, "Einheit in Sicht?" *Sdz* 110 (1985) 147-58.

[9.] K. Lehmann in an interview in *Evangelische Kommentare* 17 (1984) 689.

[10.] See the notices in *Gd* 2 (1968) 1-3, 11f., 41f.

[11.] Details in *Gd* 5 (1971) 81-94; H. Goltzen, "Ökumenische Gebets- und Bekenntnistexte," *JHL* 16 (1971) 119-33.

[12.] See the Task Force's document of December, 1984 (obtainable from, among other sources, the Liturgisches Institut of Trier).

[13.] See below, Chapter XV.

[14.] See J. G. Plöger, "Das Wort des Herrn breite sich aus. Zur Einheitsubersetzung der Heiligen Schrift," *Gd* 13 (1979) 105-8.

[15.] Text of the Report: *Growth in Agreement* (n. 6), 466-503.

[16.] Preface, *ibid.,* 466.

[17.] W. Kasper, "Auf dem Weg zur Einheit. Erklärung zum Thema Lima-Liturgie," *Gd* 12 (1985) 89f.

[18.] See Preface, 469.

[19] *Ibid.*

[20] Among others: M. Thurian (ed.), *Ecumenical Perspectives on Baptism, Eucharist and Ministry* (Faith and Order Paper 116; Geneva, 1983); W. H. Lazareth, *Zusammenwachsen in Taufe, Eucharistie und Amt* (Frankfurt, 1983); G. Voss (ed.), *Wachsende Ubereinstimmung in Taufe, Eucharistie und Amt* (Meitingen etc., 1984).

[21] W. Kasper (n. 17) 89.

[22] "The Eucharistic Liturgy of Lima," with Introduction by M. Thurian, in M. Thurian (n. 20) 226.

[23] On the Lima Liturgy: Thurian (n. 20) 225-46 (with text of the liturgy); idem, "Die eucharistiche Feier von Lima," *LJ* 34 (1984) 21-31; F. Schulz, *Die Lima-Liturgie* (Kassel, 1983); H. J. Schulz, "Die Lima-Liturgie," *Gd* 18 (1984) 27-40; R. Gronbach and L. Klein, "Überlegungen zur Lima-Liturgie," *Ökumenische Rundschau* 32 (1983) 27-40. On the problem of intercommunion see J. Höfer *et al.*, *Evangelisch-katholische Abendmahlsgemeinschaft?* (Regensburg—Gottingen, 1971), especially the essay of K. Lehmann, "Dogmatische Vorüberlegungen zum Problem der 'Interkommunion'" (pp. 77-141; also in Lehmann's *Gegenwart des Glaubens* [Mainz, 1974], 229-73).

Chapter VIII

[1] Schneider 15.

[2] The official doctrine of the seven sacraments was promulgated at the Second Council of Lyons in 1274 (DS 860; Neuner-Dupuis 28), in the *Decretum pro Armenis* (closely dependent on St. Thomas) of the Council of Florence (DS 1310: Neuner-Dupuis 1305), and at the Council of Trent in 1547 (DS 1601; Neuner-Dupuis 1311).

[3] L. Boff, *Kleine Sakramentanlehre* (Düsseldorf, 1976), who speaks of water goblets, the fag ends of cigarettes, Christmas candles, and elementary school teachers (among other persons and things) as "sacraments."

[4] Dogmatic Constitution on the Church 48 (Flannery 407).

[5] B. Häring, *A Sacramental Spirituality*, trans. R. A. Wilson (New York, 1965), 16.

[6] Sessio VII: Canones de sacramentis in genere, Can. 8 (DS 1608; Neuner-Dupuis 1318).

[7] P. Brunner, *Worship in the Name of Jesus*, trans. M. H. Bertram (St. Louis, 1968), 114.

[8] In the Middle Ages the Eucharist and baptism were also called "major sacraments" (*sacramenta maior*), an expression which in the twelfth century also served to distinguish the seven sacraments from the sacramentals (see below, Chapter XVIII, n. 1).

[9] Council of Trent, Sessio VII, can. 9 (DS 1609; Neuner-Dupuis 1319).

[10] St. Augustine, *Ep.* 98 *ad Bonifacium*, 5 (CSEL 34:526f.).

[11] St. Thomas, *Summa theologiae* III, 62, 3c.

[12] L. Boff (n. 3) 79ff.

[13] Goethe, *Dichtung und Wahrheit* VII, 2.

14. St. Thomas, *Summa theologiae* III, 65, 1c.

15. From the abundant secondary literature of recent years see, in addition to works already mentioned: J. Wiener and H. Erharter (eds.), *Zeichen des Heiles* (Vienna, 1975); A. Ganoczy, *An Introduction to Catholic Sacramental Theology* (New York, 1984) ; H. Hotz, *Sakramente im Wechselspiel zwischen Ost und West* (Einsiedeln—Gütersloh, 1979); W. Breuning, *Communio Christi* (Düsseldorf, 1980); H. Luthe (ed.), *Christusbegegnung in den Sakramenten* (Kevelaer, 1981); Th. Schnitzler, *Was die Sakramente bedeuten* (Freiburg, 1983[2]).

Chapter IX

1. E. Stauffer, *New Testament Theology,* trans. J. Marsh (New York, 1956), 160.

2. K. Rahner and H. Vorgrimler, "Baptism," in their *Concise Theological Dictionary,* trans. R. Strachan *et al.* (London, 1981[2]), 38.

3. There is a detailed description of this development in A. Stenzl, *Die Taufe. Eine genetische Erklärung der Taufliturgie* (Innsbruck, 1958).

4. The rites of baptism for both adults and children are translated in *The Rites of the Catholic Church* 1 (New York, 1990) 3-466 (Rite of Christian Initiation of Adults, 13-356; Rite of Baptism for Children, 359-466). There is a new translation of the introduction in *DOL: Christian Initiation* (*DOL* 294 nos. 2250-84); Introduction to the Rite of Baptism for Children (*DOL* 295 nos. 2285-2315); Introduction to the Rite of Christian Initiation of Adults, as well as the Introductions to the several chapters of this rite (*DOL* 301 nos. 2327-2475). The Introduction to the rite for receiving baptized Christians into full communion with the Church is in *DOL* 301 nos. 2476-88. All these new translations have been incorporated into the 1990 edition of *The Rites of the Catholic Church, 1.*

5. Origen, *Comm. in Epist. ad Rom* V, 9, on Rom 6:5-7 (PG 14:1047).

6. See W. Kasper (ed.); *Christsein ohne Entscheidung, oder soll die Kirche Kinder taufen?* (Mainz, 1970); W. Molinski, *Diskussion um die Taufe* (Munich, 1971); K. Lehmann, *Gegenwart des Glaubens* (Mainz, 1974), especially 213-28; F. Reckinger, *Kinder tufen mit Bedacht* (Steinfeld, 1979).

7. W. Ruck, *Taufgespräche* (Wurzburg, 1972); D. Emeis, "Anregungen für das Taufgespräch," *Diak* 3 (1972) 347ff.; J. Netzer, *Das Taufgesprach in der Gemeinde* (Freiburg, 1976); M. Huber, *Taufgespräche* (Regensburg, 1976); E. Werner, *Die Taufe in der Gemeinde* (Munich etc., 1981).

8. See E. Nagel, *Kindertaufe und Taufaufschub* (Frankfurt, 1980).

9. Synod of Würzburg, Breschluss: Sakramentenpastoral B 1.1.s (in *Synode* I, 244).

10. Details in A. Adam, "Erwägungen zum Patenamt bei Taufe und Firmung," in *Zeichen des Glaubens* 415-28.

11. *Ibid.*, 422-24.

12. Further literature on baptism of children: B. Fischer, "Die Intentionen bei der Reform des Erwachsenen- und Kindertaufritus," *LJ* 21 (1971) 65-75; I. Jorissen and H. B.

Meyer, *Die Taufe der Kinder* (Innsbruck, 1972).

13. Synod of Würzburg, Beschluss: Sakramentenpastoral B 2.2. (in *Synode* I, 249f.) See also the *National Statutes on the Catechumenate , Rite of Christian Initiation of Adults* (New York & Collegeville, 1988), Appendix III, no. 6. In the United States of America the Catechumenate must extend for at least one year: from before Lent in one year until Easter of the following year.

14. For details: M. Probst *et al.* (eds.), *Katechumenat heute* (Einsiedeln etc., 1976); D. Zimmermann, *Die Erneuerung des Katechumenats in Frankreich und seine Bedeutung fur Deutschland* (dissertation; Munster, 1974); G. Wainwright, "Christliche Initiation in der okumnischen Bewegung," *LJ* 27 (1977) 193-216; A. Kavanagh, "Christliche Initiation in der nachkonziliaren Kirche," *LJ* 28 (1978) 1-10. There are practical aids for baptism of children of school age in: Deutscher Katechetenverein (ed.), *Taufe un Erstkommunion* (Munich, 1984).

Chapter X

1. Extensive documentation in A. Adam, *Firmung und Seelsorge* (Dusseldorf, 1959), 3-34.

2. Dogmatic Constitution *Lument gentium* on the Church 11 (DOL 4 no. 141).

3. Introduction to the Rite of Confirmation 2 (*DOL* 305 no. 2511). The Apostolic Constitution *Divinae consortium naturae* is translated in *DOL* 303 nos. 2499-2508.

4. Jerome, *Dialogus cum Luciferianis* 9 (Pl 23:172).

5. Introduction to the Rite of Confirmation 7b (*DOL* 305 no. 2516).

6. *Ibid.*, 7. *Lumen gentium* speaks of bishops as *ministri ordinarii;* so does the new Code in Can. 882.

7. A detailed historical survey of the question of the age for confirmation is given in Adam (n. 1), 87-138; see also A. Jilek, "Die Diskussion uber das rechte Firmalter" [a survey of the literature], *LJ* 24 (1974) 31ff.

8. Introduction to the Rite of Confirmation 11 (*DOL* 305 no. 2520).

9. *Ibid.*

10. The bishops of the United States have left it to each bishop to determine the age for confirmation.

11. There is disagreement on whether this simultaneous imposition of the hand (actually of only the thumb) is an essential element in the sacramental sign. The Apostolic Constitution *Divinae consortium naturae* says that it is, as does the Introduction to the Rite of Confirmation (no. 9; *DOL* 305 no. 2518), but the actual rite of administration says nothing of it (see *The Rites of the Catholic Church 1 [New York, 1990], 491, n. 27).* The Pontifical Commission for the Interpretation of the Decrees of Vatican Council II explained, when asked, that the imposition of the hand is adequately signified by the anointing itself (AAS 64 [1972] 526; *DOL* 306 no. 2529). See J. Schmitz, "Salbung mit Chrisam auf der Stirne unter Auflegen der Hand," *LJ* 35 (1985) 58-62; H. Auf der Maur, "'Unctio quae fit manus impositione. . .,'" in *Zeichen des Glaubens* 469-83.

12. Originally used in the Frankish Church of the Middle Ages as a "reminder" that was intended to prevent the repetition of the sacrament; later on, the action was given a variety of interpretations. Details in Adam (n. 1), 218-36.

Recent studies of confirmation: D. Koster, *Die Firmung im Glaubenssinn der Kirche* (Munster, 1968); O. Betz, *Sakrament der Mudigketi* (Munich, 1969); H. B. Meyer, *Aus dem Wasser und dem Heiligen Geist* (Aschaffenburgh, 1969); A. Benning, *Gabe des Geistess* (Kevelaer, 1972); G. Biemer, *Firmung. Theologie und Praxis* (Wurzburg, 1973); J. Amoungou-Atangana, *Ein Sakrament des Geistesempfangs?* (Freiburg, 1974); P. Nordhues and H. Petri (eds.), *Die Gabe Gottes* (Paderborn, 1974). G. Austin, *Anointing with the Spirit. The Rite of confirmation: The use of Oil and Chrism* (New York, 1985); A Kavanagh, *Confirmation: Origins and Reform* (New York, 1988; J. Wilde, ed., *When Should we Confirm?* (Chicago, 1989).

13. Details in E. C. Suttner, *Taufe und Firmung* (Regensburg, 1971).

14. See K. Froer, *zur Geschichte und Ordnung der Konfirmation (Munich, 1962); M. Thurian, Die Konfirmation* (Gutersloh, 1961).

15. G. W. H. Lampe, *The Seal of the Spirit* (London, 1951), 315 and repeatedly.

Chapter XI

1. Schneider 149.

2. J. Jeremias, *The Eucharist Words of Jesus,* trans. N. Perrin (London, 1966), 189-90.

3. J. Betz, "Eucharistie," *HTG* 1:337.

4. This text was the subject of J. Betz' last study, "Das Brot des Lebens: Herzmitte des Christentums," which was published in the *Beilage zum Munchener Katholikentage 1984* of the *Deutsche Tagespost* for July 6-7, 1984, 19f. See also the commentaries on the gospel of John.

5. J. Betz, *Die Eucharistie in der Zeit der griechischen Väter II/1. Die Realpräsenz des Leibes und Blutes Jesu im Abendmahl nach dem Neuen Testament* (Freiburg, 1964^2), 201.

6. *Ibid.*, 206.

7. Justin, *Apologia I* 65-67.

8. B. Botte (ed.), *La Tradition apostolique de Saint Hippolyte: Essai de reconstitution* (LQF 39; Munster, 1963).

9. There were minor changes under Clement VIII (1604), Urban VIII (1634), and Pius X (1911).

10. *GIRM* 8 (*DOL* 208 no. 1398); see *SC* 48, 51.

11. Thus H. Noldin, *Summa theologiae moralis* II (Innsbruck, 1911^9) 278.

12. Especially helpful in understanding the individual parts of the Mass are: *MS* I-II; Lengeling, *Ordnung;* J. H. Emminghaus, *The Eucharist: Essence, Form, Celebration,* trans. M. J. O'Connell (Collegeville, 1978); J. Hermans, *Die Feier der Eucharistie* (Regensburg, 1984).

13. See *GIRM* 26 and the commentary in Lengeling, *Ordnung* 189f.

14. *PLHL* 221.

15. *GIRM* 26; see also J. Wagner, "Reflexionen uber Funktion und Stellenwert von Introitus, Kyrie und Gloria in der Messfeier," *LJ* 17 (1967) 40-47.

16. Details in Adam, *Kirchenbau* 116f.

17. *GIRM* 28 (*DOL* 208 no. 1418).

18. See the Sacramentary. On the whole subject see E. Farber, "Gemainsame Tauferrinerung vor der sonntaglichen Eucharistiefeier," in *Gemeinde im Herrenmahl* 199-208.

19. See Th. Schnitzler, "Kyrielitanei am Anfang?" in *Gemeinde im Herrenmahl* 217-21; G. Duffrer, "Das Kyrie retten. . .," *Gd* 13 (1979) 17-19.

20. Further discussion in A. Adam, "Vom Rühmen des Herrn, in *Gott feiern* 85-93.

21. See H. Büsse, "Das 'Tagesgebet' als integrierendes Element der Eröffnung," in *Gemeinde im Herrenmahl* 222-31.

22. Book of Gospels; New York: Catholic Book Publg. Co., 1984; Book of Gospels; London: G. Chapman-Collins, 1982.

23. Further discussion in A. Adam, "Die Messpredigt als Teil der eucharistischen Liturgie," in *Gemeinde in Herrenmahl* 242-50. On the place for delivery of the sermon see below, Chapter XXI.

24. The best study is P. de Clerck, *La "prière universelle" dans les liturgies latines anciennes. Témoignages patristiques et textes liturgiques* (LQF 62; Münster, 1977). For further literature see *PHLH* 157f.

25. See J. Baumgartner, "Vom Sinn der Gabenkollekte,' *Hl. Dienst* 32 (1978) 97-104; idem, "Geldspende im Gottesdienst?" *Schweiz. Kirchenzeitnung* 153 (1985) 209-11, with further bibliography.

26. DS 1303 (Neuner-Dupuis 1508).

27. Details in *MS* II, 1-100; J. A. Jungmann, "Die Gebete zur Gabenbereitung," *LJ* 23 (1973) 186-203; R. Berger, "Gabenbereitung und Gabengebet," in *Gemeinde im Herrenmahl* 264-71.

28. From the extensive literature I may mention: A. Hänggi and I. Phal (eds.), *Prex Eucharistica. Textus e Variis Liturgiis Antiquioribus Selecti* (Fribourg, 1968); Th. Schnitzler, *Die drei neuen eucharistischen Hochgebete und die neuen Praefationen* (Freiburg, 1968); B. Kleinheyer, *Erneuerung des Hochgebetes* (Regensburg, 1969); O. Nussbaum (ed.), *Die eucharistischen Hochgebete II-IV* (Münster, 1971); *PLHL* 204-9.

29. There is now an important critical edition: E. Moeller, *Corpus Praefationum* (5 vols.; CCL 161, 161A-161D; Turnhout, 1980-81).

30. See H. Eising, "Die Bedeutung des Sanctus," in *Gemeinde im Herrenmahl* 297-302.

31. See *MS* II,207-10; H. B. Meyer, "Die Elevation im deutschen Mittelalter und bei Luther," *ZKT* 85 (1963) 152-217.

32. See H. Volk and F. Wetter, *Geheimnis des Glaubens* (Mainz, 1968), 10-29.

33. Extensive documentation in Schneider 139f.; W. Stenger, "Das für alle vergossene Blut," *Gd* 4 (1970) 45ff.

34. On the theme of self-sacrifice: A. Adam, "Christlicher Gottesdienst und personliches Opfter," in *Freude am Gottesdienst* 361-70.

35. See R. Kaczynski, "Die Interzessionen im Hochgebet," in *Gemeinde im Herrenmahl* 303-13.

36. See below, Chapter XX.

37. View expressed in what was probably Jungmann's last scientific study: "Die Doxologie am Schluss der Hochgebete," in *Gemeinde im Herrenmahl* 314-22 at 321; he died on January 26, 1975.

38. The additional Eucharistic Prayers for Masses with Children and Masses of Intercessions are given in an Appendix of the second edition of the Sacramentary.

39. See H. Rennings, "Zur Diskussion über neue Hochgebete," *LJ* 23 (1973) 3-20; the same issue of *LJ* contains other articles on the subject.

40. W. Averbeck, "Die Wiedergewinnung des eucharistischen Hochgebetes im evangelischen Raum," *LJ* 18 (1968) 19-43; also the discussion of the "Lima Liturgy" in the Reformation Churches (above, Chapter VII).

41. See Justin, *Apologia I* 65 and 67.

42. W. Dürig, "Das Vaterunser in der Messe," in *Gemeinde im Herrenmahl* 326; idem, "Die Deutung der Brotbitte des Vaterunsers bei den lateinischen Vätern bis Hieronymus," *LJ* 18 (1968) 72-86.

43. For example, Cyprian, *De dominica oratione* 18 (CSEL 3/1:280f.).

44. Encyclical *Mediator Dei* (1947) 117 and 119. On the symbolism of the breaking of the bread see F. Nikolasch, "Vol geteilten Brot," in *Gott Feiern* 248-55.

45. See *MS* II, 311-13; J. A. Jungmann, *Pastoral Liturgy* 287-95.

46. O. Nussbaum, *Die Handkommunion* (Cologne, 1969); *PLHL* 192, with further bibliography.

47. Documentation and bibliography in *PLHL* 271-73.

48. On the nature and value of the blessing see J. G. Plöger, "Vom Segen des Herrn,' in *Gott feieren* 275-93.

49. The Decree *Ecclesiae semper* promulgating the *editio typica* of the rites of concelebration and of communion under both kinds is in *DOL* 222 nos. 1788-93; the Introduction to the rite of concelebration is in *DOL* 223 nos. 1794-1810.

50. The Instruction *Eucharisticum Mysterium* on worship of the Eucharist is in *DOL* 179 nos. 1230-96.

51. There is a short survey of the forms of concelebration in the Eastern Churches in *PLHL* 277f.

[52] E. von Severus, "Feiern geistlichen Gemeinschaften," *HLW* VIII, 174.

[53] *Ibid.*

[54] The *Directory for Masses with Children* is on *DOL* 276 nos. 2134-88. See the commentary of B. Fischer, *Messfeier mit kindern," in Gemeinde im Herrenmahl* 97-106.

[55] *PLHL* 247.

[56] Examples of ways of organizing children's Masses are given in B. Blasig (ed.), *Sonntag für Kinder* (9 issues; Einsiedeln, 1973ff.); M. Schegg, *Wir spielen und feiern* (Freiburg, 1984); idem, *Damit es Freude macht* (Freiburg, 1984).

[57] First published in *GD* 4 (1970) 144.

[58] Vienna, 1980. See *Diak* 11 (1980) 404-12.

[59] *Synode* I, 209.

[60] There is an instructive essay by J. Janssen, "Messfeier mit Jugendlichen," in *Gemeinde im Herrenmahl* 107-14.

[61] Published in the diocesan newspapers and in *Nachkonziliare Dokumentation* 31 (Trier, 1970), 43-47; *WGL* VIII (Freiburg, etc., 1978) 387-95.

[62] Concluding section of part I (*WGL* VIII, 390f.).

[63] *Ibid.*, II, 3 (*WGL* VIII, 392).

[64] Instruction *Actio pastoralis* 6h (*DOL* 275 no. 2127).

[65] Zurich-Einsiedeln, 1971. Literature: F. Nikolasch, "Die Feier der Messe im kleinen Kreis," *LJ* 20 (1970) 40-52; K. Richter, "Messfeiern im kleinen Kreis," *Sein und Sendung* 35 (= N. F. 2) (1970) 114-116.

[66] *GIRM* 4, citing Vatican II, Decree on the life and Ministry of Priests 13; see *SC* 26f.

[67] See E. Lengeling, *Ordnung* 342-49; K. Richter, "Messfeier ohne Gemeinde?" in *Gemeinde im Herrenmahl* 136-42.

[68] For example, Pius XII, Encyclical *Mediator Dei* (1947), no. 119, where he invokes Benedict XIV; *GIRM* 56h; *Holy Communion and Worship of the Eucharist Outside Mass* 13 (*DOL* 266 no. 2091).

[69] Detailed documentation in Nassbaum, *Aufbewahrung* 102-74; P. Browe, *Die Verehrung der Eucharistie im Mittelalter* (Munich, 1933).

[70] Instruction *Eucharisticum mysterium: DOL* 179 nos. 1230-96; *Holy Communion and Worship of the Eucharist Outside Mass* in *The Rites of the Catholic Church 1* (New York, 1976) 449-512, with new translation of the General Introduction and the Introduction to Chapter III in *DOL* 279 nos. 2193-2226.

[71] See J. Seuffert, *Kommt, wir beten ihn an* (Freiburg, 1985).

[72] Documentation in Meyer-Schermann 517-23.

[73] Bibliography in, e.g., *PLHL* 426. Most recently: O. Nussbaum, *Sonntäglicher Gemeindegottesdienst onhe Priester* (Würzburg, 1985).

[74.] The document is in *Anlage* 7 to the minutes of the plenary meeting of the German Episcopal Conference, September 19-22, 1983, at Fulda. —Help in organizing these liturgies may be found in K. Schlemmer, *Gemeinde am Sonntag. Die Feier von Wortgottesdiensten ohne Priester* (I: Freiburg, 1983; II: 1984; III in preparation).

[75.] Congregation for Divine Worship, *Directory for Sunday Celebrations in the Absence of a Priest* (Vatican City, June 2, 1988), English translation (Washington, DC, 1988).

[76.] *Sunday Celebrations in the Absence of a Priest: Leader's Edition* (Washington, DC, 1991). *Gathered in Steadfast Faith* (Washington, DC 1991).

Chapter XII

[1.] See L. Bertsch, *Busse und Bussakrament in der heutigen Kirche* (Mainz, 1970[2]), 26ff.

[2.] Chapter 21 (DS 812; Neuner-Dupuis 1608).

[3.] Recent descriptions of the historical development may be found in, among others, S. Frank, "Geschichtliche Grundlagen unserer Buss- und Beichtpraxis," in F. Schlösser (ed.), *Schuldbekenntnis—Vergebung—Umkehr* (Limburg, 1971), 39-64; K. Rahner, *Penance in the Early Church,* trans. L. Swain (New York, 1982; German original 1973); F. Nikolasch, *Die Feier der Busse. Theologie und Liturgie* (Würzburg, 1974); E. Feifel (ed.), *Busse, Bussakrament, Busspraxis* (Munster,1975)

[4.] The new Rite is in *The Rites of the Catholic Church 1* (New York, 1990), 517-629.

[5.] See R. Kaczynski, "Erneuerte Bussliturgie," *TPQ* 122 (1974) 209f.

[6.] Details in Adam, *Kirchenbau* 127-29.

[7.] During the Second World War, at the suggestion of my elderly pastor, I myself wore the vestments listed when administering the sacrament of penance; over the course of four years my impression was this practice only increased esteem for the sacrament. See also the recommendation of the Swiss Bishops in their Pastoral Letter on Penance and Confession (1970), 4. 4. 3 (published as a pamphlet with no indication of the place of publication).

[8.] *DOL* 361 nos. 3038-56.

[9.] Important aspects, including the psychological and sociophilosophical, in P. J. Cordes, "Einzelbeichte und Bussgottesdienst," *SdZ* 99 (1974) 17-33.

[10.] See J. Baumgartner, "Neuordnung der Busspraxis in der Schewiz," *Gd* 8 (1974) 169-72.

[11.] See n. 8 for the document. On the subject see K. Rahner, "Bussandacht und Einzelbeichte," *SdZ* 97 (1972) 363-72; idem, "Bussgottesdienst und Eizelbeichte," *Gd* 7 (1973) 12f., 20f.

[12.] Session XIV, chapter 5 (DS 1680; Neuner-Dupuis 1626).

[13.] See, among others, F. Nikolasch (n. 3), 91-94; R. Berger, *Bussgottesdienste. Aleitungen und Modelle* (Munich, 1974); J. Steiner and H. B. Meyer, *Eizelbeichte—Generalabsolution—Bussgottesdienst* (Innsbruck, 1975).

[14.] Session XIV, can. 6-7 (DS 1706-7; Neuner-Dupuis 1646-47).

15. F. Nikolasch, "Berechtigte Vielfalt. Plädoyer für eine erneuerte Bussliturgie," *Gd* 18 (1984) 35. The author is referring to an article of H. Jedin in *La Maison-Dieu* no. 104, pp. 88-115.

16. *Ibid.*

17. *PLHL* 88f.; greater detail in I. H. Dalmais, *Eastern Liturgies* (20th Century Encyclopedia of Catholicism 112; New York, 1966), 144ff.; S. Heitz, *Der orthodoxe Gottesdienst* (Mainz, 1965), 490-501.

18. Vol. III (Berlin, 1963^2), 94-114.

19. On the teaching of the Reformation Churches regarding penance and confession see, among others, P. Brunner, *Worship in the Name of Jesus*, trans. M. H. Bertram (St. Louis, 1968), 286ff.; G. L. Muller, *Bonhoeffers Theologie der Sakramente* (Frankfurt, 1979); J. Asmussen, I. Frank, E. Bezzel, H. Obst, and M. Mezger, "Beichte," *TRE* V, 411-39.

20. *Book of Common Prayer* (New York, 1979), 319-321, 350-353, and 446-452.

21. *Lutheran Book of Worship, Ministers Edition* (Minneapolis & Philadelphia, 1978), 33-35, 195, 318-323; *Occasional Services: A Companion to Lutheran Book of Worship* (Minneapolis and Philadelphia, 1982), 45-47.

22. *Book of Worship, United Church of Christ* (New York, 1986), 268-274 and 275-288.

23. *Services for Occasions of Pastoral Care, Supplemental Liturgical Resource 6* (Louisville, 1990), 107-113.

Chapter XIII

1. See F. Mussner, *Der Jakobusbrief* (Freiburg, 1964), 218ff.

2. Extensive documentation in A. Chavasse, *Etude sur l'onction des infirmes dans l'église latine du IIe au XIe siecle. I. Du IIe siècle au réforme carolingienne* (Lyons, 1952; only vol. I was published); idem, "Prière pour les malades et onction sacramentalle," in Martimort (1),, 580-94; E. J. Lengeling, "Todesweihe oder Krankensalbung?" *LJ* 21 (1971) 192-213.

3. From L. Deiss, *Springtime of the Liturgy. Liturgical Texts of the First Four Centuries*, trans. M. J. O'Connell (Collegeville, 1979), 206-7.

4. The new rite *Pastoral Care of the Sick: Rites of Anointing and Viaticum*, is in *The Rites of the Catholic Church* 1 (New York, 1990), 759-908.

5. See H. Spaemann, "Das Sakrament der Krakensalbung," in Th. Bogler (ed.), *Tod und Leben* (Laacher-Hefte 25; Maria Laach, 1959), 37. —G. Greshake, dogmatic theologian of Vienna, argues for a nuanced sacramental theory in his article, "Letztes Olung oder Krankensalbung?" *Geist und Leben* 56 (1983) 119-36 (a revised version of a contribution to the Festschrift for Cardinal Koning of Vienna: *Leitougia—Koinonia—Diakonia* [Vienna, 1980]). In Greshake's view this sacrament is a "sacrament of the renewal of baptism in the presence of death" (128), "the express representation, celebration, and saving presence of the eschatological center of Christian faith," the

specific effect of which is "the imparting of Christian hope" (134). Not all the links in his argument are convincing; it is therefore difficult to agree with this interpretation.

6. E. J. Lengeling, "Die Erneuerung der Krankensalbung," in M. Probst and K. Richter (eds.), *Heilssorge für die Kranken* (Freiburg, 1975[1]), 57.

7. Introduction of the German bishops to the new Ritual, 23, and in the German Ritual itself, 80-85.

8. A. Knabuer has emphatically called attention to this important aspect of the sacrament in his essay, "Gebet des Glaubens. Der personale Grundakt der Krankensalbung," *Gd* 9 (1975) 81ff.

9. E. J. Lengeling (n. 7), 60. For a critical reaction see A. Ziegenaus, "Ausdehnung der Spendevollmacht der Krankensalbung?" *MTZ* 26 (1975) 345-63.

10. Thus the Apostolic Consitution *Sacram Unctionem infirmorum* (November 30, 1972) of Paul VI (*DOL* 408 no. 3317) and the Rite of the Blessing of Oils (December 3, 1970), no. 3 (*DOL* 459 *nos.* 3861-72; see no. 3863).

11. See Ph. Holzmeinster, *Die heiligen Öle in der Morgen- und abendladischen Kirche* (Wurzburg, 1948).

12. J. Mayer-Scheu and A. Reimer, *Heilszeichen fur Kranke. Krankensalbung heute* (Kevelaer, 1975[2]), 20.

13. Introduction of the German bishops to the new Ritual, 24.

14. In addition to books and articles already mentioned the reader may consult the following more recent works: A. Knauber, *Pastoral Theology of the Anointing of the Sick,* trans. M. J. O'Connell (Collegeville, 1975) (from *HPTh* IV, 145-78); idem, "Sakrament der Kranken," *LJ* 23 (1973) 217-37; W. von Arx, *Das Sakrament der Krankensalbung* (Freiburg, 1976). — According to a communication of Autumn, 1984, from the Liturgical Institute of Trier a study group has been established to revise the celebration of the sacraments of the sick with an eye on the *Variationes.* A further point to be taken into consideration is the directive in the new Code of Canon Law (1983), can. 1007, that the anointing of the sick may not be given to "those who obstinately persist in manifest serious sin."

15. There is a translation of this rite in S. Heitz, *Der orthodoxe Gottesdienst* I (Mainz, 1965), 505-34; for further details see I. -H. Damais, *Eastern Liturgies* (20th Century Encyclopedia of Catholicism 112; New York, 1966), 101-4.

Chapter XIV

1. W. Pesch, "Kirchlicher Dienst und Neues Testament," in W. Pesch *et al., Zum Thema: Presteramt* (Stuttgart, 1970), 10; see F. Hahn, *The Titles of Jesus in Christology: Their History in the Early Church,* trans. H. Knight and G. Ogg (New York, 1969).

2. H. Volk, *Priestertum heute* (Rodenkirchen, 1976), 61; also of value is the Letter of the German Bishops on the priestly office (Trier, 1969).

3. I shall briefly discuss the varied developments in dealing with the three degrees of orders. For the rest I refer the reader to the extensive literature, for example: A.

Deissler *et al., Der priesterliche Dienst* I. *Urprung und Frühgeschichte* (Freiburg, 1970); B. Kotting, "Amt und Verfassung in der alten Kirche," in W. Pesch *et al.* (n. 1), 25-53; K. Kertelge, *Gemeinde und Amt im Neuen Testament* (Munich, 1972); J. Martin, *Die Genese des Amtspriestertums in der fruhen Kirche: Der priesterliche Dienst* III (Freiburg, 1972); H. Schutte, *Amt, Ordination und Sukzession* (Dusseldorf, 1974); H. Schutte, *Amt, Ordination und Sukzession* (Dusseldorf, 1974); J. Hainz (ed.), *Kirche im Werdern. Studien zum Thema Amt und Gemeinde im Neuen Testament* (Paderborn, 1976); G. Greshake, *Priestersein. Zur Theologie und Spiritualitat des priesterlichen Amtes* (Freiburg, 1982); B. Cooke, *Ministry to Word and Sacraments: History and Theology,* (Philadelphia, 1979); K. Osborne, *Priesthood: A History of the Ordained Miistry in the Roman Catholic Church* (New York, 1988); N. Mitchell, *Mission and Ministry; History and Theology of in the Sacrament of Orders,* (Wilmington, 1982); J. Barnett, *The Diaconate: A Full and Equal Order* (New York, 1984); P. Bradshaw, *Ordination Rites of the Ancient Churches of East and West* (New York, 1990).

4. Details in B. Kleinheyer in *HLW* VIII, 25-29; K. Richter, *Die Ordination des Bischofs von Rom* (LQF 60; Munster, 1976).

5. P. Jounel, "Ordinations," in A. G. Martimort (2), III, 164. For the details of the development see Kleinheyer (n. 4), 29-46.

6. The preliminary scientific work was done especially by A. Van Rossum, *De essentia sacramenti ordinis* (Freiburg, 1914; Rome, 1932[2]).

7. K. Rahner and H. Vorgrimler, *Kleines Konzilskompendium* (Frieburg 1968), 111.

8. The rites are in *The Rites of the Catholic Church* 2 (Collegeville, 1991), 25-108. There is a new translation of the Apostolic Constitution in *DOL* 324 nos. 2606-12.

9. Kleinheyer (n. 4), 29.

10. See Th. Klauser, *Der Ursprung der bishoflichen Insignien und Ehrenrechte* (Krefeld, n.d.).

11. See, among others, B. Kleinheyer, *Die Priesterwihe im romischen Ritus* (Trier, 1962).

12. This emerges very clearly from the parallel outlines in Kleinheyer (n. 4) 48.

13. B. Fishcer, "Das Gebet der Kirche als Wesenselement des Wihesakramentes," *LJ* 20 (1970) 176.

14. In addition to publications already mentioned see E. J. Lengeling, "Die Theologie des Weihesakraments nach dem Zeugnis des neuen Ritus," *LJ* 19 (1969) 142-66; P. Jounel, "Ordinations," in Martimort (2) III, 172-79; F. Schulz, "Dokumentation der Ordinationsliturgien," in Joint Roman Catholic and Evangelical Lutheran Commission, *Das geistliche Amt in der Kirche* (Paderborn—Frankfurt, 1981), 57-101.

15. See J. Lécuyer, "Der Diakonat nach den kirchlichen Lehräusserungen," in K. Rahner and H. Vorgrimler (eds.), *Diaconia in Christo* (Freiburg, 1962), 207-13.

16. Text in *DOL* 309 nos. 2533-46, and 319 nos. 2576-91.

17. *Ad pascendum* VI (*DOL* 319 no. 2586).

18. *Ibid.*, VIII (no. 2588).

19. On the rite: B. Kleinheyer, "Weiheliturgie in neuer Gestalt," *LJ* 18 (1968) 210-29; idem in *HLW* VIII, 57-59; O. Nussbaum, "Theologie und Ritus der Diakonenweihe," in J. G. Plöger and H. J. Weber (eds.), *Der Diakon. . .* (Freiburg, 1980), 122-46; Liturgical Commission of the German Bishops, *Der liturgische Dienst des Diakons* (Bonn, 1984). Further literature on the diaconate: G. Langgartner *et al., Der Diakon heute* (Wurzburg, 1969); A. Fischer *et al., Der Diadon* (Freiburg, 1970).

20. Documents in *DOL* 319 nos. 2576-91 and 340 nos. 2922-38.

21. The rites are in *The Rites of the Catholic Church* 2 (Collegeville, 1991).

22. *DOL* 340 nos. 2924-28.

23. *DOL* 340 no. 2932.

24. *DOL* 52 no. 525; The NCCB has decided that women are to proclaim the reading from the same place as male readers.

25. *DOL* 208 no. 1460.

26. *DOL* 264 no. 2078.

27. F. Nikolasch, "Die Neuordnung der kirchlichen Dienste," *LJ* 22 (1972) 176.

28. Beschluss: Dienste und Ämter 7. la (*Synode* I, 633).

29. *L'Osservatore Romano,* February 16, 1983, 4.

30. See *HK* 31 (1977) 152.

31. *AAS* 69 (1977) 98-116; *DOL* 321 2593-2600 at 2594. See the commentary of P. Hünermann in *HK* 31 (1977) 206-9. See also H. van der Meer, *Women Priests in the Catholic Church? A Theological-Historical Investigation*, trans. A. and L. Swidler (Philadelphia, 1973); H. Legrand and J. Vikström, "Die Zulassung der Frau zum Amt," in *Das geistliche Amt in der Kirche* (n. 14), 102-26.

32. A. G. Martimort, *Deaconesses: In Historical Study* (San Francisco, 1985). See the reviews by E. J. Lengeling in *Theologische Revue* 80 (1984) 227-30; B. Kleinheyer, "Zur Geschichte der Diakonissen," *LJ* 34 (1984) 58-64.

Chapter XV

1. M. Schmaus, *Katholische Dogmatik* IV/1 (Munich, 1952^{3-4}), 622.

2. H. Baltensweiler, "Die ehe als Glaubensgemeinschaft (in protestantischer Sicht)," *Handbuch der Elternbilung* I (Einsiedeln, 1966) 400; see idem, *Die Ehe im Neuen Testament* (Zurich, 1967). 232-35.

3. M. Schmaus (n. 1), 623.

4. *GS* 48.

5. *DOL* 354 no. 3007.

6. P. Jounel, "Le Mariage" in Martimort (1), 613.

7. *Ibid.*, 138.

8. Latin text in K. Ritzer, *Formen, Riten und religioses Brauchtum der Eheschliessung in den christlichen Kirchen des ersten Jahrtausends* (LQF 38; Munster, 1962[1]), 314.

9. Sess. XXIV (November 11, 1963), *De matrimonio*, cap. 1: *De reformatione.* Latin text in J. Alberigo *et al.*, *Conciliorum oecumenicorum decreta* (Freiburg, 1973[3]), 755ff.

10. J. Wagner, "Zum neuen deutschen Trauungsritus," *LJ* 11 (1961) 165.

11. The rite is in *The Rites of the Catholic Church* I (New York, 1976), 551-90. New translation of the Introduction in *DOL* 349 nos. 2969-86.

12. R. Köster, "Ringwechsel und Trauung," *Zeitschrift der Savigny-Stiftun fur Rechtsgeschichte. Kanon. Abt.* 22 (1933) 11.

13. K. Richter *et al.* Die Kirchliche Trauung (Freiburg, 79), 63.

14. *DOL* 354 nos. 2999-3012, espec. sect. 9)= no. 3007).

15. Pamphlet of the bishops, *Die neue Ordnung fur die konfessionsverschiedene Ehe* (November 20, 1970), no. 5; see also the regulations for implementation set down by the German episcopal conference (September 22, 1970) and published in the various disocesan bulletins (e.g., Mainz, 112 [1970] 71ff.)

16. Regensburg (Pustet) and Kassel (Stauda), 1971.

17. See H. Hammer, "Ökumenische Trauung," *Gd* 4 (1970) 97ff.

18. Zurich (Benziger and Theologischer Verlag, Zurich), 1973.

19. B. Kleinheyer, "Noch deutlichere Gemeinsamkeit," *LJ* 27 (1977) 107-23; a somewhat more succinct version in *HLW* VIII, 141-45.

20. B. Kleinheyer, in *HLW* VIII, 145.

21. *Deutsches Benediktionale* 245.

22. See B. Kleinheyer in *HLW* VIII, 146-48.

23. *Order for the Blessing of an Engaged Couple*, nos. 195-214 (pp. 59-64).

24. Documentation in B. Kleinheyer in *HLW* VIII, 148f.

25. *Order of Blessing within Mass on the Anniversary of Marriage*, nos. 94-106 (pp. 20-24).

Chapter XVI

1. Vatican II, Decree *Perfectae caritatis* on the Appropriate Renewal of Religious Life (October 28, 1965), 1.

2. *LG* 43.

3. *Ibid.*, 43f.

4. *Ibid.*, 46.

5. Detailed observations by F. Wulf in the Introduction and commentary on *Perfectae caritatis* in H. Vorgrimler (ed.), *Commentary on the Documents of Vatican II* 2 (New York, 1968) 301-70 and in the commentary of the same author on *LG*, chapter 6, in *ibid.*, 1: 273-79.

[6.] Rituale Romanum, *Ordo professionis religiosae.* The introduction is translated in *DOL* 392 nos. 3230-48. A revised English translation of the mass published in 1989: *Rite of Religious Profession* (Washington, 1989).

[7.] The rite is in *The Rites of the Catholic Church* 2 (Collegeville, 1991). New translation of the introduction in *DOL* 395 nos. 3252-62.

[8.] On this entire section see E. von Severus, "Feiern geistlicher Gemeinschafte," in *HLW* VIII, 176-81, with further bibliography.

[9.] See above no. 7.

[10.] Recent literature, in addition to *HLW* VIII (n. 8), 182-84: M. Prager, "Der neue Ritus der Jungfrauenweihe," *Heiliger Dienst* 28 (1974) 129-34; B. Albrecht, "Jungfrauenweihe fur Frauen, die in der Welt leben," *Ordenskorrespondenz* 25 (1984) 298-305.

[11.] The rites for abbot and abbess are in *The Rites of the Catholic Church* 2 (New York, 1991). New translation of the introductions in *DOL* 399 nos. 3277-91. Decree of promulgation in *DOL* 398 no. 3276.

[12.] See E. von Severus (n. 8), 185-87; U. Bomm, "Der neue Ritus der Abts- und Abtissenweihe," *Heiliger Dienst* 27 (1973) 148-52; R. Reinhardt, "Die Abtsweihe—eine 'kleine Bischofsweihe?'" *ZKG* 91 (1980) 83-88.

[13.] See the works listed in n. 12; also A. Nocent, "The Blessing of an Abbot and an Abbess Since Vatican II," in Martimort (2) III, 305-7.

Chapter XVII

[1.] *Pastoral Care of the Sick: Rites of Anointing and Viaticum* in *The Rites of the Catholic Church* I (New York, 1990) 759-908. The General Introduction is also in *DOL* 410 nos. 3321-61. The Order of *Christian Funerals* is in *The Rites* I, 909-1118.

[2.] Canon 13 (DS 129; Neuner-Dupuis 1602).

[3.] This rite is in *Holy Communion and the Worship of the Eucharist outside Mass,* Chapter II (nos. 54-78), in *The Rites* I, 659-668..

[4.] Historical documentation in R. Kaczynski, "Sterbe- und Begrabnisliturgie," *HLW VIII, 204-17; The Rites I,* 866-867.

[5.] For the history of the Christian liturgy of funerals see L. Koep and E. Stommel, "Bestattung," *RAC* II (1954), 194-219; D. Sicard, "Christian Death," in Martimort (2), III, 221-28.

[6.] John Chrysostom, *Sermo de S. Bernice et Prosdoce* (PG 50:634).

[7.] Part I (=nos. 50-127).

[8.] Part I; Funeral Liturgy (nos. 128-203); Rite of Committal (nos. 204-233).

[9.] Recent literature: H. Hollerweger, "Die erneuerte Begrabnisfeier," *LJ* 24 (1974) 13-30; K. Richter *et al., Zeinchen der Hoffnung in Tod und Trauer* (Einsiedeln—Freiburg, 1975); R. Kaczynski (n. 4), 218-24; D. Sicard (n. 5), 236-40; R. Rutherford and T. Barr, *The Death of a Christian: The Order of Christian Funerals,* revised edition (Collegeville,

1990).

10. Part II (- nos. 234-342).

11. These are the last three Masses among the Masses for the Dead.

12. *AAS* 56 (1964) 822-23; *DOL* 413 nos. 3366-70.

13. On cremation see the Appendix to the *Order of Christian Funerals,* Introduction to the "Ordo Exsequiarum" of 1969, no. 15.

Chapter XVIII

1. The same distinction was applied within the seven sacraments, baptism and Eucharist being regarded as *Maiora,* the others as *minora.* See Y. Congar, "The Notion of 'Major' or 'Principal' sacraments," *Concilium* no. 31 (1968) 21-32.

2. J. Baumgartner, "Pastorale Schwerpunkte in der Segnungspraxix," in idem (ed.), *Gläubiger Umgang mit der Welt* (Einsiedeln—Freiburg, 1976), 100.

3. G. Langgartner, *Die Sakramentalien* (Wurzburg, 1974), 10.

4. R. Kaczynski, "Die Benediktionen," *HLW* VIII, 239.

5. *Ibid.,* 240.

6. For the history of blessings: A. Franz, *Die kirchlichen Benediktionen im Mittelalter* (2 vols.; Freiburg, 1909; reprinted: Graz, 1960); E. Bartsch, *Die Sachbeschwörungen der römischen Liturgie* (LQF 46; Münster, 1967); J. Baumgartner (n. 2), especially chapters 1 and 3; R. Kaczynski (n. 4), 247-58; P. Jounel, "Blessings," in Martimort (2), III, 263-84.

7. In the German-speaking countries alone five books on the sacramentals were published in 1974: see K. Becker, "Heilige Zeichen. Kritische Anmerkungen zu fünf neuen Segnungsbüchern," *Gd* 9 (1975) 23f.

8. The guidelines were published in two documents of the Congregation for the Sacraments and Divine Worship on February 27, 1976, and Febraury 21, 1977; see Kaczynski (n. 4), 260.

9. *De Benedictionibus* (Rome, 1984 and 1985[2)]; *Book of Blessings* (New York and Collegeville, 1989). The American edition contains approximately 40 new blessings not found in the Latin edition.

10. Blessings of persons (I), buildings and the many activities of Christians (II), objects in churches (III), objects used in devotions (IV), thanksgiviing and miscellaneous (V).

11. The American edition includes a special section of 13 blessings for feasts and seasons and a much expanded section of blessings for various needs and occcasions.

12. See, e.g., H. Haag, *Abschiev vom Teufel* (Einsiedeln, 1973[4]); idem, *Teufelsglaube* (Tubingen, 1974).

13 This unsigned study appeared in *L'Osservatore Romano* for July 4, 1975 and is translated in *The Pope Speaks* 20 (1975) 209-233. Further studies: W. Kasper and K. Lehmann (eds.), *Teufel—Dämonen—Besessenheit. Zur Wirklichket des Bösen* (Mainz, 1978);

R. Schankenburg (ed.), *Die Macht des Bösen und die Glaube der Kirche* (Düsseldorf, 1979).

14. See A. Stenzl, *Die Taufe. Eine genetische Erkälrung der Taufliturgie* (Innsbruck, 1958).

15. See E. Bartsch (n. 6).

16. Details in R. Kaczynski, "Der Exorcismus," *HLW* VIII, 286-88.

17. See, e.g, the "Klingenberg Case." Documentation in M. Adler. *et al.*, *Tod und Teufel in Klingenberg* (Aschaffenburg, 1977).

18. W. Kasper, "Die Lehre der Kirche vom Bösen," in R. Schnackenburg (n. 13), 68-84 at 82.

19. See also the careful statement in the *Katholischer Erwachsenkatechismus* I (Kevelaer, 1985), 328f., which ends with the sentence: "Exorcism is never a substitute for medical treatment."

20. R. Kaczynski (n. 16), 290.

Chapter XIX

1. Mk 13:35; 14:38 par.; see Mt 24:42; 25:6; Lk 11:5-13; 12:35-40.

2. See Acts 1:14; 2:42; Rom 12:12; Eph 5:19f.; 6:18; Col 3:16f.; 4:2; 1 Thess 5:17; Heb 13:15.

3. Tertullian, *De oratione* 25:5 (CCL 1:172f.).

4. Hippolytus, *Traditio apostolica* 39 and 41 (Botte 86ff.).

5. *Constitutiones apostolorum* VIII, 35, 2—37, 7 (Funk 1:544-46); see Martimort (1) II, 815.

6. See A. Baumstark, *Nocturna laus* (LQF 32; Munster, 1957).

7. See P. Nowack, "Die Strukturelemente des Stundengebetes der *Regula Benedicti*," *ALW* 26 (1984) 253-304. On the relation of the so-called cathedral office to the monastic office see J. A. Jungmann, *The Early Liturgy to the Time of Gregory the Great*, trans. F. A. Brunner (Notre Dame, 1959) 278-87.

8. E. J. Lengeling, "*Liturgia horarum.* Zur Neuordung der Kirchlichen Stundegebetes," *LJ* 20 (1970) 146, note 22; S. Baumer, *Geschichte des Breviers* (Freiburg, 1895), 599-602, sees validity in both interpretations.

9. In the Constitution on the Liturgy only the term "divinum officium" appears, whereas the documents prefixed to the new Latin breviary prefer "liturgia horarum."

10. Details in J. A. Jungmann, "Why Was the Reform Breviary of Cardinal Quinonez a Failure?" in his *Pastoral Liturgy* (New York, 1962), 200-14.

11. Details in S. Baumer (n. 8), 529-95.

12. Righetti II, 552.

13. Documentation in E. J. Lengeling (n. 8), 142f.

[14.] Lengeling, 143f., gives a good overview of the extensive preliminary work done for this chapter.

[15.] An anticipatory version of the new breviary appeared in Paris in the summer of 1969 under the title *Priere du temps present.* See J. M. Brault, "Die Entstehung des franzosischen Breviers," *LJ* 20 (1970) 161-65.

[16.] Bd. I: *Tagezeiten* (Einsiedeln and elsewhere, 1970; Bd. II: *Geistliche Lesung* (1971).

[17.] Prayer of Christians (New York, 1971); Christian Readings (New York, 1972-73).

[18.] Liturgy of the Hours, 4 vols. (New York, 1975-76).

[19.] *Enarrationes in psalmos* 81, 1 (CCL 39:1176); cited in *GILH* 7 [from which the translation in the text is taken. —Tr.].

[20.] *Traditio apostolica* 41 (Botte 96).

[21.] K. Hemmerle, "Das Beten der Kirche," in Secretariat of the German Episcopal Conference (ed.), *Beten mit der Kirche. Hilfen zum neuen Stundengebet* (Regensburg, 1978), 24.

[22.] *SC* 85; see *GILH* 15.

[23.] The *Codex rubricarum* of 1960 had already said that it is better "to keep to the proper time for each canonical hours as far as possible" (no. 142). The *Codex* continued the permission to anticipate Matins, but withdrew it for Lauds.

[24.] E. G., H. Noldin, *Summa theologiae moralis* II (Innsbruck, 1911^9), 792f.

[25.] Suggestions for practice are given by, among others, R. Kazynski, "Schwerpunkte der allgemeinen Einfuhrung in das Stundengebet," *LJ* 27 (1977) 65-91 at 89f.

[26.] Reference must be made here to B. Fischer's valuable studies of the psalms as a Christian prayer; these are now available as a collection in his *Die Psalmen als Stimme der Kirche,* ed. A. Heinz (Trier, 1982); and see idem, *Dich will ich suchen von Tag zu Tag* (Freiburg, 1985). See also A. G. Martimort, "Vom Beten der Psalmen im Studengebet," in *Gott feiern,* 384-94; A. Merterns, "Heute Christlich Psalmen beten," in H. Becker and R. Kaczynski (eds.), *Liturgie und Dichtung* II (St. Ottilien, 1983), 497-508, where further relevant studies are listed.

[27.] Contrary to the original intention of providing a two-year cycle of scripture readings. See E. J. Lengeling (n. 8), 238-40.

[28.] *Traditio apostolica* 41 (Botte 90-92).

[29.] See B. Fischer, "Die Schlussbitten in Laudes und Vesper des neuen Stundengebetes," *LJ* 29 (1979) 14-23.

[30.] *DOL* 424 no. 3425. See, e.g., the *Didache* 8, 3 (Bihlmeyer 5). See A. A. Haussling, "Vom Gebet des Herrn," in *Gott feiern,* 444-58.

[31.] P. Parsch, *Volksliturgie. Ihr Sinn und Umfang* (Klosterneuburg—Vienna, 1940), 241f.; see H. Becker, "Poesie—Theologie—Spiritualitat. Die benediktinische komplet als Komposition," in H. Becker and R. Kaczynski (n. 25), II, 857-901.

[32.] E. von Severus, "Feiern geistlicher Gemeinschaften," *HLW* VIII, 170.

33. *Ibid.*; see also O. Lang, "Das 'monastische Stundenbuch,'" *SMGB* 94 (1983) 542-73.

34. I. Damais, *Eastern Liturgies* (20th Century Encyclopedia of Catholicism 112; New York, 1966), 125-36.

35. H. Goltzen, "Der tagliche Gottesdienst," *Leitourgia* III, 99-296.

36. H. Reinfenberg, "Anglikanische Liturgie—Anregung und Modell," *Bili* 52 (1979) 239-51; there is a brief description in L. Fendt, *Einfuhrung in der Liturgiewissenschaft* (Berlin, 1958), 253ff; M. Hatchett in *Sanctifying Life, Time and Space* (New York, 1976) gives a brief overview of the Anglican daily office (123-125; 147-150; 169-171); M. Hatchett's *Commentary on the American Prayer Book* (New York, 1980), 89-153, provides in short history of the office and a commentary on the daily office as revised in the *Book of Common Prayer* (1979).

37. D. Webb, "Les offices du matin et du soir dans l'Eglise englicane," in E. Cassien and B. Botte (eds.), *La priere des heures* (Paris, 1963), 317-81.

Chapter XX

1. *GNLYC* 17; see *SC* 102.

2. The term "paschal mystery" occurs seven times in *SC* alone. It is also used in other conciliar documents.

3. Augustine, *Ep.* 55, 24 (CSEL 34/2:195).

4. See above, Chapter I. See J. Pascher, *Mysterium paschale*—Das Ostergeheimnis im liturgischen Jahr," in A. Hanggi (ed.), *Gottesdienst nach dem Konzil* (Mainz, 1964), 80-94.

5. According to J. Pieper, *In Tune with the World: A Theory of Festivity*, trans. R. and C. Winston (New York, 1965; Chicago, 1973), "to celebrate a festival means: to live out, for some special occasion and in an uncommon manner, the universal assent to the world as a whole" (23). From the extensive literature on the theory of festivity and feasts I may metnion: J. A. Jungmann, "A 'Feast of the Church,'" in his *Pastoral Liturgy* (New York, 1962). 397-407; H. Fortman, *Von bliebenden Sinn christlicher Feste* (Vienna, 1969); G. M. Martin, *Fest und Alltag. Bausteine zu einer Theorie des Festes* (Stuttgart, 1973); W. Durig, *Das christliche Fest und seine Feier* (St. Ottilien, 1978[2]).

6. Short summary on this subject in Adam, *Liturgical Year*, 5-19, with further bibliography.

7. *CommNC*, cap. II, sect. I, 1 (p. 66).

8. See Th. Kampmann, *Das Kirchenjahr. Mysterium, Gestlt, Katechese* (Paderborn, 1964[3]), 2 and 55; G. Kunze, "Die gottesdienstliche Zeit," in *Leitourgia* I, 4-532.

9. The word *duplex* ("doubled") referred originally to the two offices that had to be recited when an important feast fell on a weekday (*feria*); both the festal and the ferial offices had to be read.

10. See E. Meyer, "Christliche Zeintrechnung," *RGG* I (1957), 1815f.

11. See 1 Cor 14 together with 1 Cor 12. See W. Thusing, "Eucharistiefeier und

Sonntagspflicht im Neuen Testament," *Gd* 5 (1971) 11.

12. *Didache* 14, 1 (Bihlmeyer 8).

13. The letter and Trajan's answer are in Kirch 22-24.

14. *Apologia I* 67, 3-6 (Goodspeed 75f.).

15. Ignatius of Antioch, *Ad Magnesios* 9, 1f. (Bihlmeyer 91).

16. *Didascalia apostolorum* II, 59, 2f. (Funk I, 170-72).

17. Can. 21 (Kirch 202).

18. Jerome, *In die dominica Paschae homilia,* in G. Morin (ed.), *Anecdota Maredsolana* III/2 (1897) 418.

19. *Codex Iustiniani* III, 12, 2, cited in F. J. Dölger, "Die Planetenwoche im Lichte des geschichtlichen Entwicklung," in his *AC* 6 (1841) 229.

20. *Ibid.*, II, 8, 1. For more information see W. Rordorf, *Sunday. The History of the Day of Rest and Worship in the Earliest Centuries of the Christian Church,* trans. A. A. K. Graham (Philiadelphia, 1968); idem, *Sabbat und Sonntag in der alten kirche* (Zurich, 1972).

21. Examples in Adam, *Liturgical Year,* 44f.

22. See H. Huber, *Geist und Buchstabe der Sonntagsruhe. Eine historisch-theologische Untersuchung über das Verbot der knechtlichen Arbeit von der Urkirche bis auf Thomas von Aquin* (Salzburg, 1957), 194-222.

23. Details in G. Troxler, *Das Kirchengebot der Sonntagsmesspflicht als moraltheologisches Problem in Geschichte und Gegenwart* (Freiburg, 1971), 159ff.

24. Documentation in "Erster oder letzter Tag der Woche?" *Gd* 9 (1975) 90ff.

25. See F. Schulz, "Gefährdeter Sonntag," *JLH* 20 (1976) 158-65.

26. *Didache* 8, 1 (Bihlmeyer 5).

27. Tertullian, *De ieiunio* 19 (CCL 2:1267f.).

28. *Didascalia apostolorum* V, 14, 1 (Funk 1:276-78).

29. Innocent I, *Epist.* 25, 5 (PL 20:255).

30. See, e.g., Honorious of Autun (d. ca. 1150), *Gemma animae* II, 67f. (PL 172:640ff.).

31. J. A. Jungmann, "The Weekly Cycle in the Liturgy," in his *Pastoral Liturgy* (New York, 1953) 253.

32. Details in *ibid.*, 254ff.

33. On the entire subject see G. Schreiber, *Die Wochentage im Erlebnis der Ostkirche und des christlichen Abendlandes* (Cologne—Opladen, 1959). There is a novel suggestion in H. Reinfenberg, *Fundamentalliturgie* (Klosterneuburg, 1978), II, 288f.

34. Details in Adam, *Liturgical Year* 57-63, with further bibliography.

35. *Ibid.*, 62-63.

36. Most important works: O. Casel, "Art und Sinn der ältesten christlichen Osterfe-

ier," *JLW* 14 (1938) 1-78; B. Fischer and J. Wagner (eds.), *Paschatis Sollemnia. Studien zur Osterfeier und Osterfrommigkeit* (Basel—Freiburg—Vienna, 1959); H. Becker, "Osterfeier—Osterglaube—Ostererfahrun," *TTZ* 88 (1979) 1-18.

37. See above, n. 3.

38. See *GNLYC* 18-19.

39. Adam, *Liturgical Year* 68.

40. A Stuiber, "Von der Pascha-Nachtwache zum Karsamstaggottesdienst," *Katechetische Blätter* 75 (1950) 99.

41. Details in Adam, *Liturgical Year* 75-77.

42. See Bonifatius Fischer, "Ambrosius der Verfasser des osterlichen Exultet?" *ALW* 2 (1952) 61-74.

43. See B. Kleinheyer, *Die neue Osterfeier* (Freiburg, 1971); R. Berger and H. Hollerweger (eds.), *Celebrating the Easter Vigil,* trans. M. J. O'Connell (New York, 1983).

44. The oldest known example is the Easter homilies of Asterios Sphistes; the best known is the five "mystagogical catecheses" of Cyril (John?" of Jerusalem. See Adam, *Liturgical Year,* 85-86.

45. See P. Hellbernd, *Die Erstkommunion der Kinder in Geschichte und Gegenwart* (Vechta, 1954).

46. *CommALI,* cap. I, sect. III, 3 (p. 63).

47. See Sacramentary (New York, 1985), Appendix to the General Instruction for the Dioceses of the United States of America, no. 331.

48. See Adam, *Liturgical Year,* 91-94.

49. *CommALI* cap. I, sect. I. 2. B. 1 (p. 58).

50. *Itinerarium Egeriae,* ed. A. Franceschini and R. Weber (Turnhout, 1968), cap. 31.

51. Adam, *Liturgical Year,* 109-10.

52. *Rite of the Blessing of Oils* 11-12, in *The Rites of the Catholic Church* I (New York, 1990), 706, or (in a slightly different translation) in *DOL* 459 nos. 3871-72.

53. See *Sacramentary* at the Chrism Mass on Holy Thursday.

54. The text and an interpretation may be found in, among others, J. Pascher, *Das liturgische Jahr* (Munich, 1963), 325-28.

55. See H. Frank, "Fruhgeschichte und Ursprung des romischen Weihnachsfestes im Lichte neuerer Forschung," *ALW* 2 (1952) 1-24; idem, "Weihnachten I. Heortologie," *LTK* X (1965) 984-88.

56. L. Duchesne, *Christian Worship: Its Origin and Evolution,* trans. M. L. McClure (London, 1903; there is a later French edition: Paris, 1925); H. Engberding, "Der 25. Dezember als Tag der Feier der Geburt des Herrn," *ALW* 2 (1952) 25-43.

57. H. Frank (n. 55), *LTK* X, 986.

58. See Adam, *Liturgical Year,* 125-26.

59. *CommALI,* cap. I, sect. II, 1 (p. 60). There are vigils of the same type for Pentecost and the Solemnities of the Birth of John the Baptist, the Apsotles Peter and Paul, and the Assumption of Mary (*ibid.*).

60. R. Berger, "Ostern und Weihnachten. Zum Grundgefuge des Kirchenjahres," *ALW* 7 (1963) 19.

61. Adam, *Liturgical Year,* 139.

62. See R. Schwarzenberger, "Die liturgische Feier des 1. Januar. Geschichte und pastoralliturgische Desiderata," *LJ* 20 (1970) 216-30; idem, "Die Liturgie ist für die Menschen da," *Gd* 4 (1970) 185-87.

63. See K. Holl, "Der Ursprung des Epiphaniefestes," *Sitzungsberichte der Preussischen Akademie der Wissenschaften,* 1917, 402-38; F. Nikolasch, "Zum Ursprung des Epiphaniefestes," *EL* 82 (1968) 393-429.

64. See *Notitiae* 13 (1977) 477.

65. For the history of Advent see W. Croce, "Die Adventsliturgie im Lichte der geschichtlichen Entwicklung," *ZKT* 70 (1954) 257-96, 440-72; J. A. Jungman, "Advent und Voradvent," in his *Liturgisches Erbe und pastorale Gegenwart. Studien und Vortrage* (Innsbruck, 1960), 232-94 [not included in the English translation, *Pastoral Liturgy].*

66. See *GNLYC* 42 and the *Commentarius.*

67. Details in J. Pascher (n. 54), 366-68.

68. N. Curti, *Volkbrauch und Voksfrommigkeit im katholischen Kirchenjahr* (Basel, 1971); H. Bausinger, *Adventskranz* (Wurzburg—Munich, 1977); H. Kirchhoff, *Christliches Brauchtum. Von Advent bis Ostern* (Munich, 1984); J. Kuster, *Worterbuch der Feste und Brauche im Jahreslauf* (Freiburg, 1985).

69. See Adam, *Liturgical Year,* 151.

70. *Ibid.,* 152.

71. The attempt to give a deeper theological reason for these various ways of counting (e.g., G. Kunze [n. 8], 256) is not very convincing.

72. Introduction to the *Lectionary for Mass* (second ed.; Collegeville, 1986), no. 82 (p. 21).

73. *Ibid.*; see *GIRM* 319.

74. A. Klaus, *Ursprung und Verbreitung der Dreifaltigkeitsmesse* (Werl, 1938); on this book see P. Browe, "Zur Geschichte des Dreifaltigkeitsfestes," *ALW* 1 (1950) 65-81.

75. See P. Browe, "Die Ausbreitung des Fronleichnamsfestes," *JLW* 8 (1928) 142f.; idem, *Die Verehrung der Eucharistie im Mittelalter* (Munich, 1933).

76. See *LJ* 11 (1961) 58.

77. A. A. Häussling, "Leitideen für Fronleichnam heute," *Gd* 3 (1969) 78-79.

78. Leo XIII, Encyclical *Annum sacrum; ASS* 31 (1899) 646-51.

79. Pius XII, Encyclical *Haurietis aquas: AAS* 48 (1956) 309-53. For the history of the Sacred Heart devotion see, among others, J. Stierli (ed.), *Heart of the Saviour: A Symposium on Devotion to the Sacred Heart,* trans. P. Andrews (New York, 1957); A. Bea and H. Rahner (eds.), *Cor Jesu. Commentations in Litteras Encyclicas Pii XII "Haurietis aquas'* (Rome, 1959). On the theology: K. Rahner, "Some Theses for a Theology of Devotion to the Sacred Heart," in Stierli 131-55 and (in a somewhat different translation) in Rahner's own *Theological Investigations* 3, trans.K.-H. and B. Kruger (Baltimore, 1967), 331-52.

80. K. Rahner (n. 79), in *Theological Investigations* 3:344.

81. New forms for the practice of the devotion in J. Seuffert, *Der Herz-Jesu-Freitag. Modelle fur Messfeiern und Andachten* (Munich, 1977).

82. Pius XI, Encyclical *Quas primas: AAS* 17 (1925) 593-610.

83. Historical evidence in Righetti II, 261.

84. *Historia ecclesiastica* X, 4 (Schwartz 370-88).

85. *Itinerarium Egeriae* (n. 50) cap. 48f.

86. See Adam, *Liturgical Year,* 186-90.

87. Twenty-five Ember Day sermons have come down to us from Leo I; See Adam (n. 86), 187.

88. Th. Klauser, *Christlicher Martyrerkult, heidnischer heroenkult und spatjudische heiligenverehrung* (Cologne—Opladen, 1960); B. Kotting, "Heiligenverehrung," *HTG* I, 633-41; P. Molinari, *Saints and Their Place in the Church,* trans, D. Maruca (New York, 1965); W. Beinert (ed.), *Die Heiligen heute ehren* (Freiburg, 1983).

89. Paul VI, Motu Proprio *Sanctitas clarior: AAS* 61 (1969) 149-53.

90. See K. Rahner, "Vom Geheimnis der Heiligkeit, der Heiligen und ihrer Verehrung,: in P. Manns (ed.), *Reformer der Kirche* (Mainz, 1970), 26; see also G. L. Muller, *Gemeinschaft un Verehrung der Heiligen* (tyepwritten Habilitationsschrift; Freiburg, 1966).

91. See W. Stählin, *Maria, die Mutter des Herrn, ihr biblisches Bild* (Dusseldorf, 1951); M. Lackmann, *Verehrung der Heiligen* (Stuttgart, 1958); M. Thurian, *Mary, Mother of all Christians,* trans. N. B. Cryer (New York, 1963).

92. The *General Norms* are in *DOL* 442 nos. 3767-3827.

93. See Adam, *Liturgical Year* 212-24. See also W. Beinert (ed.), *Maria heute ehren* (Freiburg, 1979[3]); idem, *Heute von Maria reden* (Freiburg, 1981[5]); B. Kleinheyer, "Maria in der Liturgie," in W. Beinert and H. Petri (eds.), *Handbuch der Marienkunde* (Regensburg, 1984), 404-39.

94. See Adam, *Liturgical Year* 223-24.

95. Translation in *DOL* 481 nos. 3995-4045.

96. Ph. Harnoncourt, "Erläuterungen und Kommentare," in *Nachkonziliare Dokumentation* 29 (Trier, 1975), 253.

97. Instruction on Particular Calendar (June 24, 1972), 16a (*DOL* 481 no. 4011).

[98.] *GNLYC* 52b.

[99.] Most recent Latin edition: 1956.

Chapter XXI

[1.] In order not to make this chapter excessively long and detailed I shall refer the reader to my book *Kirchenbau* (1984) for details, especially in the historical survey.

[2.] F. Mussner, "Jesus und 'das Haus des Vaters' —Jesus als 'Tempel,'" in *Freude am Gottesdienst* 272.

[3.] See H.-J. Klauck, *Hausgemeinde und Hauskirche im frühen Christentum* (Stuttgart, 1981); G. Gnilka, "Die neutestamentliche Hausgemeinde," in *Freude am Gottesdienst* 229-42.

[4.] See Adam, *Kirchenbau* 15f.

[5.] *Ibid.*, 16-19.

[6.] *Ibid.*, 29-40.

[7.] *Ibid.*, 40-47.

[8.] *Ibid.*, 48-53.

[9.] *Ibid.*, 54-61.

[10.] *Ibid.*, 61f.

[11.] *Ibid.*, 63f.

[12.] *Ibid.*, 64-77.

[13.] The Bishops' Committee on the Liturgy of the National Conference of Catholic Bishops (of the United States of America) published a statement, *Environment and Art in Catholic Worship* (Washington, 1978) to provide principles to those involved in preparing liturgical space for the worship of the Christian assembly. It is an excellent commenatary on the various provisions of the liturgical documents.

[14.] The following may be mentioned: M. Eliade, *The Sacred and the Profane: The Nature of Religion,* trans. W. R. Trask (New York, 1959); Th. Bogler (ed.), *Das Sakrale im Widerspruch* (Maria Laach, 1967); E. J. Lengeling, "Sakral—profan. Bericht über die gegenwärtige Diskussion," *LJ* 18 (1968) 164-88; H. Bartsch (ed.), *Probleme der Entsakralisierung* (Munich, 1970).

[15.] H. Mühlen, *Entsakralisierun* (Paderborn, 1970); idem, "Sakralitat und Profanitat," *HPTH* V, 477-80 (a good summary).

[16.] Y. Congar, "Reflections on the Spiritual Aspect of Church Buildings," in his *A Gospel priesthood,* trans. P.J. Hepburne-Scott (New York, 1967), 234.

[17.] Adam, *Kirchenbau* 82-86.

[18.] E.G., the Council of Tarragona (516), cap. 13; see Th. Klauser, "Kathedra," *LTK* VI, 67.

[19.] *GIRM* 276.

[20] *Ibid.*, 267.

[21] "Oratory" is also the name of two communities of secular priests: the first was founded by Philip Neri and took its name from the room in which he prayed and in which the group used to assemble in the beginning; the second was founded by French priest Pierre de Bérulle in 1611.

[22] See Adam *Kirchenbau* 93f.

[23] See the (first) Instruction *Inter Oecumenici* on the orderly carrying out of the liturgical constitution (September 26, 1964), no. 91 (*DOL* 23 no. 383); *GIRM* 258-70; Rite of the Dedication of a Church and an Altar.

[24] Details in Adam, *Kirchenbau* 103f; see also *Environment and Art in Catholic Worship*, nos. 71-73.

[25] *Ibid.*, 103-7 (with bibliography).

[26] Instruction *Inter Oecumenici* (n. 23), 91 and 95 (*DOL* 23 nos. 383 and 387).

[27] On these matters see Adam, *Kirchenbau* 109-14; see also *Environment and Art in Catholic Worship*, nos. 78-80

[28] *DOL* 550 nos. 4467-70; see *LJ* 19 (1969) 115-20.

[29] Details in J. H. Emminghaus, "Die Gestaltung des altarraumes, III: Der Vorstehersitz," *BiLi* 48 (1975) 142-52; see also *Environment and Art in Catholic Worship*, no. 70

[29a] See *Environment and Art in Catholic Worship*, nos. 74-75.

[30] See Adam, *Kirchenbau* 15f., 122.

[31] Th. Klauser, "Taufet in lebendigem Wasser!," in idem, *Pisciculi. Festschrift für F.J. Dölger* (Münster, 1939), 163f.

[32] Th. Mass-Ewerd, "Ort und Gestaltung der Taufbrunnens," in *Zeichen des Glaubens* 371.

[32a] See *Environment and Art in Catholic Worship*, nos. 75-77.

[33] For the variety for solutions see F. Ronig, "Der architektonische Ort der Kirchenmusik vom 4. Jahrhundert bis in die Gegenwart," *Kirchenmusikalische Mitteilungen* (Diocese of Rottenburg-Stuttgart), no. 38 (1980) 3-21; *Ibid., no. 39, 3-25.*

[34] Examples in Adam, *Kirchenbau* 130; see also *Environment and Art in Catholic Worship*, no. 83

[35] B. Ader, "Orgelkunde," in H. Musch (ed.), *Musik im Gottesdienst* II (Regensburg, 1983^2), 181ff.; H. Klotz, "Die kirchliche Orgelkunst," in *Leitourgia* IV, 759-804.

[36] See Adam, *Kirchenbau* 131.

[37] See H. Klotz (n. 35), 773; see also *Environment and Art in Catholic Worship*, no. 83.

[38] *Richtlinien, 1949,* Folgerung 2.

[39] Adam, *Kirchenbau* 141 and note 266.

[40]. Cap. 30, num. 1032-51.

[41]. The earliest attested example is the dedication of the church of Tyre in 314, as reported by Eusebius of Caesarea, *Historia ecclesiastica* X, 4 (Schwartz 370—88).

[42]. See *LJ* 6 (1956) 139-41.

[43]. The Rite for the Dedication of a Church and an Altar is in *The Rites of the Catholic Church* II (Collegeville, 1990), 185-293. There is a new translation of the Introductions to each chapter in *DOL* 546 nos. 4361-4445.

[44]. See J. Schmitz, "Ein qualifizierter Segen? Zur Konsekration einer benedizierten kirche," *Gd* 14 (180) 57-59.

[45]. *Code of Canon Law (Latin-English Edition),* trans. under the auspices of the Canon Law Society of America (Washington, D.C., 1983), 437.

[46]. See Adam, *Kirchenbau* 156.

Chapter XXII

[1]. See Meyer, *Liturgie.*

[2]. F. W. Weber, *Dreizehnlinden* XVII, 3 (Leipzig: Reclam, n.d.), 215.

[3]. *Munchener Kirchenzeitung,* 1972, no. 2.

[4]. Ignatius of Antioch, *Ad Smyrnaeos* VIII, 1 (Bihlmeyer 108).

[5]. Documentation in F. van der Meer, *Augustine the Bishop. Church and Society at the Dawn of the Middle Ages,* trans. B. Battershaw and G. R. Lamb (New York, 1961; rev. trans.: Harper Torchbooks, 1965), 397ff.

[6]. E. Tewes, "Romano Guardini," *Gd* 19 (1985) 17-19; see also the "Leserbrief," 50.

[7]. See *Gd* 18 (1984) 180.

[8]. R. Guardini, *Meditations Before Mass,* trans. E. C. Briefs (Westminster, Md., 1962), 5; see the whole section on the theme of stillness or silence and composure (3-34).

[9]. J. A. Jungmann, Commentary on the liturgical constitution in H. Vorgrimler (ed.), *Commentary on the Documents of Vatican II* (New York, 1967), I, 23.

[10]. See B. Fischer, "Gottesdienst als Ort der Ruhe," *Gd* 8 (1974) 185-87; 9 (1975) 4-5, 12.